Easy Grammar®: Grades 5 and 6

Author: Wanda C. Phillips

Easy Grammar Systems™
Post Office Box 25970
Scottsdale, Arizona 85255

www.easygrammar.com

Easy Grammar®: Grades 5 and 6 is dedicated to my nieces and nephew: Julie Carnell Glenn, Robyn Kuykendall, Frances Ann Rogers, Katie Rogers, and Lance Kuykendall.

"Fear thou not; For I am with thee;
be not dismayed; for I am thy God;
I will strengthen thee; yea, I will help thee; yea,
I will uphold thee with the right hand of my righteousness."

Isaiah 41:10

TABLE OF CONTENTS

Easy Grammar: Grades 5 and 6

Dear Educator,

When Easy Grammar, my non-grade level text, was introduced, it served a multitude of levels. However, I now realize that some of the materials within that text are too difficult for all fifth and sixth grade students. Easy Grammar: Grades 5 and 6 (formerly Level 1) has been designed with fewer concepts and more practice worksheets for each concept. As in Easy Grammar, the prepositional approach is introduced, and a building block method is used. Introducing concepts step-by-step helps students to comprehend more easily and helps to ensure mastery learning. For this reason, cumulative reviews are interspersed throughout the text. In addition, a test for each unit has been provided.

Easy Grammar: Grades 5 and 6 is reproducible for non-commercial use. However, for your convenience, a student workbook is available. This workbook, Easy Grammar Workbook 56, contains rule pages and all worksheets contained within Easy Grammar: Grades 5 and 6.

Wanda C. Phillips

TEACHING Easy Grammar: Grades 5 and 6:

1. **THE STUDENT MUST LEARN THE LIST OF PREPOSITIONS**. The prepositions must be **memorized** and **listed**. You may choose to divide the list into groups. For example, instruct students to learn the list of a's and then the b's. Next, have them list both a's and b's. Continue through the list until **all** prepositions have been memorized. It is absolutely imperative that all students memorize the entire list. (You may wish to have students play "preposition bingo" or do some of the included "fun" activities. Using the grid provided, each child will fill in his own preposition page. A sample has been provided.)

2. Be sure that students understand the **purpose** of deleting prepositional phrases. After a prepositional phrase has been crossed out, it will not be the subject, verb, direct object, predicate nominative, or predicate adjective.

3. In the preposition unit, review pages have been placed before worksheets that require students to use all concepts learned. This has been done as another aid in using the prepositional approach. In all other units, the review is placed directly before the cumulative review or test.

4. With the exception of capitalization, punctuation, sentence types, fragments, and friendly letters, **Easy Grammar: Grades 5 and 6** should be taught in sequence. Those units should be taught when appropriate.

5. Read the answer page before assigning a worksheet. Often, additional suggestions have been placed there for your benefit.

6. Insist on **mastery learning**. This signifies that the student fully understands the concept and is able to use it when the need arises. The additional cumulative review pages of this book should help determine if the student has mastery. If you discover that there has been a lack of understanding, it is recommended that you reteach that concept.

7. **Daily Grams: Guided Review Aiding Mastery Skills** contains ample daily review of concepts. These are extremely effective in helping to insure mastery. There are 180 reviews per book, and each page contains capitalization review, punctuation review, grammar/dictionary skills, and sentence combining for improved writing skills. (See last page for various levels.)

8. This is a lengthy text. If students master a concept with one worksheet, you may wish to skip the second one. (You can always come back to it later for a review.)

9. **If you are using a workbook**, please note that the correlating workbook page has, in most cases, been placed on the answer key page of **Easy Grammar : Grades 5 and 6**. Also, a correlation of workbook pages and teacher edition pages has been placed after this text's index.

10. Tests occur at the end of each grammar unit. However, tests are located in a separate section after the index in the student workbook.

FOR THE TEACHER:
WORKBOOK PAGE 3

PREPOSITIONS

By definition, a preposition is "a relation or function word...that connects a lexical word, usually a noun or pronoun, or a syntactic construction to another element of the sentence, as to a verb, to a noun, or to an adjective..."

-Webster's New World Dictionary

The definition is so complex that it may confuse students. If you choose to define *preposition*, do so very carefully.

PREPOSITIONAL PHRASES

A PREPOSITIONAL PHRASE BEGINS WITH A PREPOSITION AND ENDS WITH A NOUN OR PRONOUN. That noun or pronoun is called the **object of the preposition.**

with my grandfather (***with*** = preposition)
(***grandfather*** = the object of the preposition)
(***with my grandfather*** = a prepositional phrase)

At this point, students have not studied nouns or pronouns. Instruct students that a prepositional phrase will usually end with a "thing."

Example: The boy looked **at a magazine**.

Of course, this isn't always applicable. The object of the preposition may be abstract.

Example: She answered **with enthusiasm**.

However, most of the prepositional phrases will end with concrete nouns (those that can be seen).

PREPOSITIONS:

about
above
across
after
against
along
amid
among
around
at
atop
before
behind
below
beneath
beside
between
beyond
but (meaning except)
by
concerning
down
during
except
for
from
in
inside
into
like
near
of
off
on
onto
out
outside
over
past
regarding
since
through
throughout
to
toward
under
underneath
until
up
upon
with
within
without

off	beside	out	beyond	for
through	after	toward	above	up
from	into	FREE	over	of
to	with	since	within	near
below	down	outside	past	across

		FREE		

Name________________________________ **PREPOSITIONS**

WORKBOOK PAGE 4

Date________________________________

Directions: Unscramble the following prepositions.

1. tuo - **OUT**
2. hothotguru - **THROUGHOUT**
3. yb - **BY**
4. atdrow - **TOWARD**
5. fro - **FOR**
6. duiteso - **OUTSIDE**
7. ta - **AT**
8. ekil - **LIKE**
9. nices - **SINCE**
10. snidei - **INSIDE**
11. rafte - **AFTER**
12. uttiwho - **WITHOUT**
13. dargergin - **REGARDING**
14. ceetpx - **EXCEPT**
15. atubo - **ABOUT**
16. esbedi - **BESIDE**
17. tub - **BUT (MEANING EXCEPT)**
18. poat - **ATOP**
19. nnccngoeri - **CONCERNING**
20. thebean - **BENEATH**

Name________________________________

PREPOSITIONS

Date________________________________

Directions: Unscramble the following prepositions.

1. tuo -________________________________
2. hothotguru -________________________________
3. yb - ________________________________
4. atdrow - ________________________________
5. fro - ________________________________
6. duiteso - ________________________________
7. ta - ________________________________
8. ekil - ________________________________
9. nices - ________________________________
10. snidei - ________________________________
11. rafte - ________________________________
12. uttiwho -________________________________
13. dargergin - ________________________________
14. ceetpx - ________________________________
15. atubo - ________________________________
16. esbedi - ________________________________
17. tub - ________________________________
18. poat - ________________________________
19. nnccngoeri - ________________________________
20. thebean - ________________________________

Name______________________________ **PREPOSITIONS**

WORKBOOK PAGE 5

Date______________________________

Directions: Unscramble the following prepositions.

1. tub - **BUT**
2. bowle - **BELOW**
3. nulit - **UNTIL**
4. maid - **AMID**
5. oubat - **ABOUT**
6. hiwt - **WITH**
7. ondw - **DOWN**
8. rothhug - **THROUGH**
9. pu - **UP**
10. eran - **NEAR**
11. gloan - **ALONG**
12. rocass - **ACROSS**
13. fof - **OFF**
14. nithiw - **WITHIN**
15. magon - **AMONG**
16. boyend - **BEYOND**
17. twebene - **BETWEEN**
18. mfor - **FROM**
19. nirgud - **DURING**
20. sitanga - **AGAINST**

Name________________________________ **PREPOSITIONS**

Date________________________________

Directions: Unscramble the following prepositions.

1. tub - ______________________________
2. bowle - ______________________________
3. nulit - ______________________________
4. maid - ______________________________
5. oubat - ______________________________
6. hiwt - ______________________________
7. ondw - ______________________________
8. rothhug - ______________________________
9. pu - ______________________________
10. eran - ______________________________
11. gloan - ______________________________
12. rocass - ______________________________
13. fof - ______________________________
14. nithiw - ______________________________
15. magon - ______________________________
16. boyend - ______________________________
17. twebene - ______________________________
18. mfor - ______________________________
19. nirgud - ______________________________
20. sitanga - ______________________________

FOR THE TEACHER:

WORKBOOK PAGE 6

PREPOSITIONAL PHRASES WILL NOT BE THE SUBJECT OR VERB OF A SENTENCE. (This holds true 99% of the time.)

HOW TO TEACH SUBJECTS:

After crossing out all prepositional phrases, find **who** or **what** the sentence is about.

EXTREMELY IMPORTANT: When beginning the unit and working orally, be sure to ask what prepositional phrases are being deleted. Next, stress that a word crossed out cannot be the subject or verb of the sentence. Then, read that which is left in the sentence and ask **who** or **what** the sentence is about. Solicit answers. Be sure to do the beginning of the unit *and* the beginning of each lesson in this manner. Students need to become comfortable with this procedure.

A. A rabbit with long, floppy ears hopped around a cage.
   A rabbit ~~with long, floppy ears~~ hopped ~~around a cage~~.

B. One of the girls trimmed trees in her yard.
   One ~~of the girls~~ trimmed trees ~~in her yard~~.

   (Some students will need to be shown that one is a pronoun standing for one girl. If students decide that trees may be the subject, stress that the tree did not do the trimming. Later, when direct objects are introduced, students should have no trouble with this concept.)

HOW TO TEACH VERBS:

After determining the subject of the sentence, decide **what happens/happened** or **what is/was** in the sentence. *The verb will never be in a prepositional phrase.*

A. The man in the back row clapped for the singer.
   The man ~~in the back row~~ clapped ~~for the singer.~~

B. Each of the campers is happy.
   Each ~~of the campers~~ is happy.

EXTREMELY IMPORTANT: Show students that campers is not the subject because it is part of a prepositional phrase. Each is a pronoun standing for each camper. Notice that for subject and verb agreement, we use each is (not campers are). This is an important concept. Also, some students will want to make happy part of the verb. Teach them to conjugate happy by saying, "To happy: Today, I happy. Yesterday I happied. Tomorrow I shall happy." Students, usually with laughter, can readily discern that no such verb as "to happy" exists.

Name________________________________ **PREPOSITIONS**

WORKBOOK PAGE 7

Date________________________________

Directions: Cross out any prepositional phrase(s). Underline the subject once and the verb twice.

Example: Kim lives ~~in the desert~~.

1. I cleaned ~~for an hour~~.
2. His father sings ~~in the shower~~.
3. We walked ~~along a trail~~.
4. My friend lives ~~near our church~~.
5. A clerk stood ~~beside a counter~~.
6. Joyce ran ~~down the road~~.
7. Mark went ~~to the store~~.
8. Your book is ~~under the sofa~~.
9. Everyone ~~except Todd~~ left.
10. Her brush fell ~~between the seats~~.
11. A stranger walked ~~toward the policeman~~.
12. Grandma sits ~~on her patio~~.
13. Jane lives ~~with her aunt~~.
14. A dog leaped ~~off the porch~~.
15. This story is ~~about frogs~~.

Name_________________________________ **PREPOSITIONS**

Date_________________________________

Directions: Cross out any prepositional phrase(s). Underline the subject once and the verb twice.

Example: Kim lives ~~in the desert~~.

1. I cleaned for an hour.
2. His father sings in the shower.
3. We walked along a trail.
4. My friend lives near our church.
5. A clerk stood beside a counter.
6. Joyce ran down the road.
7. Mark went to the store.
8. Your book is under the sofa.
9. Everyone except Todd left.
10. Her brush fell between the seats.
11. A stranger walked toward the policeman.
12. Grandma sits on her patio.
13. Jane lives with her aunt.
14. A dog leaped off the porch.
15. This story is about frogs.

Name________________________________ **PREPOSITIONS**

WORKBOOK PAGE 8

Date________________________________

Directions: Cross out any prepositional phrase(s). Underline the subject once and the verb twice.

EXAMPLE: His keys are ~~on the table~~.

1. Jason hid ~~behind a bush~~.
2. The teenager charged ~~out the door~~.
3. His bus arrives ~~before lunch~~.
4. ~~During recess~~, her teacher works.
5. A picture hangs ~~above a small window~~.
6. Their dog ran ~~outside their gate~~.
7. Mr. Jones leaned ~~against a wall~~.
8. That cat jumps ~~over the animals~~.
9. Some children raced ~~up the hill~~.
10. Mary left ~~without his books~~.
11. A boat sailed ~~across the wide lake~~.
12. The boys flopped ~~into the water~~.
13. My mom cleans ~~throughout the day~~.
14. The picnic table is ~~beyond those trees~~.
15. Mrs. Smith stepped ~~into the bus~~.

Name________________________________ **PREPOSITIONS**

Date_________________________________

Directions: Cross out any prepositional phrase(s). Underline the subject once and the verb twice.

Example: His keys are ~~on the table~~.

1. Jason hid behind a bush.
2. The teenager charged out the door.
3. His bus arrives before lunch.
4. During recess, her teacher works.
5. A picture hangs above a small window.
6. Their dog ran outside their gate.
7. Mr. Jones leaned against a wall.
8. That cat jumps over the other animals.
9. Some children raced up the hill.
10. Mary left without her books.
11. A boat sailed across the wide lake.
12. The boys flopped into the water.
13. My mom cleans throughout the day.
14. The picnic table is beyond those trees.
15. Mrs. Smith stepped into the bus.

Name________________________________ **PREPOSITIONS**

WORKBOOK PAGE 9

Date__________________________________

Directions: Cross out any prepositional phrase(s). Underline the subject once and the verb twice.

Example: Wendy stood ~~in a long line~~.

1. This note is ~~from Mary~~.
2. Three fish swam ~~inside a bowl~~.
3. Her sister shops ~~at a mall~~.
4. A cowboy rode ~~past some cattle~~.
5. An ambulance came ~~within five minutes~~.
6. A new nurse was ~~on the telephone~~.
7. Several college students sat ~~beneath a tree~~.
8. Bill gave a report ~~about ants~~.
9. We walked ~~through the tunnel~~.
10. The papers remained ~~underneath a desk~~.
11. Their team fought ~~until the end~~.
12. A clown sat ~~upon a balloon~~.
13. His cat plays ~~among the rosebushes~~.
14. Many girls waited ~~outside the building~~.
15. My neighbor talks ~~with her mother~~ every day.

Name________________________________ **PREPOSITIONS**

Date________________________________

Directions: Cross out any prepositional phrase(s). Underline the subject once and the verb twice.

Example: Wendy stood ~~in a long line~~.

1. This note is from Mary.
2. Three fish swam inside a bowl.
3. Her sister shops at a mall.
4. A cowboy rode past some cattle.
5. An ambulance came within five minutes.
6. A new nurse was on the telephone.
7. Several college students sat beneath a tree.
8. Bill gave a report about ants.
9. We walked through the tunnel.
10. The papers remained underneath a desk.
11. Their team fought until the end.
12. A clown sat upon a balloon.
13. His cat plays among the rosebushes.
14. Many girls waited outside the building.
15. My neighbor talks with her mother every day.

Name________________________________ **PREPOSITIONS**

WORKBOOK PAGE 10

Date________________________________

Directions: Cross out any prepositional phrase(s). Underline the subject once and the verb twice.

Example: ~~During the night~~, deer lay ~~in the forest~~.

1. ~~After dinner~~ Mom went ~~to a baby shower~~.
2. We looked ~~below the sink~~ ~~for a bucket~~.
3. Some joggers ran ~~over the hill~~ and ~~past a lake~~.
4. ~~In June~~ my cousin went ~~down the Colorado River~~.
5. ~~During the blizzard~~ the children remained ~~inside the house~~.
6. They searched ~~behind the barn~~ ~~for the stray cow~~.
7. I found the jam ~~in the pantry~~ ~~beside a cereal box~~.
8. ~~Before the concert,~~ a violinist sat ~~among the guests~~.
9. ~~Throughout the summer~~ those boys waded ~~in a stream~~.
10. ~~At the bottom~~ ~~of a mine~~ is an old cart.
11. Dad drove ~~along a canal~~ and ~~over a bridge~~.
12. Every cat ~~but the gray one~~ came ~~near me~~.
13. The babysitter looked ~~out the window~~ and ~~into the yard~~.
14. These two pages are ~~about birds~~ ~~like the ostrich~~.
15. ~~By the end~~ ~~of the race~~, most ~~of the adults~~ walked.

Name______________________________

Date______________________________

PREPOSITIONS

Directions: Cross out any prepositional phrase(s). Underline the subject once and the verb twice.

Example: ~~During the night~~, <u>deer</u> <u>lay</u> ~~in the forest~~.

1. After dinner Mom went to a baby shower.
2. We looked below the sink for a bucket.
3. Some joggers ran over the hill and past a lake.
4. In June my cousin went down the Colorado River.
5. During the blizzard the children remained inside the house.
6. They searched behind the barn for the stray cow.
7. I found the jam in the pantry beside a cereal box.
8. Before the concert, a violinist sat among the guests.
9. Throughout the summer those boys waded in a stream.
10. At the bottom of a mine is an old cart.
11. Dad drove along a canal and over a bridge.
12. Every cat but the gray one came near me.
13. The babysitter looked out the window and into the yard.
14. These two pages are about birds like the ostrich.
15. By the end of the race, most of the adults walked.

FOR THE TEACHER: **Teach Part A; then, do page 23. Teach Part B and do page 25. Teach Part C and complete page 27. Do these in 3 separate lessons.**

WORKBOOK PAGE 11

VERBS

A. Teach students that to + a verb is called an infinitive. It is suggested that students place an infinitive in parentheses. This will prevent crossing out an infinitive as a prepositional phrase.

Example: James decided (to take) his bird ~~with him~~.

B. A **verb phrase** is composed of at least one helping (auxiliary) verb plus a main verb. (Use whichever term you feel is appropriate.)

Examples: The hotel maid has cleaned all ~~of the rooms~~.
Her idea was given ~~to the leader~~.

IMPORTANT NOTE: In an interrogative (question) sentence type, teach students to look for a helping (auxiliary) verb at the beginning of the sentence.

Was a man ~~with his backpack~~ sitting ~~along the road~~?

EXTREMELY IMPORTANT: Students must memorize the list of twenty-three helping verbs later when they study the unit about verbs. At this point, do not have them memorize the list of helping verbs. You may want to place a copy on the wall for easy reference. Another idea is for each child to have his own copy of the list. These auxiliary (helping) verbs have been grouped for easy learning.

LIST OF HELPING VERBS:

do	**has**	**may**	**should**	**shall**	**is**
does	**have**	**might**	**would**	**will**	**am**
did	**had**	**must**	**could**	**can**	**are**
					was
					were
					be
					being
					been

In this unit, sentences that contain helping verbs will be starred.

C. **Not (n't) is never a verb**. (Not is an adverb.) Teach students to box **not** or **n't** as soon as they read it in a sentence. (However, **not** will appear in italics on the answer key.) Make sure that each child understands that **not** or **n't** will never be double underlined as part of the verb phrase.

Examples: The attorney ~~in the black suit~~ has *not* talked ~~to the jury~~.

Has*n't* the plumber fixed the leak ~~in the toilet~~?

Name________________________________ **PREPOSITIONS**

WORKBOOK PAGE 12

Date________________________________

Directions: Place parentheses around any infinitive(s). Cross out any prepositional phrase(s). Underline the subject once and the verb twice.

REMEMBER: *to* + verb = infinitive
Place parenthesis around an infinitive; do not cross it out as a prepositional phrase.

1. She walked ~~onto the stage~~ (to sing).

2. The little girl wants (to sit) ~~between us~~.

3. Dave looked ~~beneath his chair~~ (to locate) his books.

4. A minister stood ~~amid the boys~~ (to talk).

5. ~~During the storm~~, Sally ran (to reach) her home.

6. A lady jumped ~~atop a chair~~ (to see) better.

7. ~~Before dinner~~, they go ~~into the bathroom~~ (to wash) their hands.

8. Sarah likes (to watch) programs ~~concerning plants~~.

9. A boy peeked ~~around the corner~~ (to see) his friend.

10. Dad wants (to take) a trip ~~without me~~.

11. She searched ~~underneath a pillow~~ (to find) her keys.

12. ~~After breakfast~~, they decided (to go) ~~on a picnic~~.

13. Their cousin waited ~~until the end~~ ~~of the game~~ (to leave).

14. Mrs. Sands drove ~~beyond that water tower~~ (to get) some firewood.

15. ~~At the end~~ ~~of this game~~, Kyle wants (to eat) a doughnut.

Name______________________________ **PREPOSITIONS**

Date______________________________

Directions: Place parentheses around any infinitive(s). Cross out any prepositional phrase(s). Underline the subject once and the verb twice.

REMEMBER: to + verb = infinitive
Place parentheses around an infinitive; do not cross it out as a prepositional phrase.

1. She walked onto the stage to sing.
2. The little girl wants to sit between us.
3. Dave looked beneath his chair to locate his books.
4. A minister stood amid the boys to talk.
5. During the storm, Sally ran to reach her home.
6. A lady jumped atop a chair to see better.
7. Before dinner, they go into the bathroom to wash their hands.
8. Sarah likes to watch programs concerning plants.
9. A boy peeked around the corner to see his friend.
10. Dad wants to take a trip without me.
11. She searched underneath a pillow to find her keys.
12. After breakfast, they decided to go on a picnic.
13. Their cousin waited until the end of the game to leave.
14. Mrs. Sands drove beyond that water tower to get some firewood.
15. At the end of this game, Kyle wants to eat a doughnut.

Name________________________________ **PREPOSITIONS**

WORKBOOK PAGE 13

Date________________________________

Directions: Cross out any prepositional phrase(s). Underline the subject once and the verb phrase twice.

Example: Has Tom swum ~~for an hour~~?

1. Our dog was hiding ~~under the table~~ ~~during the storm~~.
2. Their plane must have flown ~~toward Washington, D.C~~.
3. ~~After this ball~~, you may run ~~to first base~~.
4. Did Jill leave her suitcase ~~outside the door~~?
5. You may sit ~~behind me~~ or ~~on the floor~~.
6. A picture ~~of our great grandmother~~ was placed ~~above the fireplace~~.
7. Are you throwing the ball ~~onto the roof~~ or ~~over the house~~?
8. ~~At noon~~ the parade will move ~~past the courthouse~~.
9. She had hurried ~~across the busy street~~ ~~among a large crowd~~.
10. He has practiced ~~for two hours~~ ~~since the last game~~.
11. ~~By five o'clock~~, the saleslady will have driven sixty miles.
12. ~~Within an hour~~ ~~after the party~~, they had cleaned.
13. A bear might have come ~~down that trail~~ recently.
14. I shall sit ~~in the middle~~ ~~of the first row~~.
15. Everyone ~~except the bus driver~~ had gone ~~into the restaurant~~.

Name________________________________ **PREPOSITIONS**

Date________________________________

Directions: Cross out any prepositional phrase(s). Underline the subject once and the verb phrase twice.

Example: Has Tom swum ~~for an hour~~?

1. Our dog was hiding under the table during the storm.
2. Their plane must have flown toward Washington, D.C.
3. After this ball, you may run to first base.
4. Did Jill leave her suitcase outside the door?
5. You may sit behind me or on the floor.
6. A picture of our great grandmother was placed above the fireplace.
7. Are you throwing the ball onto the roof or over the house?
8. At noon the parade will move past the courthouse.
9. She had hurried across the busy street among a large crowd.
10. He has practiced for two hours since the last game.
11. By five o'clock, the saleslady will have driven sixty miles.
12. Within an hour after the party, they had cleaned.
13. A bear might have come down that trail recently.
14. I shall sit in the middle of the first row.
15. Everyone except the bus driver had gone into the restaurant.

Name________________________________ **PREPOSITIONS**

WORKBOOK PAGE 14

Date________________________________

Directions: Cross out any prepositional phrase(s). Underline the subject once and the verb phrase twice.

Example: You can*not* take the bat ~~with you~~ ~~to first base~~.

1. We could *not* leave ~~before six o'clock~~.
2. The flowers ~~from Aunt Martha~~ had been sent ~~to our family~~.
3. You can*not* jump ~~off that diving board~~.
4. The winner will *not* be chosen ~~until Friday~~.
5. That machine ~~near the window~~ would *not* take our money.
6. The box ~~inside the front door~~ must *not* be moved yet.
7. I shall *not* go ~~beyond that point~~ again.
8. They were looking ~~through binoculars~~ ~~at several birds~~.
9. The window ~~above the sink~~ must *not* be closed ~~before bedtime~~.
10. Shelly does*n't* want a sandwich ~~before bedtime~~.
11. Do*n't* you live ~~beside the library~~ ~~on Barr Lane~~?
12. She should *not* have run ~~out the door~~ and ~~down the street~~.
13. He is*n't* talking ~~to me~~ ~~about his bad score~~.
14. He did *not* look ~~below the stove~~ or ~~beneath the table~~ ~~for his coin~~.
15. May I play ~~with my friends~~ ~~on Saturday~~?

Name________________________________ **PREPOSITIONS**

Date________________________________

Directions: Cross out any prepositional phrase(s). Underline the subject once and the verb phrase twice.

Example: You can*not* take the bat ~~with you~~ ~~to first base~~.

1. We could not leave before six o'clock.
2. The flowers from Aunt Martha had been sent to our family.
3. You cannot jump off that diving board.
4. The winner will not be chosen until Friday.
5. That machine near the window would not take our money.
6. The box inside the front door must not be moved yet.
7. I shall not go beyond that point again.
8. They were looking through binoculars at several birds.
9. The window above the sink must not be closed before bedtime.
10. Shelly doesn't want a sandwich before bedtime.
11. Don't you live beside the library on Barr Lane?
12. She should not have run out the door and down the street.
13. He isn't talking to me about his bad score.
14. He did not look below the stove or beneath the table for his coin.
15. May I play with my friends on Saturday?

FOR THE TEACHER:
WORKBOOK PAGE 15

TEACHING COMPOUNDS

Compound means more than one. Be sure that students understand this. Only one example is provided for each concept. You will need to provide additional ones. ***Also, it is suggested that you teach each concept with the given lesson rather than teaching all three concepts together.***

A. **COMPOUND OBJECT OF THE PREPOSITION**: A prepositional phrase may end with two or more objects. When a prepositional phrase ends with a noun or pronoun followed by **and** or **or**, check if another noun or pronoun follows it.

Example: They went with their mom **and** dad.
They went ~~with their mom and dad~~.

B. **COMPOUND SUBJECT**: There may be a compound subject in a sentence. This means there are two or more subjects.

Example: During the game, Tom and his brother cheered.
~~During the game~~, Tom and his brother cheered.

C. **COMPOUND VERB**: Sometimes, there are two or more verbs in a sentence.

Example: Barry caught the ball and threw it ~~to second base~~.

Help students to see that Barry did two things in this sentence. Your guidance is very important.

Name________________________________

WORKBOOK PAGE 16

Date________________________________

PREPOSITIONS
Compound Object of the Preposition

Directions: Cross out any prepositional phrase(s). Underline the subject once and the verb/verb phrase twice. Starred sentences contain helping verb(s).

REMEMBER: A preposition may have more than one object.

Example: I sat ~~on the floor~~ ~~between the **couch** and the **television**~~.

1. This postcard is ~~from my aunt and uncle~~.

2. The speaker talked ~~about cars and trucks~~.

3. Joy traveled ~~with her grandmother and grandfather~~.

4. We had chicken ~~for lunch and dinner~~.

5. *~~During fall and winter~~, his family will go ~~to Boston~~.

6. This dessert ~~of apples and ice cream~~ is great.

7. Jack gave his pens ~~to Tim and me~~.

8. Sandy ran the race ~~without her shoes and socks~~.

9. His friend lives ~~near Carl or me~~.

10. Everyone ~~except Mr. Horn and Mr. Smith~~ won a prize.

11. The children decided (*to stay*)** ~~by the swings and slide~~.

12. *I am going ~~to a wedding~~ ~~on Saturday or Sunday~~.

13. *Your wallet is lying ~~under those papers and magazines~~.

14. We walked ~~around the fence and the goal posts~~.

15. *You may *not* go ~~outside the square or this line~~.

** *to stay* - Remind students that to + verb = infinitive

Name________________________________

Date________________________________

PREPOSITIONS
Compound Object of the Preposition

Directions: Cross out any prepositional phrase(s). Underline the subject once and the verb/verb phrase twice. Starred sentences contain helping verb(s).

REMEMBER: A preposition may have more than one object.

Example: I sat ~~on the floor~~ ~~between the **couch** and the **television**~~.

1. This postcard is from my aunt and uncle.
2. The speaker talked about cars and trucks.
3. Joy traveled with her grandmother and grandfather.
4. We had chicken for lunch and dinner.
5. *During fall and winter, his family will go to Boston.
6. This dessert of apples and ice cream is great.
7. Jack gave his pens to Tim and me.
8. Sandy ran the race without her shoes and socks.
9. His friend lives near Carl or me.
10. Everyone except Mr. Horn and Mr. Smith won a prize.
11. The children decided to stay by the swings and slide.
12. *I am going to a wedding on Saturday or Sunday.
13. *Your wallet is lying under those papers and magazines.
14. We walked around the fence and the goal posts.
15. *You may not go outside the square or this line.

Name______________________________

WORKBOOK PAGE 17

Date______________________________

PREPOSITIONS
Compound Subject

Directions: Cross out any prepositional phrase(s). Underline the subject once and the verb/verb phrase twice. Starred sentences contain helping verb(s).

Example: Both Jessica and her mother went ~~to the store~~.

1. Dr. Stanson and his nurse talked ~~with the patient~~.
2. *Your towel and sunglasses are lying ~~on the patio table~~.
3. Mrs. Shane and her daughter walked ~~along the pond~~.
4. ~~Around six o'clock~~, the clerk and manager count the money.
5. Gary and I crawled ~~underneath the table~~.
6. *Melissa or her brother will sit ~~beside me~~.
7. *Grandma and her friend are looking ~~through the old albums~~.
8. *Have the swimmers and their parents arrived ~~at the pool~~?
9. *~~Before the show~~, popcorn and candy were purchased.
10. *Marty, Zak, and Patty were sitting ~~behind the team~~.
11. The fireman and the ambulance driver talked ~~for a few minutes~~.
12. *Neither Ted nor his sister can come ~~until noon~~.
13. ~~Toward the end~~ ~~of the day~~, his friend and he played cards.
14. *The mayor and his wife will *not* attend the meeting ~~regarding his election~~.
15. *~~Outside the back door~~, a planter ~~of flowers~~ and a tree had been placed.

Name_______________________________

Date_______________________________

PREPOSITIONS
Compound Subject

Directions: Cross out any prepositional phrase(s). Underline the subject once and the verb/verb phrase twice. Starred sentences contain helping verb(s).

Example: Both Jessica and her mother went ~~to the store~~.

1. Dr. Stanson and his nurse talked with the patient.

2. *Your towel and sunglasses are lying on the patio table.

3. Mrs. Shane and her daughter walked along the pond.

4. Around six o'clock, the clerk and manager count the money.

5. Gary and I crawled underneath the table.

6. *Melissa or her brother will sit beside me.

7. *Grandma and her friend are looking through the old albums.

8. *Have the swimmers and their parents arrived at the pool?

9. *Before the show, popcorn and candy were purchased.

10. *Marty, Zak, and Patty were sitting behind the team.

11. The fireman and the ambulance driver talked for a few minutes.

12. *Neither Ted nor his sister can come until noon.

13. Toward the end of the day, his friend and he played cards.

14. *The mayor and his wife will not attend the meeting regarding his election.

15. *Outside the back door, a planter of flowers and a tree had been placed.

Name________________________________ **PREPOSITIONS**
WORKBOOK PAGE 18 **Compound Verb**
Date________________________________

Directions: Cross out any prepositional phrase(s). Underline the subject once and the verb/verb phrase twice. Starred sentences contain helping verb(s).

Example: The garbage man lifted the can ~~into the truck~~ and dumped it.

1. Vicky sneezed ~~during the assembly~~ and laughed softly.
2. His dog jumps ~~against their door~~ and puts scratches ~~in the wood~~.
3. A trucker stepped ~~outside his truck~~ and looked ~~at his tires~~.
4. Mr. Kunes spoke ~~about smoking~~ and showed a slide ~~concerning good health~~.
5. Everyone ~~except two players~~ ran ~~onto the field~~ and began (to practice).
6. We went ~~down several steps~~ and looked ~~into a darkened room~~.
7. *This bus travels ~~across town~~ but does not stop ~~by the train station~~.
8. ~~During the spring of each year~~, her family digs the soil and plants a garden.
9. Each student ~~but Candy~~ sang and played an instrument.
10. The chef cooks ~~throughout the day~~ and enjoys foods ~~like Cajun shrimp~~.
11. The little girl found a spider ~~below the sink~~ and yelled ~~for her mother~~.
12. *May Jake talk ~~to you~~ now or see you ~~after dinner~~?
13. *Miss Franklin will read a story ~~to the children~~ and present a puppet show.
14. Those hikers sat ~~beneath a tree~~ or rested ~~from their long trip up the mountain~~.
15. Joe raced ~~beyond the fence~~, jumped ~~over a box~~, and stood ~~near a parked car~~.

Name______________________________

Date______________________________

PREPOSITIONS
Compound Verb

Directions: Cross out any prepositional phrase(s). Underline the subject once and the verb/verb phrase twice. Starred sentences contain helping verb(s).

Example: The garbage man lifted the can ~~into the truck~~ and dumped it.

1. Vicky sneezed during the assembly and laughed softly.
2. His dog jumps against their door and puts scratches in the wood.
3. A trucker stepped outside his truck and looked at his tires.
4. Mr. Kunes spoke about smoking and showed a slide concerning good health.
5. Everyone except two players ran onto the field and began to practice.
6. We went down several steps and looked into a darkened room.
7. *This bus travels across town but does not stop by the train station.
8. During the spring of each year, her family digs the soil and plants a garden.
9. Each student but Candy sang and played an instrument.
10. The chef cooks throughout the day and enjoys foods like Cajun shrimp.
11. The little girl found a spider below the sink and yelled for her mother.
12. *May Jake talk to you now or see you after dinner?
13. *Miss Franklin will read a story to the children and present a puppet show.
14. Those hikers sat beneath a tree or rested from their long trip up the mountain.
15. Joe raced beyond the fence, jumped over a box, and stood near a parked car.

FOR THE TEACHER:
WORKBOOK PAGE 19

IMPERATIVE SENTENCES

In an imperative sentence, the subject is (you).

A. An imperative sentence gives a command.

B. (You) is termed "**You understood.**" When students give the subject of an imperative sentence, be sure to have them say you understood rather than just you.

EXAMPLES:

A. Stay here.

(You) Stay here.

B. Please look at the camera.

(You) Please look ~~at the camera~~.

C. Hang the calendar on the wall.

(You) Hang the calendar* ~~on the wall~~.

*Some students will want to underline calendar as the subject.

1. Guide students to see that this is an imperative sentence and review that (You) will be the subject.

2. Ask the question, "Is the calendar placing?" No. Help students to understand that YOU are placing.

Name________________________________

WORKBOOK PAGE 20

Date________________________________

PREPOSITIONS
Imperative Sentences

Directions: Cross out any prepositional phrase(s). Underline the subject once and the verb/verb phrase twice. Starred sentences contain helping verb(s).

Reminder: **In an imperative sentence, the subject is (You).**

1. (You) Sit ~~behind me~~.
2. (You) Toss the paper ~~into the trash~~, please.
3. (You) Brush your teeth ~~before bedtime~~.
4. (You) Listen ~~to your parents~~.
5. (You) Put the picture ~~atop the china closet~~.
6. (You) Read this newsletter ~~concerning vitamins~~.
7. (You) Open this gift ~~from Doug and Tony~~.
8. (You) ~~In the morning~~, send this ~~to your Uncle Bob~~.
9. (You) Put the puppy ~~inside the carrying cage~~.
10. (You) Throw the towels ~~like that blue one~~ ~~into the washing machine~~.
11. (You) Take this ~~with you~~ (to read) ~~on the bus~~.
12. *(You) Do *not* hang the picture ~~above the large lamp~~.
13. (You) Follow that car and drive ~~over the bridge~~.
14. (You) Walk ~~toward the back~~ ~~of the bus~~ and sit ~~by me~~.
15. *(You) Please do*n't* jump ~~over those fallen logs~~ ~~behind the shed~~.

Name________________________________

Date________________________________

PREPOSITIONS
Imperative Sentences

Directions: Cross out any prepositional phrase(s). Underline the subject once and the verb/verb phrase twice. Starred sentences contain helping verb(s).

Reminder: **In an imperative sentence, the subject is (You).**

1. Sit behind me.
2. Toss the paper into the trash, please.
3. Brush your teeth before bedtime.
4. Listen to your parents.
5. Put the picture atop the china closet.
6. Read this newsletter concerning vitamins.
7. Open this gift from Doug and Tony.
8. In the morning, send this to your Uncle Bob.
9. Put the puppy inside the carrying cage.
10. Throw the towels like that blue one into the washing machine.
11. Take this with you to read on the bus.
12. *Do not hang the picture above the large lamp.
13. Follow that car and drive over the bridge.
14. Walk toward the back of the bus and sit by me.
15. *Please don't jump over those fallen logs behind the shed.

FOR THE TEACHER:
WORKBOOK PAGE 21

PREPOSITION OR ADVERB?

Teach this concept very carefully. Do not confuse the students.

Emphasize that a preposition must be part of a prepositional phrase. In other words, it must be followed by a noun or pronoun. (Review that this noun or pronoun is called the object of the preposition.) If there is no noun or pronoun following the preposition, the preposition is not crossed out. The word then serves as an **adverb**. Have students place **ADV.** above the word. (If you believe that this is too complex for your students, you may choose not to explain that the word serves as an adverb.)

EXTREMELY IMPORTANT: Continue the process of first deleting prepositional phrases, underlining subject once, and underlining the verb/verb phrase twice. Then, look for a word that originally was learned as a preposition but does not have a noun or pronoun (object of the preposition).

EXAMPLES:

A. Janet went inside with her pets.

ADV.
Janet went **inside** ~~with her pets~~.

B. During their vacation, they camped out in the woods.

ADV.
~~During their vacation~~, they camped **out** ~~in the woods~~.

Name________________________________ **PREPOSITIONS**

WORKBOOK PAGE 22 **Preposition or Adverb?**

Date________________________________

Directions: Cross out any prepositional phrase(s). Underline the subject once and the verb/verb phrase twice. Starred sentences contain helping verb(s).
Adverbs have been labeled for your information.

Remember: A preposition must have an object (noun or pronoun) following it.

ADV.
1. The doctor came in ~~within a few minutes~~.

ADV.
2. A teacher sat down ~~between two students~~.

ADV.
3. We went up ~~into Grandma's attic~~.

ADV.
4. Lisa drove past ~~in an old black truck~~.

ADV.
5. Nick and I looked over ~~at the coach~~.

ADV.
6. *Some bikers had gone across ~~at the intersection~~.

ADV.
7. The winner danced around ~~in a circle~~.

ADV.
8. *Has the carpenter gone outside ~~for a tool~~?

ADV.
9. A player hit a ball out ~~of the ballpark~~.

ADV.
10. *She had *not* seen a llama before.

ADV.
11. Your lungs are near ~~to your heart~~.

ADV.
12. Her partner rushed by ~~in a hurry~~.

ADV.
13. (You) Jump off carefully and wait ~~for me~~ ~~at the dock~~.

ADV.
14. From ~~within the cave~~ came a cry ~~for help~~.

ADV.
15. A driver came along and asked ~~for directions~~.

Name________________________________

Date________________________________

PREPOSITIONS
Preposition or Adverb?

Directions: Cross out any prepositional phrase(s). Underline the subject once and the verb/verb phrase twice. Starred sentences contain helping verb(s).

Remember: A preposition must have an object (noun or pronoun) following it.

1. The doctor came in within a few minutes.
2. A teacher sat down between two students.
3. We went up into Grandma's attic.
4. Lisa drove past in an old black truck.
5. Nick and I looked over at the coach.
6. *Some bikers had gone across at the intersection.
7. The winner danced around in a circle.
8. *Has the carpenter gone outside for a tool?
9. A player hit a ball out of the ballpark.
10. *She had not seen a llama before.
11. Your lungs are near to your heart.
12. Her partner rushed by in a hurry.
13. Jump off carefully and wait for me at the dock.
14. From within the cave came a cry for help.
15. A driver came along and asked for directions.

Name_______________________________ **PREPOSITION REVIEW**

WORKBOOK PAGE 23

Date_______________________________

A. Directions: Cross out any prepositional phrase(s). Underline the subject once and the verb twice.

To + Verb = Infinitive: Do not cross out an infinitive.

Example: The maid wanted (to clean) the room ~~before ten o'clock~~.

1. His sister likes (*to swing*) ~~on the monkey bars~~.

2. Kyle wants (*to go*) ~~to a record shop~~ today.

3. Mr. Harmon decided (*to leave*) ~~before halftime~~.

4. ~~During the play~~, someone pretended (*to be*) a duck.

5. The banker hesitated (*to sign*) the papers.

6. We like (to watch) ~~for odd traffic signs~~.

7. The reception needs (to be) ~~in the last ballroom~~.

B. Directions: Cross out any prepositional phrase(s). Underline the subject once and the verb phrase twice.

A verb phrase consists of a helping (auxiliary) verb + a main verb.

Example: No one has seen Laura ~~for an hour~~.

1. A French poodle had run ~~into the street~~.

2. I shall scrub the floors ~~during the afternoon~~.

3. Their parents are golfing ~~after breakfast~~.

4. A forest fire had been fought ~~along a highway~~.

5. Everything ~~but the pizza~~ must be purchased ~~before the party~~.

6. A camel was leading a caravan ~~through the desert~~.

7. Should we have gone ~~without him~~?

Name________________________________ **PREPOSITION REVIEW**

Date________________________________

A. Directions: Cross out any prepositional phrase(s). Underline the subject once and the verb twice.

To + Verb = Infinitive: Do not cross out an infinitive.

Example: The maid wanted (to clean) the room ~~before ten o'clock~~.

1. His sister likes to swing on the monkey bars.

2. Kyle wants to go to a record shop today.

3. Mr. Harmon decided to leave before halftime.

4. During the play, someone pretended to be a duck.

5. The banker hesitated to sign the papers.

6. We like to watch for odd traffic signs.

7. The reception needs to be in the last ballroom.

B. Directions: Cross out any prepositional phrase(s). Underline the subject once and the verb phrase twice.

A verb phrase consists of a helping (auxiliary) verb + a main verb.

Example: No one has seen Laura ~~for an hour~~.

1. A French poodle had run into the street.

2. I shall scrub the floors during the afternoon.

3. Their parents are golfing after breakfast.

4. A forest fire had been fought along a highway.

5. Everything but the pizza must be purchased before the party.

6. A camel was leading a caravan through the desert.

7. Should we have gone without him?

Name____________________________________ **PREPOSITION REVIEW**

WORKBOOK PAGE 24

Date____________________________________

C. Directions: Cross out any prepositional phrase(s). Underline the subject once and the verb phrase twice.

Not (n't) is never a verb. Do not underline it as part of a verb phrase.

Example: The acrobat has *not* performed ~~for the audience~~.

1. These chairs were *not* painted ~~underneath the trees~~.

2. The tourist would *not* look ~~over the edge~~ ~~of the canyon~~.

3. Everyone ~~except Senator Brill~~ has spoken ~~regarding the incident~~.

4. That artist can*not* finish his painting ~~until next week~~.

5. Did the electrician lean this board ~~against the wall~~?

6. The riders may have ridden ~~toward the mountains~~.

7. Could Lenny have moved the hose ~~into the garage~~?

D. Directions: Cross out any prepositional phrase(s). Underline the subject once and the verb/verb phrase twice. Starred sentences contain helping verb(s).

Compound Object: A preposition may have more than one object.

Example: An oak tree is ~~beside a shed and a corral~~.

1. *Johnny is sitting ~~between his father and mother~~.

2. *That bus is going ~~to Baltimore or New York City~~.

3. *~~After dinner and dessert~~, you may play dominoes.

4. *Sheila does *not* study ~~with Nancy or Karen~~.

5. Mr. Lower works ~~at a video store~~ ~~in the morning and afternoon~~.

6. ~~During their field trip~~, they gathered samples ~~of leaves and flowers~~.

7. Her teacher came ~~to school~~ ~~without her glasses or grade book~~.

Name_______________________________ **PREPOSITION REVIEW**

Date_______________________________

C. Directions: Cross out any prepositional phrase(s). Underline the subject once and the verb phrase twice.

Not (n't) is never a verb. Do not underline it as part of a verb phrase.

Example: The acrobat has *not* performed ~~for the audience~~.

1. These chairs were not painted underneath the trees.

2. The tourist would not look over the edge of the canyon.

3. Everyone except Senator Brill has spoken regarding the incident.

4. That artist cannot finish his painting until next week.

5. Did the electrician lean this board against the wall?

6. The riders may have ridden toward the mountains.

7. Could Lenny have moved the hose into the garage?

D. Directions: Cross out any prepositional phrase(s). Underline the subject once and the verb/verb phrase twice. Starred sentences contain helping verb(s).

Compound Object: A preposition may have more than one object.

Example: An oak tree is ~~beside a shed and a corral~~.

1. *Johnny is sitting between his father and mother.

2. *That bus is going to Baltimore or New York City.

3. *After dinner and dessert, you may play dominoes.

4. *Sheila does not study with Nancy or Karen.

5. Mr. Lower works at a video store in the morning and afternoon.

6. During their field trip, they gathered samples of leaves and flowers.

7. Her teacher came to school without her glasses or grade book.

Name________________________________ **PREPOSITION REVIEW**

WORKBOOK PAGE 25

Date________________________________

E. Directions: Cross out any prepositional phrase(s). Underline the subject once and the verb/verb phrase twice. Starred sentences contain helping verb(s).

COMPOUND SUBJECTS: The subject tells who or what the sentence is about. Sometimes there are two or more subjects in a sentence. This is called a compound subject.

Example: A boy and his friend played ~~in the woods~~.

1. A mother and her child shopped ~~at a drugstore~~.

2. Miss Cobb and Mrs. Lunder are ~~in the tennis tournament~~.

3. Larry and I go ~~to the park~~ every day.

4. *Forests and lakes are located ~~throughout that region~~.

5. *A lemon or orange is needed ~~for this drink~~.

6. *~~After the bridge game~~, pie, cake, and ice cream were served.

7. ~~During the evening~~, a deer and her fawn walked ~~through the meadow~~.

F. Directions: Cross out any prepositional phrase(s). Underline the subject once and the verb/verb phrase twice.

COMPOUND VERBS: A verb tells what is (was) or what happens (happened). Sometimes more than one verb appears in the sentence. This is called a compound verb.

Example: You must sit and read ~~for a few minutes~~.

1. Pat hit the ball ~~into right field~~ and ran ~~for first base~~.

2. ~~In the morning~~, I comb my hair and brush my teeth.

3. Mark's frog jumped ~~onto a rock~~ and croaked.

4. ~~Before the play~~, the energetic actors learned lines and practiced.

5. *Does the new boy travel ~~by bus~~ and arrive ~~at school~~ early?

6. Mr. London takes his lunch ~~to the office~~ and eats ~~across the street~~.

7. *Rings and bracelets were cleaned and placed ~~into a special case~~.

Name__________________________________ **PREPOSITION REVIEW**

Date__________________________________

E. Directions: Cross out any prepositional phrase(s). Underline the subject once and the verb/verb phrase twice. Starred sentences contain helping verb(s).

COMPOUND SUBJECTS: The subject tells who or what the sentence is about. Sometimes there are two or more subjects in a sentence. This is called a compound subject.

Example: A boy and his friend played ~~in the woods~~.

1. A mother and her child shopped at a drugstore.
2. Miss Cobb and Mrs. Lunder are in the tennis tournament.
3. Larry and I go to the park every day.
4. *Forests and lakes are located throughout that region.
5. *A lemon or orange is needed for this drink.
6. *After the bridge game, pie, cake, and ice cream were served.
7. During the evening, a deer and her fawn walked through the meadow.

F. Directions: Cross out any prepositional phrase(s). Underline the subject once and the verb/verb phrase twice. Starred sentences contain helping verb(s).

COMPOUND VERBS: A verb tells what is (was) or what happens (happened). Sometimes more than one verb appears in a sentence. This is called a compound verb.

Example: You must sit and read ~~for a few minutes~~.

1. Pat hit the ball into right field and ran for first base.
2. In the morning, I comb my hair and brush my teeth.
3. Mark's frog jumped onto a rock and croaked.
4. Before the play, the energetic actors learned lines and practiced.
5. *Does the new boy travel by bus and arrive at school early?
6. Mr. London takes his lunch to the office and eats across the street.
7. *Rings and bracelets were cleaned and placed into a special case.

Name______________________________ **PREPOSITION REVIEW**

WORKBOOK PAGE 26

Date______________________________

G. Directions: Cross out any prepositional phrase(s). Underline the subject once and the verb twice.

IMPERATIVE SENTENCES: (YOU) is the subject of an imperative sentence. Read (You) as you understood.

Example: (You) Go ~~to bed~~ immediately.

1. (You) Keep this dollar ~~in your wallet~~.

2. (You) Erase this mark ~~from your paper~~.

3. (You) Please finish your homework ~~within the next hour~~.

4. (You) Sand the wooden duck ~~for a very smooth finish~~.

5. (You) ~~After the game~~, put the chairs ~~into the trunk~~ ~~of the car~~.

6. (You) Drill a hole ~~in the coconut~~ and drain the milk ~~into a bowl~~.

7. (You) Take this package ~~to the post office~~, please.

H. Directions: Cross out any prepositional phrase(s). Underline the subject once and the verb twice. Label any adverb-Adv.

PREPOSITION VERSUS ADVERB: A preposition must be followed by a noun or pronoun called an object of the preposition. If there is not an object of the preposition, the word is not a preposition. (It serves as an adverb.)

Adv.
Example: They walked out ~~into the rain~~.

Adv.
1. The parade went past ~~at a slow pace~~.

Adv.
2. We sat outside ~~in the sunshine~~.

Adv.
3. Their brother comes over ~~to our house~~ ~~with his friend~~.

Adv.
4. The children remained inside ~~during the snowstorm~~.

Adv. Adv.
5. He is *not* through ~~with his lunch~~.

Adv. Adv.
6. A bird flew in and out ~~among the branches~~.

Adv. Adv.
7. (You) Come in and sit down, please.

Name_______________________________ **PREPOSITION REVIEW**

Date_______________________________

G. Directions: Cross out any prepositional phrase(s). Underline the subject once and the verb twice.

IMPERATIVE SENTENCES: (YOU) is the subject of an imperative sentence. Read (You) as you understood.

Example: (You) Go ~~to bed~~ immediately.

1. Keep this dollar in your wallet.
2. Erase this mark from your paper.
3. Please finish your homework within the next hour.
4. Sand the wooden duck for a very smooth finish.
5. After the game, put the chairs into the trunk of the car.
6. Drill a hole in the coconut and drain the milk into a bowl.
7. Take this package to the post office, please.

H. Directions: Cross out any prepositional phrase(s). Underline the subject once and the verb twice. Label any adverb-Adv.

PREPOSITION VERSUS ADVERB: A preposition must be followed by a noun or pronoun called an object of the preposition. If there is not an object of the preposition, the word is not a preposition. (It serves as an adverb.)

Example: They walked out (Adv.) ~~into the rain~~.

1. The parade went past at a slow pace.
2. We sat outside in the sunshine.
3. Their brother comes over to our house with his friend.
4. The children remained inside during the snowstorm.
5. He is not through with his lunch.
6. A bird flew in and out among the branches.
7. Come in and sit down, please.

Name________________________________ **PREPOSITIONS**

WORKBOOK PAGE 27

Date________________________________

Directions: Cross out any prepositional phrase(s). Underline the subject once and the verb/verb phrase twice. Starred sentences contain helping verb(s).

1. Your tennis racket is ~~behind the green chest~~.

2. The lady walked ~~among the paintings~~ ~~at the art gallery~~.

3. *They have*n't* seen him ~~since the prom~~.

4. Mr. Barnes enjoys pictures ~~of pheasants~~ ~~in paintings and objects~~.

5. All cars ~~but that black Ford~~ are ~~at the starting line~~.

6. A zoo keeper gave a talk ~~about wolves and coyotes~~.

7. *Chicken ~~in orange sauce~~ was served ~~with creamed potatoes~~.

8. (You) Give this apple ~~to your teacher~~.

9. *Has Grandma bought a gift ~~for Sue Ellen's birthday~~?

10. The boys and girls like (to play) basketball ~~until dinner~~.

11. ~~After three tries~~, one ~~of the cowboys~~ lassoed a steer.

12. Lauren jumped ~~over the hurdles~~ and dashed ~~past her opponent~~.

13. (You) Please seal the lid ~~with this masking tape and string~~.

14. *A baton twirler had *not* competed ~~before the final show.~~

15. The dog groomer walked outside (Adv.) ~~with the shampooed dog~~.

Name________________________________ **PREPOSITIONS**

Date________________________________

Directions: Cross out any prepositional phrase(s). Underline the subject once and the verb/verb phrase twice. Starred sentences contain helping verb(s).

1. Your tennis racket is behind the green chest.
2. The lady walked among the paintings at the art gallery.
3. *They haven't seen him since the prom.
4. Mr. Barnes enjoys pictures of pheasants in paintings and objects.
5. All cars but that black Ford are at the starting line.
6. A zoo keeper gave a talk about wolves and coyotes.
7. *Chicken in orange sauce was served with creamed potatoes.
8. Give this apple to your teacher.
9. *Has Grandma bought a gift for Sue Ellen's birthday?
10. The boys and girls like to play basketball until dinner.
11. After three tries, one of the cowboys lassoed a steer.
12. Lauren jumped over the hurdles and dashed past her opponent.
13. Please seal the lid with this masking tape and string.
14. *A baton twirler had not competed before the final show.
15. The dog groomer walked outside with the shampooed dog.

Name_______________________________ **PREPOSITIONS**

WORKBOOK PAGE 28

Date________________________________

Directions: Cross out any prepositional phrase(s). Underline the subject once and the verb/verb phrase twice. Starred sentences contain helping verb(s).

Although not indicated in directions, adverbs have been labeled.

1. * Three toads were hopping ~~among the rocks~~.

2. An odor ~~of perfume~~ drifted ~~into the room~~.

3. He placed the toy ~~beyond the baby's reach~~.

4. A horse pulled a wagon ~~through the field~~.

5. This food is ~~for fish and ducks~~.

6. A pillow fell ~~off the bed~~ and ~~onto the concrete floor~~.

Adv.

7. His dime slipped down ~~through a crack~~ ~~in the boards~~.

8. *I can*not* do it ~~without your help~~.

Adv.

9. A bus ~~of screaming cheerleaders~~ drove up ~~to the school~~.

10. *A giant bird cage was placed ~~above the toilet~~ ~~in the bathroom~~.

11. ~~During the afternoon~~, pigeons hopped ~~near the dog's dish~~.

Adv.

12. (You) Wash this out and hang it ~~on the line~~.

Adv.

13. ~~In the movie~~, a wounded man crawled up ~~to a stained glass door~~.

14. Jill and her aunt like (*to travel*) ~~along the Hudson River~~.

Adv. Adv.

15. (You) Come in, but wipe your shoes off ~~on the welcome mat~~.

Name________________________________ **PREPOSITIONS**

Date________________________________

Directions: Cross out any prepositional phrase(s). Underline the subject once and the verb/verb phrase twice. Starred sentences contain helping verb(s).

1. *Three toads were hopping among the rocks.
2. An odor of perfume drifted into the room.
3. He placed the toy beyond the baby's reach.
4. A horse pulled a wagon through the field.
5. This food is for fish and ducks.
6. A pillow fell off the bed and onto the concrete floor.
7. His dime slipped down through a crack in the boards.
8. *I cannot do it without your help.
9. A bus of screaming cheerleaders drove up to the school.
10. *A giant bird cage was placed above the toilet in the bathroom.
11. During the afternoon, pigeons hopped near the dog's dish.
12. Wash this out and hang it on the line.
13. In the movie, a wounded man crawled up to a stained glass door.
14. Jill and her aunt like to travel along the Hudson River.
15. Come in, but wipe your shoes off on the welcome mat.

Name______________________________ **PREPOSITIONS**

WORKBOOK PAGE 29

Date______________________________

Directions: Cross out any prepositional phrase(s). Underline the subject once and the verb/verb phrase twice. Starred sentences contain helping verb(s).

1. A baby crawled ~~beneath a coffee table~~.

2. A family ~~with two children~~ attended church.

3. ~~Throughout the summer~~, they travel ~~to the shore~~.

4. I left ~~without my coat or hat~~.

5. ~~Before the convention~~, the women met ~~for a quick meeting~~.

Adv.

6. *The postman has come by ~~in a mail truck~~.

7. Everyone ~~except Bruce~~ dashed ~~across the street~~.

8. ~~Above the doorway~~, we hung an arrangement ~~of dry flowers~~.

9. ~~During the game~~, their team made three goals and won.

10. One ~~of the triplets~~ ran ~~into the doghouse~~ and cried.

11. A garden ~~of brightly colored flowers~~ is ~~along the western sidewalk~~.

12. Are Tim and Diana moving ~~near Houston~~?

13. ~~From Paul's knee to his ankle~~, a rash appeared.

14. The shoppers wait ~~until the sale~~ (*to buy*) sheets.

15. (You) Stand here ~~among these chairs for a family picture~~.

Name________________________________ **PREPOSITIONS**

Date________________________________

Directions: Cross out prepositional phrases. Underline the subject once and the verb/verb phrase twice. Starred sentences contain helping verb(s).

1. A baby crawled beneath a coffee table.
2. A family with two children attended church.
3. Throughout the summer, they travel to the shore.
4. I left without my coat or hat.
5. Before the convention, the women met for a quick meeting.
6. *The postman has come by in a mail truck.
7. Everyone except Bruce dashed across the street.
8. Above the doorway, we hung an arrangement of dry flowers.
9. During the game, their team made three goals and won.
10. One of the triplets ran into the doghouse and cried.
11. A garden of brightly colored flowers is along the western sidewalk.
12. Are Tim and Diana moving near Houston?
13. From Paul's knee to his ankle, a rash appeared.
14. The shoppers wait until the sale to buy sheets.
15. Stand here among these chairs for a family picture.

Name________________________________ **PREPOSITIONS**
WORKBOOK PAGE 30
Date________________________________

Directions: Cross out any prepositional phrase(s). Underline the subject once and the verb/verb phrase twice. Starred sentences contain helping verb(s).

1. The temperature is ~~below zero~~.

2. *These red pencils were given ~~to us~~ ~~by the librarian~~.

3. *A globe has been placed ~~atop the metal closet~~.

4. Mr. Jacob's car collided ~~with a truck and van~~.

5. *(You) Do *not* drink soda ~~with your meal~~.

6. Animals ~~like dogs and cats~~ are often wonderful pets.

7. The movers placed the stereo ~~between the wall and the stairway~~.

Adv.
8. The sun peaked from ~~behind the clouds~~.

9. *Did the butcher cut the meat ~~into small pieces~~?

10. A swimmer stepped ~~over me~~ and jumped ~~into the water~~.

11. The choir chose (*to stand*) ~~upon risers~~ ~~for their concert~~.

Adv.
12. A reporter and photographer ran out ~~into the street~~ ~~during the robbery~~.

13. Ten bricklayers decided (*to work*) ~~from sunrise~~ ~~until noon~~.

14. A group ~~of teachers~~ met and made plans ~~for a science fair~~.

15. * Will you please come and sit ~~behind the steering wheel~~?

Name________________________________ **PREPOSITIONS**

Date________________________________

Directions: Cross out any prepositional phrase(s). Underline the subject once and the verb/verb phrase twice. Starred sentences contain helping verb(s).

1. The temperature is below zero.
2. *These red pencils were given to us by the librarian.
3. *A globe has been placed atop the metal closet.
4. Mr. Jacob's car collided with a truck and van.
5. *Do not drink soda with your meal.
6. Animals like dogs and cats are often wonderful pets.
7. The movers placed the stereo between the wall and the stairway.
8. The sun peaked from behind the clouds.
9. *Did the butcher cut the meat into small pieces?
10. A swimmer stepped over me and jumped into the water.
11. The choir chose to stand upon risers for their concert.
12. A reporter and photographer ran out into the street during the robbery.
13. Ten bricklayers decided to work from sunrise until noon.
14. A group of teachers met and made plans for a science fair.
15. *Will you please come and sit behind the steering wheel?

Name________________________________ **PREPOSITION TEST**

WORKBOOK PAGE 319

Date________________________________

Directions: Cross out any prepositional phrase(s). Underline the subject once and the verb/verb phrase twice. Starred sentences contain helping verb(s).

1. I went ~~to a store~~ ~~at the mall~~. 4 points

2. Some islands are ~~off the coast~~ ~~of California~~. 4 points

3. A picture is ~~on the wall~~ ~~above a computer~~. 4 points

4. Mark and his cousin walked ~~down the street~~ ~~toward the loggers~~. 4 points

5. ~~After lunch~~, some ~~of the boys~~ play ping pong. 4 points

6. A swimmer dashed ~~out the door~~ and jumped ~~into the water~~. 5 points

7. ~~Throughout the day~~, many roofers rested ~~under a huge willow tree~~. 4 points

8. A letter ~~from Cindy and Sandy~~ arrived ~~in the mail~~ today. 4 points

9. ~~During the festival~~, people went ~~into the hall~~ (*to eat*). 4 points

10. An airplane rolled ~~down the runway~~ ~~without lights~~. 4 points

11. ~~Before the storm~~, our dog came inside (Adv.) ~~for shelter~~. 4 points

12. *Their friend has been ~~without electricity~~ ~~since the tornado~~. 4 points

13. *A decision ~~regarding freeways~~ will *not* be made ~~until February~~. 4 points

14. (You) Put this bag ~~of trash~~ ~~by the front door~~. 4 points

15. *The red tile was replaced ~~with white tile and carpeting~~. 3 points

Suggestion: Count 1 point for correct subject and 1 for correct verb/verb phrase. If any part of the subject or verb is incorrect, subtract one point. (For example, if not is underlined as part of the verb phrase, subtract one point for verb correctness.) All prepositional phrases are worth 1 point. If any part is incorrect, subtract a point. (For example, in #8, subtract 1 point if today is included as part of the prepositional phrase.) Total = 60 points. Recommendation: Add 1 point if inside in # 11 is labeled as an adverb.

Name________________________________ **PREPOSITION TEST**

Date________________________________

Directions: Cross out any prepositional phrase(s). Underline the subject once and the verb/verb phrase twice. Starred sentences contain helping verb(s).

1. I went to a store at the mall.

2. Some islands are off the coast of California.

3. A picture is on the wall above a computer.

4. Mark and his cousin walked down the street toward the loggers.

5. After lunch, some of the boys play ping pong.

6. A swimmer dashed out the door and jumped into the water.

7. Throughout the day, many roofers rested under a huge willow tree.

8. A letter from Cindy and Sandy arrived in the mail today.

9. During the festival, people went into the hall to eat.

10. An airplane rolled down the runway without lights.

11. Before the storm, our dog came inside for shelter.

12. *Their friend has been without electricity since the tornado.

13. *A decision regarding freeways will not be made until February.

14. Put this bag of trash by the front door.

15. *The red tile was replaced with white tile and carpeting.

FOR THE TEACHER:
WORKBOOK PAGE 31

SUGGESTIONS FOR MASTERY LEARNING

Your goal as a teacher is to insure understanding and promote **mastery learning**. Therefore, review is necessary to the program. You want students to have concepts learned in long term memory. Although the preposition unit has terminated, it is advisable to continue requiring students to cross out prepositional phrases and to underline the subject once and the verb/verb phrase twice. This text has also been designed to review previously learned material at the end of most units.

Daily Grams: Guided Review Aiding Mastery Skills is recommended as a daily review of capitalization, punctuation, grammar usage, and sentence combining. See last page for various levels.

DIRECT OBJECTS

Students must understand that direct objects receive the action of the verb. Although a prepositional phrase may serve as a direct object, it occurs so rarely that students are instructed to delete prepositional phrases.

A. The simplest way to insure an understanding of direct objects is to actually "do" an action. You may wish to drop a quarter. Write the sentence on the board:

D.O.
I dropped a quarter.

Who is the subject? *I* What is the action verb? *dropped* What was the object I dropped? *quarter* The quarter received the action.

Use other **actions** to increase learning. A few examples are provided. Be sure to write them on the board.

D.O.
1. I kicked a chair. (Object kicked = chair)

D.O.
2. The teacher wrote a note. (Object written = note)

D.O.
3. I threw paper ~~into the trash~~. (Object thrown = paper)

This latter example is extremely important. Show students that the object thrown was paper. Teach them to delete *~~into the trash~~*. Therefore, paper is the direct object. Trash cannot be the direct object because **the direct object will not be a part of a prepositional phrase.**

Note: You may wish to have students "do" examples. This allows peers to determine the direct object. Be sure that students do not hurt each other. (Example: I punched Joe.) In addition, you will need to pay close attention. An action resulting in a sentence such as "*Joe fell over a backpack.*" does not contain a direct object.

Sometimes, there will be a **compound direct object**. This means more than one.

D.O. D.O.
Example: The man bought a tie and a shirt.

B. Review the concept of direct objects by giving similar examples at the beginning of many classes. Never assume that all have mastered a concept automatically. In addition, it's advisable to have students write and mark their own examples. This will help you determine if they truly do understand the concept.

C. The **success factor** is high with direct objects. In Easy Grammar texts, direct objects are taught immediately after prepositions for four reasons.

1. In deleting prepositional phrases, fewer words remain so that students do not become so readily frustrated. The direct object is usually easy to find.

2. In sentences containing a direct object, the subject is more easily discerned. Example: John sent a letter ~~to me~~. (Letter is the direct object, not the subject.)

3. The next unit will be one about verbs. In order to understand when to use to sit/to set, to rise/to raise, and to lie/to lay, students need to identify direct objects.

4. Since the concept of direct objects can be understood easily, more success is internalized by each student.

Name________________________________

DIRECT OBJECTS

WORKBOOK PAGE 32

Date________________________________

Directions: Cross out any prepositional phrase(s). Underline the subject once and the verb/verb phrase twice. Label any direct object-D.O.

D.O.
Example: The cook makes stew ~~for winter holidays~~.

D.O.
1. Dad shines his shoes.

D.O.
2. She painted her fingernails.

D.O.
3. Lance put batteries ~~in the radio~~.

D.O.
4. A fisherman caught a large bass.

D.O.
5. The catcher threw the ball ~~to second base~~.

D.O.
6. His sister sewed a button ~~on a blouse~~.

D.O.
7. Ericka draws pictures ~~of pelicans~~.

D.O.
8. A crying toddler tossed a yellow toy ~~onto the bed~~.

D.O.
9. Mrs. Billings climbs mountains ~~for a hobby~~.

D.O.
10. They placed large pink balloons ~~on the ceiling~~.

D.O.
11. The florist has *not* yet sent flowers ~~for their wedding~~. (*Yet* is not a helping verb.)

D.O.
12. We made and ate some chocolate cupcakes.

D.O.
13. Has the plumber fixed the drain ~~in the sink~~?

D.O.
14. ~~During the wedding~~, Susan and her partner danced a polka.

D.O.
15. (You) Put the garbage ~~in the new trash can~~.

Name________________________________ **DIRECT OBJECTS**

Date________________________________

Directions: Cross out any prepositional phrase(s). Underline the subject once and the verb/verb phrase twice. Label any direct object-D.O.

D.O.
Example: The cook makes stew ~~for winter holidays~~.

1. Dad shines his shoes.
2. She painted her fingernails.
3. Lance put batteries in the radio.
4. A fisherman caught a large bass.
5. The catcher threw the ball to second base.
6. His sister sewed a button on a blouse.
7. Ericka draws pictures of pelicans.
8. A crying toddler tossed a yellow toy onto the bed.
9. Mrs. Billings climbs mountains for a hobby.
10. They placed large pink balloons on the ceiling.
11. The florist has not yet sent flowers for their wedding.
12. We made and ate some chocolate cupcakes.
13. Has the plumber fixed the drain in the sink?
14. During the wedding, Susan and her partner danced a polka.
15. Put the garbage in the new trash can.

Name________________________________ **DIRECT OBJECTS**

WORKBOOK PAGE 33

Date________________________________

Directions: Cross out any prepositional phrases. Underline the subject once and the verb/verb phrase twice. Label any direct object-D.O.

Example: They sent a telegram ~~to their aunt and uncle~~. (D.O.: telegram)

1. Robb and Anne make their beds ~~in the morning~~. (D.O.: beds)
2. Dad rubbed oil ~~on the baby's skin~~. (D.O.: oil)
3. Peter bought a candy bar ~~with nuts~~. (D.O.: bar)
4. A mother chased a child ~~across the lawn~~. (D.O.: child)
5. ~~During vacation~~, Mom took many pictures ~~of us~~. (D.O.: pictures)
6. The lady pushed the shopping cart ~~through the store~~. (D.O.: cart)
7. Micah traded baseball cards ~~at the store~~. (D.O.: cards)
8. Their dog buries bones ~~in their backyard~~. (D.O.: bones)
9. The artist carved a duck ~~with a special tool~~. (D.O.: duck)
10. The Smith family gave a party ~~for Tom's graduation~~. (D.O.: party)
11. Mindy does *not* want a mountain bike. (D.O.: bike)
12. Mr. Stone and his client ate lunch ~~at a Chinese restaurant~~. (D.O.: lunch)
13. Has that family built a new house ~~in your neighborhood~~? (D.O.: house)
14. (You) Throw that purple frisbee ~~across the street~~ immediately. (D.O.: frisbee)
15. ~~For lunch and dinner~~, Greg likes chicken ~~without the skin~~. (D.O.: chicken)

Name________________________________ **DIRECT OBJECTS**

Date________________________________

Directions: Cross out any prepositional phrases. Underline the subject once and the verb/verb phrase twice. Label any direct object-D.O.

D.O.
Example: They sent a telegram ~~to their aunt and uncle~~.

1. Robb and Anne make their beds in the morning.

2. Dad rubbed oil on the baby's skin.

3. Peter bought a candy bar with nuts.

4. A mother chased a child across the lawn.

5. During vacation, Mom took many pictures of us.

6. The lady pushed the shopping cart through the store.

7. Micah traded baseball cards at the store.

8. Their dog buries bones in their backyard.

9. The artist carved a duck with a special tool.

10. The Smith family gave a party for Tom's graduation.

11. Mindy does not want a mountain bike.

12. Mr. Stone and his client ate lunch at a Chinese restaurant.

13. Has that family built a new house in your neighborhood?

14. Throw that purple frisbee across the street immediately.

15. For lunch and dinner, Greg likes chicken without the skin.

Name________________________________

WORKBOOK PAGE 34

Date________________________________

DIRECT OBJECTS
Compound Object

Sometimes, there will be more than one direct object in a sentence. This is called a compound object.

Examples: The carpenter carried his saw (D.O.), and nail pouch (D.O.) ~~to his car~~.

We saw a clown (D.O.) and an acrobat (D.O.) ~~at the circus~~.

Directions: Cross out any prepositional phrase(s). Underline the subject once and the verb/verb phrase twice. Label any direct object(s)-D.O.

1. I want those marbles (D.O.) and a yo-yo (D.O.).
2. The secretary typed a letter (D.O.) and envelope (D.O.) ~~for the chairperson~~.
3. A cafeteria worker piled macaroni (D.O.) and a sandwich (D.O.) ~~on my tray~~.
4. Dad makes bacon (D.O.) and eggs (D.O.) ~~for breakfast~~.
5. I found a wallet (D.O.) and a comb (D.O.) ~~under the sofa cushions~~.
6. Several picnickers threw leaves (D.O.) and pebbles (D.O.) ~~into the stream~~.
7. ~~In her garden~~, Thelma Lee planted tomatoes (D.O.) and lettuce (D.O.).
8. Sally and Todd baked two pies (D.O.) and a loaf (D.O.) ~~of bread~~.
9. The waiter filled a pitcher (D.O.) and two glasses (D.O.) ~~with water~~.
10. A catcher wears a mask (D.O.) and a chest pad (D.O.) ~~for protection~~.
11. Kerry dropped a dime (D.O.) and a quarter (D.O.) ~~into the plate~~.
12. (You) Give this book (D.O.) and that magazine (D.O.) ~~to your mother~~.
13. My brother does*n't* like spinach (D.O.), mashed potatoes (D.O.), or green beans (D.O.).
14. Has the director chosen William (D.O.) or his friend (D.O.) (*to be*) ~~in the play~~?
15. ~~With Mrs. Molby's help~~, I have made a heart-shaped pillow (D.O.) and a baby's blanket (D.O.).

Name________________________________

Date________________________________

DIRECT OBJECTS
Compound Object

<u>Sometimes, there will be more than one direct object in a sentence. This is called a compound object.</u>

Examples: The carpenter carried his saw, and nail pouch ~~to his ear~~. (D.O.: saw; D.O.: pouch)

We saw a clown and an acrobat ~~at the circus~~. (D.O.: clown; D.O.: acrobat)

Directions: Cross out any prepositional phrase(s). Underline the subject once and the verb/verb phrase twice. Label any direct object(s)-D.O.

1. I want those marbles and a yo-yo.
2. The secretary typed a letter and envelope for the chairperson.
3. A cafeteria worker piled macaroni and a sandwich on my tray.
4. Dad makes bacon and eggs for breakfast.
5. I found a wallet and a comb under the sofa cushions.
6. Several picnickers threw leaves and pebbles into the stream.
7. In her garden, Thelma Lee planted tomatoes and lettuce.
8. Sally and Todd baked two pies and a loaf of bread.
9. The waiter filled a pitcher and two glasses with water.
10. A catcher wears a mask and a chest pad for protection.
11. Kerry dropped a dime and a quarter into the plate.
12. Give this book and that magazine to your mother.
13. My brother doesn't like spinach, mashed potatoes, or green beans.
14. Has the director chosen William or his friend to be in the play?
15. With Mrs. Molby's help, I have made a heart-shaped pillow and a baby's blanket.

FOR THE TEACHER:
WORKBOOK PAGE 35

VERBS

Be sure to teach this unit thoroughly. The use of verbs is important to each child's writing and speaking properly. It is highly recommended that students master the irregular verb list. Because there is not enough space for all irregular verbs, you may wish to add others. Take time to teach all verb concepts, reviewing orally, and ascertaining that mastery is being achieved.

A. **An infinitive is *to* plus a verb.** **(*to* + verb = infinitive)**

Examples:	to run	to see	to raise	to like	to enjoy
	to jump	to find	to smile	to go	to eat

Students needs to understand that *to* plus any verb is called an infinitive.

B. **A verb of a sentence expresses an action or simply states a fact.**

Examples: Martin mows the lawn each week. (action)

Mrs. Darnell cut the cake into little pieces. (action)

Jane needs a new notebook. (fact)

An apple is on the floor. (fact)

Verbs that state a fact as in the last example, are called state-of-being verbs if they are a form of the infinitive *to be.*

C. **The two main types of verbs are action and linking**. Action verbs do exactly what the term implies. Action verbs show action. (You will note that in order to have a direct object, the sentence must contain an action verb.)

Linking verbs are difficult. First, they do not show action. They do exactly what their name implies. They link two parts in the sentence. They link the subject with either a noun or pronoun (called a predicate nominative) or with an adjective (called a predicate adjective).

FOR THE TEACHER:
WORKBOOK PAGE 36

CONTRACTIONS

To contract means to draw together. In forming a contraction, we draw together two words to make one word. We do this by dropping a letter or letters and inserting an apostrophe (') where the letter or letters have been left out.

Suggestions:

A. Students need a list of contractions (located at the bottom of this page). You may wish to write the list on a chalkboard or overhead for students to copy in a notebook or to reproduce a copy for each person. Students must have a copy so that they can **memorize** and **learn** contractions.

B. Insist that the apostrophe look like an apostrophe and not a "chicken scratch" mark.

C. Insist that the apostrophe be placed exactly where the letter(s) are missing.

D. Insist that contractions be written in broken form so that mistakes are avoided.
can't Note the space between n and t. In cursive, do not attach the n and t.

CONTRACTION	= VERB	+	WORD
aren't	are	+	not
can't	can	+	not
couldn't	could	+	not
don't	do	+	not
doesn't	does	+	not
didn't	did	+	not
hasn't	has	+	not
haven't	have	+	not
hadn't	had	+	not
isn't	is	+	not
mightn't	might	+	not
mustn't	must	+	not
shouldn't	should	+	not
wasn't	was	+	not
weren't	were	+	not
won't	will	+	not
wouldn't	would	+	not

CONTRACTION	= WORD	+	VERB
he's	he	+	is
he'd	he	+	would
here's	here	+	is
I'd	I	+	would
I'll	I	+	shall*
I'm	I	+	am
it's	it	+	is
I've	I	+	have
she'd	she	+	would
she's	she	+	is
there's	there	+	is
they'll	they	+	will
they're	they	+	are
we're	we	+	are
we've	we	+	have
what's	what	+	is
where's	where	+	is
who's	who	+	is
you'd	you	+	would
you'll	you	+	will
you're	you	+	are

*or I will

Name______________________________

WORKBOOK PAGE 37

Date______________________________

CONTRACTIONS

Directions: Write the contraction.

1. could not - **couldn't**
2. you are - **you're**
3. I will - **I'll**
4. where is - **where's**
5. is not - **isn't**
6. cannot - **can't**
7. they will - **they'll**
8. you would - **you'd**
9. must not - **mustn't**
10. she is - **she's**
11. I have - **I've**
12. does not - **doesn't**
13. what is - **what's**
14. will not - **won't**
15. I am - **I'm**
16. was not - **wasn't**
17. he is - **he's**
18. have not - **haven't**
19. there is - **there's**
20. you will - **you'll**
21. did not - **didn't**
22. would not - **wouldn't**
23. here is - **here's**
24. are not - **aren't**
25. who is - **who's**
26. should not - **shouldn't**
27. do not - **don't**
28. I would - **I'd**
29. has not - **hasn't**
30. they are - **they're**

Name________________________________ **CONTRACTIONS**

Date________________________________

Directions: Write the contraction.

1. could not - ____________________
2. you are - ____________________
3. I will - ____________________
4. where is - ____________________
5. is not - ____________________
6. cannot - ____________________
7. they will - ____________________
8. you would - ____________________
9. must not - ____________________
10. she is - ____________________
11. I have - ____________________
12. does not - ____________________
13. what is - ____________________
14. will not - ____________________
15. I am - ____________________
16. was not - ____________________
17. he is - ____________________
18. have not - ____________________
19. there is - ____________________
20. you will - ____________________
21. did not - ____________________
22. would not - ____________________
23. here is - ____________________
24. are not - ____________________
25. who is - ____________________
26. should not - ____________________
27. do not - ____________________
28. I would - ____________________
29. has not - ____________________
30. they are - ____________________

Name________________________________ **CONTRACTIONS**

WORKBOOK PAGE 38

Date________________________________

Directions: Write the contraction for the italicized words in the space provided.

Example: ____You'll____ *You will* be just fine.

1. ____wasn't____ The customer *was not* happy.
2. ____hadn't____ The baby *had not* been changed.
3. ____She'd____ *She would* rather ski.
4. ____It's____ *It is* nice to meet you.
5. ____mightn't____ Mr. Coe *might not* be able to go.
6. ____weren't____ Peaches *were not* ripe yet.
7. ____I'm____ *I am* very confused.
8. ____can't____ Shelly *cannot* find the key to the lock.
9. ____He'd____ *He would* be smart to do that.
10. ____doesn't____ Their cat *does not* go outside.
11. ____Here's____ *Here is* the word in the dictionary.
12. ____haven't____ Adam and she *have not* found an apartment.
13. ____they'll____ During the holiday, *they will* fly home.
14. ____isn't____ This swimsuit *is not* on sale.
15. ____I'll____ *I shall* finish this chore later.

Name________________________________ **CONTRACTIONS**

Date________________________________

Directions: Write the contraction for the italicized words in the space provided.

Example: ______You'll______ *You will* be just fine.

1. ____________________ The customer *was not* happy.
2. ____________________ The baby *had not* been changed.
3. ____________________ *She would* rather ski.
4. ____________________ *It is* nice to meet you.
5. ____________________ Mr. Coe *might not* be able to go.
6. ____________________ Peaches *were not* ripe yet.
7. ____________________ *I am* very confused.
8. ____________________ Shelly *cannot* find the key to the lock.
9. ____________________ *He would* be smart to do that.
10. ____________________ Their cat *does not* go outside.
11. ____________________ *Here is* the word in the dictionary.
12. ____________________ Adam and she *have not* found an apartment.
13. ____________________ During the holiday, *they will* fly home.
14. ____________________ This swimsuit *is not* on sale.
15. ____________________ *I shall* finish this chore later.

Name________________________________ **CONTRACTIONS**

WORKBOOK PAGE 39

Date________________________________

Directions: Write the contraction for the italicized words in the space provided.

Example: __shouldn't__ Zack *should not* play in the street.

1. __I've__ *I have* an antique doll.
2. __Where's__ *Where is* the bag of chips, Don?
3. __didn't__ The actress *did not* perform well.
4. __What's__ *What is* the name of your favorite song?
5. __you'll__ I believe that *you will* learn to water ski easily.
6. __I'd__ *I would* prefer to take a sack lunch.
7. __who's__ Do you know *who is* the President?
8. __couldn't__ He *could not* repair the broken lock.
9. __Don't__ *Do not* go outside during the hurricane.
10. __they're__ Has Larry told you where *they are* going?
11. __you're__ Mrs. Ball is sure that *you are* right for the job.
12. __aren't__ Those soldiers *are not* training for combat now.
13. __won't__ I *will not* get my driver's license for a long time.
14. __He's__ *He is* the best basketball player I know.
15. __mustn't__ You *must not* rush through your homework.

Name________________________________

Date________________________________

CONTRACTIONS

Directions: Write the contraction for the italicized words in the space provided.

Example: ____shouldn't____ Zack *should not* play in the street.

1. ________________________ *I have* an antique doll.
2. ________________________ *Where is* the bag of chips, Don?
3. ________________________ The actress *did not* perform well.
4. ________________________ *What is* the name of your favorite song?
5. ________________________ I believe that *you will* learn to water ski easily.
6. ________________________ *I would* prefer to take a sack lunch.
7. ________________________ Do you know *who is* the President?
8. ________________________ He *could not* repair the broken lock.
9. ________________________ *Do not* go outside during the hurricane.
10. ________________________ Has Larry told you where *they are* going?
11. ________________________ Mrs. Ball is sure that *you are* right for the job.
12. ________________________ Those soldiers *are not* training for combat now.
13. ________________________ I *will not* get my driver's license for a long time.
14. ________________________ *He is* the best basketball player I know.
15. ________________________ You *must not* rush through your homework.

FOR THE TEACHER:
WORKBOOK PAGE 40

HELPING (AUXILIARY) VERBS

Students must memorize these twenty-three helping verbs and list them. Be sure that each child has complete **mastery** of these helping (auxiliary) verbs. Asking students to list them for a quiz or test may be helpful. Use methods with which you are comfortable in order to insure that the list of helping verbs has been learned.

LIST OF HELPING (AUXILIARY) VERBS

do	**have**	**may**	**should**	**shall**	**is**
does	**has**	**might**	**would**	**will**	**am**
did	**had**	**must**	**could**	**can**	**are**
					was
					were
					be
					being
					been

It is helpful to point out to students that there are "the" 3 d's, "the" 3 h's, and "the" 3 m's. Then, we note the 3 ould's. Notice that directly across from should is another sh word, shall. Across from would is another w word, will, and across from could is a c word, can. This type of pneumonics is extremely helpful.

When first introducing the list for memorization, spend time *looking* and *saying* (visual and auditory learning) them in their "groups." It is helpful to point and say the helping verbs with the students. It's also recommended that you keep the same sequence as you review each day. Students, however, may list them in any order. The goal is mastery of the twenty-three helping verbs.

EXTREMELY IMPORTANT: In the exercises in the remainder of this text, most directions concerning verb identification will state to underline the verb/verb phrase. Students will need to determine if each sentence contains any helping verb(s).

WORKBOOK PAGE 41

VERB PHRASES

A verb may be composed of one word or two or more verbs placed as a group. This group is called a verb phrase. The last word in a verb phrase is called a **main verb**. Other verbs preceding the main verb are called helping (auxiliary) verbs.

VERB PHRASE	=	HELPING VERB(S)	+	MAIN VERB
can play	=	**can**	+	**play**
has been taken	=	**has been**	+	**taken**
should have left	=	**should have**	+	**left**

Students need to understand that a verb on the helping verb list may serve both as a single verb or as a helping verb.

Examples: I **am** here. (verb)
I **am** going to a cookout. (helping verb)

Also, it's important that students understand that some verbs on the helping verb list can also serve as the main verb.

Examples: Joseph had **been** in a play. (main verb)

Her friend has **been** crying. (helping verb)

In a declarative (statement) sentence, the verb phrase is usually together.

Example: The box had been sent in the mail.

had been + sent

In an interrogative (question) sentence, the verb phrase is often split. Look for a helping verb at the beginning of most questions.

Example: Did Mario push the button?

Did + push

Name________________________________ **VERB PHRASES**

WORKBOOK PAGE 42

Date________________________________

Directions: Cross out any prepositional phrase(s). Underline the subject once and the verb phrase twice. Write the helping verb in the first column and the main verb in the second column.

Remember: **Verb Phrase =** **helping verb(s)** **+** **main verb**
may run *may* *run*

	HELPING VERB	***MAIN VERB***
1. Chris has gone ~~to the movie~~.	has	gone
2. That worker had eaten ~~in a cafe~~.	had	eaten
3. She had put the dishes ~~by the sink~~.	had	put
4. The bone was broken ~~in two places~~.	was	broken
5. These shorts were ironed today.	were	ironed
6. Karla is driving ~~to a friend's home~~.	is	driving
7. The bus should arrive soon.	should	arrive
8. This tour might require an hour.	might	require
9. Directions ~~for the test~~ were read aloud.	were	read
10. The truck was stolen ~~during the night~~.	was	stolen
11. This bread can rise ~~by the fire~~.	can	rise
12. Ellen could *not* stay ~~with us~~.	could	stay
13. Have you taken the casserole (D.O.*) ~~from the oven~~?	Have	taken
14. Bill had never (**) seen Lake Mead (D.O.*).	had	seen
15. Did one ~~of the boys~~ swim ~~across the pond~~?	Did	swim

*Although labeling the direct object is not part of the directions, this is a good place to do a quick review. (Hour in # 8 is a direct object.)

**Stress that never is not on the helping (auxiliary) verb list.

Name________________________________ **VERB PHRASES**

Date________________________________

Directions: Cross out any prepositional phrase(s). Underline the subject once and the verb phrase twice. Write the helping verb in the first column and the main verb in the second column.

Remember: Verb Phrase = helping verb(s) + main verb

may run *may* *run*

	HELPING VERB	***MAIN VERB***
1. Chris has gone to the movie.	______________	______________
2. That worker had eaten in a cafe.	______________	______________
3. She had put the dishes by the sink.	______________	______________
4. The bone was broken in two places.	______________	______________
5. These shorts were ironed today.	______________	______________
6. Karla is driving to a friend's home.	______________	______________
7. The bus should arrive soon.	______________	______________
8. This tour might require an hour.	______________	______________
9. Directions for the test were read aloud.	______________	______________
10. The truck was stolen during the night.	______________	______________
11. This bread can rise by the fire.	______________	______________
12. Ellen could not stay with us.	______________	______________
13. Have you taken the casserole from the oven?	______________	______________
14. Bill had never seen Lake Mead.	______________	______________
15. Did one of the boys swim across the pond?	______________	______________

Name_______________________________ **VERB PHRASES**

WORKBOOK PAGE 43

Date_______________________________

Directions: Cross out any prepositional phrase(s). Underline the subject once and the verb phrase twice. Write the helping verb(s) in the first column and the main verb in the second column.

Remember: **Verb Phrase = helping verb(s) + main verb**

could have sat *could have* *sat*

	HELPING VERB(S)	***MAIN VERB***
1. They will look ~~for a new home~~.	will	look
2. The train must have left ~~on time~~.	must have	left
3. Would you take me ~~to school~~?	Would	take
4. The doctor has set her leg.	has	set
5. This chair had been repaired.	had been	repaired
6. I shall leave ~~without you~~.	shall	leave
7. Flowers have been arranged ~~in a bouquet~~.	have been	arranged
8. This purse was found ~~in the closet~~.	was	found
9. His niece is leaving ~~on vacation~~.	is	leaving
10. Has Ned met the new coach?	Has	met
11. Their mother should have worn more sunblock ~~during the party~~.	should have	worn
12. Ants were crawling ~~over my foot~~.	were	crawling
13. May Sue ride ~~with Beth and you~~?	May	ride
14. My pizza might be delivered soon.	might be	delivered
15. This candle can*not* be stored here.	can be	stored

Name________________________________ **VERB PHRASES**

Date________________________________

Directions: Cross out any prepositional phrase(s). Underline the subject once and the verb phrase twice. Write the helping verb(s) in the first column and the main verb in the second column.

Remember: **Verb Phrase = helping verb(s) + main verb**
could have sat *could have* *sat*

	HELPING VERB(S)	***MAIN VERB***
1. They will look for a new home.	____________	____________
2. The train must have left on time.	____________	____________
3. Would you take me to school?	____________	____________
4. The doctor has set her leg.	____________	____________
5. This chair had been repaired.	____________	____________
6. I shall leave without you.	____________	____________
7. Flowers have been arranged in a bouquet.	____________	____________
8. This purse was found in the closet.	____________	____________
9. His niece is leaving on vacation.	____________	____________
10. Has Ned met the new coach?	____________	____________
11. Their mother should have worn more sunblock during the party.	____________	____________
12. Ants were crawling over my foot.	____________	____________
13. May Sue ride with Beth and you?	____________	____________
14. My pizza might be delivered soon.	____________	____________
15. This candle cannot be stored here.	____________	____________

Name________________________________ **VERB PHRASES**

WORKBOOK PAGE 44

Date________________________________

Directions: Cross out any prepositional phrase(s). Underline the subject once and the verb phrase twice. Write the helping verb(s) in the first column and the main verb in the second column.

Remember: **Verb Phrase** = **helping verb** + **main verb**
will be going = will be + going

	HELPING VERB(S)	***MAIN VERB***
1. Women were standing ~~in line~~.	were	standing
2. Frank has made pancakes again.	has	made
3. Can you open this jar ~~for me~~?	Can	open
4. The car had been painted blue.	had been	painted
5. Water has been poured ~~on her hair~~.	has been	poured
6. The dog's leg may have been injured ~~by the branches~~.	may have been	injured
7. Shall I remove this ~~from the table~~?	Shall	remove
8. Joy would *not* work ~~in the garden~~.	would	work
9. Trout are biting ~~in the stream~~ today.	are	biting
10. Two boys have been trying (*to surf*).	have been	trying
11. Keys might be hidden ~~under the planter~~ ~~by the front door~~.	might be	hidden
12. An athlete must practice daily.	must	practice
13. Is the roofer nailing the last tile?	Is	nailing
14. The real estate agent had *not* located a new home ~~for the family~~.	had	located
15. Shoes should be worn ~~in stores~~.	should be	worn

Name________________________________

Date________________________________

VERB PHRASES

Directions: Cross out any prepositional phrase(s). Underline the subject once and the verb phrase twice. Write the helping verb(s) in the first column and the main verb in the second column.

Remember: **Verb Phrase = helping verb + main verb**
will be going = will be + going

	HELPING VERB(S)	*MAIN VERB*
1. Women were standing in line.	____________	____________
2. Frank has made pancakes again.	____________	____________
3. Can you open this jar for me?	____________	____________
4. The car had been painted blue.	____________	____________
5. Water has been poured on her hair.	____________	____________
6. The dog's leg may have been injured by the branches.	____________	____________
7. Shall I remove this from the table?	____________	____________
8. Joy would not work in the garden.	____________	____________
9. Trout are biting in the stream today.	____________	____________
10. Two boys have been trying to surf.	____________	____________
11. Keys might be hidden under the planter by the front door.	____________	____________
12. An athlete must practice daily.	____________	____________
13. Is the roofer nailing the last tile?	____________	____________
14. The real estate agent had not located a new home for the family.	____________	____________
15. Shoes should be worn in stores.	____________	____________

FOR THE TEACHER:
WORKBOOK PAGE 45
In order to teach irregular verbs, students must first understand what a regular verb is. To do this lesson properly, a brief explanation of present and past tenses is necessary. Students need to know that *tense* means *time*. Present tense is present time; past tense is past time. Any time you list present tense, it is suggested that you use the term today for simplicity. Do likewise for past tense-using yesterday. (Tenses will be covered as a separate concept later in this unit.)

VERBS

Regular verbs are those verbs that add ed to both the past and the past participle forms.

In order to show students this concept, you will need to give them an idea of what the past participle form is. Past tense simply shows that something has already happened. Past tense does not have helping verbs. By definition, a past participle shows past time plus has a helping verb. For simplicity, *has*, *have*, and *had* are used here.

Examples: A deli clerk sliced some meat. (past tense) (tense = time)

Mother had ordered some rolls.* (past participle)

*This is the perfect tense; it will be taught in Easy Grammar.

A chart drawn like the one shown here may be helpful:

Infinitive	Today **Present**	Yesterday **Past**	has, have, or had **Past Participle**
to kick	**kick(s)** (Today I kick or he kick**s** a ball.)	**kicked** (Yesterday I kicked a ball.)	**had kicked** (I had kicked the ball.)
to talk	**talk(s)** (Today I talk or he talks to him.)	**talked** (Yesterday I talked to him.)	**had talked** (I had talked to him.)
to clean	**clean(s)** (Today I clean or he cleans.)	**cleaned** (Yesterday I cleaned.)	**had cleaned** (I had cleaned my room.)

IRREGULAR VERBS

WORKBOOK PAGE 46

Irregular verbs do not add ed to the past tense.

Examples: Today I swim. (present tense)
Yesterday I swam. (past tense)

Usually, the past tense and the past participle form are not the same.

Examples: Yesterday I ate fried chicken. (past tense)
The man had eaten three pieces. (past participle)

A chart drawn like the one shown here may be helpful.

Infinitive	Today Present	Yesterday Past	has, have, or had Past Participle
to see	**see(s)** (Today I see or he sees.)	**saw** (Yesterday I saw.)	**had seen** (I had seen.)
to speak	**speak(s)** (Today I speak or he speaks to him.)	**spoke** (Yesterday I spoke to him.)	**had spoken** (I had spoken to him.)
to bring	**bring(s)** (Today I bring or he brings cookies.)	**brought** (Yesterday I brought cookies.)	**had brought*** I had brought cookies.)

---

*You will note that the past and participle forms of *to bring* are the same (except for the addition of a helping verb in the past participle form.) However, *to bring* qualifies as an irregular verb because ed is not added to form the past tense.

EXTREMELY IMPORTANT NOTE: THE FOLLOWING PAGES CONTAIN A LIST OF IRREGULAR VERBS AND THEIR FORMS. (THIS LIST, OF COURSE, DOES NOT INCLUDE ALL IRREGULAR VERBS.) STUDENTS SHOULD BE EXPECTED TO MASTER THIS LIST.

PAGE 88 = WORKBOOK PAGE 47 ***PAGE 89 = WORKBOOK PAGE 48***

IRREGULAR VERBS

Infinitive	Present	Past	Present Participle	Past Participle*
To be	is, am, are	was, were	being	been
To beat	beat(s)	beat	beating	beaten
To begin	begin(s)	began	beginning	begun
To blow	blow(s)	blew	blowing	blown
To break	break(s)	broke	breaking	broken
To bring	bring(s)	brought	bringing	brought
To burst	burst(s)	burst	bursting	burst
To buy	buy(s)	bought	buying	bought
To choose	choose(s)	chose	choosing	chosen
To come	come(s)	came	coming	come
To do	do, does	did	doing	done
To drink	drink(s)	drank	drinking	drunk
To drive	drive(s)	drove	driving	driven
To eat	eat(s)	ate	eating	eaten
To fall	fall(s)	fell	falling	fallen
To fly	fly, flies	flew	flying	flown
To freeze	freeze(s)	froze	freezing	frozen
To give	give(s)	gave	giving	given
To go	go, goes	went	going	gone
To grow	grow(s)	grew	growing	grown
To have	have, has	had	having	had
To hang	hang(s)	hanged, hung	hanging	hanged, hung
To know	know(s)	knew	knowing	known
To lay	lay(s)	laid	laying	laid
To leave	leave(s)	left	leaving	left

*Uses a helping verb such as has, have, or had.

IRREGULAR VERBS

Infinitive	Present	Past	Present Participle	Past Participle*
To lie	lie(s)	lay	lying	lain
To ride	ride(s)	rode	riding	ridden
To ring	ring(s)	rang	ringing	rung
To rise	rises(s)	rose	rising	risen
To run	run(s)	ran	running	run
To see	see(s)	saw	seeing	seen
To set	set(s)	set	setting	set
To shake	shake(s)	shook	shaking	shaken
To sing	sing(s)	sang	singing	sung
To sink	sink(s)	sank	sinking	sunk
To sit	sit(s)	sat	sitting	sat
To speak	speak(s)	spoke	speaking	spoken
To spring	spring(s)	sprang	springing	sprung
To steal	steal(s)	stole	stealing	stolen
To swim	swim(s)	swam	swimming	swum
To swear	swear(s)	swore	swearing	sworn
To take	take(s)	took	taking	taken
To teach	teach(s)	taught	teaching	taught
To throw	throw(s)	threw	throwing	thrown
To wear	wear(s)	wore	wearing	worn
To write	write(s)	wrote	writing	written

*Uses a helping verb such as has, have, had. These may also use other helping verbs such as was or were.

Name________________________________ **IRREGULAR VERBS**

WORKBOOK PAGE 49

Date________________________________

Directions: Write the past participle form of each verb infinitive.

Remember: A past participle form will have a helping verb.

Example: past participle of *to shake* - ___had shaken___

ALTHOUGH OTHER HELPING VERBS MAY BE USED WITH THE PAST PARTICIPLE, ANSWERS HAVE BEEN GIVEN USING HAD.

1. past participle of *to begin* - had **begun**
2. past participle of *to leave* - had **left**
3. past participle of *to freeze* - had **frozen**
4. past participle of *to wear* - had **worn**
5. past participle of *to run* - had **run**
6. past participle of *to eat* - had **eaten**
7. past participle of *to swim* - had **swum**
8. past participle of *to fall* - had **fallen**
9. past participle of *to throw* - had **thrown**
10. past participle of *to drink* - had **drunk**
11. past participle of *to speak* - had **spoken**
12. past participle of *to lie* (rest) - had **lain** (Any time lie is used in this text, lie means to rest.)
13. past participle of *to bring* - had **brought** (Stress that brang and brung are not allowed.)
14. past participle of *to set* - had **set**
15. past participle of *to choose* - had **chosen**

Name________________________________ **IRREGULAR VERBS**

Date________________________________

Directions: Write the past participle form of each verb infinitive.

Remember: A past participle form will have a helping verb.

Example: past participle of *to shake* - ___had shaken___

1. past participle of *to begin* - ________________________________
2. past participle of *to leave* - ________________________________
3. past participle of *to freeze* - ________________________________
4. past participle of *to wear* - ________________________________
5. past participle of *to run* - ________________________________
6. past participle of *to eat* - ________________________________
7. past participle of *to swim* - ________________________________
8. past participle of *to fall* - ________________________________
9. past participle of *to throw* - ________________________________
10. past participle of *to drink* - ________________________________
11. past participle of *to speak* - ________________________________
12. past participle of *to lie* (rest) - ________________________________
13. past participle of *to bring* - ________________________________
14. past participle of *to set* - ________________________________
15. past participle of *to choose* - ________________________________

Name________________________________ **IRREGULAR VERBS**

WORKBOOK PAGE 50

Date________________________________

Directions: Write the past participle form of each verb infinitive.

Remember: A past participle form will have a helping verb.

Example: past participle of *to sing* - ___had sung___

ALTHOUGH OTHER HELPING VERBS MAY BE USED WITH THE PAST PARTICIPLE, ANSWERS HAVE BEEN GIVEN USING HAD.

1. past participle of *to sit* - had **sat**
2. past participle of *to grow* - had **grown**
3. past participle of *to write* - had **written**
4. past participle of *to come* - had **come**
5. past participle of *to know* - had **known**
6. past participle of *to take* - had **taken**
7. past participle of *to lay* - had **laid** Be sure that students have spelled this correctly.
8. past participle of *to buy* - had **bought**
9. past participle of *to teach* - had **taught**
10. past participle of *to rise* - had **risen**
11. past participle of *to blow* - had **blown**
12. past participle of *to go* - had **gone**
13. past participle of *to be* - had **been**
14. past participle of *to hang* - had **hanged** People are hanged; objects are hung.
    had **hung**
15. past participle of *to burst* - had **burst**

Name________________________________ **IRREGULAR VERBS**

Date________________________________

Directions: Write the past participle form of each verb infinitive.

Remember: A past participle form will have a helping verb.

Example: past participle of *to sing* - ___had sung___

1. past participle of *to sit* - ________________________________
2. past participle of *to grow* - ________________________________
3. past participle of *to write* - ________________________________
4. past participle of *to come* - ________________________________
5. past participle of *to know* - ________________________________
6. past participle of *to take* - ________________________________
7. past participle of *to lay* - ________________________________
8. past participle of *to buy* - ________________________________
9. past participle of *to teach* - ________________________________
10. past participle of *to rise* - ________________________________
11. past participle of *to blow* - ________________________________
12. past participle of *to go* - ________________________________
13. past participle of *to be* - ________________________________
14. past participle of *to hang* - ________________________________
15. past participle of *to burst* - ________________________________

Name________________________________ **IRREGULAR VERBS**

WORKBOOK PAGE 51

Date________________________________

Directions: Cross out any prepositional phrase(s). Underline the subject once and the verb phrase twice.

Example: A tennis player had (fallen, fell) ~~onto the court~~.

1. That toilet has (broke, broken) again.
2. A credit card was (stolen, stole) ~~from his wallet~~.
3. Joyce had (bought, boughten) her coat ~~on sale~~.
4. Have you (rode, ridden) your bike?
5. We should have (written, wrote) a note ~~to Mom~~.
6. The television show might have already (began, begun).
7. Those rugs have been (shaken, shook) ~~for five minutes~~.
8. The balloon had suddenly (busted, burst) ~~into many small pieces~~.
9. Victor may have (flew, flown) ~~to his aunt's place~~ today.
10. The lock ~~to the gate~~ had been (sprung, sprang).
11. I have (brung, brought) my sleeping bag ~~with me~~.
12. That dress was (wore, worn) ~~by a President's wife~~.
13. The bell has (rung, rang) ~~for the beginning of class~~.
14. Should Jo Ellen and her friend have (went, gone) ~~without permission~~?
15. They were (chose, chosen) (to ride) ~~on the float during the parade~~.

Name________________________________ **IRREGULAR VERBS**

Date________________________________

Directions: Cross out any prepositional phrase(s). Underline the subject once and the verb phrase twice.

Example: A tennis player had (fallen, fell) ~~onto the court~~.

1. That toilet has (broke, broken) again.
2. A credit card was (stolen, stole) from his wallet.
3. Joyce had (bought, boughten) her coat on sale.
4. Have you (rode, ridden) your bike?
5. We should have (written, wrote) a note to Mom.
6. The television show might have already (began, begun).
7. Those rugs have been (shaken, shook) for five minutes.
8. The balloon had suddenly (busted, burst) into many small pieces.
9. Victor may have (flew, flown) to his aunt's place today.
10. The lock to the gate had been (sprung, sprang).
11. I have (brung, brought) my sleeping bag with me.
12. That dress was (wore, worn) by a President's wife.
13. The bell has (rung, rang) for the beginning of class.
14. Should Jo Ellen and her friend have (went, gone) without permission?
15. They were (chose, chosen) to ride on the float during the parade.

Name________________________________ **IRREGULAR VERBS**

WORKBOOK PAGE 52

Date________________________________

Directions: Cross out any prepositional phrase(s). Underline the subject once and the verb phrase twice.

Example: Her arm had been (broke, broken) ~~during the fall~~.

1. The tomato plant has (grew, grown) very large.
2. Marty had (came, come) ~~to the party~~ early.
3. We could have (swam, swum) ~~for another hour~~.
4. Grandma must have (driven, drove) ~~to church~~ alone.
5. Have you (ate, eaten) all ~~of your peas~~?
6. The horseshoe had been (threw, thrown) ~~past the stake~~.
7. You should have (saw, seen) the puzzled look ~~on his face~~.

Adv. **Labeling isn't necessary.**

8. Witnesses were (sworn, swore) in ~~by a tall lady~~.
9. My grandfather may have (knew, known) Babe Ruth.
10. He was (beat, beaten) ~~at the game~~ ~~of chess~~.
11. Peaches were (froze, frozen) ~~in a small container~~.
12. Have you (drank, drunk) your apple juice?
13. That baby should *not* be (gave, given) any milk.
14. ~~During the meeting~~, someone had (spoke, spoken) ~~concerning new accounts~~.
15. The students are (teached, taught) ~~about good health practices~~.

Name________________________________

Date________________________________

IRREGULAR VERBS

Directions: Cross out any prepositional phrase(s). Underline the subject once and the verb phrase twice.

Example: Her arm had been (broke, broken) ~~during the fall~~.

1. The tomato plant has (grew, grown) very large.
2. Marty had (came, come) to the party early.
3. We could have (swam, swum) for another hour.
4. Grandma must have (driven, drove) to church alone.
5. Have you (ate, eaten) all of your peas?
6. The horseshoe had been (threw, thrown) past the stake.
7. You should have (saw, seen) the puzzled look on his face.
8. Witnesses were (sworn, swore) in by a tall lady.
9. My grandfather may have (knew, known) Babe Ruth.
10. He was (beat, beaten) at the game of chess.
11. Peaches were (froze, frozen) in a small container.
12. Have you (drank, drunk) your apple juice?
13. That baby should not be (gave, given) any milk.
14. During the meeting, someone had (spoke, spoken) concerning new accounts.
15. The students are (teached, taught) about good health practices.

Name________________________________ **IRREGULAR VERBS**
WORKBOOK PAGE 53
Date________________________________

Directions: Cross our any prepositional phrase(s). Underline the subject once and verb phrase twice.

Example: These shoes had been (bought, boughten) ~~in the wrong size~~.

1. The *U.S.S. Arizona* was (sank, sunk) ~~at Pearl Harbor~~.
2. Has the sun (rose, risen) yet?
3. We could *not* have (run, ran) another mile.
4. Doughnuts were (ate, eaten) ~~for breakfast~~.
5. Their dog has been (teached, taught) many tricks.
6. The mail should have (come, came) ~~during the morning~~.
7. His brother may have (drank, drunk) the soda.
8. David's artwork has been (chose, chosen) ~~for a prize~~.
9. A strong wind has (blown, blew) all day.
10. The tourist had never (swum, swam) ~~in the ocean~~.
11. Egg whites were (beat, beaten) ~~for five minutes~~.
12. ~~Throughout the day~~, snow cones were (gave, given) ~~to the children~~.
13. He may have (did, done) his chores ~~before breakfast~~.
14. The stewardess could have (flown, flew) ~~on another flight~~.
15. That motorcycle has been (rode, ridden) ~~across the country~~.

Name______________________________ **IRREGULAR VERBS**

Date______________________________

Directions: Cross our any prepositional phrase(s). Underline the subject once and verb phrase twice.

Example: These shoes had been (bought, boughten) ~~in the wrong size~~.

1. The *U.S.S. Arizona** was (sank, sunk) at Pearl Harbor.
2. Has the sun (rose, risen) yet?
3. We could not have (run, ran) another mile.
4. Doughnuts were (ate, eaten) for breakfast.
5. Their dog has been (teached, taught) many tricks.
6. The mail should have (come, came) during the morning.
7. His brother may have (drank, drunk) the soda.
8. David's artwork has been (chose, chosen) for a prize.
9. A strong wind has (blown, blew) all day.
10. The tourist had never (swum, swam) in the ocean.
11. Egg whites were (beat, beaten) for five minutes.
12. Throughout the day, snow cones were (gave, given) to the children.
13. He may have (did, done) his chores before breakfast.
14. The stewardess could have (flown, flew) on another flight.
15. That motorcycle has been (rode, ridden) across the country.

*name of a ship

t Object

FOR THE TEACHER:

DIRECT OBJECTS: RISE/RAISE, SIT/SET, AND LIE/LAY

In order to teach the difficult verbs lie/lay, rise/raise, and sit/set with more understanding, a review of direct objects is necessary. The next few pages contain review worksheets. (Continue crossing out prepositional phrases.)

You will be teaching that *to set*, *to raise*, and *to lay* will be followed by a direct object. Unfortunately, as in many other language areas, there are exceptions. Some have been included. However, even with the many exceptions, using the direct object approach will be helpful in mastering these confusing verbs.

Encourage students to think about the meaning of lie/lay, sit/set, and rise/raise. Students need to comprehend that *lie* and *sit* mean to rest and *set* and *lay* mean to place.

Examples: Gloria sits in the first row. Gloria *rests* in the first row.

Jim lies on the bed to read. Jim *rests* on the bed to read.

Because there are exceptions, especially with passive voice, it is vital that students comprehend the meanings and are able to insert them when necessary.

Example: The vase of flowers had been set on the table.

The vase *of flowers* had been set (placed) ~~on the table~~.

This is an example of the passive voice (an object has been acted upon). Note that *set* is the correct verb, even without a direct object, because placed can be inserted for *set*.

For this text's instruction, however, the passive voice will not be explained. All examples will use direct objects. (Students at this level do not need to comprehend passive voice; they simply need to be taught the technique of inserting verb meaning as an additional help.)

SIT/SET

WORKBOOK PAGE 54

To sit means to rest.
To set means to place or put. (Be sure students understand the meanings.)

FORMS:

Infinitive	Present	Past	Present Participle	Past Participle
to sit	sit(s)	sat	sitting	(had) sat
to set	set(s)	set	setting	(had) set

Two basic items for sit/set:

1. Both *to sit* and *to set* are irregular verbs and must be learned.
2. *Set* requires a direct object.

Examples:

They are (sitting, setting) in the front row.

They are (sitting, setting) ~~in the front row~~.

(There is no direct object in the sentence. Thus, *sitting* is used. In addition, resting can be inserted for *sitting*.)

She had (sit, set) her boots by the bed.

D.O.
She had (sit, set) her boots ~~by the bed~~.

Because boots is the direct object, the answer has to be *set*. In addition, put can be inserted for *set*.

Unfortunately, there are times when *to set* will not have a direct object. This usually occurs in passive voice. Hence, give full attention to the meaning of put or place. If place can be inserted for *set*, use a form of *to set*.

RISE/RAISE

WORKBOOK PAGE 55

To rise means to go up without help.
To raise means to lift or go up (with help).

Ask students to name objects people raise.
Possible answers: You raise your hand.
Parents raise their children.
If you live on a farm, you may raise chickens.
If you belong to a club, you may raise money.

It's important that students comprehend that these are direct objects.

Infinitive	Present	Past	Present Participle	Past Participle
to rise	rise(s)	rose	rising	(had) risen
to raise	raise(s)	raised	raising	(had) raised

If students understand direct objects, they will see that *to raise* will require a direct object.

Two basic items for rise/raise:

1. *To rise* is an irregular verb; it needs to be learned.
   To raise is a regular verb. Regular verbs add ed to the past and past participle.

2. *To raise* requires a direct object.

Examples:

Smoke was rising from the campfire.
Smoke was rising ~~from the campfire~~. Students need to see that there is no direct object. Also, smoke rises on its own.

The player raised the volleyball over his head.
D.O.
The player raised the volleyball ~~over his head~~. Students need to see that the object he placed over his head was the volleyball.

LIE/LAY

WORKBOOK PAGE 56

To lie means to rest.
To lay means to place.

Be sure that students understand that in order to place, an object is needed. One must place *something*.

Forms:

Infinitive	Present	Past	Present Participle	Past Participle
to lay	lay(s)	laid	laying	(had) laid
to lie	lie(s)	lay	lying	(had) lain

Lie/Lay is one of the most difficult concepts in the English language. The past tense of *to lie* is the same as the present tense of *to lay*. Therefore, it's imperative that students also understand that *to lie* means to rest.

Two basic items for lie/lay:

1. *To lie/lay* are irregular verbs and **must be mastered**.
2. *Lays*, *laid*, and *laying* will have direct objects.

Examples:

Anna is (lying, laying) in the sun.

Anna is (lying, laying) ~~in the sun~~. There is no direct object. *Laying* requires one. Also, you can insert resting for *lying*.

A doorman (lay, laid) a package on the floor.

D.O.

A doorman (lay, laid) a package ~~on the floor~~. There is a direct object-package. Hence, *laid* is used. Also, placed can be inserted for *laid*.

Name________________________________ **DIRECT OBJECT REVIEW**

WORKBOOK PAGE 57

Date________________________________

Directions: Cross out any prepositional phrase(s). Underline the subject once and the verb or verb phrase twice. Label any direct object-D.O.

D.O.
Example: I pushed a button ~~in the elevator.~~

D.O.
1. A receptionist answered the telephone.

D.O.
2. They built a house ~~by a lake~~.

D.O.
3. The children climbed a tree ~~in the backyard~~.

D.O.
4. Patsy cleans her room every week.

D.O.
5. Miss Jacobs sent a message ~~to her company~~.

D.O.
6. He scrubbed the floor ~~with a mop~~.

D.O.
7. Her mother baked a cake ~~for a picnic~~.

D.O.
8. The woman bought a watch ~~for her husband~~.

D.O.
9. Three waiters ~~in black suits~~ served dinner.

D.O.
10. ~~Throughout the day~~, the farmer plowed the field.

D.O.
11. We did *not* see any lions ~~at the zoo~~.

D.O.
12. An expert examined the computer disk carefully.

D.O. D.O.
13. We eat pancakes and eggs ~~for breakfast~~.

D.O.
14. (You) Buy this old chair ~~with twisted legs~~.

D.O.
15. Have you finished your homework yet?

Name________________________________ **DIRECT OBJECT REVIEW**

Date________________________________

Directions: Cross out any prepositional phrase(s). Underline the subject once and the verb or verb phrase twice. Label any direct object-D.O.

D.O.
Example: I pushed a button ~~in the elevator.~~

1. A receptionist answered the telephone.
2. They built a house by a lake.
3. The children climbed a tree in the backyard.
4. Patsy cleans her room every week.
5. Miss Jacobs sent a message to her company.
6. He scrubbed the floor with a mop.
7. Her mother baked a cake for a picnic.
8. The woman bought a watch for her husband.
9. Three waiters in black suits served dinner.
10. Throughout the day, the farmer plowed the field.
11. We did not see any lions at the zoo.
12. An expert examined the computer disk carefully.
13. We eat pancakes and eggs for breakfast.
14. Buy this old chair with twisted legs.
15. Have you finished your homework yet?

Name________________________________ **DIRECT OBJECT REVIEW**

WORKBOOK PAGE 58

Date________________________________

Directions: Cross out any prepositional phrase(s). Underline the subject once and the verb or verb phrase twice. Label any direct object-D.O.

Example: He stubbed his toe (D.O.) ~~on a step~~.

1. The small child picked a flower (D.O.) ~~for his mother~~.
2. The club planted a tree (D.O.) ~~for Arbor Day~~.
3. ~~During the afternoon~~, the boys and girls played basketball (D.O.).
4. Is the mailman delivering a package (D.O.) today?
5. I read an article (D.O.) ~~about the stock market~~.
6. Mrs. Betts and Lyle made sugarless jam (D.O.).
7. Mom and Dad washed and waxed the car (D.O.).
8. That child carries her teddy bear (D.O.) ~~with her~~ everywhere.
9. Some passengers took a plane (D.O.) ~~from Dallas~~ ~~to Atlanta~~.
10. You should have taken your sleeping bag (D.O.) ~~with you~~.
11. Did everyone ~~but Todd~~ ride his horse (D.O.) ~~to the outing~~?
12. One ~~of the students~~ wrote a letter (D.O.) ~~to a local newspaper~~.
13. The maid did *not* clean the tub (D.O.) or the shower (D.O.).
14. (You) Give this screwdriver (D.O.) ~~to your brother~~, please.
15. Has anyone seen the blue basket (D.O.) ~~without a handle~~?

Name________________________________

Date________________________________

DIRECT OBJECT REVIEW

Directions: Cross out any prepositional phrase(s). Underline the subject once and the verb or verb phrase twice. Label any direct object-D.O.

D.O.
Example: He stubbed his toe ~~on a step~~.

1. The small child picked a flower for his mother.
2. The club planted a tree for Arbor Day.
3. During the afternoon, the boys and girls played basketball.
4. Is the mailman delivering a package today?
5. I read an article about the stock market.
6. Mrs. Betts and Lyle made sugarless jam.
7. Mom and Dad washed and waxed the car.
8. That child carries her teddy bear with her everywhere.
9. Some passengers took a plane from Dallas to Atlanta.
10. You should have taken your sleeping bag with you.
11. Did everyone but Todd ride his horse to the outing?
12. One of the students wrote a letter to a local newspaper.
13. The maid did not clean the tub or the shower.
14. Give this screwdriver to your brother, please.
15. Has anyone seen the blue basket without a handle?

Name_______________________________ **SIT/SET, LIE/LAY, RISE/RAISE**

WORKBOOK PAGE 59

Date________________________________

Directions: Cross out any prepositional phrase(s). Underline the subject once and the verb/verb phrase twice. Label any direct object-D.O.

D.O.

Example: The car salesperson set a sign on the reduced car.

Remember: ***To set, to lay,* and *to raise* must have a direct object.**
***Lays, laid,* and *laying* will have a direct object.**

D.O.

1. A surfer (lay, laid) his board on the sand.

2. My grandfather (sits, sets) by a stream during fishing season.

3. The sun (rises, raises) in the east.

D.O.

4. Their neighbor (rises, raises) pigs on his farm.

5. Your taco is (lying, laying) on the kitchen table.

D.O.

6. Harold (sat, set) the table for a week.

7. That lady (lies, lays) by the pool until noon.

8. Bread (rises, raises) in a warm spot.

D.O.

9. Deanne has (laid, lain) her cards on the table.

10. Jim is (sitting, setting) with his mom and sister.

11. Nick, with a smile, (raised, rose) to his feet.

12. They (lay, laid) on the blanket (to watch) fireworks.

13. Some spectators had (sat, set) below the bleachers.

D.O.

14. The policeman (raised, rose) his hand to the traffic.

D.O.

15. The lady has been (lying, laying) papers all over the clean floor.

Name________________________________ **SIT/SET, LIE/LAY, RISE/RAISE**

Date________________________________

Directions: Cross out any prepositional phrase(s). Underline the subject once and the verb/verb phrase twice. Label any direct object-D.O.

D.O.

Example: The car salesperson set a sign ~~on the reduced car~~.

Remember: *To set*, *to lay*, and *to raise* must have a direct object. *Lays*, *laid*, and *laying* will have a direct object.

1. A surfer (lay, laid) his board on the sand.
2. My grandfather (sits, sets) by a stream during fishing season.
3. The sun (rises, raises) in the east.
4. Their neighbor (rises, raises) pigs on his farm.
5. Your taco is (lying, laying) on the kitchen table.
6. Harold (sat, set) the table for a week.
7. That lady (lies, lays) by the pool until noon.
8. Bread (rises, raises) in a warm spot.
9. Deanne has (laid, lain) her cards on the table.
10. Jim is (sitting, setting) with his mom and sister.
11. Nick, with a smile, (raised, rose) to his feet.
12. They (lay, laid) on the blanket to watch fireworks.
13. Some spectators had (sat, set) below the bleachers.
14. The policeman (raised, rose) his hand to the traffic.
15. The lady has been (lying, laying) papers all over the clean floor.

Name_________________________________ **SIT/SET, LIE/LAY, RISE/RAISE**

WORKBOOK PAGE 60

Date_________________________________

Directions: Cross out any prepositional phrase(s). Underline the subject once and the verb/verb phrase twice. Label any direct object-D.O.

Remember: ***To set*, *to lay*, and *to raise* will have a direct object. *Lays*, *laid*, and *laying* will have a direct object. *Lay* will have a direct object when its meaning is *place*.**

D.O.

Example: (You) (Lie, Lay) the clothes ~~on the couch~~.

D.O.

1. The boss (rose, raised) his salary.

2. Jenny is (laying, lying) ~~in the sun~~ ~~without a hat~~.

3. That lady always (sits, sets) ~~in the same seat~~ ~~for lunch~~.

D.O.

4. The architect has (lain, laid) the blueprint ~~on the table~~.

D.O.

5. Their grandfather (rises, raises) cattle ~~on his ranch~~.

D.O.

6. A child care worker (lay, laid) the toddler ~~in a crib~~.

7. You have (set, sat) quietly ~~for nearly ten minutes~~.

D.O.

8. ~~In the morning~~, he (rises, raises) the flag.

9. (You) (Sit, Set) ~~beside me~~ ~~with your books and papers~~.

D.O.

10. Grandma (set, sat) her open umbrella ~~near the door~~.

Adv.* Not required*

11. The patient (lies, lays) down ~~after lunch~~.

D.O.

12. Mrs. Linnwood is (rising, raising) money ~~in that booth~~ ~~beneath the elm tree~~.

13. (You) (Lie, Lay) here ~~on the floor~~ (to watch) television.

14. Has the exhausted traveler (risen, raised)?

15. This can opener has (lain, laid) ~~in the sink~~ all day.

Name________________________________ **SIT/SET, LIE/LAY, RISE/RAISE**

Date________________________________

Directions: Cross out any prepositional phrase(s). Underline the subject once and the verb/verb phrase twice. Label any direct object-D.O.

Remember: ***To set, to lay,* and *to raise* will have a direct object. *Lays, laid,* and *laying* will have a direct object. *Lay* will have a direct object when its meaning is place.**

D.O.

Example: (You) (Lie, Lay) the clothes ~~on the couch~~.

1. The boss (rose, raised) his salary.
2. Jenny is (laying, lying) in the sun without a hat.
3. That lady always (sits, sets) in the same seat for lunch.
4. The architect has (lain, laid) the blueprint on the table.
5. Their grandfather (rises, raises) cattle on his ranch.
6. A child care worker (lay, laid) the toddler in a crib.
7. You have (set, sat) quietly for nearly ten minutes.
8. In the morning, he (rises, raises) the flag.
9. (Sit, Set) beside me with your books and papers.
10. Grandma (set, sat) her open umbrella near the door.
11. The patient (lies, lays) down after lunch.
12. Mrs. Linnwood is (rising, raising) money in that booth beneath the elm tree.
13. (Lie, Lay) here on the floor to watch television.
14. Has the exhausted traveler (risen, raised)?
15. This can opener has (lain, laid) in the sink all day.

Name________________________________ **SIT/SET, LIE/LAY, RISE/RAISE**

WORKBOOK PAGE 61

Date________________________________

Directions: Cross out any prepositional phrase(s). Underline the subject once and the verb/verb phrase twice. Label any direct object-D.O.

Example: The sponge has been (lying, laying) ~~on the floor~~ all day.

Remember: ***To set*, *to lay*, and *to raise* will have a direct object. *Lays*, *laid*, and *laying* will have a direct object. *Lay* will have a direct object when its meaning is place.**

1. The painter was (sitting, setting) ~~on the curb~~.

2. A sunbather (lay, laid) ~~on his towel~~ ~~at the beach~~.

D.O.

3. Have you (raised, risen) your hand (to volunteer)?

4. Mr. Markel should have (set, sat) across ~~from me~~.

D.O.

5. My friend and I had (lain, laid) the tools ~~beside a bench~~.

6. Wilma was not (lying, laying) ~~on a lounge chair~~.

7. Prices are (rising, raising) rapidly ~~on those products~~.

D.O.

8. That boy (sits, sets) his dishes ~~in the dishwasher~~.

D.O.

9. The entire family (lay, laid) carpeting ~~in a new home~~.

10. An elderly gentleman (rose, raised) ~~from his chair~~ ~~without his cane~~.

11. A herd ~~of cows~~ had (laid, lain) ~~in the field~~ ~~for two hours~~.

D.O.

12. ~~For her 4-H project~~, Hannah is (rising, raising) a pig.

13. ~~Throughout the summer day~~, he had been (sitting, setting) ~~on a porch swing~~.

D.O.

14. (You) (Lie, Lay) the bread knife ~~below the counter~~.

D.O.

15. That taxi driver (lies, lays) his lunch ~~on the front seat~~ ~~of his taxi~~.

Name________________________________ **SIT/SET, LIE/LAY, RISE/RAISE**

Date________________________________

Directions: Cross out any prepositional phrases. Underline the subject once and the verb/verb phrase twice. Label any direct object-D.O.

Example: The sponge has been (lying, laying) ~~on the floor~~ all day.

Remember: ***To set, to lay,* and *to raise* will have a direct object. *Lays, laid,* and *laying* will have a direct object. *Lay* will have a direct object when its meaning is place.**

1. The painter was (sitting, setting) on the curb.
2. A sunbather (lay, laid) on his towel at the beach.
3. Have you (raised, risen) your hand to volunteer?
4. Mr. Markel should have (set, sat) across from me.
5. My friend and I had (lain, laid) the tools beside a bench.
6. Wilma was not (lying, laying) on a lounge chair.
7. Prices are (rising, raising) rapidly on those products.
8. That boy (sits, sets) his dishes in the dishwasher.
9. The entire family (lay, laid) carpeting in a new home.
10. An elderly gentleman (rose, raised) from his chair without his cane.
11. A herd of cows had (laid, lain) in the field for two hours.
12. For her 4-H project, Hannah is (rising, raising) a pig.
13. Throughout the summer day, he had been (sitting, setting) on a porch swing.
14. (Lie, Lay) the bread knife below the counter.
15. That taxi driver (lies, lays) his lunch on the front seat of his taxi.

VERBS

WORKBOOK PAGE 62

The verb of a sentence expresses an action or simply states a fact.

Examples: The tennis player hit the ball hard. (action)

Barry made a doll for his daughter. (action)

George became a fireman. (fact)

Their bathroom is upstairs. (fact)

Verbs that simply state a fact are often called **state of being** verbs.

IRREGULAR VERB *TO BE*

Students need to **memorize** and **master** the conjugation of *to be*:

is, **am**, **are**, **was**, **were**, **be**, **being**, **been**

Present Tense:

Singular: **is** The bread **is** in the cupboard.

am I **am** hungry.

Are is used with the singular pronoun ***you.*** You **are** nice.

Plural: **are** Those children **are** in first grade.

Past Tense:

Singular: **was** The fork **was** under the chair.

Were is used with the singular pronoun ***you.*** You **were** right!

Plural: **were** Several ducks **were** on the pond.

FOR THE TEACHER:

WORKBOOK PAGE 63 LINKING VERBS

Linking verbs do not show action. They link the subject with a noun or a pronoun, or they link the subject with an adjective (describing word).

noun

Examples: My neighbor is a *cartoonist*.

pronoun

The champion was *I*. (Students will be taught to invert this later. [I was the champion.])

adjective

The referee remained cheerful ~~throughout the game~~.

To check if a verb (other than *to be*) is serving as a linking verb in a sentence, write a form of *to be* above it. If the sentence makes sense and the meaning is not changed, the verb serves as a linking verb. (It is very important that students understand this concept. As always, give them many examples when teaching this concept.

is

Examples: The pie tastes good.

was

My friend became a missionary.

There are three easy aspects of linking verbs.

1. Linking verbs never show action.
2. Linking verbs always link the subject with something.
3. Linking verbs appear as a separate list.

The following list of linking verbs must be **memorized** and **learned**:

to feel	to appear	to seem
to taste	to become	to sound
to look	to grow	to stay
to smell	to remain	to be (is, am, are, was, were, be, being, been)

VERY IMPORTANT: These have been listed with the 4 senses in the first column, the next 7 listed alphabetically, and *to be* out of order and listed last. This is necessary so that students will also list *is*, *am*, etc. Ask students to list the first 12 infinitives (using to with the verb), and then list the conjugation of to be (*is*, *am*, *are*, etc.) without to (They are not infinitives!). The question may arise if students should list both *to be* and *be*. The answer is yes! *to be* is an infinitive, and *be* is a form of that verb. In total, ask students to list 20 answers (12 infinitives plus the 8 parts of *to be*).

FOR THE TEACHER:

LINKING VERBS: PREDICATE NOMINATIVES

In order to teach linking verbs, you must introduce two new terms: predicate nominative and predicate adjective.

A **predicate nominative (P.N.)** is a noun (naming word) or a pronoun (*I*, *he*, *she*, *we*, *they*, *you*, *it*, *who*) that is the same as the subject of the sentence.

P.N.
Examples: My dad is the principal.

P.N.
Mrs. Kimmel became their Girl Scout leader.

Predicate nominatives are easy to check. Simply invert the sentence starting with the word after the verb in a declarative sentence, tag on the verb, and add the complete subject. (Rather then repeating this somewhat complicated procedure, simply instruct students to "invert" the sentence and provide many examples. Students quickly learn how to "invert" the sentence.)

P.N.
Example: My dad is the principal.

Proof: The principal is my dad.

If a form of to be does not appear as the linking verb in the sentence, you will need to replace the existing linking verb with an appropriate form of to be.

P.N.
Example: Miss Levin remained the nurse ~~for that company~~.

Miss Levin **was** the nurse for that company.

Proof: The nurse for that company was Miss Levin.

Students must delete prepositional phrases, underline the subject once and the verb/ verb phrase twice. Prepositional phrases do not need to be included in the proof.

A sentence may contain a compound predicate nominative.

Example: Their favorite foods are pizza and steak.

Proof: Pizza and steak are their favorite foods.

FOR THE TEACHER:
WORKBOOK PAGE 64

LINKING VERBS: PREDICATE NOMINATIVES

In an interrogative sentence, the predicate nominative may be more difficult to discern. Follow this method. Turn the question into a statement, and invert the statement to prove it.

Example: Is Vic the new vice-president?

P.N.
Vic is the new vice-president.

Proof: The new vice-president is Vic.

Example: Are you the head cheerleader?

P.N.
You are the head cheerleader.

Proof: The head cheerleader is* you.

*Sometimes, the present forms of *to be* (*is*, *am*, and *are*) must be interchanged when checking for predicate nominatives.

Example: Was the artist the first person to receive the award?

P.N.
The artist was the first person to receive the award.

Proof: The first person to receive the award was the artist.

Example: Are your best friends Toby and I?

P.N. P.N.
Your best friends are Toby and I.

Proof: Toby and I are your best friends.

Name________________________________ **LINKING VERBS**
WORKBOOK PAGE 65 **Predicate Nominatives**
Date________________________________

Directions: Cross out any prepositional phrase(s). Underline the subject once and the verb/verb phrase twice. Label the predicate nominative-P.N. Then, write the inverted form of the sentence on the line provided.

P.N.
Example: Their sister is the editor ~~of the school newspaper~~.

The editor is their sister

P.N.
1. Pat was the winner ~~of the race~~.

Proof: The winner was Pat.

P.N.
2. The champion was Suzanne.

Proof: Suzanne was the champion.

P.N.
3. Dr. Post is our dentist.

Proof: Our dentist is Dr. Post.

P.N.
4. Tad's best friend is Mike.

Proof: Mike is Tad's best friend.

P.N.
5. Her favorite subject is math.

Proof: Math is her favorite subject.

P.N.
6. Their favorite dessert is a hot fudge sundae.

Proof: A hot fudge sundae is their favorite dessert.

P.N.
7. Mrs. Taber was her teacher ~~in first grade~~.

Proof: Her teacher was Mrs. Taber.

P.N.
8. Their dinner was pepperoni pizza.

Proof: Pepperoni pizza was their dinner.

Name________________________________

Date________________________________

LINKING VERBS
Predicate Nominatives

Directions: Cross out any prepositional phrase(s). Underline the subject once and the verb/verb phrase twice. Label the predicate nominative-P.N. Then, write the inverted form of the sentence on the line provided.

P.N.
Example: Their sister is the editor ~~of the school newspaper~~.

The editor is their sister

1. Pat was the winner of the race.

Proof: ______________________________

2. The champion was Suzanne.

Proof: ______________________________

3. Dr. Post is our dentist.

Proof: ______________________________

4. Tad's best friend is Mike.

Proof: ______________________________

5. Her favorite subject is math.

Proof: ______________________________

6. Their favorite dessert is a hot fudge sundae.

Proof: ______________________________

7. Mrs. Taber was her teacher in first grade.

Proof: ______________________________

8. Their dinner was pepperoni pizza.

Proof: ______________________________

Name____________________________________ **LINKING VERBS**

WORKBOOK PAGE 66 **Predicate Nominatives**

Date____________________________________

Directions: Cross out any prepositional phrase(s). Underline the subject once and the verb/verb phrase twice. Label the predicate nominative-P.N. Then, write the inverted form of the sentence on the line provided.

P.N.

Example: Mrs. Jackson is the lady ~~in the suit~~.

The lady is Mrs. Jackson.

P.N.

1. Barbara's dog is the poodle ~~with yellow bows~~.

Proof: The poodle is Barbara's dog.

P.N.

2. A Siamese is a pretty cat.

Proof: A pretty cat is a Siamese.

P.N.

3. The best car was that racer.

Proof: That racer was the best car.

P.N.

4. Her favorite show had always been Mr. Rogers.

Proof: Mr. Rogers had always been her favorite show.

P.N.

5. Burger Haven is the newest restaurant ~~in town~~.

Proof: The newest restaurant is Burger Haven.

P.N.

6. The winner ~~of the dog show~~ was a beagle.

Proof: A beagle was the winner.

P.N.

7. George remained the manager ~~for three years~~.*

Proof: The manager was George.

P.N.

8. His uncle became the newest barber ~~at Worth's~~.*

Proof: The newest barber was his uncle.

*Insert a form of *to be* (was, in this case) to prove a predicate nominative.

Name________________________________ **LINKING VERBS**
Predicate Nominatives

Date________________________________

Directions: Cross out any prepositional phrase(s). Underline the subject once and the verb/verb phrase twice. Label the predicate nominative-P.N. Then, write the inverted form of the sentence on the line provided.

P.N.
Example: Mrs. Jackson is the lady ~~in the suit~~.

The lady is Mrs. Jackson.

1. Barbara's dog is the poodle with yellow bows.

   Proof: ____

2. A Siamese is a pretty cat.

   Proof: ____

3. The best car was that racer.

   Proof: ____

4. Her favorite show had always been Mr. Rogers.

   Proof: ____

5. Burger Haven is the newest restaurant in town.

   Proof: ____

6. The winner of the dog show was a beagle.

   Proof: ____

7. George remained the manager for three years.*

   Proof: ____

8. His uncle became the newest barber at Worth's.*

   Proof: ____

*Insert a form of *to be* (was, in this case) to prove a predicate nominative.

FOR THE TEACHER:

WORKBOOK PAGE 67 **LINKING VERBS**

Predicate Adjectives:

A predicate adjective is a **describing word** that **occurs after the verb** and goes back to describe the **subject** of the sentence.

In order for a word to be a predicate adjective, you must have the following:

A. The sentence must contain a linking verb.

B. The adjective occurring after the verb must go back and describe the subject of the sentence.

Examples: The car is white. (P.A.: white) (white car)

This bread tastes stale. (P.A.: stale) (stale bread)

A baby feels soft. (P.A.: soft) (soft baby)

Be sure that the sentence contains a linking verb.

Terry rides a spotted horse. *Spotted* is not a predicate adjective. The verb *rides* is not a linking verb.* Therefore, spotted can't possibly be a predicate adjective. In addition, *spotted* describes horse. Terry, the subject, is not *spotted*.

Always run the check:

1. Is there a possible linking verb?

2. Is there a describing word (adjective) after the verb?

3. Does that describing word (adjective) go back to describe the subject?

COMPOUND PREDICATE ADJECTIVES:

There may be more than one predicate adjective in a sentence.

Examples: The Italian flag is red, white, and green. (P.A.: red, white, green)

Kirby became tired and sleepy ~~in geometry class~~. (P.A.: tired, sleepy)

*Remember that an aid in checking if a verb is linking is to see if a form of *to be* can be inserted. If this is possible, the verb generally is a linking verb.

Example: Otis remained quiet for a long time. (**was** written above *remained*)

Name_______________________________

LINKING VERBS

Date_______________________________

Directions: Make your own linking verb quiz. Scramble the letters of the linking verbs and write one per line. Give it to a friend to unscramble.

1. _______________________________
2. _______________________________
3. _______________________________
4. _______________________________
5. _______________________________
6. _______________________________
7. _______________________________
8. _______________________________
9. _______________________________
10. _______________________________
11. _______________________________
12. _______________________________
13. _______________________________
14. _______________________________
15. _______________________________
16. _______________________________
17. _______________________________
18. _______________________________
19. _______________________________
20. _______________________________

Name________________________________

WORKBOOK PAGE 69

Date________________________________

LINKING VERBS
Predicate Adjectives

Directions: Underline the subject once and the verb or verb phrase twice. Label any predicate adjective-P.A. On the line after the sentence, write the describing word (P.A.) + subject.

Example: Your teeth are shiny. (P.A. = shiny) ______ shiny teeth ______

1. The sky is cloudy. (P.A.) ______ cloudy sky ______
2. His ring is gold. (P.A.) ______ gold ring ______
3. My pants are dirty. (P.A.) ______ dirty pants ______
4. The boy was hungry. (P.A.) ______ hungry boy ______
5. Those clowns are funny. (P.A.) ______ funny clowns ______
6. A wolf is wild. (P.A.) ______ wild wolf ______
7. Her nails are pretty. (P.A.) ______ pretty nails ______
8. His shoes had been scuffed. (P.A.) ______ scuffed shoes ______
9. Their bikes are old. (P.A.) ______ old bikes ______
10. These beans are stringy. (P.A.) ______ stringy beans ______
11. The dress is new. (P.A.) ______ new dress ______
12. The bunnies were cute. (P.A.) ______ cute bunnies ______
13. Their answer was dumb. (P.A.) ______ dumb answer ______
14. His face is red and swollen. (P.A., P.A.) ______ red face / swollen face ______
15. The secretary was friendly and nice. (P.A., P.A.) ______ friendly secretary / nice secretary ______

Name_______________________________

Date_______________________________

LINKING VERBS
Predicate Adjectives

Directions: Underline the subject once and the verb or verb phrase twice. Label any predicate adjective-P.A. On the line after the sentence, write the describing word (P.A.) + subject.

Example: Your teeth are shiny. (P.A. above "shiny") ______shiny teeth______

1. The sky is cloudy. ______________________

2. His ring is gold. ______________________

3. My pants are dirty. ______________________

4. The boy was hungry. ______________________

5. Those clowns are funny. ______________________

6. A wolf is wild. ______________________

7. Her nails are pretty. ______________________

8. His shoes had been scuffed. ______________________

9. Their bikes are old. ______________________

10. These beans are stringy. ______________________

11. The dress is new. ______________________

12. The bunnies were cute. ______________________

13. Their answer was dumb. ______________________

14. His face is red and swollen. ___________/___________

15. The secretary was friendly and nice. ___________/___________

Name________________________________

WORKBOOK PAGE 70

Date________________________________

LINKING VERBS
Predicate Adjectives

Directions: This exercise requires several steps; do this page very slowly. Cross out any prepositional phrase(s). Underline the subject once and the verb/verb phrase twice. Place *is*, *am*, *are*, *was*, or *were* above any linking verb other than a form of *to be*. Label any predicate adjective-P.A. On the line after the sentence, write the describing word (P.A.) + subject.

is P.A.
Example: The man ~~in the blue car~~ sounds angry. ___angry man___

P.A.
1. The shell ~~of this egg~~ is brown. ___brown shell___

is P.A.
2. The banana yogurt tastes good. ___good yogurt___

is P.A.
3. That carved chest feels rough. ___rough chest___

is P.A.
4. Your steak smells burned. ___burned steak___

was P.A.
5. The child remained unhappy. ___unhappy child___

was P.A.
6. A hiker grew thirsty ~~in the afternoon~~. ___thirsty hiker___

are P.A.
7. Those drivers seem lost. ___lost drivers___

were P.A.
8. The bells sounded loud. ___loud bells___

is P.A.
9. His hair looks messy ~~in the back~~. ___messy hair___

P.A.
10. The watermelon is too watery. ___watery watermelon___

Name________________________________

Date________________________________

LINKING VERBS
Predicate Adjectives

Directions: This exercise requires several steps; do this page very slowly. Cross out any prepositional phrase(s). Underline the subject once and the verb/verb phrase twice. Place *is*, *am*, *are*, *was*, or *were* above any linking verb other than a form of *to be*. Label any predicate adjective-P.A. On the line after the sentence, write the describing word (P.A.) + subject.

Example: The man ~~in the blue car~~ sounds (**is**) angry (P.A.). ____angry man____

1. The shell of this egg is brown. ______________________

2. The banana yogurt tastes good. ______________________

3. That carved chest feels rough. ______________________

4. Your steak smells burned. ______________________

5. The child remained unhappy. ______________________

6. A hiker grew thirsty in the afternoon. ______________________

7. Those drivers seem lost. ______________________

8. The bells sounded loud. ______________________

9. His hair looks messy in the back. ______________________

10. The watermelon is too watery. ______________________

FOR THE TEACHER:
WORKBOOK PAGE 71

ACTION OR LINKING VERB?

Students need to "think" about the verb. Often, they will readily see that the verb shows action (walks, jumped, etc.). Because students are required to memorize linking verbs, they will immediately recognize that *to fly* is not on the linking verb list. *Fly* is an action verb.

Some verbs can serve both as action and linking verbs.

Example: The customer tasted the dessert. (action verb)

The dessert tasted sweet. (linking verb)

Suggestion: Instruct students to insert a form of *to be* (*is, am, are, was,* or *were*) for the verb. If the sentence meaning is not changed, the verb is usually linking.

was
A. Example: The customer tasted the dessert.

The customer was the dessert.

This example may produce laughter, and it will easily show students that *tasted* is not a linking verb in this sentence.

B. Example: The dessert tasted sweet.

The dessert was sweet.

This example clearly shows that *tasted* could be a linking verb. *Was* can be inserted without changing the meaning of the sentence.

Name________________________________
WORKBOOK PAGE 72
Date________________________________

LINKING VERBS
Action or Linking?

Directions: Cross out any prepositional phrase(s). Underline the subject once and the verb/verb phrase twice. Write A on the line if the verb shows action; write L on the line if the verb is linking.

were
Example: __L__ The fireworks sounded loud ~~during the show.~~

Remember: Write *is*, *am*, *are*, *was*, or *were* above the verb. If the meaning of the sentence is not changed, the verb is probably a linking verb.

was
1. __L__ The fudge became sticky.

was
2. __L__ The floor ~~behind the stove~~ grew dirty.

3. __A__ I walked ~~to the store~~. **Point out that *to walk* is not on the linking verb list; therefore, it does not qualify.**

were
4. __L__ The flowers remained fresh ~~for a week~~.

5. __A__ Justin tasted the broth ~~in the kettle~~. **Students may find inserting *was* for *tasted* rather humorous.**

is
6. __L__ The milk tastes sour.

was
7. __L__ Her hair stayed damp ~~in the heat~~.

8. __A__ She stayed ~~in the house~~ ~~for three hours~~. ***Stayed* can't be a linking verb; everything after stayed has been deleted.**

was
9. __L__ Martin sounded hoarse ~~after cheering~~.

were
10. __L__ Her fingers remained sticky ~~from the marshmallows~~.

Name________________________________

Date________________________________

LINKING VERBS
Action or Linking?

Directions: Cross out any prepositional phrase(s). Underline the subject once and the verb/verb phrase twice. Write A on the line if the verb shows action; write L on the line if the verb is linking.

were

Example: __L__ The fireworks sounded loud ~~during the show.~~

Remember: **Write *is*, *am*, *are*, *was*, or *were* above the verb. If the meaning of the sentence is not changed, the verb is probably a linking verb.**

1. _____ The fudge became sticky.

2. _____ The floor behind the stove grew dirty.

3. _____ I walked to the store.

4. _____ The flowers remained fresh for a week.

5. _____ Justin tasted the broth in the kettle.

6. _____ The milk tastes sour.

7. _____ Her hair stayed damp in the heat.

8. _____ She stayed in the house for three hours.

9. _____ Martin sounded hoarse after cheering.

10. _____ Her fingers remained sticky from the marshmallows.

Name________________________________ **LINKING VERBS**
WORKBOOK PAGE 73 **Action or Linking?**
Date________________________________

Directions: Cross out any prepositional phrase(s). Underline the subject once and the verb/verb phrase twice. Write A on the line if the verb shows action; write L on the line if the verb is linking.

was
Example: __L__ Her friend stayed upset ~~for an hour~~.

Remember: **Write *is*, *am*, *are*, *was*, or *were* above the verb. If the meaning of the sentence is not changed, the verb is usually a linking verb.**

is
1. __L__ Our cat seems sick.

was
2. __L__ His idea sounded terrific.

was
3. __L__ The floor had become sticky ~~from spilled cola~~.

is
4. __L__ This velvet feels soft ~~to the touch~~.

5. __A__ I felt my way ~~down the stairs~~.

is
6. __L__ The cellar smells musty.

7. __A__ The family smelled a strange odor ~~in their living room~~.
(Students may find inserting *was* rather humorous.)

8. __A__ The child grew three inches last year.
(Students may find inserting *was* rather humorous.)

is
9. __L__ Jim looks happy ~~about his victory~~.

10. __A__ A toddler looked ~~at me with big blue eyes~~.

Name________________________________

Date________________________________

LINKING VERBS
Action or Linking?

Directions: Cross out any prepositional phrase(s). Underline the subject once and the verb/verb phrase twice. Write A on the line if the verb shows action; write L on the line if the verb is linking.

was

Example: __L__ Her friend stayed upset ~~for an hour~~.

Remember: Write *is*, *am*, *are*, *was*, or *were* above the verb. If the meaning of the sentence is not changed, the verb is usually a linking verb.

1. _____ Our cat seems sick.

2. _____ His idea sounded terrific.

3. _____ The floor had become sticky from spilled cola.

4. _____ This velvet feels soft to the touch.

5. _____ I felt my way down the stairs.

6. _____ The cellar smells musty.

7. _____ The family smelled a strange odor in their living room.

8. _____ The child grew three inches last year.

9. _____ Jim looks happy about his victory.

10. _____ A toddler looked at me with big blue eyes.

FOR THE TEACHER:
WORKBOOK PAGE 74

SUBJECT VERB AGREEMENT

Students will need to understand that singular means one. They also need to comprehend that present tense means present time. (Today often helps students relate to present tense.)

In present time (tense): If the subject is singular (only one), the verb will be singular.

You will need to review regular verbs. **In a regular verb (one that adds ed to form past time, e.g. jump/jumped), add s to the verb when the subject is singular.**

Examples: A bird chirp**s** in the tree.

One lady work**s** at her computer.

EXCEPTION: The pronouns *I* and *you* will not add s in present tense verbs.

Examples: I walk every day.

You do that nicely.

You will need to review irregular verbs.

In present tense (time): In most irregular verbs, the same rule applies. Simply add s to the verb.

Examples: A baseball player steal**s** bases.

He know**s** the answer.

In a few irregular verbs, es is added to the verb.

Examples: The boy do**es** his homework.

My dad go**es** to work.

FOR THE TEACHER:
WORKBOOK PAGE 75

SUBJECT VERB AGREEMENT

Review present tense: Present tense means present time.

Students will need to understand the term plural.

Plural means more than one.
In present tense: If the subject is plural (more than one), do not add s to the verb.

Examples: Horses gallop through the field.
Those five boys play football.

Sometimes, the subject will be compound (two or more); do not add s if the subjects are joined by *and*.

Examples: Mickey **and** her cousin sing in a church choir.
A frog, a tadpole, **and** a crayfish live in the stream.

In most irregular verbs, do not add s to the verb if the subject is plural.

Example: Some ducks swim on the lake daily.

EXCEPTION: Some irregular verbs completely change form for the present tense.

Example: The women are in a boat on the lake.

If a compound subject (two or more) is joined by *or*, follow these rules:

A. If the subject closer to the verb is singular, add s to the verb.

Example: His daughters or **son needs** a ride home.

B. If the subject closer to the verb is plural, don't add s to the verb.

Example: His son or **daughters need** a ride home.

NOTE: The following two exercises deal with singular subjects only. Then, two exercises are given to reinforce plural subjects. The last two subject-verb agreement exercises will require students to decide if the subject is singular or plural in order to determine the correct verb.

Name_______________________________ **SUBJECT/VERB AGREEMENT**

WORKBOOK PAGE 76

Date_______________________________

Directions: Cross out any prepositional phrase(s). Underline the subject once and the verb twice.

Example: Carl (stands, stand) ~~by me~~ ~~in the lunch line~~.

Note: Although directions do not include finding direct objects, this is a good place to review that concept. Simply ask for the direct object as you go through the sentences containing one.

1. A guide (lives, live) ~~in those mountains~~.

2. Margo (stays, stay) ~~with her grandmother~~.

3. A snake (crawl, crawls) ~~in their garden~~.

4. The wind (blows, blow) ~~through that canyon~~.

5. That farmer (plant, plants) wheat ~~in his fields~~. **Direct Object? wheat**

6. A hair stylist (cut, cuts) her hair very short. **Direct Object? hair**

7. The librarian (reads, read) ~~to the children~~ ~~on Saturdays~~.

8. The reporter (writes, write) ~~about the burglaries~~ ~~in their town~~.

9. Betty (swim, swims) ~~for exercise~~.

10. A fiddler (play, plays) ~~with that band~~.

11. Our dog (lie, lies) ~~by the front door~~.

12. Her mother (go, goes) ~~to a specialist~~.

13. I (finds, find) many pennies ~~on the floor~~. **Direct Object? pennies**

14. One ~~of the girls~~ (fly, flies) ~~without her parents~~.

15. Kurt often (wear, wears) shirts ~~with flowers~~. **Direct Object? shirts**

Name________________________________ **SUBJECT/VERB AGREEMENT**

Date________________________________

Directions: Cross out any prepositional phrase(s). Underline the subject once and the verb twice.

Example: Carl (stands, stand) ~~by me~~ ~~in the lunch line~~.

1. A guide (lives, live) in those mountains.
2. Margo (stays, stay) with her grandmother.
3. A snake (crawl, crawls) in their garden.
4. The wind (blows, blow) through that canyon.
5. That farmer (plant, plants) wheat in his fields.
6. A hair stylist (cut, cuts) her hair very short.
7. The librarian (reads, read) to the children on Saturdays.
8. The reporter (writes, write) about the burglaries in their town.
9. Betty (swim, swims) for exercise.
10. A fiddler (play, plays) with that band.
11. Our dog (lie, lies) by the front door.
12. Her mother (go, goes) to a specialist.
13. I (finds, find) many pennies on the floor.
14. One of the girls (fly, flies) without her parents.
15. Kurt often (wear, wears) shirts with flowers.

Name________________________________ **SUBJECT/VERB AGREEMENT**

WORKBOOK PAGE 77

Date________________________________

Directions: Cross out any prepositional phrase(s). Underline the subject once and the verb twice.

Note: Although directions do not include finding direct objects, this is a good place to review that concept. Simply ask for the direct object as you go through the sentences containing one.

Example: A balloon (flies, fly) ~~into the air~~.

1. The dog (bark, barks) ~~throughout the night~~.
2. This document (is, are) very important.
3. Linda (drive, drives) a bus ~~for the city~~. **Direct object? bus**
4. A tiger (growls, growl) loudly.
5. My grandfather (golf, golfs) ~~during the spring~~.
6. Each ~~of the boys~~ (drink, drinks) water ~~from the large jug~~. **Direct object? water**
7. Aunt Joy (freeze, freezes) corn ~~at the end of summer~~. **Direct object? corn**
8. The child (throw, throws) pebbles ~~into the water~~. **Direct Object? pebbles**
9. Their dad (build, builds) racers ~~in the garage~~. **Direct Object? racers**
10. A rattlesnake (strikes, strike) objects ~~near him~~. **Direct Object? objects**
11. You (is, are) a friend ~~with many talents~~.
12. Miss Sanders (jogs, jog) ~~past the old mill~~.
13. The jockey (ride, rides) slowly ~~along the muddy track~~.
14. He (jumps, jump) ~~off the diving board~~.
15. Everyone (is, are) ~~across the street at the carnival~~.

Name________________________________ **SUBJECT/VERB AGREEMENT**

Date________________________________

Directions: Cross out any prepositional phrase(s). Underline the subject once and the verb twice.

Example: A balloon (flies, fly) ~~into the air~~.

1. The dog (bark, barks) throughout the night.
2. This document (is, are) very important.
3. Linda (drive, drives) a bus for the city.
4. A tiger (growls, growl) loudly.
5. My grandfather (golf, golfs) during the spring.
6. Each of the boys (drink, drinks) water from the large jug.
7. Aunt Joy (freeze, freezes) corn at the end of summer.
8. The child (throw, throws) pebbles into the water.
9. Their dad (build, builds) racers in the garage.
10. A rattlesnake (strikes, strike) objects near him.
11. You (is, are) a friend with many talents.
12. Miss Sanders (jogs, jog) past the old mill.
13. The jockey (ride, rides) slowly along the muddy track.
14. He (jumps, jump) off the diving board.
15. Everyone (is, are) across the street at the carnival.

Name________________________________ **SUBJECT/VERB AGREEMENT**

WORKBOOK PAGE 78

Date________________________________

Directions: Cross out any prepositional phrase(s). Underline the subject once and the verb twice.

Example: The swans (swim, swims) ~~on a pond~~.

Note: Although directions do not include direct objects, this is a good place to review that concept. Simply ask for the direct object as you go through the sentences containing one.

1. Those trains (travel, travels) ~~through a tunnel~~.

2. Some cooks (make, makes) lasagna ~~without meat~~. **Direct Object? lasagna**

3. Many companies (prints, print) materials ~~about smoking~~. **Direct Object? materials**

4. Several families (lives, live) ~~beyond the city limits~~.

5. Saleswomen (talk, talks) ~~to many customers~~ ~~concerning their products~~.

6. Their dog and cat (plays, play) together ~~in their backyard~~.

7. A few goats (graze, grazes) ~~on the hillside~~.

8. The carpenters (work, works) ~~before sunrise~~ ~~during the summer~~.

9. My friend and I often (run, runs) ~~around the block~~.

10. Trainers (lifts, lift) weights ~~at that gym~~. **Direct Object? weights**

11. They (bring, brings) their pets ~~to the park~~ ~~with them~~. **Direct Object? pets**

12. Some volleyball players (hits, hit) the ball ~~into the street~~. **Direct Object? ball**

13. Some baseball fans (leaves, leave) ~~toward the end~~ ~~of a game~~.

14. The relatives ~~at the reunion~~ (sits, sit) ~~underneath a tent~~.

15. Your friends and you (do, does) a great job. **Direct Object? job**

Name________________________________ **SUBJECT/VERB AGREEMENT**

Date________________________________

Directions: Cross out any prepositional phrase(s). Underline the subject once and the verb twice.

Example: The swans (swim, swims) ~~on a pond~~.

1. Those trains (travel, travels) through a tunnel.
2. Some cooks (make, makes) lasagna without meat.
3. Many companies (prints, print) materials about smoking.
4. Several families (lives, live) beyond the city limits.
5. Saleswomen (talk, talks) to many customers concerning their products.
6. Their dog and cat (plays, play) together in their backyard.
7. A few goats (graze, grazes) on the hillside.
8. The carpenters (work, works) before sunrise during the summer.
9. My friend and I often (run, runs) around the block.
10. Trainers (lifts, lift) weights at that gym.
11. They (bring, brings) their pets to the park with them.
12. Some volleyball players (hits, hit) the ball into the street.
13. Some baseball fans (leaves, leave) toward the end of a game.
14. The relatives at the reunion (sits, sit) underneath a tent.
15. Your friends and you (do, does) a great job.

Name________________________________ **SUBJECT/VERB AGREEMENT**

WORKBOOK PAGE 79

Date________________________________

Directions: Cross out any prepositional phrase(s). Underline the subject once and the verb twice.

Example: Girls (works, work) out ~~in that fitness class~~.

Note: Although directions do not include direct objects, this is a good place to review that concept. Simply ask for the direct object as you go through the sentences containing one.

1. His friends (sit, sits) ~~beside me~~ ~~on the bus~~.

2. Gold miners (search, searches) ~~for gold~~ ~~in the Superstition Mountains~~.

3. His brothers (goes, go) ~~to Penn State University~~.

4. Mrs. Glenn and she (eat, eats) lunch ~~atop a downtown building~~. **Direct Object? lunch**

5. Migrant workers (pick, picks) cherries ~~at those orchards~~. **Direct Object? cherries**

6. ~~Outside the cabin~~, the children (chases, chase) each other. **Direct object? (each) other**

7. Many ~~in the group~~ (do, does) exercises ~~in the morning~~. **Direct Object? exercises**

8. Wild geese (flies, fly) each fall ~~toward the South~~.

9. Those swimmers (lies, lie) ~~on floats~~ ~~until sunset~~.

10. The furniture movers (push, pushes) boxes ~~across the floor~~. **Direct Object? boxes**

11. Barney, Jenny, and John (likes, like) lemonade ~~with their meal~~. **Direct object? lemonade**

12. The bicycle riders (drink, drinks) water ~~along their way~~. **Direct Object? water**

13. ~~At night~~ Christina and I (place, places) our watches ~~between some books~~. **Direct Object? watches**

14. ~~Over that hill~~ (is, are) several empty houses.

15. All the men ~~but Sam~~ (appear, appears) ~~in a commercial~~.

Name______________________________ **SUBJECT/VERB AGREEMENT**

Date______________________________

Directions: Cross out any prepositional phrase(s). Underline the subject once and the verb twice.

Example: Girls (works, work) out ~~in that fitness class~~.

1. His friends (sit, sits) beside me on the bus.
2. Gold miners (search, searches) for gold in the Superstition Mountains.
3. His brothers (goes, go) to Penn State University.
4. Mrs. Glenn and she (eat, eats) lunch atop a downtown building.
5. Migrant workers (pick, picks) cherries at those orchards.
6. Outside the cabin, the children (chases, chase) each other.
7. Many in the group (do, does) exercises in the morning.
8. Wild geese (flies, fly) each fall toward the South.
9. Those swimmers (lies, lie) on floats until sunset.
10. The furniture movers (push, pushes) boxes across the floor.
11. Barney, Jenny, and John (likes, like) lemonade with their meal.
12. The bicycle riders (drink, drinks) water along their way.
13. At night Christina and I (place, places) our watches between some books.
14. Over that hill (is, are) several empty houses.
15. All the men but Sam (appear, appears) in a commercial.

Name________________________________ **SUBJECT/VERB AGREEMENT**

WORKBOOK PAGE 80

Date_________________________________

Directions: Cross out any prepositional phrase(s). Underline the subject once and the verb twice.

Example: Lights (shine, shines) ~~after dark~~.

Note: As in preceding subject/verb agreement exercises, you may wish to ask students to determine direct objects in sentences containing one.

1. Those turkeys (gobble, gobbles) loudly.

2. She (loves, love) the dog ~~with the black spots~~. **Direct Object? dog**

3. Sometimes, I (fall, falls) ~~up the steps~~.

4. Many campers (rows, row) ~~across the lake~~.

5. Balloons often (burst, bursts) ~~at a party~~.

6. We (scramble, scrambles) eggs ~~for breakfast~~. **Direct Object? eggs**

7. He (speaks, speak) English ~~without any accent~~. **Direct Object? English**

8. The secretary ~~of that company~~ (types, type) very fast.

9. Mrs. Lott or Mrs. Campbell (are, is) ~~from Canada~~.

10. His broken toy boat (sinks, sink) ~~in the bathtub~~.

11. Ned and Deanne (washes, wash) their car ~~before breakfast~~. **Direct Object? car**

12. One ~~of the cows~~ (go, goes) ~~into the barn~~.

13. That worker (sleep, sleeps) ~~on the grass~~ ~~during each break~~.

14. His sister (know, knows) ~~about the meeting~~ ~~concerning the new library~~.

15. A mother ~~with a crying child~~ often (leave, leaves) the church service. **Direct Object? service**

Name________________________________ **SUBJECT/VERB AGREEMENT**

Date________________________________

Directions: Cross out any prepositional phrase(s). Underline the subject once and the verb twice.

Example: Lights (shine, shines) ~~after dark~~.

1. Those turkeys (gobble, gobbles) loudly.
2. She (loves, love) the dog with the black spots.
3. Sometimes, I (fall, falls) up the steps.
4. Many campers (rows, row) across the lake.
5. Balloons often (burst, bursts) at a party.
6. We (scramble, scrambles) eggs for breakfast.
7. He (speaks, speak) English without any accent.
8. The secretary of that company (types, type) very fast.
9. Mrs. Lott or Mrs. Campbell (are, is) from Canada.
10. His broken toy boat (sinks, sink) in the bathtub.
11. Ned and Deanne (washes, wash) their car before breakfast.
12. One of the cows (go, goes) into the barn.
13. That worker (sleep, sleeps) on the grass during each break.
14. His sister (know, knows) about the meeting concerning the new library.
15. A mother with a crying child often (leave, leaves) the church service.

Name________________________________ **SUBJECT/VERB AGREEMENT**

WORKBOOK PAGE 81

Date________________________________

Directions: Cross out any prepositional phrase(s). Underline the subject once and the verb twice.

Example: A girl ~~in the first seat~~ (play, plays) a clarinet.

Note: As in preceding worksheets, students are not instructed to label direct objects. When going over this worksheet, you may wish to ask students to find the direct object in sentences containing one. However, #13 may be difficult; you may wish to skip it.

1. The sky (seems, seem) cloudy.
2. Those twins (dance, dances) ~~at a studio~~.
3. I (enjoys, enjoy) all sports ~~but soccer~~. **Direct object? sports**
4. The mail delivery (comes, come) ~~in the morning~~.
5. Dad and Mom (listen, listens) ~~to an oldies radio station~~.
6. That artist (paint, paints) ~~by the ocean~~.
7. We often (buy, buys) fried chicken ~~for our picnics~~. **Direct object? chicken**
8. I (am, is) ~~from the state of Florida~~.
9. She (is, am) ~~in a baton twirling contest~~.
10. We (is, are) ~~about halfway through this book~~.
11. One ~~of the children~~ (do, does) pushups ~~with his brother~~. **Direct object? pushups**
12. The Hendersons and she (sails, sail) ~~until evening~~.
13. This jar ~~of peanuts~~ (cost, costs) a dollar. **Direct object? dollar**
14. Our leaving (depend, depends) ~~on the weather~~.
15. The dinners ~~of fried shrimp~~ (taste, tastes) delicious.

Name________________________________ **SUBJECT/VERB AGREEMENT**

Date________________________________

Directions: Cross out any prepositional phrase(s). Underline the subject once and the verb twice.

Example: A girl ~~in the first seat~~ (play, plays) a clarinet.

1. The sky (seems, seem) cloudy.
2. Those twins (dance, dances) at a studio.
3. I (enjoys, enjoy) all sports but soccer.
4. The mail delivery (comes, come) in the morning.
5. Dad and Mom (listen, listens) to an oldies radio station.
6. That artist (paint, paints) by the ocean.
7. We often (buy, buys) fried chicken for our picnics.
8. I (am, is) from the state of Florida.
9. She (is, am) in a baton twirling contest.
10. We (is, are) about halfway through this book.
11. One of the children (do, does) pushups with his brother.
12. The Hendersons and she (sails, sail) until evening.
13. This jar of peanuts (cost, costs) a dollar.
14. Our leaving (depend, depends) on the weather.
15. The dinners of fried shrimp (taste, tastes) delicious.

FOR THE TEACHER:
WORKBOOK PAGE 82

VERB TENSES

PRESENT TENSE: **Tense means time. Present tense, of course, signifies present time.** Although present can mean at this moment, it is easier to use "today" as a point of reference for present tense.

PRESENT TENSE NEVER HAS A HELPING VERB (AUXILIARY VERB).
Repeat this fact until students have mastered it.

1. If students understand that present tense never has a helping verb, they will know that the following sentence cannot be present tense.

   My mom is going ~~to the mall~~.

   A. This sentence cannot be present tense although it sounds like it. The helping verb *is* makes the verb phrase *is going*.
   B. The verb phrase, *is going*, is actually a separate tense called the progressive tense.

2. To form the present tense, remove *to* from the infinitive:

   A. **If the subject is singular (one), add s to the verb.** (es to some)

   Examples: **to run**: A groundhog runs ~~across the field~~.
   to need: The fireplace needs to be cleaned.

   B. **If the subject is you, I, or is plural (more than one), simply remove the *to* from the infinitive.**

   Examples: **to chew**: His dogs chew ~~on a bone~~.
   I chew my food very slowly.
   You chew gum rapidly.

PAST TENSE: **Past tense indicates that which has happened**. Although past can mean a second ago, it is easier to use the term, Yesterday.

PAST TENSE NEVER HAS A HELPING (AUXILIARY) VERB.
Repeat this fact until students have mastered it.

WORKBOOK PAGE 83

1. If students understand that the past tense never has a helping verb, they will comprehend that the following sentence is not past tense:

   He has lost his jacket.

   A. *Has* is the helping verb. Past tense does not have a helping verb.
   B. The verb phrase, *has lost*, is actually a separate tense called the perfect tense.

2. To form the past tense, teach two rules:
   A. **To form the past tense of a regular verb, add ed to the verb.**

   to remain: remained — to practice: practiced

   B. **To form the past tense of an irregular verb, change the verb to its appropriate form.**

   to begin: began — to swear: swore

FUTURE TENSE: Future tense indicates time yet to happen.
There are two helping verbs that indicate future tense: *shall* and *will*
Although future may be any time yet to occur, using *Tomorrow* helps students comprehend it.

Be sure that students understand that *shall* or *will* must be used with the future tense.

THE FUTURE TENSE CONTAINS THE HELPING VERBS *WILL* OR *SHALL.*
Although this concept seems easy, many students have difficulty with it. Be sure that they understand and master the concept.

Note: Although it has become acceptable to use *will* with any subject, encourage students to use shall with the pronoun *I*. It may also be correctly used with the pronoun *we*.

Examples: I shall answer your question ~~in a minute~~.

The repairman will come by ~~within an hour~~.

Will you please play this game ~~with us~~?

As with all questions, teach students to search for a helping verb at the beginning of the sentence.

Name________________________________ **VERB TENSES**

WORKBOOK PAGE 84

Date________________________________

Directions: Cross out any prepositional phrase(s). Underline the subject once and the verb/verb phrase twice. Write *present*, *past*, or *future* in the space provided to indicate tense.

Example: ______future______ I shall pretend (to be) a monkey ~~in a tree~~.

1. ______**present**______ Terry rollerskates ~~to his friend's house~~.

2. ______**past**______ Terry rollerskated ~~with his sister~~.

3. ______**future**______ Tonight, Terry will rollerskate ~~around the park~~.

1. ______**present**______ She drinks juice ~~for breakfast~~.

2. ______**future**______ The lady will drink milk ~~with her meal~~.

3. ______**past**______ She drank bottled water ~~from France~~.

1. ______**future**______ ~~For my speech~~, I shall talk ~~about crime~~.

2. ______**present**______ I talk ~~with my friends~~ ~~after school~~.

3. ______**past**______ ~~During the weekend~~, I talked ~~to your sister~~.

1. ______**past**______ The cement truck driver ate his lunch.

2. ______**present**______ The cement truck driver eats ~~at a fast food place~~.

3. ______**future**______ The cement truck driver will eat dinner ~~in a few hours~~.

1. ______**future**______ That model will pose ~~in many outfits~~.

2. ______**past**______ The model posed ~~with an umbrella~~.

3. ______**present**______ The model poses ~~for a fashion catalog~~.

Name________________________________ **VERB TENSES**

Date________________________________

Directions: Cross out any prepositional phrase(s). Underline the subject once and the verb/verb phrase twice. Write *present*, *past*, or *future* in the space provided to indicate tense.

Example: ______future______ I shall pretend (to be) a monkey ~~in a tree~~.

1. ____________________ Terry rollerskates to his friend's house.
2. ____________________ Terry rollerskated with his sister.
3. ____________________ Tonight, Terry will rollerskate around the park.

1. ____________________ She drinks juice for breakfast.
2. ____________________ The lady will drink milk with her meal.
3. ____________________ She drank bottled water from France.

1. ____________________ For my speech, I shall talk about crime.
2. ____________________ I talk with my friends after school.
3. ____________________ During the weekend, I talked to your sister.

1. ____________________ The cement truck driver ate his lunch.
2. ____________________ The cement truck driver eats at a fast food place.
3. ____________________ The cement truck driver will eat dinner in a few hours.

1. ____________________ That model will pose in many outfits.
2. ____________________ The model posed with an umbrella.
3. ____________________ The model poses for a fashion catalog.

Name________________________________ **VERB TENSES**

WORKBOOK PAGE 85

Date________________________________

Directions: Cross out any prepositional phrase(s). Underline the subject once and the verb/verb phrase twice. Write *present*, *past*, or *future* in the space provided to indicate verb tense.

Example: ______past______ She laughed ~~at my joke~~.

1. ______**present**______ These girls swim ~~in the ocean~~.
2. ______**future**______ Mom will swim twenty laps.
3. ______**past**______ My cousin swam ~~on a high school team~~.

1. ______**future**______ A judge will speak ~~about courtroom conduct~~.
2. ______**past**______ The father spoke ~~to the child~~ ~~about his behavior~~.
3. ______**present**______ The professor speaks three languages.

1. ______**past**______ Darla poured honey ~~into her tea~~.
2. ______**present**______ You pour ~~with your left hand~~.
3. ______**future**______ This rain will pour ~~for another hour~~.

1. ______**present**______ Grandpa bakes apples ~~with cinnamon~~.
2. ______**future**______ I shall bake an eggless cake.
3. ______**past**______ A loaf ~~of bread~~ baked ~~in the oven~~.

1. ______**future**______ ~~Before lunch~~, a businesswoman will fly ~~to Chicago~~.
2. ______**present**______ Our bird flies all ~~over the house~~.
3. ______**past**______ Bees flew ~~around the barn~~.

Name________________________________ **VERB TENSES**

Date________________________________

Directions: Cross out any prepositional phrase(s). Underline the subject once and the verb/verb phrase twice. Write *present*, *past*, or *future* in the space provided to indicate verb tense.

Example: ____past____ She laughed ~~at my joke~~.

1. ____________________ These girls swim in the ocean.
2. ____________________ Mom will swim twenty laps.
3. ____________________ My cousin swam on a high school team.

1. ____________________ A judge will speak about courtroom conduct.
2. ____________________ The father spoke to the child about his behavior.
3. ____________________ The professor speaks three languages.

1. ____________________ Darla poured honey into her tea.
2. ____________________ You pour with your left hand.
3. ____________________ This rain will pour for another hour.

1. ____________________ Grandpa bakes apples with cinnamon.
2. ____________________ I shall bake an eggless cake.
3. ____________________ A loaf of bread baked in the oven.

1. ____________________ Before lunch, a businesswoman will fly to Chicago.
2. ____________________ Our bird flies all over the house.
3. ____________________ Bees flew around the barn.

Name________________________________ **VERB TENSES**

WORKBOOK PAGE 86

Date________________________________

Directions: Write the form of the tense on the line.

Example: present tense of *to find* - find, finds

1. past tense of *to decide* - **decided**
2. present tense of *to choose* - **choose, chooses**
3. future tense of *to turn* - **shall turn, will turn**
4. past tense of *to take* - **took**
5. present tense of *to swing* - **swing, swings**
6. future tense of *to follow* - **shall follow, will follow**
7. present tense of *to shop* - **shop, shops**
8. past tense of *to call* - **called**
9. future tense of *to skip* - **shall skip, will skip**
10. present tense of *to be* - **is, am, are**

Name________________________________ **VERB TENSES**

Date________________________________

Directions: Write the form of the tense on the line.

Example: present tense of *to find* - __________find, finds__________

1. past tense of *to decide* -______________________________

2. present tense of *to choose* - ______________________________

3. future tense of *to turn* - ______________________________

4. past tense of *to take* - ______________________________

5. present tense of *to swing* - ______________________________

6. future tense of *to follow* - ______________________________

7. present tense of *to shop* - ______________________________

8. past tense of *to call* - ______________________________

9. future tense of *to skip* - ______________________________

10. present tense of *to be* - ______________________________

Name________________________________ **VERB TENSES**

WORKBOOK PAGE 87

Date_________________________________

Directions: Write a **sentence** using the correct verb tense.

Example: present of *to lean* - ____Tom leans on his elbow when thinking.____

1. past of *to lift* - Answers will vary: **lifted**

2. future of *to go* - Answers will vary: **shall go** or **will go**

3. present of *to cut* - Answers will vary: **cut** or **cuts**

4. present of *to wash* - Answers will vary: **wash** or **washes**

5. past of *to cook* - Answers will vary: **cooked**

6. past of *to paint* - Answers will vary: **painted**

7. future of *to eat* - Answers will vary: **shall eat** or **will eat**

8. future of *to visit* - Answers will vary: **shall visit** or **will visit**

9. past of *to smile* - Answers will vary: **smiled**

10. present of *to like* - Answers will vary: **like** or **likes**

Name________________________________ **VERB TENSES**

Date________________________________

Directions: Write a **sentence** using the correct verb tense.

Example: present of *to lean* - ____Tom leans on his elbow when thinking.____

1. past of *to lift* - ________________________________

2. future of *to go* - ________________________________

3. present of *to cut* - ________________________________

4. present of *to wash* - ________________________________

5. past of *to cook* - ________________________________

6. past of *to paint* - ________________________________

7. future of *to eat* - ________________________________

8. future of *to visit* - ________________________________

9. past of *to smile* - ________________________________

10. present of *to like* - ________________________________

Name________________________________ **VERBS**

WORKBOOK PAGE 88

Date________________________________

Directions: Cross out any prepositional phrase(s). Underline the subject once and the verb/verb phrase twice.

Example: Each ~~of the boys and girls~~ enjoys ice cream cones.

1. A policewoman directs traffic ~~on Main Street~~.

2. Some daisies grow ~~under that tree~~.

3. We will travel ~~to Minnesota~~ ~~during Christmas vacation~~.

4. The tree is shedding its leaves.

5. Several steers graze ~~in the meadow.~~

6. Mickey flies a helicopter ~~for the U.S. Army~~.

7. We should have waited ~~until the end~~ ~~of the shower~~.

8. The couple has gone out ~~to dinner~~.

9. Are you studying ~~for an exam~~?

10. The lid ~~of the jigsaw puzzle~~ is lying ~~on the coffee table~~.

11. He has scrubbed and waxed the floor.

12. A teacher and a pupil had been given awards ~~by a women's club~~.

13. (You) Look ~~out the window~~ ~~at the street sweeper~~.

14. Will you be leaving ~~during Labor Day weekend~~ ~~in September~~?

15. One ~~of the paramedics~~ jumped out ~~of the fire truck~~ (to help).

Name________________________________ **VERBS**

Date________________________________

Directions: Cross out any prepositional phrase(s). Underline the subject once and the verb/verb phrase twice.

Example: Each ~~of the boys and girls~~ enjoys ice cream cones.

1. A policewoman directs traffic on Main Street.
2. Some daisies grow under that tree.
3. We will travel to Minnesota during Christmas vacation.
4. The tree is shedding its leaves.
5. Several steers graze in the meadow.
6. Mickey flies a helicopter for the U.S. Army.
7. We should have waited until the end of the shower.
8. The couple has gone out to dinner.
9. Are you studying for an exam?
10. The lid of the jigsaw puzzle is lying on the coffee table.
11. He has scrubbed and waxed the floor.
12. A teacher and a pupil had been given awards by a women's club.
13. Look out the window at the street sweeper.
14. Will you be leaving during Labor Day weekend in September?
15. One of the paramedics jumped out of the fire truck to help.

Name_______________________________ **VERBS**

WORKBOOK PAGE 89

Date________________________________

Directions: Cross out any prepositional phrase(s). Underline the subject once and the verb/verb phrase twice.

Example: Most ~~of the chickens~~ were sitting ~~in the coop~~.

1. Ted lives ~~near the beach~~.
2. The pants were ironed yesterday.
3. The vitamins had been sealed ~~for safety~~.
4. You and I should ride ~~on the roller coaster~~.
5. ~~Below the sink~~ is a drawing board.
6. ~~After the game~~, we will drive ~~to a restaurant~~.
7. A ping pong ball was pitched up ~~in the air~~.
8. (You) Sit ~~beneath the patio~~ ~~for a rest~~.
9. Sarah bought a poster and hung it ~~on her wall~~.
10. I am not ~~in this photograph~~ ~~of our family gathering~~.
11. A hummingbird flew in and sat ~~upon a branch~~.
12. Did*n't* Mayor Hines ask ~~for a map~~ ~~of Germany~~?
13. The manager ~~of the team~~ sat ~~inside the dugout~~ ~~during the game~~.
14. Marilyn, Jana, and she want (to stay) ~~until midnight~~.
15. One ~~of the triplets~~ may have been given that ring.

Name________________________________ **VERBS**

Date________________________________

Directions: Cross out any prepositional phrase(s). Underline the subject once and the verb/verb phrase twice.

Example: Most ~~of the chickens~~ were sitting ~~in the coop~~.

1. Ted lives near the beach.
2. The pants were ironed yesterday.
3. The vitamins had been sealed for safety.
4. You and I should ride on the rollercoaster.
5. Below the sink is a drawing board.
6. After the game, we will drive to a restaurant.
7. A ping pong ball was pitched up in the air.
8. Sit beneath the patio for a rest.
9. Sarah bought a poster and hung it on her wall.
10. I am not in this photograph of our family gathering.
11. A hummingbird flew in and sat upon a branch.
12. Didn't Mayor Hines ask for a map of Germany?
13. The manager of the team sat inside the dugout during the game.
14. Marilyn, Jana, and she want to stay until midnight.
15. One of the triplets may have been given that ring.

Name________________________________ **VERBS**

WORKBOOK PAGE 90

Date________________________________

Directions: Cross out any prepositional phrase(s). Underline the subject once and the verb/verb phrase twice.

Example: You must take the ice cream ~~from the freezer~~.

1. The puppets are entertaining the children.
2. That cute little puppy begs ~~for food~~.
3. A dog trainer walked ~~across the lawn~~ ~~with a collie~~.
4. A soccer player kicked the ball and made a goal.
5. ~~Before lunch~~, the cafeteria worker cleaned his hands ~~with soap and water~~.
6. May I see the slides ~~of your trip~~ ~~to Japan~~?
7. Clint and Shawna washed the clothes and hung them ~~on the clothesline~~.
8. Nobody could have known the combination ~~to the lock~~.
9. An office clerk sorts mail and distributes it ~~among the employees~~.
10. I ca*n't* bake the cake or decorate it ~~for you~~.
11. (You) Open the car door ~~for your brother and sister~~.
12. One ~~of the guards~~ must have come ~~into the building~~ early.
13. Yesterday, the kindergartner would *not* sit or stand ~~by the teacher~~.
14. A mother ~~with her children~~ ~~in a baby carriage~~ strolled ~~through the park~~.
15. Martha's mother and dad were invited ~~to the White House~~ ~~by the President~~.

Name______________________________ **VERBS**

Date______________________________

Directions: Cross out any prepositional phrase(s). Underline the subject once and the verb/verb phrase twice.

Example: You must take the ice cream ~~from the freezer~~.

1. The puppets are entertaining the children.
2. That cute little puppy begs for food.
3. A dog trainer walked across the lawn with a collie.
4. A soccer player kicked the ball and made a goal.
5. Before lunch, the cafeteria worker cleaned his hands with soap and water.
6. May I see the slides of your trip to Japan?
7. Clint and Shawna washed the clothes and hung them on the clothesline.
8. Nobody could have known the combination to the lock.
9. An office clerk sorts mail and distributes it among the employees.
10. I can't bake the cake or decorate it for you.
11. Open the car door for your brother and sister.
12. One of the guards must have come into the building early.
13. Yesterday, the kindergartner would not sit or stand by the teacher.
14. A mother with her children in a baby carriage strolled through the park.
15. Martha's mother and dad were invited to the White House by the President.

Name________________________________ **VERB REVIEW**
WORKBOOK PAGE 91
Date________________________________

A. Directions: Write the contraction.

1. I am - I'm
2. do not - don't
3. we have - we've
4. are not - aren't
5. they are - they're
6. has not - hasn't
7. I shall - I'll
8. who is - who's
9. will not - won't
10. she is - she's

B. Directions: Write the 23 helping (auxiliary) verbs on the following lines.

do, does, did   has, have, has   may, must, might   should, would, could

shall, will, can   is, am, are, was, were, be, being, been

C. Directions: Cross out any prepositional phrase(s). Underline the subject once and the verb/verb phrase twice. Write the helping verb(s) in the first column and the main verb in the second column.

	HELPING VERB(S)	MAIN VERB
1. I can leave ~~in a minute~~.	**can**	**leave**
2. That car is going too fast.	**is**	**going**
3. A light bulb was broken.	**was**	**broken**
4. His tooth had been chipped ~~in the fall~~.	**had been**	**chipped**
5. May the usher escort you?	**May**	**escort**
6. We should have arrived earlier.	**should have**	**arrived**
7. Did a tornado appear ~~near our town~~?	**Did**	**appear**

Name________________________________ **VERB REVIEW**

Date________________________________

A. Directions: Write the contraction.

1. I am - ______________________
2. do not - ______________________
3. we have - ______________________
4. are not - ______________________
5. they are - ______________________
6. has not - ______________________
7. I shall - ______________________
8. who is - ______________________
9. will not - ______________________
10. she is - ______________________

B. Directions: Write the 23 helping (auxiliary) verbs on the following lines.

____

____

____

C. Directions: Cross out any prepositional phrase(s). Underline the subject once and the verb/verb phrase twice. Write the helping verb(s) in the first column and the main verb in the second column.

	HELPING VERB(S)	**MAIN VERB**
1. I can leave in a minute.	________________	________________
2. That car is going too fast.	________________	________________
3. A light bulb was broken.	________________	________________
4. His tooth had been chipped in the fall.	________________	________________
5. May the usher escort you?	________________	________________
6. We should have arrived earlier.	________________	________________
7. Did a tornado appear near our town?	________________	________________

Name_________________________________ **VERB REVIEW**

WORKBOOK PAGE 92

Date_________________________________

D. Directions: Cross out any prepositional phrase(s). Underline the subject once and the verb/verb phrase twice. Label any direct object-D.O.

D.O.

1. He (sat, set) the carpet cleaner ~~by the couch~~.

2. The book is (lying, laying) ~~on the desk~~.

3. The sun has (risen, rose).

4. Some fans had (sat, set) ~~outside the stadium~~ ~~for an hour~~.

5. ~~Before lunch~~, the diver (lies, lays) ~~on the sand~~ ~~with his dog~~.

D.O.

6. Mrs. Sharp and Annie (raised, rose) chickens ~~in their backyard~~.

D.O.

7. She (lay, laid) the blanket ~~across the bed~~.

E. Directions: List the linking verbs (12 infinitives + 8). **to look, to feel, to taste, to smell, to appear, to become, to grow, to remain, to seem, to sound, to stay, to be, is, am, are, was, were, be, being, been**

F. Directions: Cross out any prepositional phrase(s). Underline the subject once and the verb/verb phrase twice. Write A in the space if the verb is action. Write L in the space if the verb is linking.

Remember: Write *is*, *am*, *are*, *was*, or *were* above a verb you think is linking. If the meaning is not changed, the verb is usually linking.

is

Example: __L__ The hot chocolate smells good.

1. __A__ A pelican scooped a fish ~~from the water~~.

is

2. __L__ The chili tastes very spicy.

is

3. __L__ That mother feels happy ~~about her raise~~.

4. __A__ An accountant adds numbers.

5. __A__ Krista tasted the beef stew .

was

6. __L__ A customer ~~with a return item~~ looked angry.

Name________________________________ **VERB REVIEW**

Date________________________________

D. Directions: Cross out any prepositional phrase(s). Underline the subject once and the verb/verb phrase twice. Label any direct object-D.O.

1. He (sat, set) the carpet cleaner by the couch.
2. The book is (lying, laying) on the desk.
3. The sun has (risen, rose).
4. Some fans had (sat, set) outside the stadium for an hour.
5. Before lunch, the diver (lies, lays) on the sand with his dog.
6. Mrs. Sharp and Annie (raised, rose) chickens in their backyard.
7. She (lay, laid) the blanket across the bed.

E. Directions: List the linking verbs (12 infinitives + 8).

____

____

F. Directions: Cross out any prepositional phrase(s). Underline the subject once and the verb/verb phrase twice. Write A in the space if the verb is action. Write L in the space if the verb is linking.

Remember: Write *is*, *am*, *are*, *was*, or *were* above a verb you think is linking. If the meaning is not changed, the verb is usually linking.

Example: __L__ The hot chocolate smells (**is**) good.

1. _____ A pelican scooped a fish from the water.
2. _____ The chili tastes very spicy.
3. _____ That mother feels happy about her raise.
4. _____ An accountant adds numbers.
5. _____ Krista tasted the beef stew.
6. _____ A customer with a return item looked angry.

Name________________________________ **VERB REVIEW**

WORKBOOK PAGE 93

Date________________________________

G. Directions: Cross out any prepositional phrase(s). Underline the subject once and the verb/verb phrase twice. Label any predicate nominative-P.N. Write the proof on the line provided.

P.N.

Example: Judy became the new bill collector.

Proof: The new bill collector is Judy.

P.N.

1. Paul is the leader ~~of his club~~.

Proof: The leader is Paul.

P.N.

2. His best dive was the jackknife.

Proof: The jackknife was his best dive.

P.N.

3. Lenny will be the next senator.

Proof: The next senator will be Lenny.

P.N.

4. His favorite color ~~of the rainbow~~ is red.

Proof: Red is his favorite color.

P.N.

5. Captain John Smith became a leader ~~of Jamestown~~.

Proof: A leader was Captain John Smith.

H. Directions: Cross out any prepositional phrase(s). Underline the subject once and the verb/verb phrase twice. Label any predicate adjective-P.A. Write the predicate adjective and the subject on the line to the right.

P.A.

Example: The handle ~~of the wagon~~ is yellow. yellow handle

P.A.

1. This painting looks old. old painting

P.A.

2. His jeans are black ~~with a red patch~~. black jeans

P.A.

3. Those curtains seem too long. long curtains

P.A.

4. This cement feels rough. rough cement

P.A.

5. A hurricane can be violent. violent hurricane

Name________________________________ **VERB REVIEW**

Date________________________________

G. Directions: Cross out any prepositional phrase(s). Underline the subject once and the verb/verb phrase twice. Label any predicate nominative-P.N. Write the proof on the line provided.

P.N.

Example: Judy became the new bill collector.

Proof: ___The new bill collector is Judy.___

1. Paul is the leader of his club.

   Proof: ____

2. His best dive was the jackknife.

   Proof: ____

3. Lenny will be the next senator.

   Proof: ____

4. His favorite color of the rainbow is red.

   Proof: ____

5. Captain John Smith became a leader of Jamestown.

   Proof: ____

H. Directions: Cross out any prepositional phrase(s). Underline the subject once and the verb/verb phrase twice. Label any predicate adjective-P.A. Write the predicate adjective and the subject on the line to the right.

P.A.

Example: The handle ~~of the wagon~~ is yellow. ______yellow handle______

1. This painting looks old. ____________________

2. His jeans are black with a red patch. ____________________

3. Those curtains seem too long. ____________________

4. This cement feels rough. ____________________

5. A hurricane can be violent. ____________________

Name________________________________ **VERB REVIEW**

WORKBOOK PAGE 94

Date________________________________

I. Directions: Cross out any prepositional phrase(s). Underline the subject once and the verb twice. Be sure that the subject and verb agree.

Example: One ~~of the dogs~~ (is, are) a German shepherd.

1. Wasps (build, builds) mud hives.
2. Her niece (is, are) ~~in the U.S. Navy~~.
3. The boy (carve, carves) whistles.
4. My brother and I (rinses, rinse) dishes ~~at our house~~.
5. One ~~of the roosters~~ (crow, crows) early ~~in the morning~~.
6. A lawyer (discusses, discuss) a case ~~with his client~~.
7. His sister (sneak, sneaks) ~~around the house~~.

J. Directions: Cross out any prepositional phrase(s). Underline the subject once and the verb/verb phrase twice. Write the tense, *present*, *past*, or *future* , in the space provided.

1. ______present______ Your headlight is out.
2. ______future______ I shall tell the story ~~to some children~~.
3. ______past______ Maurny called the veterinarian ~~about her sick cat~~.
4. ______present______ A mechanic repairs my car.
5. ______present______ Their grandfathers go deep-sea fishing.
6. ______future______ A dentist will speak ~~to us concerning brushing~~.
7. ______past______ A branch and a log fell ~~across the road~~.

Name________________________________ **VERB REVIEW**

Date________________________________

I. Directions: Cross out any prepositional phrase(s). Underline the subject once and the verb twice. Be sure that the subject and verb agree.

Example: One ~~of the dogs~~ (is, are) a German shepherd.

1. Wasps (build, builds) mud hives.
2. Her niece (is, are) in the U.S. Navy.
3. The boy (carve, carves) whistles.
4. My brother and I (rinses, rinse) dishes at our house.
5. One of the roosters (crow, crows) early in the morning.
6. A lawyer (discusses, discuss) a case with his client.
7. His sister (sneak, sneaks) around the house.

J. Directions: Cross out any prepositional phrase(s). Underline the subject once and the verb/verb phrase twice. Write the tense, *present*, *past*, or *future* in the space provided.

1. ____________________________ Your headlight is out.
2. ____________________________ I shall tell the story to some children.
3. ____________________________ Maurny called the veterinarian about her sick cat.
4. ____________________________ A mechanic repairs my car.
5. ____________________________ Their grandfathers go deep-sea fishing.
6. ____________________________ A dentist will speak to us concerning brushing.
7. ____________________________ A branch and a log fell across the road.

Name________________________________ **VERB REVIEW**

WORKBOOK PAGE 95

Date________________________________

K. Directions: Cross out any prepositional phrase(s). Underline the subject once and the verb/verb phrase twice.

Example: A minnow has (swam, swum) ~~into my net~~.

1. A dish ~~of sherbet~~ was (given, gave) ~~to the elderly lady~~.

2. Janice's uncle has (come, came) ~~for a visit~~.

3. We must have (taken, took) the wrong road.

4. A group ~~of Girl Scouts~~ had (rode, ridden) ~~into the forest~~.

5. My friend and I have (drank, drunk) the vanilla milkshake.

6. Should Mr. Lemon have (eaten, ate) five pieces ~~of pizza~~?

7. The tennis balls were (brought, brung) ~~onto the courts~~.

L. Directions: Cross out any prepositional phrase(s). Underline the subject once and the verb/verb phrase twice.

1. A whiff ~~of roast beef~~ floated ~~through the air~~.

2. A meal ~~of mashed potatoes, peas, and fish~~ was served ~~at six o'clock~~.

3. Has anyone seen the album ~~of family pictures~~?

4. A player can*not* be angry ~~with the umpire's call~~.

5. A janitor washed the windows and dried them ~~with newspaper~~.

6. (You) Hand this statue ~~to the lady~~ ~~in the red striped suit~~.

7. A church bulletin had been handed out ~~to all members and guests~~.

Name________________________________ **VERB REVIEW**

Date________________________________

K. Directions: Cross out any prepositional phrase(s). Underline the subject once and the verb/verb phrase twice.

Example: A minnow has (swam, swum) ~~into my net~~.

1. A dish of sherbet was (given, gave) to the elderly lady.

2. Janice's uncle has (come, came) for a visit.

3. We must have (taken, took) the wrong road.

4. A group of Girl Scouts had (rode, ridden) into the forest.

5. My friend and I have (drank, drunk) the vanilla milkshake.

6. Should Mr. Lemon have (eaten, ate) five pieces of pizza?

7. The tennis balls were (brought, brung) onto the courts.

L. Directions: Cross out any prepositional phrase(s). Underline the subject once and the verb/verb phrase twice.

1. A whiff of roast beef floated through the air.

2. A meal of mashed potatoes, peas, and fish was served at six o'clock.

3. Has anyone seen the album of family pictures?

4. A player cannot be angry with the umpire's call.

5. A janitor washed the windows and dried them with newspaper.

6. Hand this statue to the lady in the red striped suit.

7. A church bulletin had been given to all members and guests.

Name________________________________ **CUMULATIVE REVIEW**

WORKBOOK PAGE 96

Date________________________________

A. Directions: List 50 prepositions. **Students should list any 50.**

1. about
2. above
3. across
4. after
5. against
6. along
7. amid
8. among
9. around
10. at
11. atop
12. before
13. behind
14. below
15. beneath
16. beside
17. between
18. beyond
19. but (except)
20. by
21. concerning
22. down
23. during
24. except
25. for
26. from
27. in
28. inside
29. into
30. like
31. near
32. of
33. off
34. on
35. onto
36. out
37. outside
38. over
39. past
40. regarding
41. since
42. through
43. throughout
44. to
45. toward
46. under
47. underneath
48. until
49. up
50. upon

with, within, without

B. Directions: Cross out any prepositional phrase(s). Underline the subject once and the verb/verb phrase twice. Label any direct object-D.O.

1. The boy ~~in the rodeo~~ chased a steer (D.O.) ~~around the corral~~.
2. They threw snowballs (D.O.) ~~at their friend~~.
3. Mrs. Sands chose a brown carpeting (D.O.) ~~for her office~~.
4. Billy sends cards (D.O.) ~~to his grandparents in Chicago~~.
5. A small kitten chased a yarn ball (D.O.) ~~across the floor~~.

Name_______________________________ **CUMULATIVE REVIEW**

Date_______________________________

A. Directions: List 50 prepositions.

1. ____________	14. ____________	27. ____________	40. ____________
2. ____________	15. ____________	28. ____________	41. ____________
3. ____________	16. ____________	29. ____________	42. ____________
4. ____________	17. ____________	30. ____________	43. ____________
5. ____________	18. ____________	31. ____________	44. ____________
6. ____________	19. ____________	32. ____________	45. ____________
7. ____________	20. ____________	33. ____________	46. ____________
8. ____________	21. ____________	34. ____________	47. ____________
9. ____________	22. ____________	35. ____________	48. ____________
10. ____________	23. ____________	36. ____________	49. ____________
11. ____________	24. ____________	37. ____________	50. ____________
12. ____________	25. ____________	38. ____________	
13. ____________	26. ____________	39. ____________	

B. Directions: Cross out any prepositional phrase(s). Underline the subject once and the verb/verb phrase twice. Label any direct object-D.O.

1. The boy in the rodeo chased a steer around the corral.
2. They threw snowballs at their friend.
3. Mrs. Sands chose a brown carpeting for her office.
4. Billy sends cards to his grandparents in Chicago.
5. A small kitten chased a yarn ball across the floor.

Name________________________________ **VERB TEST**

WORKBOOK PAGE 320

Date________________________________

Note: You may wish to count a point for each item in parts B, C, D, and E, or you may wish to count only the answer. Use a grading system with which you are comfortable. Part F is a cumulative test. Because this test is very brief, it has been included within the unit test. You may wish to count Part F as a separate score.

A. Directions: Write the contraction.

1. had not - hadn't
2. I have - I've
3. we will - we'll
4. do not - don't
5. they are - they're
6. where is - where's
7. will not - won't
8. what is - what's
9. I am - I'm
10. he is - he's

B. Directions: Cross out any prepositional phrase(s). Underline the subject once and the verb/verb phrase twice.

1. A sunbather has (went, gone) ~~into the water~~.
2. The mail had (come, came) earlier ~~in the day~~.
3. One ~~of the sheep~~ has (lain, laid) ~~in the field~~.
4. Aaron must have (drank, drunk) a quart ~~of juice~~.
5. Our team should have (taken, took) the lead ~~from the opponents~~.
6. Clara may have (brang, brought) her brother ~~to the party~~.
7. An envelope ~~without a stamp~~ has (fallen, fell) ~~on the ground~~.
8. Have you (rode, ridden) your bike?
9. I could have (ate, eaten) more hot dogs ~~for lunch~~.
10. One ~~of the swimmers~~ must have (drove, driven) ~~to the shore~~.

Name________________________________ **VERB TEST**

Date________________________________

A. Directions: Write the contraction.

1. had not - ____________________
2. I have - ____________________
3. we will - ____________________
4. do not - ____________________
5. they are - ____________________
6. where is - ____________________
7. will not - ____________________
8. what is - ____________________
9. I am - ____________________
10. he is - ____________________

B. Directions: Cross out any prepositional phrase(s). Underline the subject once and the verb/verb phrase twice.

1. A sunbather has (went, gone) into the water.
2. The mail had (come, came) earlier in the day.
3. One of the sheep has (lain, laid) in the field.
4. Aaron must have (drank, drunk) a quart of juice.
5. Our team should have (taken, took) the lead from the opponents.
6. Clara may have (brang, brought) her brother to the party.
7. An envelope without a stamp has (fallen, fell) on the ground.
8. Have you (rode, ridden) your bike?
9. I could have (ate, eaten) more hot dogs for lunch.
10. One of the swimmers must have (drove, driven) to the shore.

C. Directions: Cross out any prepositional phrase(s). Underline the subject once and the verb/verb phrase twice. Write the tense, *present*, *past*, or *future,* in the space provided.

WORKBOOK PAGE 321

1. future — I shall demand an answer ~~from him~~.
2. present — A lizard crawls ~~up our wall~~.
3. past — A group ~~of teenagers~~ ate taffy ~~at the fair~~.
4. present — The children build castles ~~in the sand~~.
5. future — We will attend the wedding ~~during the evening~~.
6. present — Lemons are ~~in the refrigerator~~.
7. past — Matthew read the map ~~with a flashlight~~.
8. present — Linda and Danny work ~~at a factory~~.
9. past — A musician played a song ~~about love~~.
10. future — His dad will remain ~~in the service~~ ~~until his retirement.~~

D. Directions: Cross out any prepositional phrase(s). Underline the subject once and the verb twice.

1. A snail (moves, move) slowly.
2. Several ducks (waddle, waddles) ~~around that park~~.
3. Mom and Dad (shops, shop) ~~for our groceries~~.
4. These apples (tastes, taste) sour.
5. Jackie (spend, spends) so much time ~~on her hair~~.
6. Todd and I (is, are) ~~in the band~~.
7. That child (sings, sing) ~~to her little brother~~.
8. Those lifeguards (save, saves) the lives ~~of many people~~.

C. Directions: Cross out any prepositional phrase(s). Underline the subject once and the verb/verb phrase twice. Write the tense: *present*, *past*, or *future* in the space provided.

1. ______________________ I shall demand an answer from him.

2. ______________________ A lizard crawls up our wall.

3. ______________________ A group of teenagers ate taffy at the fair.

4. ______________________ The children build castles in the sand.

5. ______________________ We will attend the wedding during the evening.

6. ______________________ Lemons are in the refrigerator.

7. ______________________ Matthew read the map with a flashlight.

8. ______________________ Linda and Danny work at a factory.

9. ______________________ A musician played a song about love.

10. ______________________ His dad will remain in the service until his retirement.

D. Directions: Cross out any prepositional phrase(s). Underline the subject once and the verb twice.

1. A snail (moves, move) slowly.

2. Several ducks (waddle, waddles) around that park.

3. Mom and Dad (shops, shop) for our groceries.

4. These apples (tastes, taste) sour.

5. Jackie (spend, spends) so much time on her hair.

6. Todd and I (is, are) in the band.

7. That child (sings, sing) to her little brother.

8. Those lifeguards (save, saves) the lives of many people.

WORKBOOK PAGE 322

9. Everyone ~~of the boys~~ (are, is) ~~in my Sunday school class~~.

10. That family and she (ski, skis) ~~at a winter camp~~.

E. Directions: Cross out any prepositional phrase(s). Underline the subject once and the verb twice. Write A if the verb is action and L if the verb is linking.

1. __L__ Her hairbrush remained dirty. **was**

2. __L__ A girl ~~with long hair~~ stayed excited ~~for a long time~~. **was**

3. __A__ Several chefs tasted the winning veal dinner.

4. __L__ The chimes ~~at the tower~~ sound pretty. **are**

5. __L__ Her short story became funny. **was**

F. Directions: Cross out any prepositional phrase(s). Underline the subject once and the verb/verb phrase twice.

1. A hamster is sitting ~~on our sidewalk~~.
2. Many large hotels have been built ~~in Scottsdale~~.
3. A robber and his girlfriend fled ~~from the bank~~.
4. (You) Take this ~~to the train station with you~~.
5. Are the tourists visiting those old castles?
6. Two businessmen met and ate lunch ~~at the Kettle Inn~~.
7. You will *not* be given another dish ~~of chocolate pudding~~.
8. May we mow your grass ~~with this electric lawn mower~~?
9. Each ~~of the parents~~ had been sent a note ~~concerning flu shots~~.
10. Would you please hand this ticket ~~to the bus driver~~?

9. Everyone of the boys (are, is) in my Sunday school class.

10. That family and she (ski, skis) at a winter camp.

E. Directions: Cross out any prepositional phrase(s). Underline the subject once and the verb twice. Write A if the verb is action and L if the verb is linking.

1. _____ Her hairbrush remained dirty.

2. _____ A girl with long hair stayed excited for a long time.

3. _____ Several chefs tasted the winning veal dinner.

4. _____ The chimes at the tower sound pretty.

5. _____ Her short story became funny.

F. Directions: Cross out any prepositional phrase(s). Underline the subject once and the verb/verb phrase twice.

1. A hamster is sitting on our sidewalk.

2. Many large hotels have been built in Scottsdale.

3. A robber and his girlfriend fled from the bank.

4. Take this to the train station with you.

5. Are the tourists visiting those old castles?

6. Two businessmen met and ate lunch at the Kettle Inn.

7. You will not be given another dish of chocolate pudding.

8. May we mow your grass with this electric lawn mower?

9. Each of the parents had been sent a note concerning flu shots.

10. Would you please hand this ticket to the bus driver?

FOR THE TEACHER:
WORKBOOK PAGE 97

INTERJECTIONS

Interjections are words or phrases (group of words) that express emotion.

After an interjection, place an exclamation point (!).

Examples: **Yippee!** Our bus is here!

Heaven forbid! The boat is sinking!

The parade is coming! **Yeah!**

An interjection is a word or group of words. It is not a sentence. When an entire sentence reflects emotion, it is called an exclamatory sentence.

NOTE: Interjections are classified as a part of speech and are relatively easy to comprehend. However, they are readily forgotten. Interjections have been placed early in this text so that review can occur throughout the school year.

Name________________________________ **INTERJECTIONS**

WORKBOOK PAGE 98

Date________________________________

Note: You may choose to have students label interjections only. The complete instructions include a built-in review.

Directions: Cross out any prepositional phrase(s). Underline the subject once and the verb/verb phrase twice. Label any interjection(s)-Intj.

Example: Yippee! (Intj.) We are going ~~to the zoo~~!

1. Ouch! (Intj.) I burned my finger ~~on the pan~~!
2. Shhhh! (Intj.) A baby is sleeping ~~in that crib~~!
3. Great Scot! (Intj.) The crime has already been solved ~~by the police~~!
4. Here comes a runaway skateboard! Yikes! (Intj.)
5. This submarine sandwich has moldy bread! Yuck! (Intj.)
6. No! (Intj.) (You) Don't leave ~~without me~~!
7. Wow! (Intj.) We won the tournament!
8. Whew! (Intj.) That ball nearly hit you ~~on the arm~~!
9. Good grief! (Intj.) I've taken the man's pencil again!
10. Drats! (Intj.) I am moving ~~with my family to another state~~!
11. Those tomatoes are huge! Man! (Intj.)
12. Oh! (Intj.) No! (Intj.) We forgot the picnic lunch!
13. Far out! (Intj.) Someone has given me money ~~for a banana split~~!
14. Hurrah! (Intj.) Sharon and Sally are trying out ~~for cheerleading~~!
15. Boo! (Intj.) Hiss! (Intj.) I lost my keys ~~for the third time~~ today!

Name________________________________ **INTERJECTIONS**

Date________________________________

Directions: Cross out any prepositional phrase(s). Underline the subject once and the verb/verb phrase twice. Label any interjection(s)-Intj.

Example: Yippee! (Intj.) We are going ~~to the zoo~~!

1. Ouch! I burned my finger on the pan!
2. Shhhh! A baby is sleeping in that crib!
3. Great Scot! The crime has already been solved by the police!
4. Here comes a runaway skateboard! Yikes!
5. This submarine sandwich has moldy bread! Yuck!
6. No! Don't leave without me!
7. Wow! We won the tournament!
8. Whew! That ball nearly hit you on the arm!
9. Good grief! I've taken the man's pencil again!
10. Drats! I am moving with my family to another state!
11. Those tomatoes are huge! Man!
12. Oh! No! We forgot the picnic lunch!
13. Far out! Someone has given me money for a banana split!
14. Hurrah! Sharon and Sally are trying out for cheerleading!
15. Boo! Hiss! I lost my keys for the third time today!

FOR THE TEACHER:
WORKBOOK PAGE 99

CONJUNCTIONS

EXTREMELY IMPORTANT: Although all parts of speech have not been covered, coordinating conjunctions are introduced here so that they can be continuously reviewed throughout the year. By now, students should have an understanding of prepositions, verbs, adjectives (from predicate adjectives), and interjections. At this point, it's more important that students can identify ***and***, ***but***, and ***or***. It is also important that they understand that ***and***, ***but***, and ***or*** are connecting words.

NOTE: But is a preposition, not a conjunction, when it means except.

Conjunctions are connecting words.

The most common conjunctions are called coordinating conjunctions; they are: *and*, *but*, *or*.

Conjunctions connect prepositions: His dog ran *under* the bed **or** *into* the closet.

Conjunctions connect adjectives (describing words): I like that *blue* **and** *gray* towel.

Conjunctions connect verbs: He *made* **and** *baked* a pie.

Conjunctions connect interjections: *Wow* **and** *hurrah* ! We did it!

Conjunctions connect nouns (words that name people, places, and things):
Pizza **and** *coke* were served.

Conjunctions connect pronouns (words that take the place of nouns):
She **or** *I* will be your partner.

Conjunctions connect adverbs (words that tell, how, when, where, to what extent):
Step on the brake *quickly* **but** *carefully*.

Conjunctions connect phrases (groups of words):
The man enjoys *seeing the ocean* **and** *wading in it*.

Conjunctions connect sentences: *I like thunder*, **but** *it can be extremely loud*.

Name_______________________________ **CONJUNCTIONS**

WORKBOOK PAGE 100

Date_______________________________

Note: Conjunctions are in boldface.

Directions: Circle any conjunction(s).

1. Potatoes, onion, **and** garlic were placed on the hot coals.
2. You need to take your umbrella **or** your jacket with you.
3. Her jacket is large **but** very stylish.
4. Hamburgers **or** hot dogs were served from the grill.
5. The ship steamed out of the harbor **and** picked up speed.
6. Mr. **and** Mrs. Jenkel are coming, **but** they will be late.
7. Any food items **or** money for the needy may be given to Harriet **and** Bobby.
8. His speech was interesting, **but** it didn't help solve the problem.
9. A flamingo **or** a heron was by the island's waterlilies.
10. They like to go to Minnesota **and** Michigan, **but** New York is their favorite.
11. His aunt **or** uncle attended Shippensburg University **but** did not graduate.
12. The house was stuccoed **and** painted, **but** it wasn't completed.
13. A horse **or** a mule leads the team, **but** it isn't moving fast.
14. In the afternoon, Jason **or** his sister went to a bakery **and** a deli.
15. A minister **and** his assistant met the couple, **but** they did not have lunch with them.

Name________________________________ **CONJUNCTIONS**

Date________________________________

Directions: Circle any conjunction(s).

1. Potatoes, onion, and garlic were placed on the hot coals.
2. You need to take your umbrella or your jacket with you.
3. Her jacket is large but very stylish.
4. Hamburgers or hot dogs were served from the grill.
5. The ship steamed out of the harbor and picked up speed.
6. Mr. and Mrs. Jenkel are coming, but they will be late.
7. Any food items or money for the needy may be given to Harriet and Bobby.
8. His speech was interesting, but it didn't help solve the problem.
9. A flamingo or a heron was by the island's waterlilies.
10. They like to go to Minnesota and Michigan, but New York is their favorite.
11. His aunt or uncle attended Shippensburg University but did not graduate.
12. The house was stuccoed and painted, but it wasn't completed.
13. A horse or a mule leads the team, but it isn't moving fast.
14. In the afternoon, Jason or his sister went to a bakery and a deli.
15. A minister and his assistant met the couple, but they did not have lunch with them.

FOR THE TEACHER:
WORKBOOK PAGE 101

NOUNS

Nouns name a person, place, or thing.

CONCRETE AND ABSTRACT NOUNS:

Concrete nouns usually can be seen: board, fork, person, coyote, book

NOTE: Some concrete nouns technically cannot be seen unless examined in very small parts (atoms). Examples: air, breath

VERY IMPORTANT: TO DEMONSTRATE CONCRETE NOUNS, ASK STUDENTS TO PRETEND TO HOLD A PIECE OF CONCRETE. (Some will "hold" small pieces while others may place their hands in a weight lifting stance!) Ask them to pretend to move it around. Then, explain that concrete nouns usually can be seen. (Can they visualize their chunk of concrete?) This participation is very effective in helping students remember that concrete nouns usually can be seen.

Abstract nouns are those that cannot be seen: honesty, love, friendship

To test if a word might be an abstract noun:

A. Check to see if the word describes any other word in the sentence. If it does, STOP. It's a describing word called an adjective.

Example: This friendship ring is beautiful.

In this sentence, *friendship* is an adjective that describes ring. Thus, *friendship* is not a noun.

B. If the word does not qualify as an adjective, try placing the in front of it. If you can put the in front of the word, it is usually a noun.

Example: My friendship with Mickey is very important.

In this sentence, you can say the *friendship*; therefore, *friendship* is a noun.

Name______________________________ **NOUNS**

WORKBOOK PAGE 102 **Concrete or Abstract?**

Date______________________________

Directions: In the space provided, place C if the noun is concrete and A if the noun is abstract.

1. __C__ glass
2. __C__ letter
3. __A__ love
4. __A__ peace
5. __C__ fire
6. __C__ chain
7. __A__ justice
8. __C__ toe
9. __C__ pony
10. __C__ desert
11. __A__ laughter
12. __C__ squirrel
13. __A__ wisdom
14. __C__ mouth
15. __C__ woods
16. __A__ patience
17. __C__ lamp
18. __A__ freedom
19. __A__ loyalty
20. __C__ vitamin
21. __A__ beauty
22. __C__ thongs
23. __C__ syrup
24. __A__ happiness
25. __C__ plug

Name________________________________

Date________________________________

NOUNS
Concrete or Abstract?

Directions: In the space provided, place C if the noun is concrete and A if the noun is abstract.

1. _____ glass
2. _____ letter
3. _____ love
4. _____ peace
5. _____ fire
6. _____ chain
7. _____ justice
8. _____ toe
9. _____ pony
10. _____ desert
11. _____ laughter
12. _____ squirrel
13. _____ wisdom
14. _____ mouth
15. _____ woods
16. _____ patience
17. _____ lamp
18. _____ freedom
19. _____ loyalty
20. _____ vitamin
21. _____ beauty
22. _____ thongs
23. _____ syrup
24. _____ happiness
25. _____ plug

Name________________________________

WORKBOOK PAGE 103

Date________________________________

NOUNS
Concrete or Abstract?

Directions: Three nouns in each row are concrete; one noun is abstract. Place the letter of the abstract noun in the space provided.

Example: __D__ (A) barn (B) apple (C) lime (D) dislike

1.	__C__	(A) watch	(B) hammer	(C) loneliness	(D) disk
2.	__B__	(A) camera	(B) mercy	(C) ditch	(D) curtain
3.	__C__	(A) carrot	(B) candle	(C) kindness	(D) pilot
4.	__B__	(A) pillow	(B) pride	(C) sugar	(D) bullet
5.	__C__	(A) magazine	(B) air	(C) eagerness	(D) calf
6.	__B__	(A) spider	(B) enthusiasm	(C) bandage	(D) necklace
7.	__B__	(A) tree	(B) joy	(C) butter	(D) lipstick
8.	__A__	(A) friendship	(B) lantern	(C) heart	(D) needle
9.	__D__	(A) eyelash	(B) tire	(C) hat	(D) fear
10.	__B__	(A) window	(B) time	(C) grease	(D) vase
11.	__D__	(A) shirt	(B) bread	(C) pumpkin	(D) love
12.	__C__	(A) star	(B) desk	(C) sadness	(D) rug
13.	__C__	(A) fern	(B) rock	(C) caring	(D) book
14.	__C__	(A) smoke	(B) comb	(C) tiredness	(D) puddle
15.	__C__	(A) bag	(B) pen	(C) amazement	(D) ticket

Name______________________________

Date______________________________

NOUNS
Concrete or Abstract?

Directions: Three nouns in each row are concrete; one noun is abstract. Place the letter of the abstract noun in the space provided.

Example: __D__ (A) barn (B) apple (C) lime (D) dislike

1. _____ (A) watch (B) hammer (C) loneliness (D) disk
2. _____ (A) camera (B) mercy (C) ditch (D) curtain
3. _____ (A) carrot (B) candle (C) kindness (D) pilot
4. _____ (A) pillow (B) pride (C) sugar (D) bullet
5. _____ (A) magazine (B) air (C) eagerness (D) calf
6. _____ (A) spider (B) enthusiasm (C) bandage (D) necklace
7. _____ (A) tree (B) joy (C) butter (D) lipstick
8. _____ (A) friendship (B) lantern (C) heart (D) needle
9. _____ (A) eyelash (B) tire (C) hat (D) fear
10. _____ (A) window (B) time (C) grease (D) vase
11. _____ (A) shirt (B) bread (C) pumpkin (D) love
12. _____ (A) star (B) desk (C) sadness (D) rug
13. _____ (A) fern (B) rock (C) caring (D) book
14. _____ (A) smoke (B) comb (C) tiredness (D) puddle
15. _____ (A) bag (B) pen (C) amazement (D) ticket

FOR THE TEACHER:

NOUNS

A noun names a person, a place, or a thing.

Look around the room and classify as many nouns as possible. Divide a large piece of paper into three parts or make three columns on a chalkboard or overhead projector. Write person, place, and thing at the top of each column. As students share nouns, write them in the appropriate column.

Example:	PERSON	PLACE	THING
	Sherry	corner	books
	student	floor	globe

Sometimes the same word will serve as a noun in one sentence and as a describing word (adjective) in another sentence.

This can be a major difficulty for some students.

Example: Her *hair* was blowing in the wind. (NOUN)

That *hair* band has jewels on it. (ADJECTIVE)

In the first sentence, *hair* is a thing. Therefore, *hair* is a noun.
In the second sentence, *hair* is an adjective (describing word) because it describes band.

Example: Dan ate an *orange* for breakfast. (NOUN)

This *orange* juice is very sour. (ADJECTIVE)

In the first sentence, Dan ate a **thing**, an orange. *Orange* is a noun.
In the second sentence, *orange* describes juice. It tells what kind. *Orange* is an adjective.

FOR THE TEACHER:
WORKBOOK PAGE 104

NOUNS

Nouns name persons, places, or things.

Sometimes a word will be a noun in one sentence but be used as a verb in another sentence.

Students may have difficulty with this concept.

Example: A *steer* is standing by a watering trough. (NOUN)

The driver can *steer* in and out through traffic. (VERB)

In the first sentence, *steer*, an animal, is a noun.
Steer in the second sentence is a verb telling what the driver can do.

Example: We went to a *show* in the afternoon. (NOUN)

They show home videos to their friends. (VERB)

In the first sentence, *show* is a noun, the object of the preposition: ~~to a show~~.
In sentence two, *show* is a verb telling what they do with home videos.

IMPORTANT NOTE: This note is for your information only. Do not share it with students; you will confuse them at this point. Later, this statement will make sense to them.

A problem in understanding English and using it properly is that the part of speech depends upon the context in which it appears. This has just been verified with the same word serving as a noun, a verb, and an adjective. English can be confusing!

It is important for students to understand that grammar is a tool for speaking and writing properly. Therefore, it is important to comprehend how the language "fits together" and functions. For example, *slow* is an adjective. It is correct to say, "I am a slow runner." However, "I run slow." is incorrect. The adverb *slowly* must be used. Although our goal is not to mentally decipher every sentence we say or write, knowing such concepts will help us speak and write properly. This is the rationale for teaching grammar!

Name________________________________ **NOUNS,**

WORKBOOK PAGE 105 **Adjectives, or Verbs?**

Date________________________________

Note: Having students draw an arrow from the underlined word to the word it modifies is advised. The same is true for Part A, page 201.

A. Directions: Write N if the underlined word is a noun; write A if the underlined word is an adjective.

1. ___N___ This hamburger is tasty.
2. ___A___ My hamburger bun has become soggy.
3. ___N___ Hand me that tool, please.
4. ___A___ The tool box is in the shed beside the barn.
5. ___A___ Her jewelry case has been stolen.
6. ___N___ The queen's jewelry is very expensive.
7. ___N___ Your last grocery is a box of cereal.
8. ___A___ This grocery cart has a broken wheel.
9. ___N___ Jeanette made a craft at her friend's house.
10. ___A___ The couples enjoyed the Christmas craft show.

Note: Having students underline the subject and the verb of each sentence may help. The same is applicable for Part B, page 201.

B. Directions: Write N if the underlined word is a noun; write V if the underlined word is a verb.

1. ___N___ The answer has been written in ink.
2. ___V___ He didn't answer the first question.
3. ___V___ Would you push me on this swing?
4. ___N___ Kimberly gave Karen a push and ran off.
5. ___N___ These house plants need to be watered.
6. ___V___ She plants a garden early in the spring.
7. ___V___ Why did you slip on the floor?
8. ___N___ Someone handed the auctioneer a slip of paper.

Name________________________________

Date________________________________

NOUNS,
Adjectives, or Verbs?

A. Directions: Write N if the underlined word is a noun; write A if the underlined word is an adjective.

1. ________ This hamburger is tasty.
2. ________ My hamburger bun has become soggy.
3. ________ Hand me that tool, please.
4. ________ The tool box is in the shed beside the barn.
5. ________ Her jewelry case has been stolen.
6. ________ The queen's jewelry is very expensive.
7. ________ Your last grocery is a box of cereal.
8. ________ This grocery cart has a broken wheel.
9. ________ Jeanette made a craft at her friend's house.
10. ________ The couples enjoyed the Christmas craft show.

B. Directions: Write N if the underlined word is a noun; write V if the underlined word is a verb.

1. ________ The answer has been written in ink.
2. ________ He didn't answer the first question.
3. ________ Would you push me on this swing?
4. ________ Kimberly gave Karen a push and ran off.
5. ________ These house plants need to be watered.
6. ________ She plants a garden early in the spring.
7. ________ Why did you slip on the floor?
8. ________ Someone handed the auctioneer a slip of paper.

Name________________________________

WORKBOOK PAGE 106

Date________________________________

NOUNS, Adjectives, or Verbs?

A. Directions: Write N if the underlined word is a noun; write A if the underlined word is an adjective.

1. ___A___ The garage sale had been successful.
2. ___N___ The two mechanics pushed the car into the garage.
3. ___N___ Would you like a banana with your cereal?
4. ___A___ Did you fall on a banana peel?
5. ___N___ A bear roams through those woods.
6. ___A___ A bear trap was found by some campers.
7. ___N___ The nurse laid the baby on his stomach.
8. ___A___ My stomach ache seems to be getting worse.

B. Directions: Write N on the line if the underlined word is a noun; write V on the line if the underlined word is a verb.

1. ___N___ Take this change and put it in the machine.
2. ___V___ He will change the knobs on the cupboard doors.
3. ___V___ When the snow ends, we will shovel the sidewalk.
4. ___N___ The construction worker used a shovel to smooth some dirt.
5. ___N___ She has a run in her stocking.
6. ___V___ Their quarterback had run the length of the field.
7. ___V___ Lift the latch and open the gate, please.
8. ___N___ That was her first ride on a ski lift.
9. ___N___ A load of hay was pulled by a large red tractor.
10. ___V___ Did you load the dishwasher yet?

Name________________________________

Date________________________________

NOUNS, Adjectives, or Verbs?

A. Directions: Write N if the underlined word is a noun; write A if the underlined word is an adjective.

1. ________ The garage sale had been successful.
2. ________ The two mechanics pushed the car into the garage.
3. ________ Would you like a banana with your cereal?
4. ________ Did you fall on a banana peel?
5. ________ A bear roams through those woods.
6. ________ A bear trap was found by some campers.
7. ________ The nurse laid the baby on his stomach.
8. ________ My stomach ache seems to be getting worse.

B. Directions: Write N on the line if the underlined word is a noun; write V on the line if the underlined word is a verb.

1. ________ Take this change and put it in the machine.
2. ________ He will change the knobs on the cupboard doors.
3. ________ When the snow ends, we will shovel the sidewalk.
4. ________ The construction worker used a shovel to smooth some dirt.
5. ________ She has a run in her stocking.
6. ________ Their quarterback had run the length of the field.
7. ________ Lift the latch and open the gate, please.
8. ________ That was her first ride on a ski lift.
9. ________ A load of hay was pulled by a large red tractor.
10. ________ Did you load the dishwasher yet?

FOR THE TEACHER:

WORKBOOK PAGE 107

NOUNS

Nouns name persons, places, and things.

Although noun determiners are really adjectives and will be reintroduced in the adjective unit, they help students identify nouns. It is wise to have students learn determiners under nouns. After teaching the concept, you will need to review daily for several lessons. Ask questions such as "What are the 4 demonstrative determiners? Remember that they are the T determiners." Students will respond: *this*, *that*, *those*, and *these*.

Another suggestion to help students learn the three determining articles is to have them do the hula while singing, "*A*, *an*, *the* (swaying to the right) are articles," (swaying to the left). Perhaps this idea sounds silly; however, it's amazing how much students remember when actions are involved. Also, do this throughout the year (once every month, at least). Try it!

Noun Determiners

Determiners help to identify nouns. Determiners are like RED lights. When you see a determiner, STOP and check to see if a noun follows it. The noun may be the next word or several words after the determiner.

Classification of Determiners:

A. Articles: **a**, **an**, **the**
B. Demonstratives: **this, that, those, these**
C. Numbers: examples: **two** pizzas, **fifty** dollars
D. Possessive adjectives (also called possessive pronouns used as adjectives):
my, **his**, **her**, **your**, **its**, **our**, **their**
E. Possessive nouns (used as adjectives): examples: Barry's van, ladies' club
F. Indefinites: examples: **some**, **few**, **many**, **several**, **no**, **any**

A. ***A***, ***an***, and ***the*** will come before a noun and occasionally a pronoun. There may be other words between them.

Examples:	**a** city **park**	**(place)**
	an officer	**(person)**
	the pencil **sharpener**	**(thing)**

B. The demonstratives are: **this**, **that**, **those**, and **these.** Demonstratives may signal for a noun to follow. However, they may stand alone. When ***this***, ***that***, ***those***, or ***these*** does not have a noun following closely, it will not be a determiner.

noun
Examples: **This** door is extremely heavy.

WORKBOOK PAGE 108

noun
These potato chips are too salty.

That is funny!
That is not a determiner; a noun doesn't follow it.
What is funny? The answer is not given.

C. Numbers may signal a noun. Stop to determine if a person, place, or thing follows a number.

noun
Examples: The mail carrier delivered **two** large envelopes.

noun
The concert ticket costs **twelve** dollars.

I want **two**!
Two is not a determiner here. Two what? The answer isn't given.

D. Possessive pronouns used as determiners are: **my**, **his**, **her**, **its**, **your**, **our**, and **their.** These usually signal a noun. Always STOP and check if a noun (person, place, or thing) follows it. Remember: Sometimes, other words will separate the possessive pronoun and the noun.

noun
Examples: **My** big brother is nice. (person)

noun
Your home is very close to the school (place)

E. Possessive nouns often signal other nouns. They show ownership.

poss. noun noun **poss. noun noun**
Examples: **Marilyn's** parrot **boys'** locker **room**

F. Indefinites include **some**, **any**, **no**, **many**, **few**, **several**, and others. Stop at all indefinites. Check to see if a noun follows it. There may be a few words between the indefinite and the noun.

noun
Examples: **Several** tornadoes were spotted. (things)

noun
No new actresses were hired. (persons)

Some left early. (*Some* is not a determiner. Some what? No noun is given.)

Several ~~of the loons~~ are gone. *Several* is not a determiner. *Loons* has been crossed out.

Name________________________________ **NOUNS**
WORKBOOK PAGE 109 **Determiners**
Date________________________________

Directions: In the space provided, write the underlined determiner and the noun that it modifies (goes over to):

Example: Our family likes to watch old movies. ______Our family______

1. The Arctic region is rather cold. ______The region______
2. Keep your essay in this notebook. ______your essay______
3. We'd like two doughnuts for breakfast. ______two doughnuts______
4. Tina will become a bride in June. ______a bride______
5. May we buy some candy? ______some candy______
6. He has changed his plans again. ______his plans______
7. This machines needs more paper. ______This machine______
8. Have you read Julie's letter? ______Julie's letter______
9. No money was raised for the trip. ______No money______
10. The ponies' master is kind. ______ponies' master______
11. They put an ornament on the tree. ______an ornament______
12. How do you operate that computer? ______that computer______
13. Our favorite dessert is a brownie. ______Our dessert______
14. Are many caves found in Kentucky? ______many caves______
15. These sunglasses have been found. ______These sunglasses______

Name________________________________

Date________________________________

NOUNS
Determiners

Directions: In the space provided, write the underlined determiner and the noun that it modifies (goes over to):

Example: Our family likes to watch old movies. ______Our family________

1. The Arctic region is rather cold. ________________________________
2. Keep your essay in this notebook. ________________________________
3. We'd like two doughnuts for breakfast. ________________________________
4. Tina will become a bride in June. ________________________________
5. May we buy some candy? ________________________________
6. He has changed his plans again. ________________________________
7. This machine needs more paper. ________________________________
8. Have you read Julie's letter? ________________________________
9. No money was raised for the trip. ________________________________
10. The ponies' master is kind. ________________________________
11. They put an ornament on the tree. ________________________________
12. How do you operate that computer? ________________________________
13. Our favorite dessert is a brownie. ________________________________
14. Are many caves found in Kentucky? ________________________________
15. These sunglasses have been found. ________________________________

Name________________________________

WORKBOOK PAGE 110

Date________________________________

NOUNS
Determiners

Directions: In the space provided, write the underlined determiner with the noun it modifies (goes over to).

Example: Tree trimmers piled many branches there. ___many branches___

1. Please don't take my new shoes. ___my shoes___
2. We found a few grasshoppers. ___few grasshoppers___
3. An award for sportsmanship is given. ___An award___
4. Did you see those two large hornets? ___two hornets___
5. Brian's friend is learning to be an umpire. ___Brian's friend___
6. He removed fat from the piece of meat. ___the piece___
7. The telephone is in her closet. ___her closet___
8. You need not do any hard work today. ___any work___
9. They haven't been here for several years. ___several years___
10. That one-way street has been closed. ___That street___
11. In twelve days, we are going to Iowa. ___twelve days___
12. A chipmunk has lost its way. ___its way___
13. May I have some mashed potatoes? ___some potatoes___
14. A boys' club offered basketball games. ___boys' club___
15. Campers put their gear by the van. ___their gear___

Name________________________________

Date________________________________

NOUNS
Determiners

Directions: In the space provided, write the underlined determiner with the noun it modifies (goes over to).

Example: Tree trimmers piled many branches there. ____many branches____

1. Please don't take my new shoes. ________________________________
2. We found a few grasshoppers. ________________________________
3. An award for sportsmanship is given. ________________________________
4. Did you see those two large hornets? ________________________________
5. Brian's friend is learning to be an umpire. ________________________________
6. He removed fat from the piece of meat. ________________________________
7. The telephone is in her closet. ________________________________
8. You need not do any hard work today. ________________________________
9. They haven't been here for several years. ________________________________
10. That one-way street has been closed. ________________________________
11. In twelve days, we are going to Iowa. ________________________________
12. A chipmunk has lost its way. ________________________________
13. May I have some mashed potatoes? ________________________________
14. A boys' club offered basketball games. ________________________________
15. Campers put their gear by the van. ________________________________

PAGE 216 = WORKBOOK PAGE 115
PAGE 217 = WORKBOOK PAGE 116

FOR THE TEACHER:
WORKBOOK PAGE 111

NOUNS

COMMON AND PROPER NOUNS

A common noun refers to any person, place, or thing.
Do not capitalize common nouns.

person: boy   place: zoo   thing: building

A type of something is also a common noun.
A type of building is a bank. A bank is still a common noun.
(There are many banks in the world.)

A proper noun names a specific person, place, or thing.
Capitalize a proper noun. Common and proper nouns are easier to show by example than to define:

Common Noun: beach

Proper Noun: **H**untington **B**each

Common Noun: dog
Common Noun: collie (type of dog--still a common noun)

Proper Noun: Bowser (name of a particular dog)

Common Noun: state

Proper Noun: North Carolina (name of a specific state)

Common Noun: airport

Proper Noun: Dulles International Airport

NOTE: Be sure that students comprehend the difference between common nouns and proper nouns. A good way is to say a common noun such as restaurant, reinforcing there are many restaurants in the world. Then, ask for the name of a particular restaurant. Reinforce that this is the name of a specific restaurant, a proper noun, and will be capitalized when written.

Name________________________________

WORKBOOK PAGE 112

Date________________________________

NOUNS
Common and Proper

Directions: In the space provided, write a proper noun for each common noun.

Example: creek - ____________ Beaver Creek ____________

ANSWERS WILL VARY.

1. person - ________________________________
2. street - ________________________________
3. lake - ________________________________
4. park - ________________________________
5. restaurant - ________________________________
6. athlete - ________________________________
7. store - ________________________________
8. river - ________________________________
9. country - ________________________________
10. company - ________________________________

Name________________________________

Date________________________________

NOUNS
Common and Proper

Directions: In the space provided, write a proper noun for each common noun.

Example: creek - ____________ Beaver Creek ____________

1. person - ________________________________
2. street - ________________________________
3. lake - ________________________________
4. park - ________________________________
5. restaurant - ________________________________
6. athlete - ________________________________
7. store - ________________________________
8. river - ________________________________
9. country - ________________________________
10. company - ________________________________

Name________________________________

WORKBOOOK PAGE 113

Date________________________________

NOUNS
Common or Proper?

Directions: Write C if the noun is a common noun; write P if the noun is a proper noun.

1. __C__ MOUNTAIN
2. __P__ MT. BALDY
3. __P__ JOHN WAYNE
4. __C__ ACTOR
5. __C__ BANK
6. __P__ THUNDERBIRD BANK
7. __C__ RIVER
8. __P__ COLORADO RIVER
9. __P__ PASTOR KLEGG
10. __C__ MINISTER
11. __C__ WRITER
12. __P__ MARK TWAIN
13. __P__ SANDRA DAY O'CONNER
14. __C__ JUDGE
15. __P__ REHOBOTH BEACH
16. __C__ BEACH
17. __C__ PLANET
18. __P__ SATURN
19. __P__ KANSAS
20. __C__ STATE
21. __P__ PACIFIC OCEAN
22. __C__ OCEAN
23. __C__ ISLAND
24. __P__ HAWAII
25. __P__ TED'S BODY SHOP
26. __C__ SHOP
27. __C__ RACE
28. __P__ INDIANAPOLIS 500
29. __P__ DISNEYLAND
30. __C__ PARK
31. __P__ AMY GRANT
32. __C__ SINGER

Name________________________________

Date________________________________

NOUNS
Common or Proper?

Directions: Write C if the noun is a common noun; write P if the noun is a proper noun.

1. _____ MOUNTAIN
2. _____ MT. BALDY
3. _____ JOHN WAYNE
4. _____ ACTOR
5. _____ BANK
6. _____ THUNDERBIRD BANK
7. _____ RIVER
8. _____ COLORADO RIVER
9. _____ PASTOR KLEGG
10. _____ MINISTER
11. _____ WRITER
12. _____ MARK TWAIN
13. _____ SANDRA DAY O'CONNER
14. _____ JUDGE
15. _____ REHOBOTH BEACH
16. _____ BEACH
17. _____ PLANET
18. _____ SATURN
19. _____ KANSAS
20. _____ STATE
21. _____ PACIFIC OCEAN
22. _____ OCEAN
23. _____ ISLAND
24. _____ HAWAII
25. _____ TED'S BODY SHOP
26. _____ SHOP
27. _____ RACE
28. _____ INDIANAPOLIS 500
29. _____ DISNEYLAND
30. _____ PARK
31. _____ AMY GRANT
32. _____ SINGER

Name________________________________

WORKBOOK PAGE 114

Date________________________________

NOUNS
Common or Proper?

Directions: Write C if the noun is a common noun; write P if the noun is a proper noun.

Remember: **A common noun doesn't name a specific person, place or thing. There are usually many of a common noun: dog. Types are still common: poodle.**
A proper noun names a particular person, place, or thing: Fido.

IMPORTANT:

WHEN SOLICITING ANSWERS, HAVE STUDENTS EXPLAIN WHY THE WORD IS COMMON. (EXAMPLE: THERE ARE MANY FLOWERS IN THE WORLD.) HAVE STUDENTS EXPLAIN ALSO ABOUT PROPER NOUNS. (EXAMPLE: GLEN'S DINER NAMES A PARTICULAR DINER.)

1. C FLOWER
2. C DAFFODIL
3. P SEARS TOWER
4. C CUSHION
5. P BETSY ROSS
6. P GREAT SALT LAKE
7. C MOTEL
8. P LONDON BRIDGE
9. C ENCYCLOPEDIA
10. P FAITH CHURCH
11. P DR. SABO
12. C BAY
13. C DIME
14. C POST CARD
15. C COMB
16. P ELM STREET
17. P GLEN'S DINER
18. P GREENWAY ROAD
19. P SALVATION ARMY
20. C BALLET
21. P FREEDOM TRAIL
22. C WALLET
23. C SEAMSTRESS
24. P GRAND CANYON
25. C FLAG
26. P MR. ADAMS
27. P HEARTHSIDE INN
28. C KITE
29. P CANADA
30. C FAIR
31. P LAKE ONTARIO
32. C TERRIER

Name________________________________

Date________________________________

NOUNS
Common or Proper?

Directions: Write C if the noun is a common noun; write P if the noun is a proper noun.

Remember: A common noun doesn't name a specific person, place or thing. There are usually many of a common noun: dog. Types are still common: poodle.
A proper noun names a particular person, place, or thing: Fido.

1. _____ FLOWER
2. _____ DAFFODIL
3. _____ SEARS TOWER
4. _____ CUSHION
5. _____ BETSY ROSS
6. _____ GREAT SALT LAKE
7. _____ MOTEL
8. _____ LONDON BRIDGE
9. _____ ENCYCLOPEDIA
10. _____ FAITH CHURCH
11. _____ DR. SABO
12. _____ BAY
13. _____ DIME
14. _____ POST CARD
15. _____ COMB
16. _____ ELM STREET
17. _____ GLEN'S DINER
18. _____ GREENWAY ROAD
19. _____ SALVATION ARMY
20. _____ BALLET
21. _____ FREEDOM TRAIL
22. _____ WALLET
23. _____ SEAMSTRESS
24. _____ GRAND CANYON
25. _____ FLAG
26. _____ MR. ADAMS
27. _____ HEARTHSIDE INN
28. _____ KITE
29. _____ CANADA
30. _____ FAIR
31. _____ LAKE ONTARIO
32. _____ TERRIER

NOUNS

SINGULAR AND PLURAL NOUNS

Singular means one.
Plural means more than one.

Rule 1: **The plural of most nouns is made by adding s to the noun.**

door/doors   star/stars   window/windows   gate/gates

Rule 2: **When a singular noun ends in s, sh, ch, x, or z, add es to form the plural.**

gas/gases   dish/dishes   punch/punches   wax/waxes   buzz/buzzes

Rule 3: **When a singular noun ends in a vowel + y, add s to form the plural.**

bay/bays   guy/guys   toy/toys   monkey/monkeys

Rule 4: **When a singular noun ends in consonant + y, change the y to i and add es to form the plural.**

strawberry/strawberries   cry/cries   filly/fillies

Rule 5: **Some nouns totally change in the plural form.**

woman/women   child/children   ox/oxen

Use a dictionary to check the plural form of nouns. If the word totally changes to form the plural, the dictionary will spell out the plural. pl. = plural

Example: tooth (n), pl. teeth - 1. hard, bonelike structure...

Rule 6: **Some nouns are the same in both the singular and plural form.**

deer/deer   sheep/sheep

Use a dictionary to check the plural form of nouns. If the noun does not change, the dictionary will show it.

Example: sheep (n), pl. sheep 1. a cud-chewing bovine animal...

Rule 7: **Some nouns ending in f, change the f to v and add es to form the plural.**

leaf/leaves calf/calves life/lives

Use a dictionary to check the plural form of nouns. If there is a change, the dictionary will show it.

Example: life (n), pl. lives [ME...] a living being

Rule 8: **Some nouns ending in f, simply add s to form the plural.**

gulf/gulfs staff/staffs huff/huffs

Use a dictionary to check the plural form of nouns. If s is added, no special entry (*pl.*) will be given.

Rule 9: **Some nouns ending in o, add s to form the plural.**
Some nouns ending in o, add es to form the plural.

Use a dictionary to check the plural form of nouns. If s should be added, no special plural entry will be given. If es should be added, the entry with *pl.* will be given.

Example: tomato (n), pl. *-toes* {Sp...] 1. a red or yellow fruit

Rule 10: **Some hyphenated nouns add s to the first part when forming the plural. The same applies to some non-hyphenated nouns.**

Check your dictionary for the correct plural form.

mother-in-law/mothers-in-law

IMPORTANT NOTE: If two plural forms are given in a dictionary entry, the first listed is the more acceptable.

Example: cactus (n), pl. cacti, cactuses 1. desert plant

Name________________________________ **NOUNS**
WORKBOOK PAGE 117 **Plurals**
Date________________________________

Directions: Write the plural form in the space after the noun. In the first space, write the number of the rule.

Example: 4 berry - berries

NOTE: DICTIONARIES ARE INCONSISTENT WITH THEIR PLURAL RULES. IF STUDENTS FIND A DIFFERENT ANSWER, ACCEPT IT. (HAVE THEM SHOW YOU THE ENTRY.) BE SURE STUDENTS UNDERSTAND THE IMPORTANCE OF USING A DICTIONARY!

1. 1 post - posts
2. 1 gate - gates
3. 2 toothbrush - toothbrushes
4. 3 guy - guys
5. 6 sheep - sheep
6. 2 buzz - buzzes
7. 1 pencil - pencils
8. 4 penny - pennies
9. 5 child - children
10. 2 bus - buses
11. 2 box - boxes
12. 1 pea - peas
13. 7 calf - calves
14. 2 lunch - lunches
15. 9 tomato - tomatoes

Name______________________________

Date______________________________

NOUNS
Plurals

Directions: Write the plural form in the space after the noun. In the first space, write the number of the rule.

Example: __4__ berry - ______berries______________________

1. ______ post - ______________________________
2. ______ gate - ______________________________
3. ______ toothbrush - __________________________
4. ______ guy - ______________________________
5. ______ sheep - ______________________________
6. ______ buzz - ______________________________
7. ______ pencil - ______________________________
8. ______ penny - ______________________________
9. ______ child - ______________________________
10. ______ bus - ______________________________
11. ______ box - ______________________________
12. ______ pea - ______________________________
13. ______ calf - ______________________________
14. ______ lunch - ______________________________
15. ______ tomato - ______________________________

Name________________________________ **NOUNS**

WORKBOOK PAGE 118 **Plurals**

Date________________________________

Directions: Write the plural form in the space after the noun. In the first space, write the number of the rule.

Example: __9__ potato - ______potatoes______

NOTE: DICTIONARIES ARE INCONSISTENT WITH THEIR PLURAL RULES. IF STUDENTS FIND A DIFFERENT ANSWER, ACCEPT IT. (HAVE THEM SHOW YOU THE ENTRY.) BE SURE STUDENTS UNDERSTAND THE IMPORTANCE OF USING A DICTIONARY!

1. __4__ baby - ______babies______
2. __1__ page - ______pages______
3. __1__ nephew - ______nephews______
4. __5__ tooth - ______teeth______
5. __9__ banjo - ______banjos, (banjoes -less preferred)______
6. __8__ whiff - ______whiffs______
7. __2__ watch - ______watches______
8. __3__ clay - ______clays______
9. __1__ lesson - ______lessons______
10. __2__ mess - ______messes______
11. __2__ flash - ______flashes______
12. __5__ goose - ______geese______
13. __6__ shrimp - ______shrimp______
14. __1__ tear - ______tears______
15. __10__ brother-in-law - ______brothers-in-law______

Name______________________________

Date______________________________

NOUNS
Plurals

Directions: Write the plural form in the space after the noun. In the first space, write the number of the rule.

Example: __9__ potato - ______potatoes______________________

1. _____ baby - ______________________________
2. _____ page - ______________________________
3. _____ nephew - ______________________________
4. _____ tooth - ______________________________
5. _____ banjo - ______________________________
6. _____ whiff - ______________________________
7. _____ watch - ______________________________
8. _____ clay - ______________________________
9. _____ lesson - ______________________________
10. _____ mess - ______________________________
11. _____ flash - ______________________________
12. _____ goose - ______________________________
13. _____ shrimp - ______________________________
14. _____ tear - ______________________________
15. _____ brother-in-law - ______________________________

Name________________________________

WORKBOOK PAGE 119

Date________________________________

NOUNS

Plurals

Directions: Write the plural form in the space after the noun. In the first space, write the number of the rule.

Example: __1__ ski - ______skis______

NOTE: DICTIONARIES ARE INCONSISTENT WITH THEIR PLURAL RULES. IF STUDENTS FIND A DIFFERENT ANSWER, ACCEPT IT. (HAVE THEM SHOW YOU THE ENTRY.) BE SURE STUDENTS UNDERSTAND THE IMPORTANCE OF USING A DICTIONARY.

1. __2__ ditch - ______ditches______
2. __3__ play - ______plays______
3. __1__ house - ______houses______
4. __8__ gulf - ______gulfs______
5. __1__ fern - ______ferns______
6. __4__ cherry - ______cherries______
7. __2__ wish - ______wishes______
8. __5__ mouse - ______mice______
9. __2__ class - ______classes______
10. __9__ studio - ______studios______
11. __1__ greeting - ______greetings______
12. __7__ thief - ______thieves______
13. __5__ man - ______men______
14. __2__ fez - ______fezes______
15. __3__ key - ______keys______

Name______________________________

Date______________________________

NOUNS
Plurals

Directions: Write the plural form in the space after the noun. In the first space, write the number of the rule.

Example: __1__ ski - ______skis______

1. ______ ditch - ______________________________
2. ______ play - ______________________________
3. ______ house - ______________________________
4. ______ gulf - ______________________________
5. ______ fern - ______________________________
6. ______ cherry - ______________________________
7. ______ wish - ______________________________
8. ______ mouse - ______________________________
9. ______ class - ______________________________
10. ______ studio - ______________________________
11. ______ greeting - ______________________________
12. ______ thief - ______________________________
13. ______ man - ______________________________
14. ______ fez - ______________________________
15. ______ key - ______________________________

FOR THE TEACHER:
PAGE 225 = WORKBOOK PAGE 120

NOUNS

POSSESSIVE NOUNS

Students need to comprehend that possessives show ownership. Be sure that they understand the difference between the term plural and the term possessive.

An easy approach is to ask students to say their own name and add something owned.

Examples: Terry's bike

Tammi's notebook

Crystal's jacket

Next, ask students what objects might own. Hold up a book. What might a book own? Write the answers on the board.

Examples: a book's cover

a book's pages

a book's table of contents

Do this with other objects in the room. You may want students to write three objects. When the student says the object, another student volunteer makes it show ownership and adds something the object might own. Write student examples on the board.

Examples: door - door's knob

desk - desk's legs

wall - wall's paint

A page containing rules for forming the possessive is provided. However, before teaching the rules, make sure students comprehend that the possessive form of a noun shows that something belongs or is owned.

When teaching the rules for showing possession, be sure that students understand that which is owned is not important. In determining placement of the apostrophe, it doesn't matter if John owns one dog or two dogs. All that is important is whether the possessive noun is singular or plural.

NOUNS

POSSESSIVE NOUNS

RULE A: To form the possessive of a singular noun, add 's to the noun.

Examples: baby + rattle = baby'**s** rattle

dog + leash = dog'**s** leash

cup + handle = cup'**s** handle

This rule applies to all singular nouns, even those ending in s.

Examples: class + teacher = class'**s** teacher

Mrs. Jones + son = Mrs. Jones'**s** son

RULE B: To form the possessive of a plural noun ending in s, add ' after the s.

Examples: (more than one boy) boy**s**' bathroom

(more than one horse) horse**s**' corral

(more than one cow) cow**s**' pasture

RULE C: To form the possessive of a plural noun that does NOT end in s, add 's to the word.

Examples: one woman/two women

women'**s** meeting

one mouse/two mice

mice'**s** hole

Name________________________________

WORKBOOK PAGE 121

Date________________________________

NOUNS
Possessives

Directions: Write the possessive form.

Example: a hose belonging to firemen: ____firemen's hose____

1. a hamster belonging to Fran: ____Fran's hamster____
2. books belonging to Spencer: ____Spencer's books____
3. a coach belonging to a team: ____team's coach____
4. a car belonging to two officers: ____officers' car____
5. a party hat belonging to a child: ____child's party hat____
6. a swing belonging to children: ____children's swing____
7. dishes belonging to Mrs. Cass: ____Mrs. Cass's dishes____
8. a baseball belonging to Miss Arl: ____Miss Arl's baseball____
9. papers belonging to a teller: ____teller's papers____
10. a cage belonging to two birds: ____birds' cage____

Name_______________________________

Date_______________________________

NOUNS
Possessives

Directions: Write the possessive form.

Example: a hose belonging to firemen: ________firemen's hose________

1. a hamster belonging to Fran: _______________________________
2. books belonging to Spencer: _______________________________
3. a coach belonging to a team: _______________________________
4. a car belonging to two officers: _______________________________
5. a party hat belonging to a child: _______________________________
6. a swing belonging to children: _______________________________
7. dishes belonging to Mrs. Cass: _______________________________
8. a baseball belonging to Miss Arl: _______________________________
9. papers belonging to a teller: _______________________________
10. a cage belonging to two birds: _______________________________

Name________________________________

WORKBOOK PAGE 122

Date________________________________

NOUNS
Possessives

Directions: Write the possessive form.

Example: nuts belonging to a chipmunk: ___chipmunk's nuts___

1. a lunch box belonging to a worker: ___worker's lunch box___
2. ice skates belonging to Caleb: ___Caleb's ice skates___
3. a store belonging to two ladies: ___ladies' store___
4. glasses belonging to Sis: ___Sis's glasses___
5. a canoe belonging to two men: ___men's canoe___
6. a fishing pole belonging to Brenda: ___Brenda's fishing pole___
7. a frame belonging to a picture: ___picture's frame___
8. trash belonging to all the neighbors: ___neighbors' trash___
9. freeway belonging to a city: ___city's freeway___
10. oranges belonging to many growers: ___growers' oranges___

Name________________________________

Date________________________________

NOUNS
Possessives

Directions: Write the possessive form.

Example: nuts belonging to a chipmunk: ________chipmunk's nuts________

1. a lunch box belonging to a worker: ______________________________

2. ice skates belonging to Caleb: ______________________________

3. a store belonging to two ladies: ______________________________

4. glasses belonging to Sis: ______________________________

5. a canoe belonging to two men: ______________________________

6. a fishing pole belonging to Brenda: ______________________________

7. a frame belonging to a picture: ______________________________

8. trash belonging to all the neighbors: ______________________________

9. freeway belonging to a city: ______________________________

10. oranges belonging to many growers: ______________________________

Name________________________________ **NOUNS**

WORKBOOK PAGE 123 **Possessives**

Date________________________________

Directions: Write the possessive form.

Example: leader belonging to a few girls: ________girls' leader__________

1. tap shoes belonging to a dancer: ______dancer's tap shoes________________
2. a cage belonging to two birds: ________birds' cage_______________________
3. notes belonging to a student: _________student's notes____________________
4. a lounge belonging to all workers: _____workers' lounge____________________
5. feathers belonging to a heron: _________heron's feathers___________________
6. a banana split belonging to Miss Liss: __Miss Liss's banana split_____________

Point out that the answer would be the same for more than one deer.

7. a meadow belonging to one deer: _____deer's meadow______________________
8. a trail for joggers: ____________________joggers' trail______________________
9. pearls belonging to a princess: ________princess's pearls___________________
10. a center for many visitors: ______________visitors' center____________________

Name____________________________

Date____________________________

NOUNS
Possessives

Directions: Write the possessive form.

Example: leader belonging to a few girls: ______girls' leader______

1. tap shoes belonging to a dancer: ____________________________

2. a cage belonging to two birds: ____________________________

3. notes belonging to a student: ____________________________

4. a lounge belonging to all workers: ____________________________

5. feathers belonging to a heron: ____________________________

6. a banana split belonging to Miss Liss: ____________________________

7. a meadow belonging to one deer: ____________________________

8. a trail for joggers: ____________________________

9. pearls belonging to a princess: ____________________________

10. a center for many visitors: ____________________________

Name________________________________ **NOUNS**
WORKBOOK PAGE 124 **Identification**
Date________________________________

Determiners are in italics; nouns are boldfaced.

Directions: Circle any determiner(s). Look for a noun that closely follows each determiner. Box any noun.

DETERMINERS:

1. a, an, the
2. this, that, those, these
3. numbers: example: fifteen sleeping bags
4. my, his, her, your, its, our, their
5. possessives: example: frog's legs
6. several, few, many, some, any, no

Reminder: Read each sentence. Then, go back and look for determiners. When you see a determiner, STOP, and check if a noun is closely following it. Say the determiner to yourself and add what to it. If you can answer, the word that completes the what is a noun.

Example: That ring is pretty.
That is a possible determiner.
That what? Answer: that ring
Therefore, *ring* is a noun and should be boxed.

Next, go through the sentence and decide if there are any nouns that do not have a determiner. (Not all nouns have determiners in front of them.)

1. *A* **swallow** flew into *an* **orchard**.

2. *Her* **gerbil** is in *the* **bedroom**.

3. ***Debbie's*** **mother** talked to *a* **neighbor**.

4. *Some* **cars** drove through *a* **tunnel**.

5. I made *six* **hamburgers** and *that* **salad** for **lunch**. (Lunch has no determiner; point out that it is the object of the preposition which will be a noun or pronoun.)
(Point out that I is always a pronoun.)

6. *Many* **children** asked *their* **parents** for *a* **ride** on *the* Ferris **wheel**.

7. *A* **parade** of *five* **bands** and *several* **floats** passed by.

8. *These* **jacks** and *this* **ball** should be put away.

9. *The* ***boys'*** **group** doesn't have *any* **equipment** for *the* **game**.

10. *Your* **sister** needs *this* **baton** for *a* **competition** in **Philadelphia**.

Name_______________________________

Date_______________________________

NOUNS
Identification

Directions: Circle any determiner(s). Look for a noun that closely follows each determiner. Box any noun.

DETERMINERS:
1. a, an, the
2. this, that, those, these
3. numbers: example: fifteen sleeping bags
4. my, his, her, your, its, our, their
5. possessives: example: frog's legs
6. several, few, many, some, any, no

Reminder: Read each sentence. Then, go back and look for determiners. When you see a determiner, STOP, and check if a noun is closely following it. Say the determiner to yourself and add what to it. If you can answer, the word that completes the what is a noun.

Example: That ring is pretty.
That is a possible determiner.
That what? Answer: that ring
Therefore, *ring* is a noun and should be boxed.

Next, go through the sentence and decide if there are any nouns that do not have a determiner. (Not all nouns have determiners in front of them.)

1. A swallow flew into an orchard.
2. Her gerbil is in the bedroom.
3. Debbie's mother talked to a neighbor.
4. Some cars drove through a tunnel.
5. I made six hamburgers and that salad for lunch.
6. Many children asked their parents for a ride on the Ferris wheel.
7. A parade of five bands and several floats passed by.
8. These jacks and this ball should be put away.
9. The boys' group doesn't have any equipment for the game.
10. Your sister needs this baton for a competition in Philadelphia.

Name________________________________

NOUNS
Identification

WORKBOOK PAGE 125

Date________________________________

Determiners are in italics; nouns are boldfaced.

Directions: Circle any determiner(s). Look for a noun that closely follows each determiner. Box any noun.

DETERMINERS:
1. a, an, the
2. this, that, those, these
3. numbers: example: fifteen sleeping bags
4. my, his, her, your, its, our, their
5. possessives: example: frog's legs
6. several, few, many, some, any, no

Reminder: Read each sentence. Then, go back and look for determiners. When you see a determiner, STOP, and check if a noun is closely following it. Say the determiner to yourself and add what to it. If you can answer, the word that completes the what is a noun.

Example: Many buses arrived.
Many is a possible determiner.
Many what? Answer: Many buses
Therefore, *buses* is a noun and should be boxed.

Next, go through the sentence and decide if there are any nouns that do not have a determiner. (Not all nouns have determiners in front of them.)

1. *Your* **television** has *three* **knobs**.

2. ***Lennie's*** **cousin** has *many* **guppies**.

3. Are *thirty* **waiters** serving at *that* **luncheon**?

4. *Their* lawn **mower** has *an* electric **switch**.

5. *A* ***porcupine's*** **quills** are thin with sharp **points**.

6. *Those* **butterflies** spread *their* **wings** and flew off.

7. *The* ***skeleton's*** **bones** have been assembled for science **class**.

8. Do *the* **secretaries** in *that* **office** have *any* vacation **days** left?

9. During *our* first **summer** in *this* **home**, we painted *my* **bedroom** with *a* blue **paint**.

10. *Some* **tourists** at *the* **museum** asked to see ***Monet's*** **paintings**.

Name________________________________

Date________________________________

NOUNS
Identification

Directions: Circle any determiner(s). Look for a noun that closely follows each determiner. Box any noun.

DETERMINERS:

1. a, an, the
2. this, that, those, these
3. numbers: example: fifteen sleeping bags
4. my, his, her, your, its, our, their
5. possesseives: example: frog's legs
6. several, few, many, some, any, no

Reminder: Read each sentence. Then, go back and look for determiners. When you see a determiner, STOP, and check if a noun is closely following it. Say the determiner to yourself and add what to it. If you can answer, the word that completes the what is a noun.

Example: Many buses arrived.
Many is a possible determiner.
Many what? Answer: many buses
Therefore, *buses* is a noun and should be boxed.

Next, go through the sentence and decide if there are any nouns that do not have a determiner. (Not all nouns have determiners in front of them.)

1. Your television has three knobs.
2. Lennie's cousin has many guppies.
3. Are thirty waiters serving at that luncheon?
4. Their lawn mower has an electric switch.
5. A porcupine's quills are thin with sharp points.
6. Those butterflies spread their wings and flew off.
7. The skeleton's bones have been assembled for science class.
8. Do the secretaries in that office have any vacation days left?
9. During our first summer in this home, we painted my bedroom with a blue paint.
10. Some tourists at the museum asked to see Monet's paintings.

Name________________________________ **NOUNS**

WORKBOOK PAGE 126 **Identification**

Date________________________________

<u>Determiners are in italics; nouns are boldfaced.</u>

Directions: Circle any determiner(s). Look for a noun that closely follows each determiner. Box any noun.

DETERMINERS:

1. a, an, the
2. this, that, those, these
3. numbers: example: fifteen sleeping bags
4. my, his, her, your, its, our, their
5. possessives: example: frog's legs
6. several, few, many, some, any, no

Reminder: Read each sentence. Then, go back and look for determiners. When you see a determiner, STOP, and check if a noun is closely following it. Say the determiner to yourself and add <u>what</u> to it. If you can answer, the word that completes the <u>what</u> is a noun.

Example: Two girls laughed.
Two is a possible determiner.
Two <u>what?</u> Answer: two girls
Therefore, *girls* is a noun and should be boxed.

Next, go through the sentence and decide if there are any nouns that do not have a determiner. (<u>Not all nouns have determiners in front of them.</u>)

1. *His* **answer** was written in *the* first **column**.

2. ***Joyann's*** **house** has *no* **curtains** in *the* front **window**.

3. *Their* **mother** yelled across *the* **street** to *her* **friend**.

4. *These* **baskets** contain **blueberries** and **bananas**.

5. *That* ***boy's*** **bicycle** has *several* **dents** and *a* **hole** in *its* **frame**.

6. *Some* **parents** with small **children** sat in *an* open **area** of *the* **woods**.

7. *An* **orange** and *several* **lemons** are needed for *this* **recipe**.

8. *Many* **squirrels** gathered **nuts** for *their* long **winter** ahead.

9. *A* **caterpillar** crawled up *the* **flower** and slid beneath *its* **leaf**.

10. They have purchased *four* **ribbons**, *some* **lace**, and *two* **bolts** of silky **fabric**.

Name________________________________

Date________________________________

NOUNS
Identification

Directions: Circle any determiner(s). Look for a noun that closely follows each determiner. Box any noun.

DETERMINERS:
1. a, an, the
2. this, that, those, these
3. numbers: example: fifteen sleeping bags
4. my, his, her, your, its, our, their
5. possessives: example: frog's legs
6. several, few, many, some, any, no

Reminder: Read each sentence. Then, go back and look for determiners. When you see a determiner, STOP, and check if a noun is closely following it. Say the determiner to yourself and add what to it. If you can answer, the word that completes the what is a noun.

Example: Two girls laughed.
Two is a possible determiner.
Two what? Answer: two girls
Therefore, *girls* is a noun and should be boxed.

Next, go through the sentence and decide if there are any nouns that do not have a determiner. (Not all nouns have determiners in front of them.)

1. His answer was written in the first column.
2. Joyann's house has no curtains in the front window.
3. Their mother yelled across the street to her friend.
4. These baskets contain blueberries and bananas.
5. That boy's bicycle has several dents and a hole in its frame.
6. Some parents with small children sat in an open area of the woods.
7. An orange and several lemons are needed for this recipe.
8. Many squirrels gathered nuts for their long winter ahead.
9. A caterpillar crawled up the flower and slid beneath its leaf.
10. They have purchased four ribbons, some lace, and two bolts of silky fabric.

Name____ **NOUNS**

WORKBOOK PAGE 127 **Predicate Nominatives**

Date____

NOTE: A REVIEW HAS BEEN PROVIDED HERE; HENCE, THIS PAGE CONTAINS ONLY THREE SENTENCES FOR FINDING PREDICATE NOMINATIVES. THE FOLLOWING PAGE WILL CONTAIN MANY SENTENCES. THIS CONCEPT WILL **NOT** BE TESTED ON THE END OF UNIT TEST.

You have learned about predicate nominatives in the verb unit. Let's review. **A predicate nominative is a noun or pronoun that occurs after a linking verb and means the same as the subject.** (In this unit, a P.N. will be a noun.)

Linking Verbs:	to feel	to become	to remain
	to taste	to seem	to appear
	to look	to sound	to stay
	to smell	to grow	to be (is, am, are, was, were, be, being, been)

P.N.

Example: Ludwig is the best swimmer.

Proof: The best swimmer is Ludwig.

Remember: To prove the predicate nominative, invert the sentence. Begin with the word(s) after the verb, include the predicate nominative, and, then, go to the beginning of the sentence. This is called inverting the sentence.

Directions: Cross out any prepositional phrase(s). Underline the subject once and the verb/verb phrase twice. Label any predicate nominative-P.N. Write the proof for the predicate nominative on the line provided.

P.N.

1. Tahiti is a beautiful island ~~in the South Pacific~~.

   Proof: A beautiful island is Tahiti.

P.N.

2. Their favorite baseball player was Ken Griffey, Jr.

   Proof: Ken Griffey, Jr. was their favorite baseball player.

P.N.

3. A planet ~~with rings~~ is Saturn.

   Proof: Saturn is a planet.

Name______________________________

Date______________________________

NOUNS
Predicate Nominatives

You have learned about predicate nominatives in the verb unit. Let's review. **A predicate nominative is a noun or pronoun that occurs after a linking verb and means the same as the subject.** (In this unit, a P.N. will be a noun.)

Linking Verbs:	to feel	to become	to remain
	to taste	to seem	to appear
	to look	to sound	to stay
	to smell	to grow	to be (is, am, are, was, were, be, being, been)

P.N.

Example: Ludwig is the best swimmer.

Proof: The best swimmer is Ludwig.

Remember: To prove the predicate nominative, invert the sentence. Begin with the word(s) after the verb, include the predicate nominative, and, then, go to the beginning of the sentence. This is called inverting the sentence.

Directions: Cross out any prepositional phrase(s). Underline the subject once and the verb/verb phrase twice. Label any predicate nominative-P.N. Write the proof for the predicate nominative on the line provided.

1. Tahiti is a beautiful island in the South Pacific.

   Proof: ____

2. Their favorite baseball player was Ken Griffey, Jr.

   Proof: ____

3. A planet with rings is Saturn.

   Proof: ____

Name________________________________

WORKBOOK PAGE 128

Date________________________________

NOUNS
Predicate Nominatives

Note: Predicate nominatives may not be mastered at this point. Therefore, they will not be included in the unit test.

Directions: Cross out any prepositional phrase(s). Underline the subject once and the verb/verb phrase twice. Label any predicate nominative-P.N. Write the proof for the predicate nominative on the line provided.

1. A green precious gem is an emerald. (P.N.)

   Proof: An emerald is a green precious gem.

2. The last person ~~in the race~~ was their teacher. (P.N.)

   Proof: Their teacher was the last person.

3. A penguin is a flightless bird ~~of the Southern Hemisphere~~. (P.N.)

   Proof: A flightless bird is a penguin.

4. Janeen Holloway is the president ~~of the Aviators' Club~~. (P.N.)

   Proof: The president is Janeen Holloway.

5. Karen's favorite book remains Black Beauty. (P.N.)

   Proof: Black Beauty remains (is) Karen's favorite book.

6. Joe's cousin is the manager ~~of his high school's football team~~. (P.N.)

   Proof: The manager is Joe's cousin.

7. Jody's favorite part ~~of math~~ became fractions. (P.N.)

   Proof: Fractions became (are) Jody's favorite part (of math).

Name_______________________________

Date_______________________________

NOUNS
Predicate Nominatives

Directions: Cross out any prepositional phrase(s). Underline the subject once and the verb/verb phrase twice. Label any predicate nominative-P.N. Write the proof for the predicate nominative on the line provided.

1. A green precious gem is an emerald.

Proof: ____

2. The last person in the race was their teacher.

Proof: ____

3. A penguin is a flightless bird of the Southern Hemisphere.

Proof: ____

4. Janeen Holloway is the president of the Aviators' Club.

Proof: ____

5. Karen's favorite book remains Black Beauty.

Proof: ____

6. Joe's cousin is the manager of his high school's football team.

Proof: ____

7. Jody's favorite part of math became fractions.

Proof: ____

Name________________________________
WORKBOOK PAGE 129
Date________________________________

NOUNS
Direct Objects

Direct objects receive the action of the verb.

D.O.
Example: He bought a straw hat. The object he bought is a *hat*.

Sometimes, the direct object is compound (more than one).

D.O. **D.O.**
Example: Volunteers served strawberries and cream ~~at the fund raiser~~.

Directions: Cross out any prepositional phrase(s). Underline the subject once and the verb/verb phrase twice. Label any direct object-D.O.

1. Lynnsey received a puppy ~~for her birthday~~. (**D.O.** puppy)
2. Ida pushed a penny ~~across the table~~. (**D.O.** penny)
3. The librarian forgot her umbrella today. (**D.O.** umbrella)
4. That typist finished ten letters ~~in an hour~~. (**D.O.** letters)
5. Those pigeons ate all the food ~~in the dog's dish~~. (**D.O.** food)
6. Patty's mom plays tennis every day. (**D.O.** tennis)
7. We cleaned the bathroom and the kitchen. (**D.O.** bathroom, **D.O.** kitchen)
8. Are you buying new clothes ~~for vacation~~? (**D.O.** clothes)
9. Misty needed five stitches ~~in her knee~~. (**D.O.** stitches)
10. The girl ~~beside me~~ sings different tunes ~~to herself~~. (**D.O.** tunes)
11. Gloria wants a new bike and a chain lock ~~with a secret code~~. (**D.O.** bike, **D.O.** lock)
12. (You) Put these tapes and credit cards ~~in a safe place~~. (**D.O.** tapes, **D.O.** cards)

Name________________________________

Date________________________________

NOUNS
Direct Objects

Direct objects receive the action of the verb.

D.O.
Example: He bought a straw hat. The object he bought is a *hat*.

Sometimes, the direct object is compound (more than one).

D.O. D.O.
Example: Volunteers served strawberries and cream ~~at the fund raiser~~.

Directions: Cross out any prepositional phrase(s). Underline the subject once and the verb/verb phrase twice. Label any direct object-D.O.

1. Lynnsey received a puppy for her birthday.
2. Ida pushed a penny across the table.
3. The librarian forgot her umbrella today.
4. That typist finished ten letters in an hour.
5. Those pigeons ate all the food in the dog's dish.
6. Patty's mom plays tennis every day.
7. We cleaned the bathroom and the kitchen.
8. Are you buying new clothes for vacation?
9. Misty needed five stitches in her knee.
10. The girl beside me sings different tunes to herself.
11. Gloria wants a new bike and a chain lock with a secret code.
12. Put these tapes and credit cards in a safe place.

FOR THE TEACHER:
PAGE 245 = WORKBOOK PAGE 130

NOUNS

Indirect Objects

This concept is very difficult. It will be introduced here, reviewed during cumulative reviews, and reintroduced during the teaching of pronouns.

This concept will not be part of the unit test.

If students understand direct objects, they will find indirect objects less difficult.

Students need to understand that in order to have an indirect object, a direct object must be present in the sentence. (This can be confusing because most sentences with direct objects do not contain an indirect object.)

You will teach students that either ***to*** or ***for*** must be inserted **mentally** before a noun in order for that noun to function as an indirect object. If ***to*** or ***for*** is written, a prepositional phrase occurs.

Example: Jamie gave his sister a lizard.

to **I.O. D.O.**
Jamie gave / his sister a lizard.

Jamie gave a lizard to Mia. — to Mia = prepositional phrase
There is no indirect object.

STEPS FOR TEACHING INDIRECT OBJECTS:

1. Ask students to cross out any prepositional phrase(s).
2. Ask students to underline the subject once.
3. Ask students to underline the verb/verb phrase twice.
4. Ask students to label the direct object.
5. Search for a noun in front of which either ***to*** or ***for*** can be inserted mentally. The placement may be before an adjective or several adjectives.

to **I.O. D.O.**
Example: Joyce handed /the bus driver two quarters.

for **I.O. D.O.**
The chef baked /the daughter ~~of the owner~~ a carrot cake.

NOUNS

Indirect Objects

The indirect object is the receiver of some direct objects.

Example: He handed the clerk ten dollars.

I.O. D.O.
He handed the **clerk** ten dollars.

RULES FOR INDIRECT OBJECTS:

1. In order to have an indirect object in the sentence, you must have a direct object.

2. You must be able to insert ***to*** or ***for*** **mentally** in front of an indirect object.

to **I.O.** **D.O.**
Examples: The hotel clerk handed / the guest his key.

for **I.O.** **D.O.**
Mr. Jackson prepared/ the family his famous chili.

NOTE: If *to* or *for* is actually **written** in the sentence, the noun is not an indirect object.
Example: Mr. Jackson made his famous chili **for** his family.

A. A sentence containing a direct object does not always contain an indirect object.

D.O.
Examples: The florist delivered flowers. (no indirect object)

I.O. **D.O.**
The florist delivered Hannah flowers. (indirect object)

B. Some sentences may contain compound indirect objects.

I.O. **I.O.** **D.O.**
Example: Ty's mother made Ginger and her brother some fudge.

Name________________________________ **NOUNS**

WORKBOOK PAGE 131 **Indirect Objects**

Date________________________________

Directions: Read each sentence. Decide if you could **mentally** insert *to* or *for* above the slash (/). Write *to* or *for*, whichever makes sense, on the line.

to
1. Bill handed / Mrs. Johnson papers.

for
2. Aunt Vestal has quilted / her niece a small blanket.

to
3. Dad handed / Mom a wrench for the sink.

for
4. That graphic artist designed / the company a logo.

to
5. The usher handed / Jerry and Nicki colorful programs.

Directions: Cross out any prepositional phrase(s). Underline the subject once and the verb/verb phrase twice. Label a direct object-D.O. and an indirect object-I.O.

I.O. D.O.
Example: The mayor presented her the key ~~to the city~~.

I.O. D.O.
1. Bill handed Mrs. Johnson papers.

I.O. D.O.
2. Aunt Vestal has quilted her nieces a small blanket.

I.O. D.O.
3. Dad handed Mom a wrench ~~for the sink~~.

I.O. D.O.
4. That graphic artist designed the company a logo.

I.O. I.O. D.O.
5. The usher handed Jerry and Nicki colorful programs.

Name________________________________

Date________________________________

NOUNS
Indirect Objects

Directions: Read each sentence. Decide if you could **mentally** insert *to* or *for* above the slash (/). Write *to* or *for*, whichever makes sense, on the line.

1. Bill handed / Mrs. Johnson papers.

2. Aunt Vestal has quilted / her niece a small blanket.

3. Dad handed / Mom a wrench for the sink.

4. That graphic artist designed / the company a logo.

5. The usher handed / Jerry and Nicki colorful programs.

Directions: Cross out any prepositional phrase(s). Underline the subject once and the verb/verb phrase twice. Label a direct object-D.O. and an indirect object-I.O.

I.O. D.O.

Example: The mayor presented her the key ~~to the city~~.

1. Bill handed Mrs. Johnson papers.

2. Aunt Vestal has quilted her niece a small blanket.

3. Dad handed Mom a wrench for the sink.

4. That graphic artist designed the company a logo.

5. The usher handed Jerry and Nicki colorful programs.

Name_______________________________

WORKBOOK PAGE 132

Date_______________________________

NOUNS
Indirect Objects

Directions: Read each sentence. Decide if you could mentally insert *to* or *for* above the slash (/). Write *to* or *for*, whichever makes sense, on the line.

for
1. That company provides / its salespeople a car.

to
2. Miss Anders sent / her nephew a statue from Peru.

to
3. The parcel service delivers / Dad packages of books.

for
4. His sister baked / her church group some brownies.

for
5. Marshall makes / his family breakfast every morning.

Directions: Cross out any prepositional phrase(s). Underline the subject once and the verb/verb phrase twice. Label a direct object-D.O. and an indirect object-I.O.

I.O. D.O.
Example: Ken ironed Melissa a blouse.

I.O. D.O.
1. That company provides its salespeople a car.

I.O. D.O.
2. Miss Anders sent her nephew a statue ~~from Peru~~.

I.O. D.O.
3. The parcel service delivers Dad packages ~~of books~~.

I.O. D.O.
4. His sister baked her church group some brownies.

I.O. D.O.
5. Marshall makes his family breakfast every morning.

Name________________________________

Date________________________________

NOUNS
Indirect Objects

Directions: Read each sentence. Decide if you could mentally insert *to* or *for* above the slash (/). Write *to* or *for*, whichever makes sense, on the line.

1. That company provides / its salespeople a car.

2. Miss Anders sent / her nephew a statue from Peru.

3. The parcel service delivers / Dad packages of books.

4. His sister baked / her church group some brownies.

5. Marshall makes / his family breakfast every morning.

Directions: Cross out any prepositional phrase(s). Underline the subject once and the verb/verb phrase twice. Label a direct object-D.O. and an indirect object-I.O.

I.O. **D.O.**

Example: Ken ironed Melissa a blouse.

1. That company provides its salespeople a car.

2. Miss Anders sent her nephew a statue from Peru.

3. The parcel service delivers Dad packages of books.

4. His sister baked her church group some brownies.

5. Marshall makes his family breakfast every morning.

Name________________________________ **NOUNS**
WORKBOOK PAGE 133 **Indirect Objects**
Date________________________________

Directions: Cross out any prepositional phrase(s). Underline the subject once and the verb/verb phrase twice. Label a direct object-D.O. and an indirect object-I.O.

I.O. D.O.
Example: The clown gave the children some popcorn.

I.O. D.O.
1. Sandy gave her friend a bracelet.

I.O. D.O.
2. The waitress handed Mom the bill.

I.O. D.O.
3. Scott gave Jill a ring ~~for an engagement present~~.

I.O. D.O.
4. The girl ~~in the back row~~ passes her friends notes.

I.O. D.O.
5. That barber gives his customers free combs.

I.O. D.O.
6. I shall bake my friends a cherry cake ~~with cream cheese icing~~.

I.O. D.O.
7. A zoo keeper fed the lions their daily food.

I.O. D.O.
8. The coach gave each boy a trophy.

I.O D.O.
9. A carnival attendant handed the boy three balls ~~for the game~~.

I.O. D.O.
10. (You) Hand the food seller this dollar ~~for a cola~~.

Name________________________________

Date________________________________

NOUNS
Indirect Objects

Directions: Cross out any prepositional phrase(s). Underline the subject once and the verb/verb phrase twice. Label a direct object-D.O. and an indirect object-I.O.

I.O. **D.O.**

Example: The clown gave the children some popcorn.

1. Sandy gave her friend a bracelet.

2. The waitress handed Mom the bill.

3. Scott gave Jill a ring for an engagement present.

4. The girl in the back row passes her friends notes.

5. That barber gives his customers free combs.

6. I shall bake my friends a cherry cake with cream cheese icing.

7. A zoo keeper fed the lions their daily food.

8. The coach gave each boy a trophy.

9. A carnival attendant handed the boy three balls for the game.

10. Hand the food seller this dollar for a cola.

Name_______________________________

NOUN REVIEW

WORKBOOK PAGE 134

Date_______________________________

Be sure to discuss answers with students.

Each page has a space for a name if you wish to span the review over a few days.

A. Directions: Write A if the noun is abstract; write C if the noun is concrete.

1. __C__ sock
2. __C__ brick
3. __A__ hope
4. __C__ polish
5. __C__ tin
6. __A__ love
7. __C__ blossom
8. __C__ air

B. Directions: Write C if the noun is common; write P if the noun is proper.

1. __C__ BIRD
2. __C__ ROBIN
3. __C__ BUILDING
4. __C__ SCHOOL
5. __P__ LINCOLN SCHOOL
6. __P__ GOLDEN GATE BRIDGE
7. __C__ BOOK
8. __P__ ROANOKE ISLAND

C. Directions: Write A if the underlined word serves as an adjective (describing word); write N if the underlined word serves as a noun.

1. __N__ They enjoy working on their computer.
2. __A__ Mrs. Jamison is a computer programmer.
3. __N__ Please sit on the carpet and talk to us.
4. __A__ Grandmother has an antique carpet beater.
5. __A__ The young woman wore a striped hair band.
6. __N__ Her hair had been dyed a golden blonde with brown highlights.
7. __A__ The ceiling fan helps to cool the house in the summer.
8. __N__ Some flies were walking across the ceiling of the old shed.

Name________________________________ **NOUN REVIEW**

Date________________________________

A. Directions: Write A if the noun is abstract; write C if the noun is concrete.

1. _____	sock	5. _____	tin
2. _____	brick	6. _____	love
3. _____	hope	7. _____	blossom
4. _____	polish	8. _____	air

B. Directions: Write C if the noun is common; write P if the noun is proper.

1. _____	BIRD	5. _____	LINCOLN SCHOOL
2. _____	ROBIN	6. _____	GOLDEN GATE BRIDGE
3. _____	BUILDING	7. _____	BOOK
4. _____	SCHOOL	8. _____	ROANOKE ISLAND

C. Directions: Write A if the underlined word serves as an adjective (describing word); write N if the underlined word serves as a noun.

1. _____ They enjoy working on their computer.
2. _____ Mrs. Jamison is a computer programmer.
3. _____ Please sit on the carpet and talk to us.
4. _____ Grandmother has an antique carpet beater.
5. _____ The young woman wore a striped hair band.
6. _____ Her hair had been dyed a golden blonde with brown highlights.
7. _____ The ceiling fan helps to cool the house in the summer.
8. _____ Some flies were walking across the ceiling of the old shed.

Name________________________________ **NOUN REVIEW**

WORKBOOK PAGE 135

Date________________________________

D. Directions: Write V if the underlined word serves as a verb; write N if the underlined word serves as a noun.

1. __N__ The man began his washing after he came home from work.
2. __V__ Are you washing the floors before you leave for vacation?
3. __N__ Mr. and Mrs. Fisher enjoyed the talk about New Zealand.
4. __V__ Did Congressman Keats talk to the class today?

E. Directions: Write the plural:

1. fence - fences
2. eyelash - eyelashes
3. half - halves
4. mix - mixes
5. boy - boys
6. library - libraries
7. list - lists
8. hunch - hunches
9. moose - moose
10. peach - peaches

F. Directions: Write the possessive form.

1. a net belonging to a fisherman: fisherman's net
2. food belonging to James: James's food
3. a vase for some flowers: flowers' vase
4. a herd of cattle led by ranchers: ranchers' herd (of cattle)
5. kittens belonging to an elderly lady: an elderly lady's kittens
6. a company owned by five men: (five) men's company

Name________________________________ **NOUN REVIEW**

Date________________________________

D. Directions: Write V if the underlined word serves as a verb; write N if the underlined word serves as a noun.

1. _____ The man began his washing after he came home from work.

2. _____ Are you washing the floors before you leave for vacation?

3. _____ Mr. and Mrs. Fisher enjoyed the talk about New Zealand.

4. _____ Did Congressman Keats talk to the class today?

E. Write the plural:

1. fence - ____________________
2. eyelash - ____________________
3. half - ____________________
4. mix - ____________________
5. boy - ____________________
6. library - ____________________
7. list - ____________________
8. hunch - ____________________
9. moose - ____________________
10. peach - ____________________

F. Directions: Write the possessive form.

1. a net belonging to a fisherman: ______________________________

2. food belonging to James: ______________________________

3. a vase for some flowers: ______________________________

4. a herd of cattle led by ranchers: ______________________________

5. kittens belonging to an elderly lady: ______________________________

6. a company owned by five men: ______________________________

Name______________________________ **NOUN REVIEW**

WORKBOOK PAGE 136

Date______________________________

G. Directions: Write the determiner and the noun in the space provided.

Determiners will be italicized; nouns will be in boldface.

1. My relatives live there. _*My* **relatives**_
2. Jennifer's professor is coming. _***Jennifer's**** **professor**_
   *This is a possessive noun that serves as a determining adjective.
3. Have you seen a pyramid? _*a* **pyramid**_
4. Many cases had been decided. _*Many* **cases**_
5. That suitcase is new. _*That* **suitcase**_
6. I would like two brownies. _*two* **brownies**_
7. He sold me these boots. _*these* **boots**_

H. Directions: Box any nouns.

Nouns are in bold print.

1. **Jeremy** placed two **straws** in his **soda**.
2. His **mother** wiped the **stain** from the **jacket**.
3. Two tall **trees** with white **lights** stood in ceramic **containers**.
4. Several silk **ties** were reduced to ten **dollars** at the department **store**.
5. Her **love** for her **children** is shown in her kind **speech** and **gentleness**.
6. The **grocer** delivers our **milk** and **bread** to our **home** each **week**.

Name________________________________

Date________________________________

NOUN REVIEW

G. Directions: Write the determiner and the noun in the space provided.

1. My relatives live there. ________________________________
2. Jennifer's professor is coming. ________________________________
3. Have you seen a pyramid? ________________________________
4. Many cases had been decided. ________________________________
5. That suitcase is new. ________________________________
6. I would like two brownies. ________________________________
7. He sold me these boots. ________________________________

H. Directions: Box any nouns.

1. Jeremy placed two straws in his soda.
2. His mother wiped the stain from the jacket.
3. Two tall trees with white lights stood in ceramic containers.
4. Several silk ties were reduced to ten dollars at the department store.
5. Her love for her children is shown in her kind speech and gentleness.
6. The grocer delivers our milk and bread to our home each week.

Name______________________________
WORKBOOK PAGE 137
Date______________________________

CUMULATIVE REVIEW

A. Directions: List 50 prepositions. **Students should list any 50.**

1. about
2. above
3. across
4. after
5. against
6. along
7. amid
8. among
9. around
10. at
11. atop
12. before
13. behind
14. below
15. beneath
16. beside
17. between
18. beyond
19. but (except)
20. by
21. concerning
22. down
23. during
24. except
25. for
26. from
27. in
28. inside
29. into
30. like
31. near
32. of
33. off
34. on
35. onto
36. out
37. outside
38. over
39. past
40. regarding
41. since
42. through
43. throughout
44. to
45. toward
46. under
47. underneath
48. until
49. up
50. upon

with, within, without

B. Directions: Cross out any prepositional phrase(s). Underline the subject once and the verb/verb phrase twice.

1. A scarf was wrapped ~~around her head~~.

2. ~~During the dust storm~~, some cars did *not* pull ~~off the road~~.

3. He walked in ~~among the fans~~ and sat down.

4. Jonathan and his mom waited ~~at the airport~~ ~~for two hours~~.

5. One ~~of the workers~~ had gone ~~to a local market~~ (*to buy*) chips.

Name_______________________________ **CUMULATIVE REVIEW**

Date_______________________________

A. Directions: List 50 prepositions.

1. ____________	14. ____________	27. ____________	40. ____________
2. ____________	15. ____________	28. ____________	41. ____________
3. ____________	16. ____________	29. ____________	42. ____________
4. ____________	17. ____________	30. ____________	43. ____________
5. ____________	18. ____________	31. ____________	44. ____________
6. ____________	19. ____________	32. ____________	45. ____________
7. ____________	20. ____________	33. ____________	46. ____________
8. ____________	21. ____________	34. ____________	47. ____________
9. ____________	22. ____________	35. ____________	48. ____________
10. ____________	23. ____________	36. ____________	49. ____________
11. ____________	24. ____________	37. ____________	50. ____________
12. ____________	25. ____________	38. ____________	
13. ____________	26. ____________	39. ____________	

B. Directions: Cross out any prepositional phrase(s). Underline the subject once and the verb/verb phrase twice.

1. A scarf was wrapped around her head.
2. During the dust storm, some cars did not pull off the road.
3. He walked in among the fans and sat down.
4. Jonathan and his mom waited at the airport for two hours.
5. One of the workers had gone to a local market to buy chips.

Name________________________________ **CUMULATIVE REVIEW**

WORKBOOK PAGE 138

Date________________________________

C. Directions: List the 23 helping (auxiliary) verbs:

do, does, did **have, has, had** **may, must, might**

should, would, could **shall, will, can** **is, am, are, was, were, be, being, been**

D. Directions: Cross out any prepositional phrase(s). Underline the subject once and the verb/verb phrase twice. Label any direct object-D.O.

1. A clerk dropped a dollar (D.O.) ~~on the floor~~
2. Sean wants a puppy (D.O.) ~~for his birthday~~.
3. Their dentist gave toothbrushes (D.O.) ~~to them~~.
4. Millicent sings lullabies (D.O.) ~~to her baby at night~~.
5. The butler showed the guests (D.O.) ~~to the huge dining room~~.
6. The masons finished the wall (D.O.) ~~after sundown~~.
7. (You) Please empty that trash can (D.O.) ~~into the huge dumpster~~.

E. Directions: Cross out any prepositional phrase(s). Underline the subject once and the verb/verb phrase twice.

1. The French designer has (chose, chosen) a new print.
2. His brother has (ridden, rode) his motorcycle today.
3. They had (swam, swum) ~~across the pool~~ three times.
4. Have you (drank, drunk) ~~from this cup~~?
5. Jacob's meal had been (brought, brung) ~~to him~~.
6. The city bus should have (come, came) ~~by noon~~

Name________________________________ **CUMULATIVE REVIEW**

Date________________________________

C. Directions: List the 23 helping (auxiliary) verbs:

____

____

____

D. Directions: Cross out any prepositional phrase(s). Underline the subject once and the verb/verb phrase twice. Label any direct object-D.O.

1. A clerk dropped a dollar on the floor.
2. Sean wants a puppy for his birthday.
3. Their dentist gave toothbrushes to them.
4. Millicent sings lullabies to her baby at night.
5. The butler showed the guests to the huge dining room.
6. The masons finished the wall after sundown.
7. Please empty that trash can into the huge dumpster.

E. Directions: Cross out any prepositional phrase(s). Underline the subject once and the verb/verb phrase twice.

1. The French designer has (chose, chosen) a new print.
2. His brother has (ridden, rode) his motorcycle today.
3. They had (swam, swum) across the pool three times.
4. Have you (drank, drunk) from this cup?
5. Jacob's meal had been (brought, brung) to him.
6. The city bus should have (come, came) by noon.

Name________________________________ **CUMULATIVE REVIEW**
WORKBOOK PAGE 139
Date________________________________

F. Directions: Cross out any prepositional phrase(s). Underline the subject once and the verb/verb phrase twice.

1. The listener (sits, sets) ~~with his hands~~ ~~on his head~~.

D.O.
2. A tourist (lay, laid) his camera ~~on the seat~~ ~~of the bus~~.

D.O.
3. (You) (Sit, Set) your foot ~~on this board~~.

4. Those cinnamon buns are (raising, rising) ~~in the pantry~~.

5. Her robe is (lying, laying) ~~by the bed~~.

6. Charlotte (lies, lays) ~~on a hammock~~ often.

D.O.
7. Has Mr. Charter (raised, risen) money ~~for his club~~?

8. Those triplets have (laid, lain) ~~on a raft~~ ~~in the water~~ ~~for an hour~~.

G. Directions: List the 20 linking verbs (12 infinitives + 8):
to feel, to taste, to look, to smell, to become, to seem, to sound, to grow, to remain, to appear, to stay, to be
is, am, are, was, were, be, being, been

H. Directions: Cross out any prepositional phrase(s). Underline the subject once and the verb twice. Write A if the verb is action; write L if the verb is linking.
Remember: If you can place *is, am, are, was,* or *were* above the verb without changing the sentence meaning, it is usually a linking verb.

was
Example: __L__ His aunt became a journalist.

was
1. __L__ The sea remained calm ~~throughout the day~~.

2. __A__ That child smelled the flowers ~~along the path~~.

is
3. __L__ My Mexican food tastes too hot ~~for me~~ (*to eat*).

4. __A__ The witness answered all the questions quietly.

Name________________________________ **CUMULATIVE REVIEW**

Date________________________________

F. Directions: Cross out any prepositional phrase(s). Underline the subject once and the verb/verb phrase twice.

1. The listener (sits, sets) with his hands on his head.
2. A tourist (lay, laid) his camera on the seat of the bus.
3. (Sit, Set) your foot on this board.
4. Those cinnamon buns are (raising, rising) in the pantry.
5. Her robe is (lying, laying) by the bed.
6. Charlotte (lies, lays) on a hammock often.
7. Has Mr. Charter (raised, risen) money for his club?
8. Those triplets have (laid, lain) on a raft in the water for an hour.

G. Directions: List the 20 linking verbs (12 infinitives + 8):

____

____

H. Directions: Cross out any prepositional phrase(s). Underline the subject once and the verb twice. Write A if the verb is action; write L if the verb is linking.

Remember: If you can place *is*, *am*, *are*, *was*, or *were* above the verb without changing the sentence meaning, it is usually a linking verb.

was

Example: __L__ His aunt became a journalist.

1. _____ The sea remained calm throughout the day.
2. _____ That child smelled the flowers along the path.
3. _____ My Mexican food tastes too hot for me to eat.
4. _____ The witness answered all the questions quietly.

Name________________________________ **CUMULATIVE REVIEW**

WORKBOOK PAGE 140

Date________________________________

Note: You may need to provide examples for students. These exercises are difficult. You also may wish to do them orally. Be sure to discuss each part.

I. Directions: Cross out any prepositional phrase(s). Underline the subject once and the verb/verb phrase twice. Label any predicate nominative-P.N. Write the proof on the line.

P.N.
1. Margaret was the leader ~~of her club~~.

Proof: The leader was Margaret.

P.N.
2. Her best friend is the boy ~~in the red sweater~~.

Proof: The boy is her best friend.

P.N.
3. *Spring Party* ~~by Janet Fish~~ became Mom's favorite artwork.

Proof: Mom's favorite artwork (became) is *Spring Party.*

P.N.
4. Mr. Sanders remained the president ~~of that organization~~ ~~for four years~~.

Proof: The president (remained) was Mr. Sanders.

J. Directions: Cross out any prepositional phrase(s). Underline the subject once and the verb twice. Label any predicate adjective-P.A. Write the predicate adjective and the subject of the sentence on the line provided.

P.A.
1. The little red wagon is old. old wagon

P.A.
2. Her ruffled blouse is white. white blouse

P.A.
3. His shirt is blue ~~with green stripes~~. blue shirt

4. Those boys ~~in black jackets~~ seem
P.A.
nervous ~~about their performance~~. nervous boys

Name________________________________

Date________________________________

CUMULATIVE REVIEW

I. Directions: Cross out any prepositional phrase(s). Underline the subject once and the verb/verb phrase twice. Label any predicate nominative-P.N. Write the proof on the line.

1. Margaret was the leader of her club.

   Proof: ____

2. Her best friend is the boy in the red sweater.

   Proof: ____

3. *Spring Party* by Janet Fish became Mom's favorite artwork.

   Proof: ____

4. Mr. Sanders remained the president of that organization for four years.

   Proof: ____

J. Directions: Cross out any prepositional phrase(s). Underline the subject once and the verb twice. Label any predicate adjective-P.A. Write the predicate adjective and the subject of the sentence on the line provided.

1. The little red wagon is old. ______________________________

2. Her ruffled blouse is white. ______________________________

3. His shirt is blue with green stripes. ______________________________

4. Those boys in black jackets seem nervous about their performance. ______________________________

Name________________________________ **CUMULATIVE REVIEW**

WORKBOOK PAGE 141

Date________________________________

K. Directions: Write the contraction:

1. it is - it's
2. we are - we're
3. will not - won't
4. what is - what's
5. cannot - can't
6. he would - he'd
7. you will - you'll
8. I have - I've
9. could not - couldn't
10. I will - I'll

L. Directions: Cross out any prepositional phrase(s). Underline the subject once and the verb/verb phrase twice. Determine the tense and write *present*, *past*, or *future* in the space provided.

1. future — I shall *not* decide ~~until Monday~~.
2. present — The patient reads magazines ~~in the doctor's office~~.
3. past — A grocery clerk handed us our bags.
4. present — We watch whales ~~from a pier~~.
5. past — Lance and Stephani made pizza ~~for everyone~~.
6. present — That real estate agent sells homes ~~in my area~~.
7. future — Cy's family will never forget their trip ~~to Arkansas~~.

M. Directions: Write *conj.* above any conjunction; write *intj.* above any interjection.

1. **Wow!** (intj.) Andy **and** (conj.) I had never seen an Egyptian tomb **or** (conj.) a mummy!
2. **Yikes!** (intj.) This cliff is steep, **but** (conj.) we will make it!

Name_______________________________ **CUMULATIVE REVIEW**

Date_______________________________

K. Directions: Write the contraction.

1. it is - ______________________
2. we are - ______________________
3. will not - ______________________
4. what is - ______________________
5. cannot - ______________________
6. he would - ______________________
7. you will - ______________________
8. I have - ______________________
9. could not - ______________________
10. I will - ______________________

L. Directions: Cross out any prepositional phrase(s). Underline the subject once and the verb/verb phrase twice. Determine the tense and write *present*, *past*, or *future* in the space provided.

1. ______________________ I shall not decide until Monday.
2. ______________________ The patient reads magazines in the doctor's office.
3. ______________________ A grocery clerk handed us our bags.
4. ______________________ We watch whales from a pier.
5. ______________________ Lance and Stephani made pizza for everyone.
6. ______________________ That real estate agent sells homes in my area.
7. ______________________ Cy's family will never forget their trip to Arkansas.

M. Directions: Write *conj.* above any conjunction; write *intj.* above any interjection.

1. Wow! Andy and I had never seen an Egyptian tomb or a mummy!
2. Yikes! This cliff is steep, but we will make it.

Name________________________________ **NOUN TEST**

WORKBOOK PAGE 323

Date________________________________

A. Directions: Write A if the noun is abstract; write C if the noun is concrete.

1. __A__ grace
2. __C__ ladder
3. __C__ marshmallow
4. __A__ safety
5. __C__ bulb
6. __A__ happiness
7. __C__ window
8. __C__ air
9. __C__ pamphlet
10. __A__ patience

B. Directions: Write C if the noun is common; write P if the noun is proper.

1. __P__ LONDON BRIDGE
2. __C__ SOUP
3. __C__ SNAKE
4. __C__ COPPERHEAD SNAKE
5. __P__ PHOENIX ART MUSEUM
6. __C__ MUSEUM
7. __C__ PLUM
8. __P__ SENATOR JONES
9. __C__ FRUIT
10. __P__ MEXICO

C. Directions: Write A if the underlined word serves as an adjective (describing word); write N if the word serves as a noun.

1. __N__ The dog chewed a bone.
2. __A__ This catalog offers bone china.
3. __A__ The cave explorer has arrived.
4. __N__ Would you like to visit a cave in Kentucky?

Name________________________________

NOUN TEST

Date________________________________

A. Directions: Write A if the noun is abstract; write C if the noun is concrete.

1. _____ grace
2. _____ ladder
3. _____ marshmallow
4. _____ safety
5. _____ bulb
6. _____ happiness
7. _____ window
8. _____ air
9. _____ pamphlet
10. _____ patience

B. Directions: Write C if the noun is common; write P if the noun is proper.

1. _____ LONDON BRIDGE
2. _____ SOUP
3. _____ SNAKE
4. _____ COPPERHEAD SNAKE
5. _____ PHOENIX ART MUSEUM
6. _____ MUSEUM
7. _____ PLUM
8. _____ SENATOR JONES
9. _____ FRUIT
10. _____ MEXICO

C. Directions: Write A if the underlined word serves as an adjective (describing word); write N if the word serves as a noun.

1. _____ The dog chewed a bone.
2. _____ This catalog offers bone china.
3. _____ The cave explorer has arrived.
4. _____ Would you like to visit a cave in Kentucky?

WORKBOOK PAGE 324

D. Directions: Write V if the underlined word serves as a verb; write N if the underlined word serves as a noun.

1. ___V___ The girls laugh together often.

2. ___N___ My laugh is soft but funny.

3. ___N___ They made a paste from flour and water.

4. ___V___ Paste this magazine picture on the white paper.

E. Directions: Write the possessive form.

1. a chicken belonging to Susie: ___Susie's chicken___

2. books belonging to that boy: ___boy's books___

3. parents belonging to Chris: ___Chris's parents___

4. a playground belonging to children: ___children's playground___

5. a horse path for riders: ___riders' (horse) path___

6. a master of more than one ox: ___oxen's master___

F. Directions: Write the plural form:

1. dash - ___dashes___

2. fly - ___flies___

3. sock - ___socks___

4. leaf - ___leaves___

5. bench - ___benches___

6. box - ___boxes___

7. toy - ___toys___

8. table - ___tables___

9. pass - ___passes___

10. sheep - ___sheep___

D. Directions: Write V if the underlined word serves as a verb; write N if the underlined word serves as a noun.

1. _____ The girls laugh together often.

2. _____ My laugh is soft but funny.

3. _____ They made a paste from flour and water.

4. _____ Paste this magazine picture on the white paper.

E. Directions: Write the possessive form.

1. a chicken belonging to Susie: ______________________________

2. books belonging to that boy: ______________________________

3. parents belonging to Chris: ______________________________

4. a playground belonging to children: ______________________________

5. a horse path for riders: ______________________________

6. a master of more than one ox: ______________________________

F. Directions: Write the plural form:

1. dash - ____________________
2. fly - ____________________
3. sock - ____________________
4. leaf - ____________________
5. bench - ____________________
6. box - ____________________
7. toy - ____________________
8. table - ____________________
9. pass - ____________________
10. sheep - ____________________

WORKBOOK PAGE 325

G. Directions: Write the determiner and the noun in the space provided.

1. Some wild geese flew overhead. Some (wild) geese
2. He ate three bread sticks. Three (bread) sticks
3. Give me your money, please. your money
4. They didn't like the movie. the movie
5. Arnie's uncle left today. Arnie's uncle

H. Directions: Box any noun.

Nouns are in boldfaced print.

1. The **volunteers** picked up some **garbage** in the **alley**.
2. The **man** had thirteen **stitches** in his right **leg**.
3. Several **actors** perform on a **stage** without a **microphone**.
4. An **elephant** walked through the **jungle** during a **rainstorm**.
5. **Jimmy's** roller **blades** and his **bike** are on a **pile** beside the **garage**.
6. Their **aunt** made apple **pies**, a **cake**, and **punch** for the **party**.
7. **Carla** showed her **concern** for the **child** with a gentle **hug**.
8. **Grandma** showed **pictures** of her **friends' homes** in **Denver.**
9. Many **bugs** were crawling in our **flowers** by those **sheds**.
10. Your **love** for the **outdoors** was shown during that camping **trip**.

G. Directions: Write the determiner and the noun in the space provided.

1. Some wild geese flew overhead. ______________________

2. He ate three bread sticks. ______________________

3. Give me your money, please. ______________________

4. They didn't like the movie. ______________________

5. Arnie's uncle left today. ______________________

H. Directions: Box any noun.

1. The volunteers picked up some garbage in the alley.
2. The man had thirteen stitches in his right leg.
3. Several actors perform on a stage without a microphone.
4. An elephant walked through the jungle during a rainstorm.
5. Jimmy's roller blades and his bike are on a pile beside the garage.
6. Their aunt made apple pies, a cake, and punch for the party.
7. Carla showed her concern for the child with a gentle hug.
8. Grandma showed pictures of her friends' homes in Denver.
9. Many bugs were crawling in our flowers by those sheds.
10. Your love for the outdoors was shown during that camping trip.

Name________________________________

WORKBOOK PAGE 326

Date________________________________

CUMULATIVE TEST
Nouns

A. Directions: Cross out any prepositional phrase(s). Underline the subject once and the verb twice.

1. Two children dashed ~~up the hill~~ ~~in a race~~.
2. Everyone ~~except the mother~~ ~~of the bride~~ was ready.
3. ~~Underneath the palm tree~~ sat a beachcomber.
4. The car backed out ~~of the driveway~~ very slowly.
5. One ~~of the puppets~~ has brown hair ~~with red bows~~.
6. The band director and music teacher sing ~~in our church choir~~.
7. (You) Take this bag ~~of popcorn~~ ~~to the baseball game~~ tonight.

B. Directions: Cross out any prepositional phrase(s). Underline the subject once and the verb/verb phrase twice. Label any direct object -D.O.

D.O.

1. A burglar ~~in a white car~~ had (stole, stolen) a television.
2. One ~~of the bags~~ has (broke, broken) ~~at the bottom~~.

D.O.

3. Mrs. Jansen had (laid, lay) the dress ~~in the box~~.
4. The pilot must have (flown, flew) ~~to Turkey~~.

D.O.

5. My brother might have (ate, eaten) the roast beef sandwich.
6. Darla's mother has (risen, rose) ~~to a supervisor~~ ~~in the company~~.

C. Directions: Cross out any prepositional phrase(s). Underline the subject once and the verb/verb phrase twice. Write the tense, *present*, *past*, or *future*, in the space provided.

1. present   His sister teaches their dog tricks.
2. past   Mr. Jacobson fell ~~into the pool~~ recently.
3. future   The soccer players will practice ~~before the game~~.
4. present   Two wrestlers are ~~in the state championship~~.
5. present   Some shrubs and flowers grow better ~~in the shade~~.

Name______________________________

Date______________________________

CUMULATIVE TEST
Nouns

A. Directions: Cross out any prepositional phrase(s). Underline the subject once and the verb twice.

1. Two children dashed up the hill in a race.

2. Everyone except the mother of the bride was ready.

3. Underneath the palm tree sat a beachcomber.

4. The car backed out of the driveway very slowly.

5. One of the puppets has brown hair with red bows.

6. The band director and music teacher sing in our church choir.

7. Take this bag of popcorn to the baseball game tonight.

B. Directions: Cross out any prepositional phrase(s). Underline the subject once and the verb/verb phrase twice. Label any direct object -D.O.

1. A burglar in a white car had (stole, stolen) a television.

2. One of the bags has (broke, broken) at the bottom.

3. Mrs. Jansen had (laid, lay) the dress in the box.

4. The pilot must have (flown, flew) to Turkey.

5. My brother might have (ate, eaten) the roast beef sandwich.

6. Darla's mother has (risen, rose) to a supervisor in the company.

C. Directions: Cross out any prepositional phrase(s). Underline the subject once and the verb/verb phrase twice.Write the tense, *present*, *past*, or *future*, in the space provided.

1. ______________ His sister teaches their dog tricks.
2. ______________ Mr. Jacobson fell into the pool recently.
3. ______________ The soccer players will practice before the game.
4. ______________ Two wrestlers are in the state championship.
5. ______________ Some shrubs and flowers grow better in the shade.

FOR THE TEACHER:
PAGE 277 = WORKBOOK PAGE 142

REMINDER:

You may teach the capitalization unit when you wish.*

You may teach the punctuation unit when you wish.*

You may teach friendly letter when appropriate.

You may teach sentence types when appropriate.

You may wish to teach sentences, fragments, and run-ons when appropriate.

A section entitled IMPORTANT WORDS may be taught when you wish. However, you may want to teach this section before the adjective unit or immediately after it.
IMPORTANT WORDS includes exercises dealing with:
may and can
their, they're, and there
to, two, and too

When you return to parts of speech, teach those concepts in order. For example, do not teach pronouns before adjectives. Sequence is important.

***Daily Grams at your grade level is highly recommended. Students are provided with daily capitalization and punctuation reviews. See the last page of this book.**

ADJECTIVES

There are two general types of adjectives: descriptive adjectives and limiting adjectives.

A. Descriptive adjectives are describing words. They often tell what kind.

Examples:	**pumpkin** pie	What kind of pie?	pumpkin pie
	soft, **velvet** dress	What kind of dress?	soft dress velvet dress
	red sponge ball	What kind of ball?	red ball sponge ball

B. Limiting adjectives include determiners. Determiners are actually called determining adjectives. These must be memorized and learned.

1. **Determining adjectives**:

   a. Articles: **a**, **an**, **the**
   b. Demonstratives: **this**, **that**, **those**, **these**
   c. **Numbers**: twenty-five days third base
   d. Possessive pronouns (used as adjectives): **my**, **his**, **her**, **its**, **your**, **our**, **their**
   e. **Possessive nouns** (used as adjectives): Niki's cow teachers' meeting
   f. Indefinites: **many**, **some**, **few**, **several**, **no**, **any**...

2. In order to be a determining adjective, a noun must follow it. A determining (also called limiting) adjective modifies a noun. Modifies means *goes over to.*

   Examples: Several laser printers were purchased.

   Several is an adjective because it modifies or goes over to printers. (*Several* what? several printers)

   She had been hired as an architect.

   An is an adjective because it modifies or goes over to architect. (a/*an* what? an architect)

When a word that may serve as a limiting adjective does not modify a noun, that word serves as a pronoun.

That is funny? *That* is not an adjective. *That* what? We don't know; there is no noun. Therefore, *that* is a pronoun.

Name________________________________
WORKBOOK PAGE 143
Date_________________________________

ADJECTIVES
Limiting Adjectives

Directions: In the space provided, write the italicized limiting adjective(s) with the noun that it modifies (goes to).

Example: Do you have *any* paper? any paper

1. *Two* alligators swam through deep water. two alligators
2. Do you have a *few* dollars to loan me? few dollars
3. Please bring *your* swimsuit with you. your swimsuit
4. A *boys'* club was begun there. boys' club
5. Has Mrs. Little seen *these* new shoes? these shoes
6. They floated down *the* river on rafts. the river
7. *An* apple is filled with pectin. An apple
8. Sometimes, he has *no* patience. no patience
9. Hand me *that* basket of fruit, please. that basket
10. *His* jeep is in *the* parking lot. His jeep
    the lot
11. *Jay's* toads are in *a* special garden. Jay's toads
    a garden
12. Have you seen *my* binoculars? my binoculars
13. Chad paid *fifteen* dollars for *a* ticket. fifteen dollars
    a ticket
14. *This* gum smells like spearmint. This gum

Name________________________________

Date________________________________

ADJECTIVES
Limiting Adjectives

Directions: In the space provided, write the italicized limiting adjective(s) with the noun that it modifies (goes to).

Example: Do you have *any* paper? ______any paper______

1. *Two* alligators swam through deep water. ____________________
2. Do you have a *few* dollars to loan me? ____________________
3. Please bring *your* swimsuit with you. ____________________
4. A *boys'* club was begun there. ____________________
5. Has Mrs. Little seen *these* new shoes? ____________________
6. They floated down *the* river on rafts. ____________________
7. *An* apple is filled with pectin. ____________________
8. Sometimes, he has *no* patience. ____________________
9. Hand me *that* basket of fruit, please. ____________________
10. *His* jeep is in *the* parking lot. ____________________

    ____
11. *Jay's* toads are in *a* special garden. ____________________

    ____
12. Have you seen *my* binoculars? ____________________
13. Chad paid *fifteen* dollars for *a* ticket. ____________________

    ____
14. *This* gum smells like spearmint. ____________________

Name______________________________

WORKBOOK PAGE 144

Date______________________________

ADJECTIVES
Limiting Adjectives

Directions: In the space provided, write the italicized limiting adjective with the noun that it modifies (goes to).

Example: Kimberly left *her* bowl on the table. her bowl

1. *Charlene's* mouse is cute. Charlene's mouse
2. *A* free pass was given to him. A pass
3. Have you taken *her* napkin? her napkin
4. *This* broken watch must be returned. This watch
5. Wait *twenty* minutes for us. twenty minutes
6. *Several* children played happily. Several children
7. I don't want *my* dessert. my dessert
8. The *girls'* dad listened carefully. girls' dad
9. The teacher requested *an* answer immediately. an answer
10. Did *any* telephone operator stay late? any operator
11. *Those* apricots are spoiled. Those apricots
12. She reached up for *some* cookies. some cookies
13. An eagle spread *its* wings and flew off. its wings
14. Please give Allen *these* sandals. these sandals
15. *The* computer chip is very tiny. The chip

Name______________________________

Date______________________________

ADJECTIVES
Limiting Adjectives

Directions: In the space provided, write the italicized limiting adjective with the noun that it modifies (goes to).

Example: Kimberly left *her* bowl on the table. her bowl

1. *Charlene's* mouse is cute. ____________________
2. *A* free pass was given to him. ____________________
3. Have you taken *her* napkin? ____________________
4. *This* broken watch must be returned. ____________________
5. Wait *twenty* minutes for us. ____________________
6. *Several* children played happily. ____________________
7. I don't want *my* dessert. ____________________
8. The *girls'* dad listened carefully. ____________________
9. The teacher requested *an* answer immediately. ____________________
10. Did *any* telephone operator stay late? ____________________
11. *Those* apricots are spoiled. ____________________
12. She reached up for *some* cookies. ____________________
13. An eagle spread *its* wings and flew off. ____________________
14. Please give Allen *these* sandals. ____________________
15. *The* computer chip is very tiny. ____________________

Name________________________________

WORKBOOK PAGE 145

Date________________________________

ADJECTIVES
Limiting Adjectives

Directions: Write A in the first space if the underlined word is an adjective; write P if the underlined word is a pronoun. After the sentence, write the limiting adjective and the noun it modifies. After P, the line will be blank.

Examples: __A__ Her shampoo is all gone. ____her shampoo____

__P__ Will you go with her? ____________

1. __A__ This orange is sour. ____This orange____
2. __P__ Do you want this? ____________
3. __P__ I'll take a few! ____________
4. __A__ He ate a few pancakes. ____few pancakes____
5. __P__ Forty came to the reunion. ____________
6. __A__ There are forty jellybeans in this jar. ____forty jellybeans____
7. __P__ Margie said that she doesn't have any. ____________
8. __A__ Has Doug bought any carmels? ____any carmels____
9. __P__ That is funny. ____________
10. __A__ Tell me that joke again. ____that joke____
11. __P__ Take two with you. ____________
12. __A__ The baby has two teeth. ____two teeth____
13. __P__ Several will be elected. ____________
14. __A__ Several blueberry muffins were eaten. ____Several muffins____

Name________________________________

Date________________________________

ADJECTIVES
Limiting Adjectives

Directions: Write A in the first space if the underlined word is an adjective; write P if the underlined word is a pronoun. After the sentence, write the limiting adjective and the noun it modifies. After P, the line will be blank.

Examples: __A__ Her shampoo is all gone. ______her shampoo______

__P__ Will you go with her? ____________________

1. ______ This orange is sour. ____________________
2. ______ Do you want this? ____________________
3. ______ I'll take a few! ____________________
4. ______ He ate a few pancakes. ____________________
5. ______ Forty came to the reunion. ____________________
6. ______ There are forty jellybeans in this jar. ____________________
7. ______ Margie said that she doesn't have any. ____________________
8. ______ Has Doug bought any carmels? ____________________
9. ______ That is funny. ____________________
10. ______ Tell me that joke again. ____________________
11. ______ Take two with you. ____________________
12. ______ The baby has two teeth. ____________________
13. ______ Several will be elected. ____________________
14. ______ Several blueberry muffins were eaten. ____________________

PAGE 285 = WORKBOOK PAGE 146

ADJECTIVES

There are two general types of adjectives: limiting adjectives and descriptive adjectives.

Descriptive Adjectives:

1. Descriptive adjectives **describe**: yellow, large, plain

2. Descriptive adjectives answer the question **WHAT KIND**.

   Example: stale bread What kind of bread? *stale*

3. Some suffixes help to identify descriptive adjectives:

   a. **able** - believable, capable, reliable
   b. **al** - critical, unusual
   c. **ar** - muscular, regular
   d. **ible** - digestible, responsible
   e. **ic** - fantastic, basic
   f. **ive** - festive, sensitive
   g. **ful** - playful, careful, colorful
   h. **less** - careless, restless
   i. **ous** - delicious, spacious, luscious
   j. **some** - handsome, burdensome

(Always look for a noun following words with these endings. Some words ending with these suffixes will not serve as adjectives.)

Descriptive adjectives modify (go over to) a noun (or pronoun).

1. Descriptive adjectives often come before the noun or pronoun.

   Examples: A ***red*** carnation was given to Sue.
   Red describes carnation.

   This ***gas*** lamp still works.
   Gas describes lamp.

2. Descriptive adjectives sometimes come after the noun or pronoun.

   Examples: His leg, ***swollen*** and ***cut***, was treated for minor injuries.

   This syrup is very ***watery***. (predicate adjective)

Name________________________________ **ADJECTIVES**

WORKBOOK PAGE 147

Date________________________________

<u>Recommendation: Do this exercise orally. Throughout this unit, instruct students to draw an arrow from each adjective to the noun or pronoun it modifies.</u>

Directions: First, read each sentence. Circle any limiting adjective(s). Then, reread each sentence and circle any describing adjective(s).

Answers are in boldfaced print.

1. **Her second** child takes **jazz** dancing.

2. **Derek's** friend has **brown wavy** hair.

3. **A cherry ice** drink costs **seventy-five** cents.

4. Have you found **a small silver** bracelet?

5. **The girls' cocker** spaniel has **black** fur.

6. Later, we ate **several toasted** marshmallows.

7. **Their cheerful** smiles welcomed **the tired** visitors.

8. On **the next rainy** day, we will make **chocolate** pudding.

9. **Tom's** cousin made **a silly** face at **the upset** girls.

10. **The hot fudge** sundae was topped with **whipping** cream.

11. **Our last basketball** game was **long** but **fun**.

12. **An elegant** dress with **blue** sequins was purchased for **the holiday** party.

Name________________________________

Date________________________________

ADJECTIVES

Directions: First, read each sentence. Circle any limiting adjective(s). Then, reread each sentence and circle any describing adjective(s).

1. Her second child takes jazz dancing.

2. Derek's friend has brown wavy hair.

3. A cherry ice drink costs seventy-five cents.

4. Have you found a small silver bracelet?

5. The girls' cocker spaniel has black fur.

6. Later, we ate several toasted marshmallows.

7. Their cheerful smiles welcomed the tired visitors.

8. On the next rainy day, we will make chocolate pudding.

9. Tom's cousin made a silly face at the upset girls.

10. The hot fudge sundae was topped with whipping cream.

11. Our last basketball game was long but fun.

12. An elegant dress with blue sequins was purchased for the holiday party.

Name________________________________ **ADJECTIVES**

WORKBOOK PAGE 148

Date________________________________

Directions: First, read each sentence. Circle any limiting adjective(s). Then, reread each sentence and circle any describing adjective(s).

Answers are in boldfaced print.

1. **Anne's first fruit** drink contained **ice** cubes and **pink** lemonade.

2. **Spicy** food is always **a** treat in **Kerry's** family.

3. Miss Sills wore **a fashionable cotton** jacket with **green** stripes.

4. **That old** road has **dangerous** curves and **high** shoulders.

5. **This coconut cream** pie is **good** but **watery**.

6. **That** group ate **raspberry sugarless** popsicles.

7. **Seventeen beautiful** girls sang in **the charity** show.

8. **A young** girl wrote **a special** letter to **her elderly great** aunt.

9. **Several shiny silver** dollars were given to **an eighth** grader.

10. **Their favorite** toy is **a sponge** football with **bright** stars.

11. **A tall, thin** man was sleeping under **the weeping willow** tree.

12. **Many gorgeous** ponies are being shown at **the annual firemen's** carnival.

Name________________________________ **ADJECTIVES**

Date________________________________

Directions: First, read each sentence. Circle any limiting adjective(s). Then, reread each sentence and circle any describing adjective(s).

1. Anne's first fruit drink contained ice cubes and pink lemonade.

2. Spicy food is always a treat in Kerry's family.

3. Miss Sills wore a fashionable cotton jacket with green stripes.

4. That old road has dangerous curves and high shoulders.

5. This coconut cream pie is good but watery.

6. That group ate raspberry sugarless popsicles.

7. Seventeen beautiful girls sang in the charity show.

8. A young girl wrote a special letter to her elderly great aunt.

9. Several shiny silver dollars were given to an eighth grader.

10. Their favorite toy is a sponge football with bright stars.

11. A tall, thin man was sleeping under the weeping willow tree.

12. Many gorgeous ponies are being shown at the annual firemen's carnival.

Name________________________________ **ADJECTIVES**

WORKBOOK PAGE 149

Date________________________________

Directions: Circle any adjectives.

Remember: Search for any limiting adjective(s) first. Then, reread the sentence and find any descriptive adjective(s).

Answers are in boldfaced print.

1. **Their blue** bike is **old** and **rusty**.

2. **The quiet** child sat near **a wide, open** window.

3. **Mrs. Kilper's short** speech included **colorful** slides of **tropical** fish.

4. **Many cheering** fans sat on **the comfortable padded** benches.

5. **The** businessman, **happy** and **rested**, made notes on **his yellow legal** pad.

6. **Your favorite** actor will be appearing at **an expensive charity** ball.

7. **A small yellow** canary fluttered among **those leafless** branches.

8. **A brightly colored** kimono was given as **a Christmas** gift to **his older** sister.

9. **A lovely christening** outfit had been knitted for **their new** baby.

10. **My festive** decorations included **green crepe** paper and **foil** streamers.

11. **Several diamond** rings had been stolen by **a short, blonde** woman.

12. Have you traded **five baseball** cards for **that valuable autographed** copy?

Name________________________________ **ADJECTIVES**

Date________________________________

Directions: Circle any adjectives.

Remember: Search for any limiting adjective(s) first. Then, reread the sentence and find any descriptive adjective(s).

1. Their blue bike is old and rusty.

2. The quiet child sat near a wide, open window.

3. Mrs. Kilper's short speech included colorful slides of tropical fish.

4. Many cheering fans sat on the comfortable padded benches.

5. The businessman, happy and rested, made notes in his yellow legal pad.

6. Your favorite actor will be appearing at an expensive charity ball.

7. A small yellow canary fluttered among those leafless branches.

8. A brightly colored kimono was given as a Christmas gift to his older sister.

9. A lovely christening outfit had been knitted for their new baby.

10. My festive decorations included green crepe paper and foil streamers.

11. Several diamond rings had been stolen by a short, blonde woman.

12. Have you traded five baseball cards for that valuable autographed copy?

PAGE 293 = WORKBOOK PAGE 150
PAGE 300 = WORKBOOK PAGE 154
PAGE 301 = WORKBOOK PAGE 155
PAGE 306 = WORKBOOK PAGE 158
PAGE 307 = WORKBOOK PAGE 159

ADJECTIVES

Proper Adjectives

A proper adjective is a descriptive word derived from a proper noun. Proper nouns are capitalized; therefore, proper adjectives are capitalized.

A. Often, a proper adjective will be similar to the proper noun:

PROPER NOUN	PROPER ADJECTIVE	
Japan	Japanese	(Japanese gardens)
Canada	Canadian	(Canadian bacon)
Arab	Arabian	(Arabian horses)

B. Some proper adjectives will be very different from the proper noun:

PROPER NOUN	PROPER ADJECTIVE	
Switzerland	Swiss	(Swiss chocolate)
Holland	Dutch	(Dutch tulips)

C. Sometimes, the proper adjective is the same as the proper noun:

PROPER NOUN	PROPER ADJECTIVE	
Ford	Ford	(Ford van)
General Electric	General Electric	(General Electric light bulbs)
Scottsdale	Scottsdale	(Scottsdale police)

Name____________________

WORKBOOK PAGE 151

Date____________________

ADJECTIVES
Proper Adjectives

Directions: Underline any proper adjective. Capitalize it. In the space provided, write the proper adjective and the noun it modifies (goes to).

Example: They went to a new jersey amusement park. (N J) ____New Jersey park____

Answers that should be underlined are in boldfaced print.
Be sure students capitalize the proper adjective but not the ensuing noun.

1. The **Arizona** flag has a large star. ____Arizona flag____

2. A **French** poodle is for sale. ____French poodle____

3. Granny made a **Christmas** dinner. ____Christmas dinner____

4. Do you like **Swiss** cheese? ____Swiss cheese____

5. John's father lives in an **Italian** village. ____Italian village____

6. That **Los Angeles** store offers discounts. ____Los Angeles store____

7. Have you ridden a **New York** subway? ____New York subway____

8. Uncle Fred has learned to make **Mexican** tortillas. ____Mexican tortillas____

9. A **Sears** catalog came in the mail today. ____Sears catalog____

10. We are invited to a **Greek** wedding. ____Greek wedding____

Name________________________________

Date________________________________

ADJECTIVES
Proper Adjectives

Directions: Underline any proper adjective. Capitalize it. In the space provided, write the proper adjective and the noun it modifies (goes to).

Example: They went to a new jersey amusement park. ____New Jersey park____

(Above "new jersey" in the example the capitals N and J are written in.)

1. The arizona flag has a large star. ______________________

2. A french poodle is for sale. ______________________

3. Granny made a christmas dinner. ______________________

4. Do you like swiss cheese? ______________________

5. John's father lives in an italian village. ______________________

6. That los angeles store offers discounts. ______________________

7. Have you ridden a new york subway? ______________________

8. Uncle Fred has learned to make mexican tortillas. ______________________

9. A sears catalog came in the mail today. ______________________

10. We are invited to a greek wedding. ______________________

Name________________________________ **ADJECTIVES**
WORKBOOK PAGE 152 **Proper Adjectives**
Date________________________________

Directions: Underline any proper adjective. Capitalize it. In the space provided, write the proper adjective and the noun it modifies (goes to).

S F
Example: Have you seen a san francisco trolley? San Francisco trolley

Answers that should be underlined are in boldfaced print.
Be sure students capitalize the proper adjective but not not the ensuing noun.

1. We went to an **Easter** service. Easter service

2. Stan went to a **Canadian** wilderness to photograph moose. Canadian wilderness

3. Shanna attended a **Hawaiian** luau. Hawaiian luau

4. Did you attend a **St. Patrick's** party? St. Patrick's party

5. Is there an **Atlanta** football team? Atlanta team

6. Have you seen **Alaskan** king crab? Alaskan crab

7. Cynthia enjoys **Dannon** yogurt. Dannon yogurt

8. His friend lives in a **Maine** apartment. Maine apartment

9. Beth goes to the **African** nation of Egypt. African nation

10. The Bolston family loves **Jewish** rye bread. Jewish bread

Name____________________________________

Date_____________________________________

ADJECTIVES
Proper Adjectives

Directions: Underline any proper adjective. Capitalize it. In the space provided, write the proper adjective and the noun it modifies (goes to).

Example: Have you seen a san francisco trolley? (S F written above "san francisco") ____San Francisco trolley____

1. We went to an easter service. ______________________

2. Stan went to a canadian wilderness to photograph moose. ______________________

3. Shanna attended a hawaiian luau. ______________________

4. Did you attend a st. patrick's party? ______________________

5. Is there an atlanta football team? ______________________

6. Have you seen alaskan king crab? ______________________

7. Cynthia enjoys dannon yogurt. ______________________

8. His friend lives in a maine apartment. ______________________

9. Beth goes to the african nation of Egypt. ______________________

10. The Bolston family loves jewish rye bread. ______________________

Name________________________________ **ADJECTIVES**

WORKBOOK PAGE 153

Date________________________________

Directions: Read each sentence. First, circle limiting adjectives. Then, circle descriptive adjectives. Be sure to circle proper adjectives.

Answers that should be circled are in boldfaced print.

1. **A Boston** rocker is for sale at **that antique** shop.

2. **The Edison** home is on **a quiet** street in Ohio.

3. Has **your** uncle seen **the new Chevrolet** truck?

4. They chose **a pink Valentine's Day** card for **their** friend.

5. For breakfast, we ate **scrambled** eggs and **crisp Canadian** bacon.

6. **Some enthusiastic** people talked eagerly about **Sargent's** painting.

7. **Billy's youngest** nephew works on **a southern Kansas** farm.

8. **Lipton iced** tea was served with **fat lemon** wedges.

9. **An old oak** table was topped with **a white lace** tablecloth and **clear crystal** goblets.

10. **Several Danish sweet** rolls and **assorted fresh** fruit are available in **the next** room.

11. **Santa's** helpers were dressed in **short red velvet** dresses and **green tennis** shoes.

12. **A tall, confused** man asked **the** grocer for directions to **the Chinese food** aisle.

13. **Two college** roommates attending **their class** party had made **a lasting** friendship.

Name________________________________ **ADJECTIVES**

Date________________________________

Directions: Read each sentence. First, circle limiting adjectives. Then, circle descriptive adjectives. Be sure to circle proper adjectives.

1. A Boston rocker is for sale at that antique shop.

2. The Edison home is on a quiet street in Ohio.

3. Has your uncle seen the new Chevrolet truck?

4. They chose a pink Valentine's Day card for their friend.

5. For breakfast, we ate scrambled eggs and crisp Canadian bacon.

6. Some enthusiastic people talked eagerly about Sargent's painting.

7. Billy's youngest nephew works on a southern Kansas farm.

8. Lipton iced tea was served with fat lemon wedges.

9. An old oak table was topped with a white lace tablecloth and clear crystal goblets.

10. Several Danish sweet rolls and assorted fresh fruit are available in the next room.

11. Santa's helpers were dressed in short red velvet dresses and green tennis shoes.

12. A tall, confused man asked the grocer for directions to the Chinese food aisle.

13. Two college roommates attending their class party had made a lasting friendship.

ADJECTIVES

Predicate Adjectives

A predicate adjective is a describing word that occurs in the predicate of the sentence and describes the subject.

The predicate starts at the **verb** and **goes to the end of the sentence.**

Examples: Mary likes to ride her bike in the park.

likes to ride her bike in the park = predicate

The man in the blue tie lives near me.

lives near me = predicate

Steps in identifying a predicate adjective:

1. Look for a linking verb. A predicate adjective will occur after a linking verb.

Linking verbs:	to feel	to appear	to sound
	to taste	to become	to stay
	to look	to grow	to be (is, am, are, was,
	to smell	to remain	were, be, being, been)

Remember: To check for a linking verb, try replacing the verb with a form of to be:

is, *am*, *are*, *was*, or *were*. If you can do this without changing the meaning of the sentence, the verb is usually linking.

Examples: Joe **looks** happy today.

Joe **is** happy today.

The shopper **became** concerned about her lost child.

The shopper **was** concerned about her lost child.

2. If the sentence contains a linking verb, check if a word in the predicate describes the subject. The adjective must describe the subject, not another word in the predicate.

P.A.

Examples: That girl is very funny. (funny girl)
(funny = predicate adjective)

His dad was a silver medal winner.

(*Silver* occurs in the predicate. However, *silver* describes winner. Dad is not silver! Therefore, *silver* is not a predicate adjective.)

3. If there is a linking verb and the adjective in the predicate (after the verb) describes the subject, the word is a predicate adjective.

This soup tastes delicious.

P.A.

This soup tastes delicious. (delicious soup)

NOTE: A question (interrogative sentence) usually has the predicate adjective and the noun after the verb.

Is your bathroom clean?

To determine a predicate adjective more easily, change the question to a statement.

Your bathroom is clean.

Then, go through the steps by asking the following questions:

1. Is there a possible linking verb?
2. Is there an adjective in the predicate (after the verb)?
3. Does the adjective in the predicate go back and describe the subject?

P.A.

Your bathroom is clean. (clean bathroom)

Use this method to help identify any predicate adjective. However, be sure to change a question to a statement first.

Name________________________________ **ADJECTIVES**
WORKBOOK PAGE 156 **Predicate Adjectives**
Date________________________________

Directions: Cross out any prepositional phrase(s). Underline the subject once and the verb/verb phrase twice. Label any predicate adjective-P.A. Write the predicate adjective and the noun it modifies on the line provided.

P.A.
Example: His pliers are rusty. rusty pliers

P.A.
1. The baseball shoes are black. black shoes

P.A.
2. Those tarts taste sweet. sweet tarts

P.A.
3. Her hair had been kinky. kinky hair

P.A.
4. This pickle tastes sweet. sweet pickle

P.A.
5. Your voice seems hoarse ~~from yelling~~. hoarse voice

P.A.
6. The man remained silent. silent man

P.A.
7. The drawer is full ~~of old clothes~~. full drawer

P.A.
8. Your face appears swollen. swollen face

P.A.
9. That horn sounds too loud. loud horn

P.A.
10. The dog grew excited ~~by the stranger's voice~~. excited dog

Name________________________________

Date________________________________

ADJECTIVES
Predicate Adjectives

Directions: Cross out any prepositional phrase(s). Underline the subject once and the verb/verb phrase twice. Label any predicate adjective-P.A. Write the predicate adjective and the noun it modifies on the line provided.

Example: His pliers are rusty. (P.A.) ______rusty pliers______

1. The baseball shoes are black. ______________________

2. Those tarts taste sweet. ______________________

3. Her hair had been kinky. ______________________

4. This pickle tastes sweet. ______________________

5. Your voice seems hoarse from yelling. ______________________

6. The man remained silent. ______________________

7. The drawer is full of old clothes. ______________________

8. Your face appears swollen. ______________________

9. That horn sounds too loud. ______________________

10. The dog grew excited by the stranger's voice. ______________________

Name____________________________________

WORKBOOK PAGE 157

Date____________________________________

ADJECTIVES
Predicate Adjectives

Directions: Cross out any prepositional phrase(s). Underline the subject once and the verb/verb phrase twice. Label any predicate adjective-P.A. Write the predicate adjective and the noun it modifies on the line provided.

Example: The crackers ~~in the soup~~ are mushy. (P.A.) ____mushy crackers____

1. His thumb was feeling numb. (P.A.) ____numb thumb____
2. The edge ~~of that knife~~ is sharp. (P.A.) ____sharp edge____
3. Her foot became enlarged ~~from the spider bite~~. (P.A.) ____enlarged foot____
4. A waitress appeared upset ~~by the customer's remark~~. (P.A.) ____upset waitress____
5. That riverbed is dry again. (P.A.) ____dry riverbed____
6. His hair is blonde. (P.A.) ____blonde hair____
7. ~~After the argument~~, the two ladies were friendly. (P.A.) ____friendly ladies____
8. Their socks had become holey. (P.A.) ____holey socks____
9. ~~Throughout the winter~~, the walks had remained icy. (P.A.) ____icy walks____
10. Her finger became sore ~~around the joint~~. (P.A.) ____sore finger____

Name____________________________

Date____________________________

ADJECTIVES
Predicate Adjectives

Directions: Cross out any prepositional phrase(s). Underline the subject once and the verb/verb phrase twice. Label any predicate adjective-P.A. Write the predicate adjective and the noun it modifies on the line provided.

Example: The crackers ~~in the soup~~ are mushy. (P.A.) ____mushy crackers____

1. His thumb was feeling numb. ____________________
2. The edge of that knife is sharp. ____________________
3. Her foot became enlarged from the spider bite. ____________________
4. A waitress appeared upset by the customer's remark. ____________________
5. That riverbed is dry again. ____________________
6. His hair is blonde. ____________________
7. After the argument, the two ladies were friendly. ____________________
8. Their socks had become holey. ____________________
9. Throughout the winter, the walks had remained icy. ____________________
10. Her finger became sore around the joint. ____________________

ADJECTIVES

Degrees of Adjectives

Adjectives are used to make comparisons.

A. The **comparative form** compares **two**.

B. The **superlative form** compares **three or more**.

Examples: This thumb nail is shorter than my index finger nail.

Of all the nails, the thumb nail is shortest.

There are several ways to form the comparative and superlative forms:

A. **Comparative**:

1. Add **er** to most one-syllable adjectives:

   low/lower strong/stronger

2. Add **er** to some two-syllable adjectives:

   sincere/sincerer pretty/prettier

3. Place **more** (or less) before some two-syllable adjectives:

   famous/more famous special/more special

IMPORTANT: Use your DICTIONARY to determine if er should be added to a two-syllable adjective.

4. Before adjectives of three or more syllables, add **more** (or less) to make comparisons.

   responsible/more responsible expensive/more expensive

5. Some adjectives completely change form.

good/better bad/worse

B. **Superlative**:

1. Add **est** to most one-syllable adjectives:

low/lowest strong/strongest

2. Add **est** to some two-syllable adjectives:

sincere/sincerest pretty/prettiest

3. Place **most** (or least) before some two-syllable adjectives:

famous/most famous special/most special

IMPORTANT: Use a DICTIONARY to determine if est should be added to a two-syllable adjective.

4. Place **most** (or least) before three-syllable adjectives.

responsible/most responsible expensive/most expensive

5. Some adjectives totally change form.

good/best bad/worst

Remember:

1. **Use the comparative form when comparing 2 items.**

Example: He is friendlier than his sister.

2. **Use the superlative form when comparing 3 items or more.**

Example: He is tallest of the five boys.

Name________________________________ **ADJECTIVES**

WORKBOOK PAGE 160 **Degrees of Adjectives**

Date________________________________

You may wish for students to raise 2 fingers for comparative and 3 for superlative.

Directions: Write the required comparative or superlative form of the given adjective in the space provided.

Allow students to use dictionaries. Sometimes, dictionaries differ. If a student has a different answer, allow him to show you the dictionary entry.

Example: comparative of beautiful - more beautiful

1. comparative form of lively - livelier
2. superlative form of sticky - stickiest
3. comparative form of fast - faster
4. superlative form of disinterested - most disinterested
5. comparative form of creative - more creative
6. comparative form of dull - duller
7. superlative form of thrilling - most thrilling
8. comparative form of dangerous - more dangerous
9. comparative form of white - whiter
10. superlative form of happy - happiest

Name______________________________

Date______________________________

ADJECTIVES
Degrees of Adjectives

Directions: Write the required comparative or superlative form of the given adjective in the space provided.

Example: comparative of beautiful - ____more beautiful____

1. comparative form of lively - ______________________________

2. superlative form of sticky - ______________________________

3. comparative form of fast - ______________________________

4. superlative form of disinterested - ______________________________

5. comparative form of creative - ______________________________

6. comparative form of dull - ______________________________

7. superlative form of thrilling - ______________________________

8. comparative form of dangerous - ______________________________

9. comparative form of white - ______________________________

10. superlative of happy - ______________________________

Name________________________________
WORKBOOK PAGE 161
Date________________________________

ADJECTIVES
Degrees of Adjectives

You may wish for students to raise 2 fingers for comparative and 3 for superlative.

Directions: Write the required comparative or superlative form of the given adjective in the space provided.

Allow students to use dictionaries. Sometimes, dictionaries differ. If a student has a different answer, allow him to show you the dictionary entry.

Example: superlative of wise - wisest

1. comparative of small - smaller
2. superlative form of honest - most honest
3. comparative of angry - angrier
4. comparative of careless - more careless
5. superlative of good - best
6. superlative of courageous - most courageous
7. comparative of delicious - more delicious
8. comparative of funny - funnier
9. superlative of hard - hardest
10. superlative of careless - most careless

Name________________________________

Date________________________________

ADJECTIVES
Degrees of Adjectives

Directions: Write the required comparative or superlative form of the given adjective in the space provided.

Example: superlative of wise - ____wisest____________

1. comparative of small - ________________________________
2. superlative form of honest - ________________________________
3. comparative of angry - ________________________________
4. comparative of careless - ________________________________
5. superlative of good - ________________________________
6. superlative of courageous - ________________________________
7. comparative of delicious - ________________________________
8. comparative of funny - ________________________________
9. superlative of hard - ________________________________
10. superlative of careless - ________________________________

Name_______________________________

WORKBOOK PAGE 162

Date_______________________________

ADJECTIVES
Degrees

Answers are in boldfaced print.

Directions: Choose the correct form in each sentence.

Example: His uncle is the (taller, **tallest**) in that quartet.

1. This watermelon is (**bigger**, biggest) than that one.
2. That cucumber is (**largest**, larger) of all the ones in the bin.
3. My barbecue sandwich is (**tastier**, tastiest) than the one I ate yesterday.
4. The whirlpool tub is (**deeper**, deepest) than the regular one.
5. Mrs. Yales is (**taller**, tallest) than her sister.
6. The drawer at the bottom is (more spacious, **most spacious**) of the entire chest.
7. Those twins are cute; however, the taller one is (**more demanding**, most demanding).
8. This pack of football cards is (badder, **worse**) than your pack.
9. Is the Atlantic Ocean (**more peaceful**, most peaceful) than the Pacific Ocean?
10. Her living room is the (fancier, **fanciest**) room of the entire house.
11. Of the two brothers, Harvey is (**younger**, youngest).
12. This painting is (more abstract, **most abstract**) of all the ones in the museum.
13. Miss Shales is the (more talkative, **most talkative**) woman in her college class.
14. This blue wagon is (**smaller**, smallest) than the red wagon that was given away.
15. Of the four girls, Jolene is the (more energetic, **most energetic**).

Name_______________________________

Date_______________________________

ADJECTIVES
Degrees

Directions: Choose the correct form in each sentence.

Example: His uncle is the (taller, **tallest**) in that quartet.

1. This watermelon is (bigger, biggest) than that one.
2. That cucumber is (largest, larger) of all the ones in the bin.
3. My barbecue sandwich is (tastier, tastiest) than the one I ate yesterday.
4. The whirlpool tub is (deeper, deepest) than the regular one.
5. Mrs. Yales is (taller, tallest) than her sister.
6. The drawer at the bottom is (more spacious, most spacious) of the entire chest.
7. Those twins are cute; however, the taller one is (more demanding, most demanding).
8. This pack of football cards is (badder, worse) than your pack.
9. Is the Atlantic Ocean (more peaceful, most peaceful) than the Pacific Ocean?
10. Her living room is the (fancier, fanciest) room of the entire house.
11. Of the two brothers, Harvey is (younger, youngest).
12. This painting is (more abstract, most abstract) of all the ones in the museum.
13. Miss Shales is the (more talkative, most talkative) woman in her college class.
14. This blue wagon is (smaller, smallest) than the red wagon that was given away.
15. Of the four girls, Jolene is the (more energetic, most energetic).

Name________________________________ **ADJECTIVES**
WORKBOOK PAGE 163 **Degrees**
Date________________________________
Answers are in boldface.

Directions: Choose the correct form in each sentence.

Example: That wrench is (**older**, oldest) than this hammer.

1. This paper is (**shorter**, shortest) than the regular size.
2. This floor is (**dirtier**, dirtiest) than it was yesterday.
3. Mike is the (more comical, **most comical**) member of that comedy club.
4. This horse is (gentler, **gentlest**) of all the horses in the barn.
5. He wanted the (better, **best**) shirt on the rack.
6. Laura chose the (heavier, **heaviest**) bowling ball at the alley.
7. That old car was (**more dependable**, most dependable) than this new one.
8. Which choir member do you think is (more talented, **most talented**)?
9. That salesman was (friendlier, **friendliest**) of all conference attendees.
10. Of all the balls in the bin, this one is (more inflated, **most inflated**).
11. Joanne and Troy have the (cuter, **cutest**) cat in the neighborhood.
12. The small parrot seems (**noisier**, noisiest) than the large one.
13. Mandy's school pictures are (**prettier**, prettiest) than last year's pictures.
14. Mrs. Jamison is wearing the (more beautiful, **most beautiful**) dress at the dance.
15. Is Mel the (more daring, **most daring**) diver you have ever seen?

Name____________________________________

Date_____________________________________

ADJECTIVES
Degrees

Directions: Choose the correct form in each sentence.

Example: That wrench is (**older**, oldest) than this hammer.

1. This paper is (shorter, shortest) than the regular size.
2. This floor is (dirtier, dirtiest) than it was yesterday.
3. Mike is the (more comical, most comical) member of that comedy club.
4. This horse is (gentler, gentlest) of all the horses in the barn.
5. He wanted the (better, best) shirt on the rack.
6. Laura chose the (heavier, heaviest) bowling ball at the alley.
7. That old car is (more dependable, most dependable) than this new one.
8. Which choir member do you think is (more talented, most talented)?
9. That salesman was (friendlier, friendliest) of all conference attendees.
10. Of all the balls in the bin, this one is (more inflated, most inflated).
11. Joanne and Troy have the (cuter, cutest) cat in the neighborhood.
12. The small parrot seems (noisier, noisiest) than the large one.
13. Mandy's school pictures are (prettier, prettiest) than last year's pictures.
14. Mrs. Jamison is wearing the (more beautiful, most beautiful) dress at the dance.
15. Is Mel the (more daring, most daring) diver you have ever seen?

Name________________________________ **ADJECTIVE REVIEW**

WORKBOOK PAGE 164

Date________________________________

A. Directions: In the space provided, write the underlined adjective with the noun that it modifies (goes over to).

Example: Does his shirt need to be ironed? his shirt

1. Do you have any juice? any juice
2. These nuts are too salty. These nuts
3. Will you hand me an orange? an orange
4. Is this your yellow sweater? your sweater
5. Penny's laugh is very loud. Penny's laugh
6. Several leasing agents helped everyone. Several agents
7. I'll take three hard pretzels, please. three pretzels

B. Directions: Write A in the space provided if the underlined word is an adjective; write P if the underlined word is a pronoun (stands alone). After the sentence, write the limiting adjective and the noun it modifies. (After P, the line will be blank.)

Example: A This desk is maple. This desk

P This is easy. ______

1. A Do you want these marbles? these marbles
2. P I found these in the closet. ______
3. P Have many been invited? ______
4. A Many flowers are in bloom. Many flowers
5. P Would you like one? ______
6. A I want one ice cream cone. one cone

Name________________________________

Date________________________________

ADJECTIVE REVIEW

A. Directions: In the space provided, write the underlined adjective with the noun that it modifies (goes over to).

Example: Does his shirt need to be ironed? ______his shirt______

1. Do you have any juice? ________________

2. These nuts are too salty. ________________

3. Will you hand me an orange? ________________

4. Is this your yellow sweater? ________________

5. Penny's laugh is very loud. ________________

6. Several leasing agents helped everyone. ________________

7. I'll take three hard pretzels, please. ________________

B. Directions: Write A in the space provided if the underlined word is an adjective; write P if the underlined word is a pronoun (stands alone). After the sentence, write the limiting adjective and the noun it modifies. (After P, the line will be blank.)

Example: __A__ This desk is maple. ______This desk______

__P__ This is easy. ________________

1. _____ Do you want these marbles? ________________

2. _____ I found these in the closet. ________________

3. _____ Have many been invited? ________________

4. _____ Many flowers are in bloom. ________________

5. _____ Would you like one? ________________

6. _____ I want one ice cream cone. ________________

Name_______________________________ **ADJECTIVE REVIEW**

WORKBOOK PAGE 165

Date_______________________________

C. Directions: Underline any proper adjective and capitalize it. In the space provided, write the proper adjective and the noun it modifies.

Proper adjectives will be in boldfaced print.

M

Example: Shirley went to a missouri town. ___Missouri town___

1. They rode bikes along a **California** beach. ___California beach___
2. Their family ate at a **Houston** deli. ___Houston deli___
3. Ben lives near a **Mexican** restaurant. ___Mexican restaurant___
4. Does he go to a **Walmart** store? ___Walmart store___
5. They are part of a **Rocky Mountain** hiking team. ___Rocky Mountain team___
6. The lady purchased **Nabisco** crackers today. ___Nabisco crackers___

D. Directions: Cross out any prepositional phrase(s). Underline the subject once and the verb/verb phrase twice. Label any predicate adjective-P.A. Write the predicate adjective and the noun it modifies on the line.

P.A.

Example: The pillars ~~in this museum~~ are high. ___high pillars___

P.A.

1. The sky remained dark ~~during the storm~~. ___dark sky___

P.A.

2. An Arizona sunset is colorful. ___colorful sunset___

P.A.

3. Those sidewalks are icy ~~near the edges~~. ___icy sidewalks___

P.A.

4. His friend's mom seems fearful ~~of some dogs~~. ___fearful mom___

P.A.

5. My answer was very careless. ___careless answer___

P.A.

6. His back became quite sunburned . ___sunburned back___

P.A.

7. Her bracelet became rusty ~~from water~~. ___rusty bracelet___

Name_______________________________ **ADJECTIVE REVIEW**

Date_______________________________

C. Directions: Underline any proper adjective and capitalize it. In the space provided, write the proper adjective and the noun it modifies.

M
Example: Shirley went to a missouri town. ______Missouri town______

1. They rode bikes along a california beach. ____________________

2. Their family ate at a houston deli. ____________________

3. Ben lives near a mexican restaurant. ____________________

4. Does he go to a walmart store? ____________________

5. They are part of a rocky mountain hiking team. ____________________

6. The lady purchased nabisco crackers today. ____________________

D. Directions: Cross out any prepositional phrase(s). Underline the subject once and the verb/verb phrase twice. Label any predicate adjective-P.A. Write the predicate adjective and the noun it modifies on the line.

P.A.
Example: The pillars ~~in this museum~~ are high. ______high pillars______

1. The sky remained dark during the storm. ____________________

2. An Arizona sunset is colorful. ____________________

3. Those sidewalks are icy near the edges. ____________________

4. His friend's mom seems fearful of some dogs. ____________________

5. My answer was very careless. ____________________

6. His back became quite sunburned . ____________________

7. Her bracelet became rusty from water. ____________________

Name________________________________

WORKBOOK PAGE 166

Date________________________________

ADJECTIVE REVIEW

E. Directions: Circle any adjectives.

Answers are in boldface.

Remember: First circle any limiting adjective(s). Next, circle descriptive adjective(s).

1. **A fake fur** hat was worn by **a German** woman.

2. **The brown** carpeting is being replaced by **marble** tile.

3. **Several lovable** retrievers played near **the French** doors.

4. Has **his youngest** cousin ever gone to **that water** park?

5. **Kyle's** car was taken across **a peaceful** lake by **that ferry** boat.

6. **Their carved glass** plate is in **a lighted china** cupboard.

7. **The delicious** lunch consists of **a sliced beef** sandwich, **two celery** sticks, and **an egg** roll.

F. Directions: Choose the correct form.

1. I think this plaid scarf is (**prettier**, more pretty) than the striped one.

2. This groomer is (patienter, **more patient**) than his assistant.

3. Your foot is (**longer**, longest) than mine.

4. Jay's cousin is (most determined, **more determined**) to win than Jay is.

5. The employee received an award for being the (more dependable, **most dependable**) reservationist in the entire office.

6. Of their family, she is (more helpful, **most helpful**) to her grandfather.

7. Shirley's suitcase is (**more durable**, most durable) than her duffel bag.

8. This is the (better, **best**) handwriting example in the entire book.

Name______________________________

Date______________________________

ADJECTIVE REVIEW

E. Directions: Circle any adjectives.

Remember: First circle any limiting adjective(s). Next, circle descriptive adjective(s).

1. A fake fur hat was worn by a German woman.
2. The brown carpeting is being replaced by marble tile.
3. Several lovable retrievers played near the French doors.
4. Has his youngest cousin ever gone to that water park?
5. Kyle's car was taken across a peaceful lake by that ferry boat.
6. Their carved glass plate is in a lighted china cupboard.
7. The delicious lunch consists of a sliced beef sandwich, two celery sticks, and an egg roll.

F. Directions: Choose the correct form.

1. I think this plaid scarf is (prettier, more pretty) than the striped one.
2. This groomer is (patienter, more patient) than his assistant.
3. Your foot is (longer, longest) than mine.
4. Jay's cousin is (most determined, more determined) to win than Jay is.
5. The employee received an award for being the (more dependable, most dependable) reservationist in the entire office.
6. Of their family, she is (more helpful, most helpful) to her grandfather.
7. Shirley's suitcase is (more durable, most durable) than her duffel bag.
8. This is the (better, best) handwriting example in the entire book.

Name_______________________________ **CUMULATIVE REVIEW**

WORKBOOK PAGE 167

Date_______________________________

Section A contains compounds. You may wish to do it orally.

A. Directions: Cross out any prepositional phrase(s). Underline the subject once and the verb/verb phrase twice. Label any direct object-D.O.

D.O.
1. Everyone ~~except the man~~ ~~in the back row~~ left the theater.

D.O.
2. Len tossed the frisbee ~~past his sister and her friend~~.

D.O.
3. The women prepared dinner and read ~~for an hour~~.

D.O. D.O.
4. We collect shells and small pebbles ~~at the beach~~.

D.O.
5. (You) Take this empty box ~~to the garbage can~~.

••

B. Directions: Cross out any prepositional phrase(s). Underline the subject once and the verb/verb phrase twice. Label any direct object-D.O. Label any indirect object-I.O. **Indirect objects are difficult; you may wish to do this section orally.**

I.O. D.O.
1. The father gave his son ten dollars.

I.O. D.O.
2. A florist designed the new store a huge silk arrangement.

I.O. D.O. *infinitive*
3. We sent Grandma tickets (*to visit*).

I.O. D.O.
4. He will make Jonathan a new outfit.

••

C. Directions: List the 23 helping verbs: **do, does, did have, has, had may, might, must should, would, could, shall, will, can, is, am, are was, were, be, being, been**

••

D. Directions: Cross out any prepositional phrase(s). Underline the subject once and the verb/verb phrase twice.

1. The man has (rode, ridden) the camel ~~across the desert~~.
2. Have you (brought, brung) your skates ~~with you~~?
3. They should have (flew, flown) earlier.
4. His sister-in-law might have (went, gone) ~~to the zoo~~.
5. The joggers must have (ran, run) ~~for an hour~~.

Name________________________________ **CUMULATIVE REVIEW**

Date________________________________

A. Directions: Cross out any prepositional phrase(s). Underline the subject once and the verb/verb phrase twice. Label any direct object-D.O.

1. Everyone except the man in the back row left the theater.

2. Len tossed the frisbee past his sister and her friend.

3. The women prepared dinner and read for an hour.

4. We collect shells and small pebbles at the beach.

5. Take this empty box to the garbage can.

B. Directions: Cross out any prepositional phrase(s). Underline the subject once and the verb/verb phrase twice. Label any direct object-D.O. Label any indirect object-I.O.

1. The father gave his son ten dollars.

2. A florist designed the new store a huge silk arrangement.

3. We sent Grandma tickets to visit.

4. He will make Jonathan a new outfit.

C. Directions: List the 23 helping verbs: ________________________________

____

D. Directions: Cross out any prepositional phrase(s). Underline the subject once and the verb/verb phrase twice.

1. The man has (rode, ridden) the camel across the desert.

2. Have you (brought, brung) your skates with you?

3. They should have (flew, flown) earlier.

4. His sister-in-law might have (went, gone) to the zoo.

5. The joggers must have (ran, run) for an hour.

Name________________________________ **CUMULATIVE REVIEW**

WORKBOOK PAGE 168

Date________________________________

E. Directions: Cross out any prepositional phrase(s). Underline the subject once and the verb/verb phrase twice. Write the helping verb(s) and the main verb in the correct column.

	helping verb(s)	main verb
1. Mr. Lindner has chosen a new office.	has	chosen
2. I shall leave ~~in the morning~~.	shall	leave
3. This balloon is leaking.	is	leaking
4. She cannot take anyone ~~to the station~~.	can	take

F. Directions: Cross out any prepositional phrase(s). Underline the subject once and the verb/verb phrase twice. Label any direct object-D.O.

Remember: To set, to raise, and to lay (lays, laid, laying) will have a direct object.

1. The portable telephone is (lying, laying) ~~by the television~~.
2. That student (rises, raises) his hand constantly. (D.O.)
3. Jonah (sits, sets) ~~in the back pew at church~~.
4. Do you (sit, set) an alarm clock ~~at bedtime~~? (D.O.)

G. Directions: List the 20 linking verbs. **to feel, to taste, to look, to smell, to appear, to become, to grow, to remain, to seem, to sound, to stay, to be: is, am, are, was, were, be, being, been**

H. Directions: Cross out any prepositional phrase(s). Underline the subject once and the verb twice. Write A if the verb is action; write L if the verb is linking.

Remember: A linking verb can be replaced by a form of to be: is, am, are, was, or were.

1. __L__ These chips taste terrible. (**are**)
2. __A__ A guest tasted the dip ~~with a finger~~.
3. __L__ The family remained calm ~~during the fire~~. (**was**)
4. __A__ A customer felt the texture ~~of the tweed suit~~.

Name________________________________ **CUMULATIVE REVIEW**

Date________________________________

E. Directions: Cross out any prepositional phrase(s). Underline the subject once and the verb/verb phrase twice. Write the helping verb(s) and the main verb in the correct column.

	helping verb(s)	**main verb**
1. Mr. Lindner has chosen a new office.	____________	____________
2. I shall leave in the morning.	____________	____________
3. This balloon is leaking.	____________	____________
4. She cannot take anyone to the station.	____________	____________

F. Directions: Cross out any prepositional phrase(s). Underline the subject once and the verb/verb phrase twice. Label any direct object-D.O.

Remember: To set, to raise, and to lay (lays, laid, laying) will have a direct object.

1. The portable telephone is (lying, laying) by the television.
2. That student (rises, raises) his hand constantly.
3. Jonah (sits, sets) in the back pew at church.
4. Do you (sit, set) an alarm clock at bedtime?

G. Directions: List the 20 linking verbs. ________________________________

____

H. Directions: Cross out any prepositional phrase(s). Underline the subject once and the verb twice. Write A if the verb is action; write L if the verb is linking.

Remember: A linking verb can be replaced by a form of to be: is, am, are, was, or were.

1. _____ These chips taste terrible.
2. _____ A guest tasted the dip with a finger.
3. _____ The family remained calm during the fire.
4. _____ A customer felt the texture of the tweed suit.

Name________________________________ **CUMULATIVE REVIEW**

WORKBOOK PAGE 169

Date________________________________

I. Directions: Write the contraction.

1. they are - they're
2. does not - doesn't
3. I am - I'm
4. we have - we've
5. there is - there's
6. will not - won't
7. she is - she's
8. would not - wouldn't

J. Directions: Cross out any prepositional phrase(s). Underline the subject once and the verb/verb phrase twice. Determine the tense and write *present*, *past*, or *future* in the space provided.

1. present — Shelby lives ~~in Montana~~.
2. future — I shall send you some money.
3. past — The toddler swam ~~to the side of the pool~~.
4. present — Bo and he dive ~~for oysters~~.
5. future — Will you have a garage sale soon?

K. Directions: Write intj. above any interjection.

1. **Yippee!** (intj.) We're moving at last!
2. You forgot the tickets again! **Oh no!** (Intj.)

L. Directions: Write conj. above any conjunction.

1. The front door **or** (conj.) the back one needs to be oiled.
2. We ordered pizza **and** (conj.) cola, **but** (conj.) it arrived too late.

M. Directions: Write A if the word is abstract; write C if it is concrete.

1. A love
2. C applesauce
3. C scissors
4. C water
5. A hope
6. C fountain

Name________________________________ **CUMULATIVE REVIEW**

Date________________________________

I. Directions: Write the contraction.

1. they are - ______________________ 5. there is - ______________________

2. does not - ______________________ 6. will not - ______________________

3. I am - ______________________ 7. she is - ______________________

4. we have - ______________________ 8. would not - ______________________

J. Directions: Cross out any prepositional phrase(s). Underline the subject once and the verb/verb phrase twice. Determine the tense and write *present*, *past*, or *future* in the space provided.

1. ____________________ Shelby lives in Montana.

2. ____________________ I shall send you some money.

3. ____________________ The toddler swam to the side of the pool.

4. ____________________ Bo and he dive for oysters.

5. ____________________ Will you have a garage sale soon?

K. Directions: Write intj. above any interjection.

1. Yippee! We're moving at last!

2. You forgot the tickets again! Oh no!

L. Directions: Write conj. above any conjunction.

1. The front door or the back one needs to be oiled.

2. We ordered pizza and cola, but it arrived too late.

M. Directions: Write A if the word is abstract; write C if it is concrete.

1. _____ love 3. _____ scissors 5. _____ hope

2. _____ applesauce 4. _____ water 6. _____ fountain

Name______________________________ **CUMULATIVE REVIEW**

WORKBOOK PAGE 170

Date______________________________

N. Directions: Write C if the noun is common; write P if it is proper.

1. __C__ PERSON 3. __C__ FOOD 5. __P__ CANADA

2. __P__ JOHN ADAMS 4. __C__ GOAT 6. __C__ COUNTRY

O. Directions: Write A if the underlined word serves as an adjective; write N if the underlined word serves as a noun.

1. __N__ The catcher threw the baseball to second base.

2. __A__ She grasped the baseball bat very tightly.

3. __A__ This trash can is full.

4. __N__ Will trash be picked up soon?

P. Directions: Write V if the underlined word serves as a verb; write N if the underlined word serves as a noun.

1. __V__ In tense situations, she handles herself well.

2. __N__ Several handles on the chest are broken.

3. __V__ Those boys often fall around to be funny.

4. __N__ Leaves change colors in the fall.

Q. Directions: Write the possessive form.

1. a jump rope belonging to Lisa - Lisa's (jump) rope

2. shoes belonging to Mrs. Jones - Mrs. Jones's shoes

3. luggage belonging to travelers - travelers' luggage

4. toys belonging to children - children's toys

5. tools belonging to one man - man's tools

Name________________________________ **CUMULATIVE REVIEW**

Date________________________________

N. Directions: Write C if the noun is common; write P if it is proper.

1.	_____	PERSON	3. _____	FOOD	5.	_____	CANADA
2.	_____	JOHN ADAMS	4. _____	GOAT	6.	_____	COUNTRY

O. Directions: Write A if the underlined word serves as an adjective; write N if the underlined word serves as a noun.

1. _____ The catcher threw the baseball to second base.

2. _____ She grasped the baseball bat very tightly.

3. _____ This trash can is full.

4. _____ Will trash be picked up soon?

P. Directions: Write V if the underlined word serves as a verb; write N if the underlined word serves as a noun.

1. _____ In tense situations, she handles herself well.

2. _____ Several handles on the chest are broken.

3. _____ Those boys often fall around to be funny.

4. _____ Leaves change colors in the fall.

Q. Directions: Write the possessive form.

1. a jump rope belonging to Lisa - ________________________________

2. shoes belonging to Mrs. Jones - ________________________________

3. luggage belonging to travelers - ________________________________

4. toys belonging to children - ________________________________

5. tools belonging to one man - ________________________________

Name________________________________ **CUMULATIVE REVIEW**

WORKBOOK PAGE 171

Date________________________________

R. Directions: Write the plural of the noun.

1. fence - fences
2. mass - masses
3. calf - calves
4. story - stories
5. eyelash - eyelashes
6. delay - delays
7. poem - poems
8. punch - punches

S. Directions: Box any nouns. (Determining adjectives will help you find many.)
Note: Nouns will be boldfaced. (Encourage students to look for determiners to help identify nouns. Determiners have been underlined for you.)

1. A single **rose** bloomed on the **bush**.
2. Two **deer** and an enormous **squirrel** live in that **forest**.
3. Some **papers** and several **booklets** are in his **briefcase**.
4. **Grandma's house** has yellow **siding** and a brown **roof**.
5. Their science **professor** is a small **man** with large **glasses**.
6. A **lawyer** talked with three **jurists** on the third **floor** of the **courthouse**.

T. Directions: Cross out any prepositional phrase(s). Underline the subject once and the verb/verb phrase twice. Label any predicate nominative-P.N. Then, write the proof on the line provided.

Note: Some students may be able to do an exercise using an example but not understand the concept. Hence, no example is provided.

1. The winners ~~of the badminton game~~ were Hope (P.N.) and Cecil (P.N.).

   Proof: Hope and Cecil were the winners.

2. Mrs. Tarbell is the mother (P.N.) ~~of these four children~~.

   Proof: The mother is Mrs. Tarbell.

3. Their favorite national park is Yellowstone (P.N.).

   Proof: Yellowstone is their favorite national park.

Name________________________________ **CUMULATIVE REVIEW**

Date________________________________

R. Directions: Write the plural of the noun.

1. fence - ______________________
2. mass - ______________________
3. calf - ______________________
4. story - ______________________
5. eyelash - ______________________
6. delay - ______________________
7. poem - ______________________
8. punch - ______________________

S. Directions: Box any nouns. (Determining adjectives will help you find many nouns.)

1. A single rose bloomed on the bush.
2. Two deer and an enormous squirrel live in that forest.
3. Some papers and several booklets are in his briefcase.
4. Grandma's house has yellow siding and a brown roof.
5. Their science professor is a small man with large glasses.
6. A lawyer talked with three jurists on the third floor of the courthouse.

T. Directions: Cross out any prepositional phrase(s). Underline the subject once and the verb/verb phrase twice. Label any predicate nominative-P.N. Then, write the proof on the line provided.

1. The winners of the badminton game were Hope and Cecil.

   Proof: ____

2. Mrs. Tarbell is the mother of those four children.

   Proof: ____

3. Their favorite national park is Yellowstone.

   Proof: ____

Name________________________________ **ADJECTIVE TEST**

WORKBOOK PAGE 327

Date________________________________

A. Directions: Circle any proper adjective and capitalize it. In the space provided, write the proper adjective and the noun it modifies.

1. Winter snows block some **Arizona** highways. ______Arizona highways______
2. A **Japanese** bonsai tree is pretty. ______Japanese tree______
3. Did they take a taxi to the **Denver** hotel? ______Denver hotel______
4. The tourists admired the **English** countryside. ______English countryside______
5. Come to my house for a **Christmas** feast. ______Christmas feast______
6. Pedro rides a **Schwinn** bicycle. ______Schwinn bicycle______

B. Directions: Cross out any prepositional phrase(s). Underline the subject once and the verb/verb phrase twice. Label any predicate adjective-P.A. Write the predicate adjective and the noun it modifies on the line.

Example: The mud flaps ~~on this car~~ are too low. (P.A.) ______low flaps______

1. His voice suddenly sounded squeaky. (P.A.) ______squeaky voice______

2. The battery ~~in the yellow car~~ is dead. (P.A.) ______dead battery______

3. Her knee becomes painful ~~during rain~~. (P.A.) ______painful knee______

4. Those towels are damp ~~from baths~~. (P.A.) ______damp towels______

5. The apple cobbler smells good. (P.A.) ______good cobbler______

Name________________________________ **ADJECTIVE TEST**

Date________________________________

A. Directions: Circle any proper adjective and capitalize it. In the space provided, write the proper adjective and the noun it modifies.

1. Winter snows block some arizona highways. ________________________
2. A japanese bonsai tree is pretty. ________________________
3. Did they take a taxi to the denver hotel? ________________________
4. The tourists admired the english countryside. ________________________
5. Come to my house for a christmas feast. ________________________
6. Pedro rides a schwinn bicycle. ________________________

B. Directions: Cross out any prepositional phrase(s). Underline the subject once and the verb/verb phrase twice. Label any predicate adjective-P.A. Write the predicate adjective and the noun it modifies on the line.

Example: The mud flaps ~~on this car~~ are too low. (P.A.) ___low flaps___________

1. His voice suddenly sounded squeaky. ____________________________
2. The battery in the yellow car is dead. ____________________________
3. Her knee becomes painful during rain. ____________________________
4. Those towels are damp from baths. ____________________________
5. The apple cobbler smells good. ____________________________

Answers are in boldfaced print. ***WORKBOOK PAGE 328***

C. Directions: Circle any adjectives.

Remember: First, circle any limiting adjective(s). Next, reread the sentence and circle any descriptive adjective(s).

1. Venus is **a brilliant** planet in **our solar** system.
2. **His final** payment on **the ruby** ring was **twenty** dollars.
3. **A few** toads hopped along **the dusty country** lane.
4. **Erin's first Easter** basket was shaped like **a gigantic** egg.
5. They wore **wet** suits in **the icy** waters on **that foggy** day.
6. **These large greeting** cards with **the funny** kittens are **cute**.
7. **An orange** tricycle was given to **the surprised** child on **his fourth** birthday.
8. **Several paper** towels were scattered on **the dirty** floor of **the boys'** bathroom.

D. Directions: Circle the correct adjective form.

1. Jeremiah is the (**smaller**, smallest) twin.
2. Jim Thorpe was one of the (faster, **fastest**) runners in the world.
3. Roy is (cheerfuler, **more cheerful**) than his older brother.
4. She is the (more pleasant, **most pleasant**) prom queen ever.
5. The first swimmer has a (**better**, best) stroke than his opponent.
6. Of the three tires, this one is (more damaged, **most damaged**.)
7. My mother is (**more patient**, most patient) with me than my sister.
8. This is the (more beautiful, **most beautiful**) spot in the world.

C. Directions: Circle any adjectives.

Remember: **First, circle any limiting adjective(s). Next, reread the sentence and circle any descriptive adjective(s).**

1. Venus is a brilliant planet in our solar system.
2. His final payment on the ruby ring was twenty dollars.
3. A few toads hopped along the dusty country lane.
4. Erin's first Easter basket was shaped like a gigantic egg.
5. They wore wet suits in the icy waters on that foggy day.
6. These large greeting cards with the funny kittens are cute.
7. An orange tricycle was given to the surprised child on his fourth birthday.
8. Several paper towels were scattered on the dirty floor of the boys' bathroom.

D. Directions: Circle the correct adjective form.

1. Jeremiah is the (smaller, smallest) twin.
2. Jim Thorpe was one of the (faster, fastest) runners in the world.
3. Roy is (cheerfuler, more cheerful) than his older brother.
4. She is the (more pleasant, most pleasant) prom queen ever.
5. The first swimmer has a (better, best) stroke than his opponent.
6. Of the three tires, this one is (more damaged, most damaged.)
7. My mother is (more patient, most patient) with me than my sister.
8. This is the (more beautiful, most beautiful) spot in the world.

Name______________________________

WORKBOOK PAGE 329

Date______________________________

CUMULATIVE TEST
Adjectives

A. Directions: Cross out any prepositional phrase(s). Underline the subject once and the verb/verb phrase twice. Label any direct object-D.O.

1. The hot air balloon ~~with red stripes~~ left ~~before dawn~~.

2. The argument ~~between the two men~~ was ~~about higher taxes~~.

3. Some ~~of the boys~~ picked berries (D.O.) ~~along the country road~~.

4. ~~Beneath the bridge~~ the woman sat ~~during hot summer days~~.

5. All the children ~~but Lenny~~ found Easter eggs (D.O.) ~~among the various plants~~.

B. Directions: Cross out any prepositional phrase(s). Underline the subject once and the verb/verb phrase twice.

1. Only one man (travel, travels) alone.
2. His truck has (fell, fallen) ~~into a ditch~~.
3. Has Jim (took, taken) a tent ~~on his camping trip~~?
4. The sun has already (risen, rose).
5. A large pink balloon ~~without any ribbon~~ has (burst, busted).
6. Those bowlers (score, scores) strikes often.
7. Does Jane (sit, set) ~~in the middle of the front row~~?
8. One ~~of the hotel guests~~ (eat, eats) meals ~~by the pool~~.
9. Kirby (lay, laid) an apple ~~under some papers near the sink~~.
10. Mr. Greer (rose, raised) ~~until the end of the national anthem~~.
11. An alligator had (swam, swum) ~~past the small boat in the Everglades~~.
12. Should you have (knew, known) the man ~~across the street~~?
13. Many people (go, goes) ~~through that mountain tunnel~~.
14. The lady was (swore, sworn) in ~~during the trial~~.
15. This package has been (lying, laying) here all afternoon.

Name_______________________________

CUMULATIVE TEST
Adjectives

Date_______________________________

A. Directions: Cross out any prepositional phrase(s). Underline the subject once and the verb/verb phrase twice. Label any direct object-D.O.

1. The hot air balloon with red stripes left before dawn.
2. The argument between the two men was about higher taxes.
3. Some of the boys picked berries along the country road.
4. Beneath the bridge the woman sat during hot summer days.
5. All the children but Lenny found Easter eggs among the various plants.

B. Directions: Cross out any prepositional phrase(s). Underline the subject once and the verb/verb phrase twice.

1. Only one man (travel, travels) alone.
2. His truck has (fell, fallen) into a ditch.
3. Has Jim (took, taken) a tent on his camping trip?
4. The sun has already (risen, rose).
5. A large pink balloon without any ribbon has (burst, busted).
6. Those bowlers (score, scores) strikes often.
7. Does Jane (sit, set) in the middle of the front row?
8. One of the hotel guests (eat, eats) meals by the pool.
9. Kirby (lay, laid) an apple under some papers near the sink.
10. Mr. Greer (rose, raised) until the end of the national anthem.
11. An alligator had (swam, swum) past the small boat in the Everglades.
12. Should you have (knew, known) the man across the street?
13. Many people (go, goes) through that mountain tunnel.
14. The lady was (swore, sworn) in during the trial.
15. This package has been (lying, laying) here all afternoon.

C. Directions: Write the contraction on the line. **_WORKBOOK PAGE 330_**

1. I have - **I've** 3. you are - **you're** 5. cannot - **can't**

2. was not - **wasn't** 4. who is - **who's** 6. we will - **we'll**

D. Directions: Cross out any prepositional phrase(s). Underline the subject once and the verb/verb phrase twice. Write the tense: *present*, *past*, or *future* on the line.

1. future Paul will send this ~~for you~~.

2. past A mason laid bricks ~~during the afternoon~~.

3. present Those tree limbs are ~~by the dumpster~~.

4. present My friend's dad walks several miles ~~before breakfast~~.

E. Directions: Fill in the blank:

1. Write an interjection: ANSWERS WILL VARY (Wow!, Yuck!, Yeah!, Yippee!).

2. The three coordinating conjunctions are and, but, and or.

3. Write an abstract noun: ANSWERS WILL VARY (love, peace, patience, kindness).
Be sure that proper nouns are capitalized.

4. Write a proper noun: ANSWERS WILL VARY (George, Mormon Lake, Alabama).

5. *He had not gone.*: verb phrase: had gone, main verb: gone

F. Directions: Write the plural. **Be sure students have learned that es is added to nouns ending is s, sh, ch, z, and x. Also, 1 and 3 should reflect if the concepts of consonant + y and vowel + y have been mastered.**

1. cemetery - cemeteries
2. prayer - prayers
3. monkey - monkeys
4. half - halves
5. tomato - tomatoes
6. mouse - mice

G. Directions: Write the possessive form.

1. turtles belonging to a girl - girl's turtles

2. whiffle ball belonging to two boys - boys' (whiffle) ball

3. meeting belonging to more than one woman - women's meeting

C. Directions: Write the contraction on the line.

1. I have - ____________ 3. you are - ____________ 5. cannot - ____________

2. was not - ____________ 4. who is - ____________ 6. we will - ____________

D. Directions: Cross out any prepositional phrase(s). Underline the subject once and the verb/verb phrase twice. Write the tense: *present*, *past*, or *future* on the line.

1. ________________ Paul will send this for you.

2. ________________ A mason laid bricks during the afternoon.

3. ________________ Those tree limbs are by the dumpster.

4. ________________ My friend's dad walks several miles before breakfast.

E. Directions: Fill in the blank:

1. Write an interjection: ________________________

2. The three coordinating conjunctions are _______, _______, and _______.

3. Write an abstract noun: ________________________

4. Write a proper noun: ________________________

5. *He had not gone.:* verb phrase:______________, main verb:______________

F. Directions: Write the plural.

1. cemetery - ________________ 4. half - ________________

2. prayer - ________________ 5. tomato - ________________

3. monkey - ________________ 6. mouse - ________________

G. Directions: Write the possessive form.

1. turtles belonging to a girl - ________________________________

2. whiffle ball belonging to two boys - ____________________________

3. meeting belonging to more than one woman -_______________________

WORKBOOK PAGE 331

Answers are in boldfaced print; limiting adjectives have been underlined although this was not part of the directions.

H. Directions: Box any nouns.

Remember: Determining (limiting) adjectives often help you find nouns.

1. Two baby **teeth** are sticking out of his swollen **gums**.
2. **Mo's mother** lives in **Texas** with twelve **cats** and an oversized **dog**.
3. A **letter** from **Mrs. Kelly** arrived by special **delivery** in the **afternoon**.
4. Many little **monkeys** were swinging from large **bars**.
5. Her **response** was a happy **scream** and a **hug** for all her **friends**.
6. I camped beside a **lake** in the **mountains** of **Missouri**.
   Be sure that students understand that *I* is a pronoun.

I. Directions: Fill in the blank.

1. *Put this envelope on the desk.* The subject of this sentence is (You).
2. Write the past participle form of the following verbs:

   A. to come - (had) come
   B. to live - (had) lived
   C. to teach - (had) taught
   D. to walk - (had) walked
   E. to sink - (had) sunk
   F. to give - (had) given

Be sure to discuss answers when reviewing the test. Remember, at this point, these are additional points.

Free A: (one additional point for each correct answer)

1. Not is never a verb. **(Technically, other parts of speech could be accepted.)**
2. The word that ends a prepositional phrase is called the object of the preposition. Example: down the **street** **(This is an important concept for teaching pronouns later.)**
3. A regular verb adds ed at the end in both the past tense and the past participle form. Write an example of a regular verb: ANSWERS WILL VARY: examples: to walk (walked), to bounce (bounced), to yell (yelled)
4. To + verb is called an infinitive.
5. *Mr. Hamilton handed Molly a check.* The indirect object of this sentence is Molly. **Direct object = check; Mr. Hamilton handed (to) Molly a check.**

H. Directions: Box any nouns.

Remember: Determining (limiting) adjectives often help you find nouns.

1. Two baby teeth are sticking out of his swollen gums.
2. Mo's mother lives in Texas with twelve cats and an oversized dog.
3. A letter from Mrs. Kelly arrived by special delivery in the afternoon.
4. Many little monkeys were swinging from large bars.
5. Her response was a happy scream and a hug for all her friends.
6. I camped beside a lake in the mountains of Missouri.

I. Directions: Fill in the blank.

1. *Put this envelope on the desk.* The subject of this sentence is _______________.
2. Write the past participle form of the following verbs:

   A. to come - (had) _______________

   B. to live - (had) _______________

   C. to teach - (had) _______________

   D. to walk - (had) _______________

   E. to sink - (had) _______________

   F. to give - (had) _______________

Free A: (one additional point for each correct answer)

1. Not is never a ____________________.
2. The word that ends a prepositional phrase is called the __________ of the preposition. Example: down the **street**
3. A regular verb adds ________ to the end in both the past tense and the past participle form. Write an example of a regular verb: ____________________
4. To + verb is called an __________________________.
5. *Mr. Hamilton handed Molly a check.* The indirect object of this sentence is __________________________.

FOR THE TEACHER: **If friendly letter, sentence types, and important words have not been taught, it is recommended that they be taught before the pronoun unit. The cumulative review at the end of the pronoun unit will include questions from these. Use the index for location in text.**

REMINDER:

You may teach the capitalization unit when you wish.*

You may teach the punctuation unit when you wish.*

You may teach friendly letter when appropriate.

You may teach sentence types when appropriate.

A section entitled IMPORTANT WORDS may be taught when you wish.
IMPORTANT WORDS includes exercises dealing with:
may and can
their, they're, and there
to, two, and too

When you return to parts of speech, teach all concepts in order. Sequence is important.

***Daily Grams at your grade level is highly recommended. Students are provided with daily capitalization and punctuation reviews. See the last page of this book.**

WORKBOOK PAGE 177

FOR THE TEACHER: **Be patient and thorough in teaching adverbs. This page will provide an overview and help you to teach "how" adverbs.**

ADVERBS

Overview:

The "textbook" definition of adverbs: Adverbs are words that tell how, when, where, and to what extent. They modify verbs, adjectives, and other adverbs.

1. Most students will be overwhelmed and confused by this definition. Rather than giving this definition, one will be provided with each concept.

2. Students will be asked to delete prepositional phrases. (Adverbs telling **how**, **when**, and **where** aren't located in a prepositional phrase. When teaching **to what extent**, students will be instructed to first look for those adverbs.) Also, students will be asked to determine the subject and verb/verb phrase. This will help them to answer **how**, **when**, and **where**.

How:

Some adverbs tell **how**. These usually modify verbs. They often end in **ly**.

Example: Tracy talks quickly. (*Quickly* tells **how** Tracy talks.)
Tracy runs fast. (*Fast* tells **how** Tracy runs.)

ADVERB OR ADJECTIVE:

Before continuing with this explanation, it's important for students to use the adverb form rather than the adjective one. Write a list of adjectives on the board. Then, have students give the adverb form. Use a dictionary to check the form.

	Adjective	**Adverb** (telling how someone does something)
Examples:	careful (person)	carefully
	happy	happily
	slow	slowly
	fast	fast (Some do not change.)

How, cont.:

In teaching **how**, it is recommended that you write on the board the following:

My aunt (or some other person) runs ________________.

Allow students to respond. **Request one word answers.**

Representative answers: slowly

(If someone says *slow*, show him that the aunt is a slow runner. However, she runs slowly. **In fact, this concept is important for students to speak and write properly, the ultimate goal in studying grammar.**)

quickly carefully
weirdly fast

Name________________________________
WORKBOOK PAGE 178
Date________________________________

ADVERBS
Adverb or Adjective?

A. Directions: Write the adverb. Use a dictionary if necessary.

	ADJECTIVE	ADVERB
1.	easy	easily
2.	smooth	smoothly
3.	fine	finely
4.	careless	carelessly
5.	peaceful	peacefully
6.	beautiful	beautifully
7.	slow	slowly
8.	patient	patiently

B. Directions: Select the correct word:

1. That neighbor is a (**kind**, kindly) woman.
2. She speaks (kind, **kindly**) to us.
3. That man is very (**hungry**, hungrily).
4. That man ate his meal (hungry, **hungrily**).
5. He spoke (angry, **angrily**).
6. The (**angry**, angrily) child refused the lollipop.
7. Senator Harving speaks (loud, **loudly**).
8. Senator Harving has a (**loud**, loudly) voice.
9. The (**merry**, merrily) children climbed the slide.
10. The children slid (merry, **merrily**) down the slide during the afternoon recess.

Name________________________________

Date________________________________

ADVERBS
Adverb or Adjective?

A. Directions: Write the adverb. Use a dictionary if necessary.

	ADJECTIVE	ADVERB
1.	easy	____________________
2.	smooth	____________________
3.	fine	____________________
4.	careless	____________________
5.	peaceful	____________________
6.	beautiful	____________________
7.	slow	____________________
8.	patient	____________________

B. Directions: Select the correct word:

1. That neighbor is a (kind, kindly) woman.
2. She speaks (kind, kindly) to us.
3. That man is very (hungry, hungrily).
4. That man ate his meal (hungry, hungrily).
5. He spoke (angry, angrily).
6. The (angry, angrily) child refused the lollipop.
7. Senator Harving speaks (loud, loudly).
8. Senator Harving has a (loud, loudly) voice.
9. The (merry, merrily) children climbed the slide.
10. The children slid (merry, merrily) down the slide during the afternoon recess.

Name________________________________ **ADVERBS**

WORKBOOK PAGE 179 **Adverb or Adjective?**

Date________________________________

A. Directions: Write the adverb. Use a dictionary if necessary.

	ADJECTIVE	**ADVERB**
1.	loving	lovingly
2.	weird	weirdly
3.	fast	fast
4.	helpless	helplessly
5.	faithful	faithfully
6.	timid	timidly
7.	dangerous	dangerously
8.	lucky	luckily

B. Directions: Select the correct word:

1. Jay hits the ball (powerful, **powerfully**) to the outfield.
2. Jay is a (**powerful**, powerfully) hitter.
3. The judge can be very (**stern**, sternly) to witnesses.
4. The judge spoke (stern, **sternly**) to the witness.
5. The (**demanding**, demandingly) child grabbed the candy and ran.
6. A child who grabs candy acts (demanding, **demandingly**).
7. The woman looked (sad, **sadly**) at the telephone bill.
8. The (**sad**, sadly) woman doesn't know how she will pay her telephone bill.
9. The (**joyful**, joyfully) participants waited for the winners' names to be announced.
10. They jumped up (**joyfully**, joyful) when their names were called.

Name________________________________

Date________________________________

ADVERBS
Adverb or Adjective?

A. Directions: Write the adverb. Use a dictionary if necessary.

	ADJECTIVE	**ADVERB**
1.	loving	____________________
2.	weird	____________________
3.	fast	____________________
4.	helpless	____________________
5.	faithful	____________________
6.	timid	____________________
7.	dangerous	____________________
8.	lucky	____________________

B. Directions: Select the correct word:

1. Jay hits the ball (powerful, powerfully) to the outfield.
2. Jay is a (powerful, powerfully) hitter.
3. The judge can be very (stern, sternly) to witnesses.
4. The judge spoke (stern, sternly) to the witness.
5. The (demanding, demandingly) child grabbed the candy and ran.
6. A child who grabs candy acts (demanding, demandingly).
7. The woman looked (sad, sadly) at the telephone bill.
8. The (sad, sadly) woman doesn't know how she will pay her telephone bill.
9. The (joyful, joyfully) participants waited for the winners' names to be announced.
10. They jumped up (joyfully, joyful) when their names were called.

Name________________________________ **ADVERBS**
WORKBOOK PAGE 180 **How?**
Date________________________________

Directions: Cross out any prepositional phrase(s). Underline the subject once and the verb/verb phrase twice. Label any adverb (ADV.) that tells **HOW**. In the space provided, explain the use of the adverb in the sentence.

ADV.
Example: A roadrunner goes quickly ~~across open highways~~.

Quickly tells HOW a roadrunner goes.

ADV.
1. A new employee listened carefully ~~to the directions~~.

Carefully tells HOW a new employee listened.

ADV.
2. The college students walked slowly ~~to class~~.

Slowly tells HOW the college students walked.

ADV.
3. Fans cheer enthusiastically ~~for their team~~.

Enthusiastically tells HOW fans cheer.

ADV.
4. The child peeped timidly ~~around the corner~~.

Timidly tells HOW the child peeped.

ADV.
5. A truck was weaving dangerously ~~through heavy traffic~~.

Dangerously tells HOW a truck was weaving.

ADV.
6. Their mom cries softly ~~during some movies~~.

Softly tells HOW their mom cries.

ADV.
7. The train whistle blew loudly.

Loudly tells HOW the train whistle blew.

ADV.
8. A racquetball player hit the ball hard ~~against the wall~~.

Hard tells HOW the racquetball player hit the ball.

Name________________________________

Date________________________________

ADVERBS
How?

Directions: Cross out any prepositional phrase(s). Underline the subject once and the verb/verb phrase twice. Label any adverb (ADV.) that tells **HOW**. In the space provided, explain the use of the adverb in the sentence.

Example: A roadrunner goes quickly ~~across open highways~~.
(ADV. above "quickly")

Quickly tells HOW a roadrunner goes.

1. A new employee listened carefully to the directions.

____

2. The college students walked slowly to class.

____

3. Fans cheer enthusiastically for their team.

____

4. The child peeped timidly around the corner.

____

5. A truck was weaving dangerously through heavy traffic.

____

6. Their mom cries softly during some movies.

____

7. The train whistle blew loudly.

____

8. A racquetball player hit the ball hard against the wall.

____

Name________________________________

WORKBOOK PAGE 181

Date________________________________

ADVERBS
How?

Directions: Cross out any prepositional phrase(s). Underline the subject once and the verb/verb phrase twice. Label any adverb (ADV.) that tells **HOW**. In the space provided, explain the use of the adverb in the sentence.

Example: The athlete wheezed mildly ~~after the event~~. (ADV. = mildly)

Mildly tells HOW the athlete wheezed.

1. A jet zoomed fast ~~toward the ocean~~. (ADV. = fast)

   Fast tells HOW a jet zoomed.

2. A deer lay silently ~~near a tree~~. (ADV. = silently)

   Silently tells HOW a deer lay.

3. Birds chirped noisily ~~in a flowering bush~~. (ADV. = noisily)

   Noisily tells HOW birds chirped.

4. Each morning, she stretches lazily ~~by her bed~~. (ADV. = lazily)

   Lazily tells HOW she stretches each morning.

5. His dog lay quietly ~~under his desk~~. (ADV. = quietly)

   Quietly tells HOW his dog lay.

6. Bicycle riders pulled their bikes cautiously ~~to the curb~~. (ADV. = cautiously)

   Cautiously tells HOW the riders pulled their bikes.

7. Cheerfully, she pumped gas ~~at the local garage~~. (ADV. = Cheerfully)

   Cheerfully tells HOW she pumped gas.

8. The animal ~~with the hurt leg~~ whined softly. (ADV. = softly)

   Softly tells HOW the animal whined.

Name________________________________ **ADVERBS**
How?

Date________________________________

Directions: Cross out any prepositional phrase(s). Underline the subject once and the verb/verb phrase twice. Label any adverb (ADV.) that tells **HOW**. In the space provided, explain the use of the adverb in the sentence.

ADV.
Example: The athlete wheezed mildly ~~after the event~~.

Mildly tells HOW the athlete wheezed.

1. A jet zoomed fast toward the ocean.

____

2. A deer lay silently near a tree.

____

3. Birds chirped noisily in a flowering bush.

____

4. Each morning, she stretches lazily by her bed.

____

5. His dog lay quietly under his desk.

____

6. Bicycle riders pulled their bikes cautiously to the curb.

____

7. Cheerfully, she pumped gas at the local garage.

____

8. The animal with the hurt leg whined softly.

____

Name________________________________
WORKBOOK PAGE 182
Date________________________________

ADVERBS
How?

Directions: Cross out any prepositional phrase(s). Underline the subject once and the verb/verb phrase twice. Label any adverb (ADV.) that tells **HOW**. In the space provided, explain the use of the adverb in the sentence.

Example: The wind blows gently ~~through that canyon~~. (ADV. = gently)

Gently tells HOW the wind blows.

1. The child stomped his foot angrily. (ADV. = angrily)

Angrily tells HOW the child stomped his foot.

2. Abruptly, the car stopped ~~at the intersection~~. (ADV. = Abruptly)

Abruptly tells HOW the car stopped.

3. ~~After his bath~~, Fido shook himself briskly. (ADV. = briskly)

Briskly tells HOW Fido shook himself.

4. Her corsage slowly wilted ~~during the dance~~. (ADV. = slowly)

Slowly tells HOW her corsage wilted.

5. The travelers ate hungrily ~~at the Wayside Inn~~. (ADV. = hungrily)

Hungrily tells HOW the travelers ate.

6. That Corvette turns corners sharply. (ADV. = sharply)

Sharply tells HOW that Corvette turns corners.

7. The teenage girl spoke harshly ~~to her brother with the squirt gun~~. (ADV. = harshly)

Harshly tells HOW the teenage girl spoke.

8. A child ~~in the airport~~ laid his head sleepily ~~on the back of a chair~~. (ADV. = sleepily)

Sleepily tells HOW a child laid his head.

Name________________________________

Date________________________________

ADVERBS
How?

Directions: Cross out any prepositional phrase(s). Underline the subject once and the verb/verb phrase twice. Label any adverb (ADV.) that tells **HOW**. In the space provided, explain the use of the adverb in the sentence.

ADV.
Example: The wind blows gently ~~through that canyon~~.

Gently tells HOW the wind blows.

1. The child stomped his foot angrily.

____

2. Abruptly, the car stopped at the intersection.

____

3. After his bath, Fido shook himself briskly.

____

4. Her corsage slowly wilted during the dance.

____

5. The travelers ate hungrily at the Wayside Inn.

____

6. That Corvette turns corners sharply.

____

7. The teenage girl spoke harshly to her brother with the squirt gun.

____

8. A child in the airport laid his head sleepily on the back of a chair.

____

FOR THE TEACHER:

A. This has been produced on the following page (without teaching notes) for the student. Additional examples of comparative forms have been given. This has been done to facilitate student learning.

B. When teaching *well*, be sure that students understand that actions are performed well. It is suggested that students be called on to tell something they do well. Requiring the student to express his thought in a complete sentence helps to insure understanding of this concept.

WORKBOOK PAGE 183

ADVERBS

Good or Well?

Good is an adjective.

Good will describe a noun or a pronoun.

Examples: He is a **good** high jumper.
That last show was a **good** one.
These cookies are **good**.

Remember: A linking verb such as *to feel*, *to taste*, *to look*, *to become*, or *to seem* will use **good**.

First, determine if the verb is linking by inserting *is*, *am*, *are*, *was*, or *were* above it. If the sentence makes sense, use good instead of well.

Examples: This soup tastes (**is**) **good**. ____good soup____

The jockey became (**was**) **good** ~~at riding~~. ____good jockey____

The forms for comparing **good**: good, better (2), and best (3 or more).

Well is an adverb.

Well tells how and modifies the verb.
Anytime someone tells how they performed an *ACTION*, **well** is used.

Examples: He speaks **well**.

The clerk operates the cash register **well**.

Has he done his job **well**? (Make sure students understand why *"You did good !"* is **WRONG**.)

Exception: Use **well** to signify one's physical condition.
Example: I don't feel **well**.

The forms for comparing **well**: well, better (2), and best (3 or more)

ADVERBS
Good or Well?

Good is an adjective.
Good will describe a noun or a pronoun.

Examples: He is a **good** high jumper.

That last show was a **good** one.

These cookies are **good**.

Remember: A linking verb such as *to feel, to taste, to look, to become*, or *to seem* will use **good**.

First, determine if the verb is linking by inserting *is, am, are, was*, or *were* above it. If the sentence makes sense, use good instead of well.

is

Examples: This soup tastes **good**. ______good soup______

was

The jockey became **good** ~~at riding~~. ______good jockey______

The forms for comparing **good**: good, better (2), and best (3 or more).

That baby is a **good** sleeper.
This baby is a **better** sleeper than his sister. (2)
He is the **best** sleeper in the entire church nursery. (3 or more)

Well is an adverb.
Well tells how and modifies the verb.
Anytime someone tells how they performed an *ACTION*, **well** is used.

Examples: He speaks **well**.

The clerk operates the cash register **well**.

Has he done his job **well**?

Exception: Use **well** to signify one's physical condition.
Example: I don't feel **well**.

The forms for comparing **well**: well, better (2), and best (3 or more)

She swims **well**.
Joan's sister swims **better** than she does. (2)
Blake swims **best** of all the boys in his 4-H club.

Name_______________________________

WORKBOOK PAGE 184

Date_______________________________

ADVERBS
Good or Well?

Directions: Write **good** or **well** in the space provided.

1. You are a ___good___ singer.

   You sing ___well___.

2. Amanda flies ___well___.

   Amanda is a ___good___ pilot.

3. Councilman Jackson speaks ___well___.

   Councilman Jackson is a ___good___ speaker.

4. Aunt Edna and Uncle Frank are ___good___ cooks.

   Aunt Edna and Uncle Frank cook ___well___.

5. Scooter is a ___good___ catcher.

   Scooter catches ___well___.

6. Grandma Moses painted ___well___.

   Grandma Moses was a ___good___ artist.

7. That lady sews ___well___.

   That lady is a ___good___ seamstress.

8. The maid is a ___good___ cleaner.

   The maid cleans ___well___.

Name________________________________

Date________________________________

ADVERBS
Good or Well?

Directions: Write **good** or **well** in the space provided.

1. You are a ________________ singer.

   You sing ________________.

2. Amanda flies ________________.

   Amanda is a ________________ pilot.

3. Councilman Jackson speaks ________________.

   Councilman Jackson is a ________________ speaker.

4. Aunt Edna and Uncle Frank are ________________ cooks.

   Aunt Edna and Uncle Frank cook ________________.

5. Scooter is a ________________ catcher.

   Scooter catches ________________.

6. Grandma Moses painted ________________.

   Grandma Moses was a ________________ artist.

7. That lady sews ________________.

   That lady is a ________________ seamstress.

8. The maid is a ________________ cleaner.

   The maid cleans ________________.

Name________________________________

WORKBOOK PAGE 185

Date________________________________

ADVERBS
Good or Well?

Directions: Write **good** or **well** in the space provided.

1. She washes her car ____well____.
2. Nan is a ____good____ shoe shiner.
3. I don't feel ____well____.
4. His teacher writes ____well____.
5. Please be a ____good____ listener.
6. Her mom plays baseball ____well____.
7. The gardener trimmed the bushes ____well____ last week.
8. Mr. Howell is a ____good____ chiropractor.
9. You did so ____well____.
10. That cowboy is a ____good____ rancher.
11. A ____good____ babysitter is important.
12. Harvey doesn't pack a suitcase too ____well____.
13. The boys threw the balls ____well____ and won purple stuffed animals.
14. Frances Ann, a member of the swimming team, swims very ____well____.
15. The kindergartner says her *ABC's* ____well____.

Name_______________________________

Date________________________________

ADVERBS
Good or Well?

Directions: Write **good** or **well** in the space provided.

1. She washes her car _________________.
2. Nan is a _________________ shoe shiner.
3. I don't feel _________________.
4. His teacher writes _________________.
5. Please be a _________________ listener.
6. Her mom plays baseball _________________.
7. The gardener trimmed the bushes _________________ last week.
8. Mr. Howell is a _________________ chiropractor.
9. You did so _________________.
10. That cowboy is a _________________ rancher.
11. A _________________ babysitter is important.
12. Harvey doesn't pack a suitcase too _________________.
13. The boys threw the balls _________________ and won purple stuffed animals.
14. Frances Ann, a member of the swimming team, swims very _________________.
15. The kindergartner says her *ABC's* _________________.

Name________________________________
WORKBOOK PAGE 186
Date_________________________________

ADVERBS
Good or Well?

Directions: Write **good** or **well** in the space provided.

1. A road construction crew cleaned up ____well__________ after the storm.

2. Sometimes a newborn baby doesn't sleep ____well__________.

3. You have done a ____good__________ job with that.

4. Martha doesn't feel ____well__________ tonight.

5. This pencil has not been sharpened____well__________.

6. Lori and Dawn are ____good__________ volleyball players.

7. Fasten this gate ____well__________for security.

8. The spaghetti and garlic bread taste ____good__________. **(Note: Be sure to discuss that *to taste* is a linking verb. Hence, *good* is used: good spaghetti and garlic bread.)**

9. Carmen is ____good__________ at making dolls. **(Note: Carmen makes dolls well; however, she is good at it.)**

10. Your shoelaces aren't tied ____well__________.

11. Did your parents tell you to wash your face ____well__________ in the morning?

12. We had a ____good__________ time at the party.

13. Have you done ____well__________ on the test?

14. His condition remained ____good__________ after surgery. **(Note: *To remain* is a linking verb; therefore, *good* is used: good condition.)**

15. Olivia needs a ____good__________ job with enough money to pay the rent.

Name_______________________________

Date_______________________________

ADVERBS
Good or Well?

Directions: Write **good** or **well** in the space provided.

1. A road construction crew cleaned up ________________ after the storm.
2. Sometimes a newborn baby doesn't sleep ________________.
3. You have done a ________________ job with that.
4. Martha doesn't feel ________________ tonight.
5. This pencil has not been sharpened ________________.
6. Lori and Dawn are ________________ volleyball players.
7. Fasten this gate ________________ for security.
8. The spaghetti and garlic bread taste ________________.
9. Carmen is ________________ at making dolls.
10. Your shoelaces aren't tied ________________.
11. Did your parents tell you to wash your face ________________ in the morning?
12. We had a ________________ time at the party.
13. Have you done ________________ on the test?
14. His condition remained ________________ after surgery.
15. Olivia needs a ________________ job with enough money to pay the rent.

FOR THE TEACHER:
WORKBOOK PAGE 187

ADVERBS
Where?

Some adverbs tell where.
An adverb that tells where usually modifies (goes over to) a verb.

1. Instruct students to fill in the blank with a word that tells where. This must be **one word** only.

   My aunt (or another person) walks ________________________.

2. Ask students to write at least five words that would tell where an aunt might walk.

3. After giving students ample time to write, solicit one-word responses.
   (*Down the street* is a phrase.)

   Representative answers:

here	in*	inside
there	out	outside
somewhere	up	around
everywhere	down	upstream
nowhere	uptown	far
where	downtown	nearby

---

*Keep in mind that some adverbs that tell **where** were learned originally as prepositions.

Example: The boy rolled ~~**down** the hill~~. (preposition)

The boy fell **down** ~~on the wet floor~~. (adverb telling where)

A boat driver leaned **over** and whispered to a passenger. (adverb)

That athlete jumps ~~**over** hurdles~~ well. (preposition)

Exercises will be provided to reinforce this concept which had been introduced in the preposition unit.

Steps in determining adverbs that tell where:
1. Have students delete prepositional phrases. Adverbs telling where will not be in a prepositional phrase.
2. Underline the subject once and the verb/verb phrase twice.
3. Look for any adverb(s) that tells where.

Name________________________________ **ADVERBS**

WORKBOOK PAGE 188 **Where?**

Date________________________________

Directions: Cross out any prepositional phrase(s). Underline the subject once and the verb/verb phrase twice. Label any adverb (ADV.) that tells **WHERE**. In the space provided, explain the use of the adverb in the sentence.

ADV.
Example: I took my form over ~~to that nurse~~ ~~with the white hat~~.

Over tells WHERE I took my form.

ADV.
1. Jerry fell down ~~on his scooter~~.

Down tells WHERE Jerry fell.

ADV.
2. Ellen is coming here ~~in the morning~~.

Here tells WHERE Ellen is coming.

ADV.
3. We have searched everywhere ~~for the lost puppy~~.

Everywhere tells WHERE we have searched.

ADV.
4. The astronomer looked up ~~into the telescope~~.

Up tells WHERE the astronomer looked.

ADV.
5. Would you like to sit there ~~by the window~~?

There asks WHERE you would like to sit.

ADV.
6. Our raft had floated far ~~into the bay~~.

Far tells WHERE our raft had floated.

ADV.
7. A security guard looked around ~~in the hotel~~.

Around tells WHERE a security guard looked.

ADV.
8. They played inside ~~on a rainy day~~.

Inside tells WHERE they played.

Name________________________________

Date________________________________

ADVERBS
Where?

Directions: Cross out any prepositional phrase(s). Underline the subject once and the verb/verb phrase twice. Label any adverb (ADV.) that tells **WHERE**. In the space provided, explain the use of the adverb in the sentence.

ADV.
Example: I took my form over ~~to that nurse~~ ~~with the white hat~~.

Over tells WHERE I took my form.

1. Jerry fell down on his scooter.

____

2. Ellen is coming here in the morning.

____

3. We have searched everywhere for the lost puppy.

____

4. The astronomer looked up into the telescope.

____

5. Would you like to sit there by the window?

____

6. Our raft had floated far into the bay.

____

7. A security guard looked around in the hotel.

____

8. They played inside on a rainy day.

____

Name________________________________ **ADVERBS**

WORKBOOK PAGE 189 **Where?**

Date________________________________

Directions: Cross out any prepositional phrase(s). Underline the subject once and the verb/verb phrase twice. Label any adverb (ADV.) that tells **WHERE**. In the space provided, explain the use of the adverb in the sentence.

ADV.

Example: She pointed westward ~~toward the setting sun~~.

Westward tells WHERE she pointed.

ADV.

1. They must have gone somewhere.

Somewhere tells WHERE they must have gone.

ADV.

2. A passenger came aboard.

Aboard tells WHERE a passenger came.

ADV.

3. Where are you going?

Where asks WHERE you are going.

ADV.

4. The sports club members waded upstream to fish.

Upstream tells WHERE the members waded.

ADV.

5. I can**not** find my books anywhere.

Remind students to box *not*.

Anywhere tells WHERE I can (not) find my books.

ADV.

6. Do you live nearby?

Nearby asks WHERE you live.

ADV.

7. That freeway goes downtown ~~to the business section~~.

Downtown tells WHERE the freeway goes.

ADV.

8. (You) Do **not** come in ~~without your shoes~~.

This is a difficult sentence. Remind students that it is a command.

In tells WHERE you do (not) come.

Name________________________________

Date_________________________________

ADVERBS
Where?

Directions: Cross out any prepositional phrase(s). Underline the subject once and the verb/verb phrase twice. Label any adverb (ADV.) that tells **WHERE**. In the space provided, explain the use of the adverb in the sentence.

ADV.
Example: She pointed westward ~~toward the setting sun~~.

Westward tells WHERE she pointed.

1. They must have gone somewhere.

____

2. A passenger came aboard.

____

3. Where are you going?

____

4. The sports club members waded upstream to fish.

____

5. I can't find my books anywhere.

____

6. Do you live nearby?

____

7. That freeway goes downtown to the business section.

____

8. Do not come in without your shoes.

____

Name________________________________ **ADVERBS**
WORKBOOK PAGE 190 **Where?**
Date________________________________

Directions: Cross out any prepositional phrase(s). Underline the subject once and the verb/verb phrase twice. Label any adverb (ADV.) that tells **WHERE**. In the space provided, explain the use of the adverb in the sentence.

ADV.
Example: The couple lives farther ~~down the winding road~~.

Farther tells WHERE the couple lives.

ADV.
1. I should have stayed home.

Home tells WHERE I should have stayed.

ADV.
2. A gull glided downward ~~over the ocean~~.

Downward tells WHERE a gull glided.

ADV.
3. His hat fell off ~~into the water~~.

Off tells WHERE his hat fell.

ADV.
4. You may sit here ~~by the window~~.

Here tells WHERE you may sit.

ADV.
5. This hallway ~~in the Winchester House~~ goes nowhere.

Nowhere tells WHERE this hallway goes.

ADV.
6. There are no dolphins ~~in this area~~.

Students need to know that there is always an adverb.

There tells WHERE no dolphins are.

ADV.
7. A man ~~in his late twenties~~ skipped out ~~of the library~~ ~~with an armload~~ ~~of books~~.

Out tells WHERE a man skipped.

ADV.
8. She approached the finish line and dashed across ~~to victory~~.

Across tells WHERE she dashed.

Name________________________________

Date________________________________

ADVERBS
Where?

Directions: Cross out any prepositional phrase(s). Underline the subject once and the verb/verb phrase twice. Label any adverb (ADV.) that tells **WHERE**. In the space provided, explain the use of the adverb in the sentence.

ADV.
Example: The couple lives farther ~~down the winding road~~.

Farther tells WHERE the couple lives.

1. I should have stayed home.

____

2. A gull glided downward over the ocean.

____

3. His hat fell off into the water.

____

4. You may sit here by the window.

____

5. This hallway in the Winchester House goes nowhere.

____

6. There are no dolphins in this area.

____

7. A man in his late twenties skipped out of the library with an armload of books.

____

8. She approached the finish line and dashed across to victory.

____

FOR THE TEACHER:
WORKBOOK PAGE 191

ADVERBS
When?

Some adverbs tell when.

An adverb that tells ***when*** usually modifies (or goes over to) the verb/verb phrase. It will be only one word.

Examples: Yesterday he went home. (*Yesterday* tells when he went.)

I shall buy a gift ~~for you~~ later. (*Later* tells when I shall buy a gift.)

1. Give students these sentences:
   My aunt (or another person) walks ________________.
   My aunt (or another person) walked ________________.
   My aunt (or another person) will walk ________________.

2. Ask students to write adverbs that tell **when** to finish the sentences.

3. Write the answers in a list. Be sure to take only one-word answers. *During the snowstorm* is not acceptable.

Representative answers:

tonight	soon	ever	nightly
today	sooner	never	daily
now	when	forever	hourly
late	always	whenever	early
later	yet	then	afterwards

Steps students should use to determine adverbs that tell ***when***.

1. Cross out any prepositional phrase(s).

2. Underline the subject once and the verb/verb phrase twice.

3. Look for any word that tells when.

Example: The nurse immediately (ADV.) rushed ~~to the patient's room~~.

Name________________________________ **ADVERBS**
WORKBOOK PAGE 192 **When?**
Date________________________________

Directions: Cross out any prepositional phrase(s). Underline the subject once and the verb/verb phrase twice. Label any adverb (ADV.) that tells **WHEN**. In the space provided, explain the use of the adverb in the sentence.

ADV.
Example: They always brush their teeth ~~in the morning~~.

Always tells WHEN they brush their teeth.

ADV.
1. Suddenly, the truck swerved ~~off the road~~.

Suddenly tells WHEN the truck swerved.

ADV.
2. Tonight, I shall read ~~for a few hours~~.

Tonight tells WHEN I shall read.

ADV.
3. She never leaves ~~for work~~ ~~before nine o'clock~~.

Never tells WHEN she leaves.

ADV.
4. The gentleman frequently feeds the pigeons ~~in the park~~.

Frequently tells WHEN the gentleman feeds the pigeons.

ADV.
5. Their family goes ~~to church~~ regularly.

Regularly tells WHEN their family goes (to church).

ADV.
6. A physical exam was recommended yesterday.

Yesterday tells WHEN a physical exam was recommended.

ADV.
7. That store operates daily.

Daily tells WHEN that store operates.

ADV.
8. They often surf ~~in the afternoon~~.

Often tells WHEN they surf.

Name________________________________

Date________________________________

ADVERBS
When?

Directions: Cross out any prepositional phrase(s). Underline the subject once and the verb/verb phrase twice. Label any adverb (ADV.) that tells **WHEN**. In the space provided, explain the use of the adverb in the sentence.

ADV.
Example: They always brush their teeth ~~in the morning~~.

Always tells WHEN they brush their teeth.

1. Suddenly, the truck swerved off the road.

____

2. Tonight, I shall read for a few hours.

____

3. She never leaves for work before nine o'clock.

____

4. The gentleman frequently feeds the pigeons in the park.

____

5. Their family goes to church regularly.

____

6. A physical exam was recommended yesterday.

____

7. That store operates daily.

____

8. They often surf in the afternoon.

____

Name________________________________

WORKBOOK PAGE 193

Date________________________________

ADVERBS
When?

Directions: Cross out any prepositional phrase(s). Underline the subject once and the verb/verb phrase twice. Label any adverb (ADV.) that tells **WHEN**. In the space provided, explain the use of the adverb in the sentence.

ADV.
Example: Will this rain last forever?

Forever tells WHEN this rain will last.

ADV.
1. You always seem happy.

Always tells WHEN you seem happy.

ADV.
2. Martin goes ~~to Oregon~~ yearly.

Yearly tells WHEN Martin goes.

ADV.
3. Someday, you must visit Heard Museum.

Someday tells WHEN you must visit Heard Museum.

ADV.
4. When will he be finished?

When asks WHEN he will be finished.

ADV.
5. The toddler seldom takes a nap.

Seldom tells WHEN the toddler takes a nap.

ADV.
6. Mom and Dad usually donate used clothes ~~to charity~~.

Usually tells WHEN Mom and Dad donate used clothes.

ADV.
7. The children take baths nightly.

Nightly tells WHEN the children take baths.

ADV.
8. I shall go ~~with you~~ later.

Later tells WHEN I shall go.

Name________________________________

Date________________________________

ADVERBS
When?

Directions: Cross out any prepositional phrase(s). Underline the subject once and the verb/verb phrase twice. Label any adverb (ADV.) that tells **WHEN**. In the space provided, explain the use of the adverb in the sentence.

Example: Will this rain last forever? (ADV. over "forever")

Forever tells WHEN this rain will last.

1. You always seem happy.

____

2. Martin goes to Oregon yearly.

____

3. Someday, you must visit Heard Museum.

____

4. When will he be finished?

____

5. The toddler seldom takes a nap.

____

6. Mom and Dad usually donate used clothes to charity.

____

7. The children take baths nightly.

____

8. I shall go with you later.

____

Name________________________________ **ADVERBS**
WORKBOOK PAGE 194 **When?**
Date________________________________

Directions: Cross out any prepositional phrase(s). Underline the subject once and the verb/verb phrase twice. Label any adverb (ADV.) that tells **WHEN**. In the space provided, explain the use of the adverb in the sentence.

ADV.
Example: Is Santa coming soon?

Soon tells WHEN Santa is coming .

ADV.
1. They left the fast food restaurant suddenly.

Suddenly tells WHEN they left the fast food restaurant.

ADV.
2. Kevin burned the cookies again.

Again tells WHEN Kevin burned the cookies.

ADV.
3. (You) Please do that now.

Now tells WHEN to do that.

ADV.
4. Duane recently moved ~~to San Diego~~.

Recently tells WHEN Duane moved.

ADV. ADV.
5. We enjoy a circus now and then.

Now/then tell WHEN we enjoy a circus.

ADV.
6. She pulled weeds immediately ~~after lunch~~.

Immediately tells WHEN she pulled weeds.

ADV. ADV.
7. Sooner or later, Dad must make a decision ~~about the job~~.

Sooner/later tells WHEN Dad must make a decision.

ADV. ADV.
8. Susan will save her money now and buy a home soon.

Now tells WHEN Susan will save her money. Soon tells WHEN Susan will buy a home.

Name________________________________

Date________________________________

ADVERBS
When?

Directions: Cross out any prepositional phrase(s). Underline the subject once and the verb/verb phrase twice. Label any adverb (ADV.) that tells **WHEN**. In the space provided, explain the use of the adverb in the sentence.

ADV.
Example: Is Santa coming soon?

Soon tells WHEN Santa is coming.

1. They left the fast food restaurant suddenly.

____

2. Kevin burned the cookies again.

____

3. Please do that now.

____

4. Duane recently moved to San Diego.

____

5. We enjoy a circus now and then.

____

6. She pulled weeds immediately after lunch.

____

7. Sooner or later, Dad must make a decision about the job.

____

8. Susan will save her money now and buy a home soon.

____

PAGE 388 = WORKBOOK PAGE 200
PAGE 389 = WORKBOOK PAGE 201

FOR THE TEACHER:
WORKBOOK PAGE 195

ADVERBS

To What Extent?

Some adverbs tell to what extent.

There are seven common adverbs that tell to what extent: not, so, very, too, quite, rather, somewhat. Students need to memorize them. Say them together repeatedly, put them to music, or make up a song. The point is that students must learn them.

There are other adverbs that tell **to what extent** (examples: extremely, unusually).

These adverbs can modify (go over to) a **verb**, an **adjective**, or another **adverb**:

VERB
Examples: I would **rather** stay here. (Rather tells **to what extent** I would stay.)

ADJ.
This is a **very** pretty picture. (Very tells **to what extent** pretty.)

ADV.
Don't walk **so** slowly. (So tells **to what extent** slowly.)

Occasionally, an adverb that tells *to what extent* will occur within a prepositional phrase. Hence, the following steps need to be taken in determining these adverbs.

1. First, delete prepositional phrases. Check each prepositional phrase to see if an adverb telling to what extent is in it.

   ADV.
   Example: The door ~~by the bedroom~~ did not open ~~onto a~~ very ~~large patio~~.

2. Underline the subject once and the verb/verb phrase twice.

   ADV.
   Example: The door ~~by the bedroom~~ did not open ~~onto a~~ very ~~large patio~~.

3. Look for any other adverbs in the sentence that tell *to what extent.*

   ADV. ADV.
   Example: The door ~~by the bedroom~~ did not open ~~onto a~~ very ~~large patio~~.

Name________________________________

WORKBOOK PAGE 196

Date________________________________

ADVERBS
To What Extent?

There are seven adverbs that commonly tell *to what extent.* These are **not (n't)**, **so**, **very**, **too**, **quite**, **rather**, and **somewhat**. Although there are others, these seven appear repeatedly and tell *to what extent.* (Others may include *completely, extremely,* or *unusually.*) Be sure to memorize **not (n't)**, **so**, **very**, **too**, **quite**, **rather**, and **somewhat**.

Answers will be in boldfaced print.

Directions: Circle any adverb(s) telling ***to what extent.***

1. You look **so** sad.
2. The parents were **very** upset.
3. Those painters are **too** busy to come today.
4. Do **not** waste your time with that.
5. He is a **rather** calm jockey.
6. Debra is **quite** happy to sit and knit.
7. Do**n't** become **so** fearful.
8. Mr. and Mrs. Little are **rather** concerned about the concert.
9. The boat left the harbor **very** suddenly.
10. He looks at me **rather** strangely.
11. Sydney is **completely** interested in the deal.
12. The child appears **extremely** sleepy.
13. We felt **somewhat** ill after eating the salad.
14. You are **too** worried about driving to Tulsa.
15. Do **not** spend **so** much time in the bathroom.

Name________________________________

Date________________________________

ADVERBS
To What Extent?

There are seven adverbs that commonly tell *to what extent.* These are **not (n't)**, **so**, **very**, **too**, **quite**, **rather**, and **somewhat**. Although there are others, these seven appear repeatedly and tell *to what extent*. (Others may include *completely*, *extremely*, or *unusually*.) Be sure to memorize **not (n't)**, **so**, **very**, **too**, **quite**, **rather**, and **somewhat**.

Directions: Circle any adverb(s) telling ***to what extent***.

1. You look so sad.
2. The parents were very upset.
3. Those painters are too busy to come today.
4. Do not waste your time with that.
5. He is a rather calm jockey.
6. Debra is quite happy to sit and knit.
7. Don't become so fearful.
8. Mr. and Mrs. Little are rather concerned about the concert.
9. The boat left the harbor very suddenly.
10. He looks at me rather strangely.
11. Sydney is completely interested in the deal.
12. The child appears extremely sleepy.
13. We felt somewhat ill after eating the salad.
14. You are too worried about driving to Tulsa.
15. Do not spend so much time in the bathroom.

Name________________________________

WORKBOOK PAGE 197

Date________________________________

ADVERBS
To What Extent?

There are seven adverbs that commonly tell *to what extent*. These are **not (n't)**, **so**, **very**, **too**, **quite**, **rather**, and **somewhat**. Although there are others, these appear repeatedly and tell *to what extent*. (Others may include *completely*, *extremely*, or *unusually*.) Be sure to memorize the seven commonly used adverbs.

Answers are in boldfaced print.

Directions: Circle any adverb that tells ***to what extent***.

1. These clothes are **too** worn out to sell.
2. Mrs. Hand is **so** excited about skydiving.
3. Her friend is **somewhat** timid.
4. That forest is **rather** beautiful.
5. This doughnut is **too** sticky.
6. A glass of lemonade can be **very** refreshing.
7. The **somewhat** burned egg was scraped from the pan.
8. This telephone is **extremely** old.
9. A radio is playing **too** loudly for me.
10. I would **not** like to go there this summer.
11. His answer was **not very** clear.
12. Her sister is **unusually** tall.
13. He is **somewhat** shy, but his brother is **rather** outgoing.
14. Jenny seems **quite** perturbed by John's **rather** funny remark.
15. Do**n't** give up **so** easily.

Name____________________________

Date____________________________

ADVERBS
To What Extent?

There are seven adverbs that commonly tell *to what extent*. These are **not (n't)**, **so**, **very**, **too**, **quite**, **rather**, and **somewhat**. Although there are others, these appear repeatedly and tell *to what extent*. (Others may include *completely*, *extremely*, or *unusually*.) Be sure to memorize the seven commonly used adverbs.

Directions: Circle any adverb(s) telling ***to what extent***.

1. These clothes are too worn out to sell.
2. Mrs. Hand is so excited about skydiving.
3. Her friend is somewhat timid.
4. That forest is rather beautiful.
5. This doughnut is too sticky.
6. A glass of lemonade can be very refreshing.
7. The somewhat burned egg was scraped from the pan.
8. This telephone is extremely old.
9. A radio is playing too loudly for me.
10. I would not like to go there this summer.
11. His answer was not very clear.
12. Her sister is unusually tall.
13. He is somewhat shy, but his brother is rather outgoing.
14. Jenny seems quite perturbed by John's rather funny remark.
15. Don't give up so easily.

Name________________________________ **ADVERBS**

WORKBOOK PAGE 198

Date________________________________

Directions: Label **any** adverb(s) in each sentence.

Recommendation: Do this worksheet orally. Students should soon understand the suggested pattern.

Remember: Adverbs tell **HOW**, **WHEN**, **WHERE**, AND **TO WHAT EXTENT**.

Suggestion: Cross out any prepositional phrase(s). However, check to see if one of the 7 adverbs that tell *to what extent* may be in any prepositional phrase. If it is, label that adverb. Underline the subject once and the verb/verb phrase twice. Next, go through the sentence looking specifically for any adverbs that tell **how**. Reread the sentence, searching for any adverbs that tell **when**. Next, look for any adverbs that tell **where**. Finally, look for any adverbs that tell **to what extent** and are not located in a prepositional phrase. This process may sound long, but once you do it step-by-step, it will become fast and will help you to determine adverbs.

Example: Yesterday (ADV.), a man ~~with a very lovely wife~~ snorkled (ADV.) here (ADV.).

1. That customer comes **in** (ADV.) **daily** (ADV.).

2. Her mother ~~in South Dakota~~ will **not** (ADV.) visit **soon** (ADV.).

3. Monica stayed **there** (ADV.) **alone** (ADV.).

4. Those children play **nicely** (ADV.) **together** (ADV.).

5. Dr. Hubbard **often** (ADV.) seems **very** (ADV.) tired. (Tired is an adjective.)

6. **Later** (ADV.), some citizens wrote **rather** (ADV.) long letters ~~to their senator~~.

7. **Afterwards** (ADV.), the family went **up** (ADV.) ~~into an observation tower~~.

8. ~~At the family gathering~~, they sat **everywhere** (ADV.) ~~on the lawn~~ and chatted ~~about their~~ ~~**somewhat** (ADV.) unusual pets~~.

Name________________________________ **ADVERBS**

Date________________________________

Directions: Label **any** adverb(s) in each sentence.

Remember: Adverbs tell **HOW**, **WHEN**, **WHERE**, AND **TO WHAT EXTENT**.

Suggestion: Cross out any prepositional phrase(s). However, check to see if one of the 7 adverbs that tell *to what extent* may be in any prepositional phrase. If it is, label that adverb. Underline the subject once and the verb/verb phrase twice. Next, go through the sentence looking specifically for any adverbs that tell **how**. Reread the sentence, searching for any adverbs that tell **when**. Next, look for any adverbs that tell **where**. Finally, look for any adverbs that tell **to what extent** and are not located in a prepositional phrase. This process may sound long, but once you do it step-by-step, it will become fast and will help you to determine adverbs.

ADV. ADV. ADV.
Example: Yesterday, a man ~~with a very lovely wife~~ snorkled here.

1. That customer comes in daily.

2. Her mother in South Dakota will not visit soon.

3. Monica stayed there alone.

4. Those children play nicely together.

5. Dr. Hubbard often seems very tired.

6. Later, some citizens wrote rather long letters to their senator.

7. Afterwards, the family went up into an observation tower.

8. At the family gathering, they sat everywhere on the lawn and chatted about their somewhat unusual pets.

Name________________________________ **ADVERBS**

WORKBOOK PAGE 199

Date________________________________

Directions: Label **any** adverb(s) in each sentence.

Remember: Adverbs tell **HOW**, **WHEN**, **WHERE**, AND **TO WHAT EXTENT**.

Suggestion: Cross out any prepositional phrase(s). However, check to see if one of the 7 adverbs that tell *to what extent* may be in any prepositional phrase. If it is, label that adverb. Underline the subject once and the verb/verb phrase twice. Next, go through the sentence looking specifically for any adverbs that tell **how**. Reread the sentence, searching for any adverbs that tell **when**. Next, look for any adverbs that tell **where**. Finally, look for any adverbs that tell **to what extent** and are not located in a prepositional phrase. This process may sound long, but once you do it step-by-step, it will become fast and will help you to determine adverbs.

ADV. ADV.
Example: Their coach sat there silently ~~with his head~~ ~~in his hands~~.

ADV. ADV.
1. **Yesterday**, clouds rolled **in** ~~from the west~~.

ADV. ADV.
2. He reacted **so strangely** ~~to the news~~.

ADV. ADV.
3. The bride smiled **down** ~~at her **somewhat** frightened flower girl~~.

ADV. ADV.
4. **Very** heavy rains **rapidly** flooded the area.

ADV. ADV.
5. You may sit **somewhere nearby**.

ADV. ADV. ADV.
6. **There** are **not** any snakes ~~in the Dayhoff's pond~~ **now.**

ADV. ADV.
7. The bathroom has been cleaned **too hurriedly**.

ADV. ADV.
8. Their uncle **always** travels **everywhere** ~~during his summer vacation~~.

Name________________________________ **ADVERBS**

Date________________________________

Directions: Label **any** adverb(s) in each sentence.

Remember: Adverbs tell **HOW**, **WHEN**, **WHERE**, AND **TO WHAT EXTENT**.

Suggestion: Cross out any prepositional phrase(s). However, check to see if one of the 7 adverbs that tell *to what extent* may be in any prepositional phrase. If it is, label that adverb. Underline the subject once and the verb/verb phrase twice. Next, go through the sentence looking specifically for any adverbs that tell **how**. Reread the sentence, searching for any adverbs that tell **when**. Next, look for any adverbs that tell **where**. Finally, look for any adverbs that tell **to what extent** and are not located in a prepositional phrase. This process may sound long, but once you do it step-by-step, it will become fast and will help you to determine adverbs.

ADV. ADV.

Example: Their coach sat there silently ~~with his head~~ ~~in his hands~~.

1. Yesterday, clouds rolled in from the west.

2. He reacted so strangely to the news.

3. The bride smiled down at her somewhat frightened flower girl.

4. Very heavy rains rapidly flooded the area.

5. You may sit somewhere nearby.

6. There are not any snakes in the Dayhoff's pond now.

7. The bathroom has been cleaned too hurriedly.

8. Their uncle always travels everywhere during his summer vacation.

ADVERBS

Degrees of Adverbs

Adverbs often make comparisons:

The **comparative** form compares two things.

The **superlative** form compares three things or more.

comparative: The first batter hit the ball **harder** than the second one. (Two are being compared for how the ball was hit.)

superlative: Cameron hit the ball **hardest** during the game. (A comparison with Cameron and everyone else who hit the ball during the game is being made.)

There are three ways to form the comparative and the superlative:

A. **Comparative** - comparing 2:

1. Add **er** to most one-syllable adverbs:

   hard/harder fast/faster

2. Place **more** before most two or more syllable adverbs:

   gently/more gently recently/more recently

3. Some adverbs totally change form:

   badly/worse well/better

B. **Superlative** - comparing <u>3</u> or more:

1. Add **<u>est</u>** to most one-syllable adverbs:

   hard/hardest fast/fastest

2. Place **<u>most</u>** before most two or more syllable adverbs:

   gently/most gently recently/most recently

3. Some adverbs totally change form:

   badly/worst well/best

Adverb	Comparative	Superlative
well	better	best
lazily	more lazily	most lazily
hurriedly	more hurriedly	most hurriedly
sleepily	more sleepily	most sleepily

*Less for the comparative and least for the superlative may also be used.

Name_______________

ADVERBS

WORKBOOK PAGE 202

Degrees of Adverbs

Date_______________

Directions: An adjective form has been given. Write the adverb form in the first blank. Then, write the comparative form in B and the superlative form in C.

You may wish to do this exercise orally and have students write in answers. It's important that they also hear the correct usage.

Example: Margo did her work ___rapidly___ (rapid).
However, Kent does his work ___more rapidly___ than Margo.
Of all the office workers, Helen does her work ___most rapidly___

1. A. Penny walks ___**slowly**___ (slow).

   B. Her brother walks ___**more slowly**___ .

   C. Of the entire family, their dad walks ___**most slowly**___.

2. A. An acrobat flipped ___**smoothly**___ (smooth).

   B. This acrobat flips ___**more smoothly**___ than his partner.

   C. That acrobat flips ___**most smoothly**___ during her third act.

3. A. I spoke ___**kindly**___ (kind) to the new neighbor.

   B. Roberto speaks ___**more kindly**___ to his friends than Kurt.

   C. Of all the girls on the cheering squad, Franny speaks ___**most kindly**___.

4. A. The cafeteria server works ___**carefully**___ (careful).

   B. Of the two gardeners, the tall one works ___**more carefully**___.

   C. You worked hard on the three assignments, but you did the first one ___**most carefully**___.

5. A. The athlete standing by the coach runs ___**fast**___ (fast).

   B. However, the one getting a drink runs ___**faster**___.

   C. The athlete without his helmet runs ___**fastest**___ of the whole team.

Name________________________________

Date________________________________

ADVERBS
Degrees of Adverbs

Directions: An adjective form has been given. Write the adverb form in the first blank. Then, write the comparative form in B and the superlative form in C.

Examples: Margo did her work _____rapidly_______ (rapid).
However, Kent does his work ____more rapidly___ than Margo.
Of all the office workers, Helen does her work __most rapidly__.

1. A. Penny walks __________________ (slow).

   B. Her brother walks ___________________________.

   C. Of the entire family, their dad walks ___________________________.

2. A. An acrobat flipped ___________________ (smooth).

   B. This acrobat flips _____________________________ than his partner.

   C. That acrobat flips _____________________________ during her third act.

3. A. I spoke ____________________ (kind) to the new neighbor.

   B. Roberto speaks ____________________________ to his friends than Kurt.

   C. Of all the girls on the cheering squad, Franny speaks ____________________.

4. A. The cafeteria server works _________________________ (careful).

   B. Of the two gardeners, the tall one works ___________________________.

   C. You worked hard on the three assignments, but you did the first one _________

   ______________________________.

5. A. The athlete standing by the coach runs ___________________ (fast).

   B. However, the one getting a drink runs ____________________.

   C. The athlete without his helmet runs ____________________ of the whole team.

Name_______________________________ **ADVERBS**

WORKBOOK PAGE 203 **Degrees of Adverbs**

Date_______________________________

You may wish to do this orally (as students write in answers). Hearing proper usage is very important.

Directions: An adjective form has been given. Write the adverb form in the first blank. Then, write the comparative form in B and the superlative form in C.

Examples: Carlo sits ___restlessly___ (restless).
He sits even ___more restlessly___ than his little brother.
His older brother sits ___most restlessly___ of the family.

1. A. She does that ___**easily**___ (easy).

   B. Lauren does the trick ___**more easily**___ than I.

   C. Of the triplets, Dee Dee does the trick ___**most easily**___.

2. A. Heyward hits the ball ___**hard**___ (hard).

   B. His younger son hits it ___**harder**___ than Heyward.

   C. However, his oldest son hits it ___**hardest**___ of the entire family.

3. A. Joel moved ___**recently**___ (recent).

   B. Tammi moved ___**more recently**___ than her friend.

   C. Of all their travels, the Clarks enjoyed the trip taken ___**most recently**___.

4. A. A visitor stepped onto the ladder bridge ___**hesitantly**___ (hesitant).

   B. Brad climbed on the horse ___**more hesitantly**___ than his sister did.

   C. He jumps ___**most hesitantly**___ of their skydiving team.

5. A. Don't answer so ___**sharply**___ (sharp).

   B. This fire bell rings ___**more sharply**___ than the old one.

   C. The parent answered ___**most sharply**___ the third time he said no.

Name________________________________

Date________________________________

ADVERBS
Degrees of Adverbs

Directions: An adjective form has been given. Write the adverb form in the first blank. Then, write the comparative form in B and the superlative form in C.

Examples: Carlo sits ____restlessly____ (restless).
He sits even ____more restlessly____ than his little brother.
His older brother sits ____most restlessly____ of the family.

1. A. She does that ____________________ (easy).

   B. Lauren does the trick ________________________ than I.

   C. Of the triplets, Dee Dee does the trick ______________________________.

2. A. Heyward hits the ball _______________________ (hard).

   B. His younger son hits it ______________________ than Heyward.

   C. However, his oldest son hits it ____________________ of the entire family.

3. A. Joel moved _______________________ (recent).

   B. Tammi moved __________________________ than her friend.

   C. Of all their travels, the Clarks enjoyed the trip taken _____________________.

4. A. A visitor stepped onto the ladder bridge ______________________ (hesitant).

   B. Brad climbed on the horse __________________________ than his sister did.

   C. He jumps _________________________ of their skydiving team.

5. A. Don't answer so ______________________ (sharp).

   B. This fire bell rings _______________________ than the old one.

   C. The parent answered ______________________ the third time he said no.

Name________________________________ **ADVERBS**
WORKBOOK PAGE 204 **Degrees of Adverbs**
Date________________________________

Directions: Select the correct adverb form.

Example: Loni walks (**more slowly**, most slowly) than his teammate.

1. Jacob answered (**more quickly**, most quickly) than his friend.
2. He fell down (**harder**, hardest) the second time he fell.
3. The student reciting a speech spoke (more confidently, **most confidently**) during the third practice.
4. In that family, the oldest speaks (more softly, **most softly**).
5. That patient went home (**earlier**, more early) than his roommate.
6. The carpet layer takes breaks (**more often**, oftener) than his helper.
7. That raccoon climbed the tree (faster, **fastest**) of all the animals.
8. Morning storms seem to occur (**more suddenly**, most suddenly) than afternoon ones.
9. This last check in the checkbook has been written (more legibly, **most legibly**).
10. Bean plants grow (**taller**, tallest) than corn in their garden.
11. The customer behaved (**more rudely**, most rudely) the second time she explained the problem to the clerk.
12. The boys and girls played (more roughly, **most roughly**) during the third game.
13. That volcano erupted (**more violently**, most violently) the second time.
14. Of all the gifts, she likes her tennis shoes (better, **best**).
15. In the round of golf, she hit the ball (more swiftly, **most swiftly**) at hole four.

Name________________________________

Date________________________________

ADVERBS
Degrees of Adverbs

Directions: Select the correct adverb form.

Example: Ron walks (**more slowly**, most slowly) than his teammate.

1. Jacob answered (more quickly, most quickly) than his friend.
2. He fell down (harder, hardest) the second time he fell.
3. The student reciting a speech spoke (more confidently, most confidently) during the third practice.
4. In that family, the oldest speaks (more softly, most softly).
5. That patient went home (earlier, more early) than his roommate.
6. The carpet layer takes breaks (more often, oftener) than his helper.
7. That raccoon climbed the tree (faster, fastest) of all the animals.
8. Morning storms seem to occur (more suddenly, most suddenly) than afternoon ones.
9. This last check in the checkbook has been written (more legibly, most legibly).
10. Bean plants grow (taller, tallest) than corn in their garden.
11. The customer behaved (more rudely, most rudely) the second time she explained the problem to the clerk.
12. The boys and girls played (more roughly, most roughly) during the third game.
13. That volcano erupted (more violently, most violently) the second time.
14. Of all the gifts, she likes her tennis shoes (better, best).
15. In the round of golf, she hit the ball (more swiftly, most swiftly) at hole four.

Name________________________________
WORKBOOK PAGE 205
Date________________________________

ADVERBS
Degrees of Adverbs

Directions: Select the correct adverb form.

Example: The actress reacted (**more tearfully**, most tearfully) the second time.

1. The little girl plays (**more quietly**, most quietly) than her older sister.
2. The teenager did (**worse**, worst) on the second driving test.
3. A black kitten chased the ball (**more playfully**, most playfully) than the white one.
4. He shook the third rug (more furiously, **most furiously**).
5. The wind blew (**more strongly**, most strongly) during the second storm.
6. That girl smiles (more brightly, **most brightly**) of the three models.
7. A large kite soared (**higher**, highest) than the smaller one.
8. This ballet dancer moves (more gracefully, **most gracefully**) of all the performers.
9. The runners cut the corner (more sharply, **most sharply**) during the third try.
10. This new canoe glides (**more slowly**, most slowly) than the old one.
11. At the party, they arrived (**sooner**, soonest) than the Smith family.
12. Dick sleds (**more frequently**, most frequently) than he toboggans.
13. The model smiled (more brightly, **most brightly**) for the fifth commercial.
14. I feel (badly, **worse**) today than I did yesterday.
15. That driver stopped his car (**more recklessly**, most recklessly) at the second traffic light than at the first one.

Name_______________________________

Date_______________________________

ADVERBS
Degrees of Adverbs

Directions: Select the correct adverb form.

Example: The actress reacted (**more tearfully**, most tearfully) the second time.

1. The little girl plays (more quietly, most quietly) than her older sister.
2. The teenager did (worse, worst) on the second driving test.
3. A black kitten chased the ball (more playfully, most playfully) than the white one.
4. He shook the third rug (more furiously, most furiously).
5. The wind blew (more strongly, most strongly) during the second storm.
6. That girl smiles (more brightly, most brightly) of the three models.
7. A large kite soared (higher, highest) than the smaller one.
8. This ballet dancer moves (more gracefully, most gracefully) of all the performers.
9. The runners cut the corner (more sharply, most sharply) during the third try.
10. This new canoe glides (more slowly, most slowly) than the old one.
11. At the party, they arrived (sooner, soonest) than the Smith family.
12. Dick sleds (more frequently, most frequently) than he toboggans.
13. The model smiled (more brightly, most brightly) for the fifth commercial.
14. I feel (badly, worse) today than I did yesterday.
15. That driver stopped his car (more recklessly, most recklessly) at the second traffic light than at the first one.

FOR THE TEACHER: The concept of double negatives is easily understood by students. However, the problem arises that some students have heard double negatives used (misused) at home. Therefore, they use them, and double negatives sound "right." This is a challenging situation.

WORKBOOK PAGE 206

ADVERBS
Double Negatives

Negative words include: no, not (n't), never, none, no one, nobody, nothing, nowhere, scarcely, hardly.

Don't use two negatives in a sentence.
(Actually, this is true for an independent clause not containing a subordinate clause. At this point, you do not want to teach subordinate clauses; therefore, it's best to stick with simple sentences.) A subordinate clause is in boldface in the following sentence.

Because Bill didn't register, he can't attend college this fall.

Two *nots* are perfectly acceptable in this sentence because the first negative word occurs in a subordinate clause.

However, in independent clauses, two negatives should not be used.

Examples: **WRONG:** I don't want nothing.
RIGHT: I don't want anything.
OR
I want nothing.

WRONG: She won't give nobody money.
RIGHT: She won't give anybody money.
OR
She will give nobody money.

WRONG: I hardly get no time to myself.
RIGHT: I hardly get any time to myself.
OR
I get no time to myself.

Neither is also a negative word and should not be used with another negative.

Examples: **WRONG:** Neither wants to go nowhere.
RIGHT: Neither wants to go anywhere.

Neither may be used with *nor*: Neither Mother nor her friends are bowling today.

It is acceptable to use *no* as a response at the beginning of a sentence and then use another negative word after it.

Example: **No**, I do **not** want a cookie.

<u>ADVERBS</u>
Double Negatives

Negative words include: no, not (n't), never, none, no one, nobody, nothing, nowhere, scarcely, hardly.

Don't use two negatives in a sentence.

Examples: **WRONG:** I don't want nothing.

RIGHT: I don't want anything.

OR

I want nothing.

WRONG: She won't give nobody money.

RIGHT: She won't give anybody money.

OR

She will give nobody money.

WRONG: I hardly get no time to myself.

RIGHT: I hardly get any time to myself.

OR

I get no time to myself.

Neither is also a negative word and should not be used with another negative.

Examples: **WRONG:** Neither wants to go nowhere.
RIGHT: Neither wants to go anywhere.

Neither may be used with *nor*: Neither Mother nor her friends are bowling today.

It is acceptable to use *no* as a response at the beginning of a sentence and then use another negative word after it.

Example: **No**, I do **not** want a cookie.

Name________________________________
WORKBOOK PAGE 207
Date________________________________

ADVERBS
Double Negatives

A. Directions: Select the correct word.

1. He never leaves me (**any**, no) money.
2. This isn't (**anybody's**, nobody's) business.
3. He (**can**, can't) hardly hear you.
4. I can't find a quarter (nowhere, **anywhere**).
5. We have not eaten (no, **any**) potatoes.
6. She doesn't want (nothing, **anything**) to drink.
7. You're not allowed to go (nowhere, **anywhere**) alone.
8. The man didn't have (no, **any**) trouble fixing his car.
9. They never do (**anything**, nothing).
10. I don't want (none, **any**).

B. Each sentence contains double negatives. Rewrite each sentence correctly.

1. She doesn't want none. **She doesn't want any. OR She wants none.**
2. I never want nothing. **I never want anything. OR I want nothing.**
3. They scarcely go nowhere. **They scarcely go anywhere. OR They go nowhere.**
4. Nobody wants none. **Nobody wants any.**
5. Don't go with no one. **Don't go with anyone. OR Go with no one.**

Name________________________________

Date________________________________

ADVERBS
Double Negatives

A. Directions: Select the correct word.

1. He never leaves me (any, no) money.
2. This isn't (anybody's, nobody's) business.
3. He (can, can't) hardly hear you.
4. I can't find a quarter (nowhere, anywhere).
5. We have not eaten (no, any) potatoes.
6. She doesn't want (nothing, anything) to drink.
7. You're not allowed to go (nowhere, anywhere) alone.
8. The man didn't have (no, any) trouble fixing his car.
9. They never do (anything, nothing).
10. I don't want (none, any).

B. Each sentence contains double negatives. Rewrite each sentence correctly.

1. She doesn't want none. ________________________________
2. I never want nothing. ________________________________
3. They scarcely go nowhere. ________________________________
4. Nobody wants none. ________________________________
5. Don't go with no one. ________________________________

Name________________________________ **ADVERBS**
WORKBOOK PAGE 208 **Double Negatives**
Date________________________________

A. Directions: Select the correct word.

1. The soda fountain doesn't have (no, **any**) chairs.
2. I hadn't (**ever**, never) seen that.
3. That store scarcely has (no, **any**) products.
4. Nobody wants to go (**anywhere**, nowhere).
5. Don't do that (never, **ever**) again.
6. He hardly earned (**anything**, nothing) last summer.
7. No one ever wants (**any**, none).
8. You aren't supposed to do (nobody's, **anybody's**) work.
9. This lawn mower (**has**, hasn't) hardly been used.
10. Don't drink (no, **any**) water from the creek.

B. Each sentence contains double negatives. Rewrite each sentence correctly.

1. He's not mad at nobody. **He's not mad at anybody. OR He's mad at nobody.**

2. His mother doesn't want nothing. **His mother doesn't want anything. OR His mother wants nothing.**

3. Don't try that never again. **Don't try that ever again.**

4. This computer doesn't have no keyboard. **This computer doesn't have any keyboard. OR This computer has no keyboard.**

5. There isn't hardly any time to do that. **There isn't any time to do that. OR There is no time to do that. OR There is hardly any time to do that.**

Name________________________________

Date________________________________

ADVERBS
Double Negatives

A. Directions: Select the correct word.

1. The soda fountain doesn't have (no, any) chairs.
2. I hadn't (ever, never) seen that.
3. That store scarcely has (no, any) products.
4. Nobody wants to go (anywhere, nowhere).
5. Don't do that (never, ever) again.
6. He hardly earned (anything, nothing) last summer.
7. No one ever wants (any, none).
8. You aren't supposed to do (nobody's, anybody's) work.
9. This lawn mower (has, hasn't) hardly been used.
10. Don't drink (no, any) water from the creek.

B. Each sentence contains double negatives. Rewrite each sentence correctly.

1. He's not mad at nobody. ________________________________
2. His mother doesn't want nothing. ________________________________
3. Don't try that never again. ________________________________
4. This computer doesn't have no keyboard. ________________________________
5. There isn't hardly any time to do that. ________________________________

Name________________________________ **ADVERB REVIEW**

WORKBOOK PAGE 209

Date________________________________

Adverbs are in boldfaced print.

Directions: Choose **any** adverb(s) in each sentence.

Example: We can go **there later** ~~for a very brief workout~~.

Note: You may wish to instruct students to use the process included in previous lessons. Answers have been provided.

1. Her hair is **very** curly **today**.

2. Those sand dunes are **quite** steep ~~for me~~ (to steer) **easily**.

3. **Abruptly**, she stood **up** and yelled ~~with too much anger in her voice~~.

4. The welder **carefully** placed two pieces ~~of steel~~ **sideways**.

5. Several **very** large tumbleweeds twirled **fiercely around** ~~in the air~~.

6. That deli owner does **not** cut his pickles **lengthwise**.

7. **When** has Mrs. Stanford gone **somewhere** ~~without her children~~?

8. (You) **Tomorrow**, don't go **outside** ~~until lunch~~.

Directions: Select the correct answer.

1. This new machine works (**more steadily**, most steadily) than the old one.

2. Anita climbs the tree (more easily, **most easily**) of the four girls.

3. Did you arrive (**later**, latest) than Miss Calhoun?

4. The third car stopped (suddener, **most suddenly**).

Directions: Select the correct answer.

1. He never goes (**anywhere**, nowhere) without his hat.

2. Nobody wants (none, **any**) right now.

3. She hardly has (no, **any**) money.

Name_________________________________ **ADVERB REVIEW**

Date_________________________________

Directions: Choose **any** adverb(s) in each sentence.

Example: We can go **there** (ADV.) **later** (ADV.) ~~for a **very** (ADV.) brief workout~~.

1. Her hair is very curly today.

2. Those sand dunes are quite steep for me to steer easily.

3. Abruptly, she stood up and yelled with too much anger in her voice.

4. The welder carefully placed two pieces of steel sideways.

5. Several very large tumbleweeds twirled fiercely around in the air.

6. That deli owner does not cut his pickles lengthwise.

7. When has Mrs. Stanford gone somewhere without her children?

8. Tomorrow, don't go outside until lunch.

Directions: Select the correct answer.

1. This new machine works (more steadily, most steadily) than the old one.

2. Anita climbs the tree (more easily, most easily) of the four girls.

3. Did you arrive (later, latest) than Miss Calhoun?

4. The third car stopped (suddener, most suddenly).

Directions: Select the correct answer.

1. He never goes (anywhere, nowhere) without his hat.

2. Nobody wants (none, any) right now.

3. She hardly has (no, any) money.

Name________________________________ **CUMULATIVE REVIEW**
WORKBOOK PAGE 210
Date________________________________

A. Directions: Cross out any prepositional phrase(s). Underline the subject once and the verb/verb phrase twice.

1. One ~~of the birds~~ flew ~~among the branches~~.

2. A lizard had crawled ~~under a rock~~ ~~in the garden~~.

3. ~~After the beginning~~ ~~of the third quarter~~, the snack bar was closed.

4. (You) Please move the boxes ~~toward the middle~~ ~~of the garage~~.

****

B. Directions: Write the contraction.

1. will not - ___won't___ 3. has not - ___hasn't___

2. we have - ___we've___ 4. we are - ___we're___

****

C. Directions: Write the tense in the blank provided.

1. ___future___ The council will meet to discuss the plans.

2. ___present___ Those Native Americans weave beautiful baskets.

3. ___past___ The mason laid bricks for the patio.

****

D. Write intj. above any interjection and conj. above any conjunction.

1. The janitor pushed the door open **and** (**conj.**) propped it with a broom.

2. **Good grief!** (**intj.**) The pen has leaked all over my shirt!

****

E. Write A if the noun is abstract; write C if the noun is concrete.

1. ___C___ butterfly 2. ___A___ patience 3. ___A___ anger 4. ___C___ air

****

F. Directions: Write C if the noun is common; write P if it is proper.

1. ___P___ LAKE ERIE 2. ___C___ BELL 3. ___C___ BUILDING 4. ___P___ SEARS TOWER

Name_______________________________ **CUMULATIVE REVIEW**

Date_______________________________

A. Directions: Cross out any prepositional phrase(s). Underline the subject once and the verb/verb phrase twice.

1. One of the birds flew among the branches.

2. A lizard had crawled under a rock in the garden.

3. After the beginning of the third quarter, the snack bar was closed.

4. Please move the boxes toward the middle of the garage.

****

B. Directions: Write the contraction.

1. will not - ____________________ 3. has not - ____________________

2. we have - ____________________ 4. we are - ____________________

****

C. Directions: Write the tense in the blank provided.

1. ________________ The council will meet to discuss the plans.

2. ________________ Those Native Americans weave beautiful baskets.

3. ________________ The mason laid bricks for the patio.

****

D. Write intj. above any interjection and conj. above any conjunction.

1. The janitor pushed the door open and propped it with a broom.

2. Good grief! The pen has leaked all over my shirt!

****

E. Write A if the noun is abstract; write C if the noun is concrete.

1. ____ butterfly 2. ____ patience 3. ____ anger 4. ____ air

****

F. Directions: Write C if the noun is common; write P if it is proper.

1. ___ LAKE ERIE 2. ___ BELL 3. ___ BUILDING 4. ___ SEARS TOWER

Name________________________________ **CUMULATIVE REVIEW**

WORKBOOK 211

Date________________________________

G. Directions: Write **N** if the underlined word is a noun. Write **A** if the underlined word is an adjective. Write **V** if the underlined word is a verb.

1. _N_ The elderly ladies go for a walk every day.

2. _V_ The first four pupils will walk to the end of the line.

3. _A_ A cat dish has been placed by the door.

4. _N_ The Simpson family has been given a cat.

****

H. Directions: Write the possessive form.

1. clothes belonging to a man - ___a man's clothes___

2. a ball belonging to Chris - ___Chris's ball___

3. a hole belonging to mice - ___mice's hole___

4. popsicles belonging to girls - ___girls' popsicles___

****

I. Directions: Write the plural.

1. lash - __lashes__ 2. bug - __bugs__ 3. child - __children__

4. box - __boxes__ 5. list - __lists__ 6. lens- __lenses__

****

J. Directions: Box any nouns:

Nouns are in boldfaced print.

1. Several **lights** have been broken near that **alley**.
2. His **bike** has a loose **seat**.
3. **Jolene's dad** is having a **party** for some **friends**.

****

K. Directions: Write **D.O**. if the underlined word is a direct object, **P.N.** if the underlined word is a predicate nominative, and **P.A.** if the underlined word is a predicate adjective.

Be sure to discuss answers.

1. _D.O._ The child threw a ball to his friend.

2. _P.N._ The winner is Juan. (Juan is the winner.)

3. _P.A._ This bread tastes stale.

Name________________________________ **CUMULATIVE REVIEW**

Date________________________________

G. Directions: Write **N** if the underlined word is a noun. Write **A** if the underlined word is an adjective. Write **V** if the underlined word is a verb.

1. _____ The elderly ladies go for a walk every day.

2. _____ The first four pupils will walk to the end of the line.

3. _____ A cat dish has been placed by the door.

4. _____ The Simpson family has been given a cat.

****

H. Directions: Write the possessive form.

1. clothes belonging to a man - ________________________________

2. a ball belonging to Chris - ________________________________

3. a hole belonging to mice - ________________________________

4. popsicles belonging to girls - ________________________________

****

I. Directions: Write the plural.

1. lash - ____________ 2. bug - ____________ 3. child - ____________
4. box - ____________ 5. list - ____________ 6. lens- ____________

****

J. Directions: Box any nouns:

1. Several lights have been broken near that alley.
2. His bike has a loose seat.
3. Jolene's dad is having a party for some friends.

****

K. Directions: Write **D.O.** if the underlined word is a direct object, **P.N.** if the underlined word is a predicate nominative, and **P.A.** if the underlined word is a predicate adjective.

1. ______ The child threw a ball to his friend.

2. ______ The winner is Juan.

3. ______ This bread tastes stale.

Name________________________________ **ADVERB TEST**

WORKBOOK PAGE 332

Date________________________________

A cumulative test has been placed after the pronoun unit.

A. Directions: Choose any adverb(s).

1. You must sign **here carefully**, but write **quickly**.

2. **Tonight,** they will be taking a **rather** short walk **up** into the mountains.

3. He **always** writes **neatly**, but he drops papers **everywhere**.

4. Sal arises **early** and fishes **upstream daily**.

5. Harvey hit the ball **very hard out** into left field.

6. The attendant **clearly** announced that the flight would **not** arrive **late**.

B. Directions: Choose the correct adverb.

1. That announcer speaks (**more rapidly**, most rapidly) than his friend.

2. Jill runs (fast, **faster**) than her sister.

3. Of the four, this large balloon rose (more quickly, **most quickly**).

4. Mark walks (**more slowly**, most slowly) than I.

5. Chelsea arrived (earlier, **earliest**) of all the students.

6. Of all the diagrams, this one was drawn (more carefully, **most carefully**).

C. Directions: Select the correct word.

1. Mrs. Reno doesn't eat (**any**, no) chicken.

2. That girl swims so (good, **well**).

3. He never has (no, **any**) money.

4. Nobody wants (**anything**, nothing) from the snack bar.

5. Their sister hasn't felt (good, **well**) all week.

Name________________________________ **ADVERB TEST**

Date________________________________

A. Directions: Circle any adverb(s).

1. You must sign here carefully, but write quickly.
2. Tonight they will be taking a rather short walk up into the mountains.
3. He always writes neatly, but he drops his papers everywhere.
4. Sal arises early and fishes upstream daily.
5. Harvey hit the ball very hard out into left field.
6. The attendant clearly announced that the flight would not arrive late.

B. Directions: Choose the correct adverb.

1. That announcer speaks (more rapidly, most rapidly) than his friend.
2. Jill runs (faster, faster) than her sister.
3. Of the four, this large balloon rose (more quickly, most quickly).
4. Mark walks (more slowly, most slowly) than I.
5. Chelsea arrived (earlier, earliest) of all the students.
6. Of all the diagrams, this one was drawn (more carefully, most carefully).

C. Directions: Select the correct word.

1. Mrs. Reno doesn't eat (any, no) chicken.
2. That girl swims so (good, well).
3. He never has (no, any) money.
4. Nobody wants (anything, nothing) from the snack bar.
5. Their sister hasn't felt (good, well) all week.

PAGE 413 = WORKBOOK PAGE 213
PAGE 418 = WORKBOOK PAGE 216
PAGE 419 = WORKBOOK PAGE 217
PAGE 420 = WORKBOOK PAGE 218
PAGE 422 = WORKBOOK PAGE 219
PAGE 423 = WORKBOOK PAGE 220

SENTENCE TYPES

The four types of sentences are declarative, interrogative, imperative, and exclamatory.

1. A **declarative** sentence makes a **statement.**
   A declarative sentence ends with a period.

   Examples: Spain and Portugal are on the same peninsula.

   Roberta eats ketchup on crackers.

2. An **interrogative** sentence asks a **question**.
   An interrogative sentence ends with a question mark.

   Examples: How many taste buds does a human have?

   Are there any bees in that hive?

3. An **imperative** sentence gives a **command**.
   An imperative sentence ends with a period.

   Examples: Pass the salt, please.

   Take this home with you.

4. An **exclamatory** sentence shows **emotion**.
   An exclamatory sentence ends with an exclamation point.

   Examples: The water is flooding the kitchen!

   Yuck! You threw that on the floor!

****

An entire interrogative sentence will ask a question.

Example: Can you fix the car?

A sentence will be declarative if part of the sentence infers a question.

Example: Mr. Hanes asked the mechanic if he could fix the car.

Name________________________________

SENTENCE TYPES

WORKBOOK PAGE 214

Date________________________________

Directions: Write the sentence type on the line.

1. declarative — Groceries were purchased early in the morning.
2. interrogative — Is a dove a sign of peace?
3. exclamatory — You're here!
4. imperative — Please read this.
5. declarative — A peacock displays his feathers.
6. exclamatory — Yeah! We're finished!
7. declarative — Cabbage is a very healthy vegetable.
8. imperative — Put your papers in this trash.
9. interrogative — What game are they playing?
10. declarative — Jane asked if she could go.
11. declarative — We've lost the gas cap.
12. interrogative — May we watch television for an hour?

Name________________________________

SENTENCE TYPES

Date________________________________

Directions: Write the sentence type on the line.

1. ______________________ Groceries were purchased early in the morning.

2. ______________________ Is a dove a sign of peace?

3. ______________________ You're here!

4. ______________________ Please read this.

5. ______________________ A peacock displays his feathers.

6. ______________________ Yeah! We're finished!

7. ______________________ Cabbage is a very healthy vegetable.

8. ______________________ Put your papers in this trash.

9. ______________________ What game are they playing?

10. ______________________ Jane asked if she could go.

11. ______________________ We've lost the gas cap.

12. ______________________ May we watch television for an hour?

Name________________________________

SENTENCE TYPES

WORKBOOK PAGE 215

Date________________________________

Directions: Write the sentence type on the line.

1. ___declarative___ Bee hives are very clean.

2. ___interrogative___ Have you ever eaten kale?

3. ___imperative___ Grab the fire extinguisher.

4. ___exclamatory___ We won!

5. ___imperative___ Stop at the red line.

6. ___declarative___ They listen well.

7. ___interrogative___ Would you like a hot dog?

8. ___imperative___ Clean your room.

9. ___declarative___ The closet was cleaned once a year.

10. ___interrogative___ Have you finished your homework?

11. ___declarative___ Virgil wanted to know if Lou Ann had finished her homework.

12. ___exclamatory___ I can't believe it!

Name________________________________ **SENTENCE TYPES**

Date________________________________

Directions: Write the sentence type on the line.

1. ______________________ Bee hives are very clean.

2. ______________________ Have you ever eaten kale?

3. ______________________ Grab the fire extinguisher.

4. ______________________ We won!

5. ______________________ Stop at the red line.

6. ______________________ They listen well.

7. ______________________ Would you like a hot dog?

8. ______________________ Clean your room.

9. ______________________ The closet was cleaned once a year.

10. ______________________ Have you finished your homework?

11. ______________________ Virgil wanted to know if Lou Ann had finished her homework.

12. ______________________ I can't believe it!

FRIENDLY LETTER

The parts of a friendly letter are the heading, the greeting, the body, the closing, and the signature. The greeting is also called the salutation.

A three-lined formal heading will be used. In informal letters, the date is frequently the only item included. However, the formal heading is important to know.

In a formal letter, as in all formal writing, abbreviations are not used. The **exception** to this is the postal code for states. A postal code is capitalized, and no punctuation is used.

Examples: New Mexico = NM   Maine = ME
Arizona = AZ   Florida = FL

••

FRIENDLY LETTER PARTS:

POST OFFICE BOX
or
HOUSE NUMBER AND STREET NAME
heading CITY, STATE ZIP CODE
COMPLETE DATE (not abbreviated)

greeting Dear (Person),

body The message is written here. Note that you indent at least five letters. You may wish to skip a line between the greeting and the body. Note that you maintain margins on each side of the paper.
Remember that every time you change topics, you begin a new paragraph.

closing Your friend,
signature Writer's Name

••

IMPORTANT NOTES:

1. Notice the **use of commas** in the heading (between city and state), in the greeting, and in the closing. Also, note that **no comma** is placed between the state and the zip code.

2. Capitalize only the first word of a closing. Be sure you know the spelling of *sincerely* and *truly*.

3. Note that the first word of each line of the heading begins at the same place. The same is true of the closing and signature. Also, the heading, closing, and

signature are lined up. You should be able to place a ruler in front of the heading, the closing, and the signature and draw a straight line.

4. Any friendly letter should be spaced down the page. A letter should not be crowded at the top of a page. The number of lines skipped between the heading and body will depend on the length of the message. Again, the letter should be spaced down the page.

5. Be sure to keep margins on both sides of the paper. The heading needs to be set up so that the street name (unabbreviated) will not flow out into the margin.

••

SAMPLE FRIENDLY LETTER:

12321 North Cedar Hill Drive
Scottsdale, AZ 85254
August 14, 20--

Dear Dan and Anne,

We are so excited about your visit this Christmas. Plans are already being made. Our annual Christmas open house is now planned for December 22nd; we want all of our friends to meet you two. Bring some dressy clothes for that occasion. Of course, Christmas Eve service is important to our family. We are glad that you want to attend with us; this is an important night for our family. As we discussed, let's open gifts Christmas morning.

After Christmas, we want to show you our state. If the weather isn't snowy, we'd like to take you to see the Grand Canyon. Prescott and Tucson are interesting. Of course, Phoenix has much to offer, too. I'm sending several brochures so that you can choose what you want to see.

We are so excited about your visit. Let us know what we can do to make this a memorable Christmas vacation.

Love,
Janell

ENVELOPE

The envelope for a friendly letter usually is in block form. That means that each line is exactly below the line before it.

YOUR NAME ********
HOUSE NUMBER AND STREET ADDRESS **return address** STAMP
CITY, STATE ZIP CODE ********

PERSON TO WHOM YOU ARE SENDING LETTER
HOUSE NUMBER AND STREET ADDRESS
CITY, STATE ZIP CODE

Janell Batsworth *********
5454 East Elm Street STAMP
Phoenix, AZ 85032 *********

Mr. and Mrs. Don Landon
4545 East Jackson Way
Clearwater, SC 29822

IMPORTANT NOTES:

1. In a formal envelope, abbreviations are not used.

2. A variation of the block style allows for indentation of each line. If this is chosen, both the return address and the regular address must be indented.

FOR THE TEACHER: This page contains suggestions for teaching sentences, fragments, and run-ons.

WORKBOOK PAGES 219-220

SENTENCES, FRAGMENTS and RUN-ONS

A. **Sentences**: Make a cooperative decision with your students to talk in complete sentences. This helps them to recognize complete sentences in print. (This may be more difficult than you think.)

B. **Fragments**:

1. To teach fragments, the following is suggested. Walk up to a student, look him straight in the eye, (smile, of course), say the fragment, and walk away. After taking a few steps, pause, turn around, and gesture to imply that you are waiting for an answer (perhaps, in mock disbelief that the student isn't answering). This simple method works! Over a period of days, do it often. Try it when students are in line or are near you in a social situation. They may think you're strange, but they will understand the concept.

   Examples: Walking down the street.
   The man in the back of the police car.
   Fell over a fire hydrant.
   When I was little.

2. Students will be asked to cross out prepositional phrases, to underline the subject once, and to underline the verb or verb phrase twice. This procedure will help to determine fragments.

C. **Run-Ons**

1. Run-ons are easy to spot if they are lengthy. A good rule of thumb, so to speak, is to use a specific conjunction only once in a sentence. In other words, *and* and *but* may work; however, avoid more than one *and* in a sentence.

   Avoid this: I went to the store *and* bought some ice cream *and* then went home *and* made a float.

2. Short run-ons are easy to spot if students understand that two sentences are run together. You need to make them see that this is occurring. It is suggested that you say the first sentence, take a step in whichever direction you are comfortable, and say the second part of the run-on. This helps students recognize that two (or more) sentences are together. Another suggestion is to visually determine the subject and verb of each part by underlining the subject once and the verb/verb phrase twice.

   Examples: I enjoy horses Taffy is my favorite.

   I enjoy horses. (step) Taffy is my favorite.

   I enjoy horses. Taffy is my favorite.

3. Show students how to correct run-ons by using the rules on the ensuing pages.

4. Suggest that students read their own work aloud and pause after each sentence. It's amazing how readily they recognize fragments and run-ons. This can be done cooperatively as well.

NOTE: You may feel that your students aren't ready for dependent and independent clauses. If this is the case, refer to independent clauses as sentences and refer to dependent clauses as fragments.

SENTENCES
FRAGMENTS
RUN-ONS

Sentences:

Clauses:

A. **Independent clauses:**

1. An independent clause contains subject and verb.
2. An independent clause expresses a complete thought.
3. An independent clause can stand alone as a sentence.

Example: Your shirt has some missing buttons.

B. **Dependent clauses:**

1. A dependent clause contains subject and verb.
2. A dependent clause does not express a complete thought.
3. A dependent clause cannot stand alone as a sentence.
4. A dependent clause without an independent clause is a fragment.

Example: Before you eat lunch.

Fragments:

A. A sentence may be missing a subject. This creates a fragment.

Example: A running down the street.

B. A sentence may be missing a verb. This creates a fragment.

Example: The driver of the speed boat.

C. Some fragments are missing both subject and verb.

Examples: This.
Recently.
In the middle of the night.

D. An imperative sentence (command) is not a fragment. Some commands may be only one word, but the subject is (You) meaning "you understood."

Examples: Stop! (You) Stop.

Hold these, please. (You) Hold these, please.

Run-Ons:

A. A run-on may consist of two independent clauses (sentences) run together.

Example: This car is dirty we will wash it.

B. A run-on may consist of two independent clauses joined by a comma.

Example: This car is dirty, we will wash it.

Note: This is often used incorrectly. Even with the comma, the sentence is still a run-on.

C. A run-on may consist of a group of sentences combined with too many conjunctions.

Example: Mom bought groceries home **and** we had to carry them in **but** she was in a hurry **and** we had to put them away.

Note: Avoid using more than two different conjunctions in a sentence. Also, do not use two or more ***and's*** in the same sentence. (Although the use of two ***and's*** is sometimes fine, it's best, at this point, to avoid using two or more in a sentence.)

D. A run-on may consist of a group of sentences combined with commas.

Example: Last year our friends went to Denver, then they went to Colorado Springs, next they went to Utah to see some relatives.

Correcting Run-ons:

1. **Use a period between the independent clauses (sentences).**

Example: The car is dirty. We will wash it.

2. **Use a semicolon between the independent clauses (sentences).**

Example: The car is dirty; we will wash it.

Note: However, the two sentences must be closely related.
WRONG: The car is dirty; I like pizza.

3. **Use a comma and a conjunction between the independent clauses.**

Example: This car is dirty, and we will wash it.

4. **Sometimes, the sentence can be changed.**

Examples: We will wash the dirty car.
Because the car is dirty, we will wash it.

Name________________________________ **SENTENCES**
WORKBOOK PAGE 221 **FRAGMENTS**
Date________________________________ **RUN-ONS**

Note: Be sure to discuss all sentences. Determine what is missing in fragments. Discuss how to correct fragments and run-ons.

Directions: Cross out any prepositional phrase(s). Underline the subject once and the verb/verb phrase twice. In the space provided, write S for sentence, F for fragment, and R-O for run-on.

Example: __F__ ~~With his brother and friend~~.

1. __**F**__ ~~Down the hall~~.
2. __**F**__ The sheets and pillowcases. **Technically, this may be interpreted differently and not underlined as subject.**
3. __**F**__ My sister and I.
4. __**S**__ A chimpanzee walked ~~along the wall~~.
5. __**R-O**__ A policeman searched a shed and went ~~into the house~~ and he checked the back porch and then left ~~in his car~~.
6. __**F**__ Standing ~~in line~~.
7. __**R-O**__ She peeked ~~into the box~~, she began (to laugh).
8. __**F**__ The visited Mt. Rushmore.
9. __**S**__ (You) Stay ~~with me~~. **(imperative sentence)**
10. __**R-O**__ The movie director began to speak, everyone looked restless and began (to look) around and smile at each other and not listen.
11. __**F**__ ~~For the first time in two years~~.
12. __**S**__ He sits ~~in the park~~ daily.
13. __**R-O**__ The alarm rang at six, he didn't rise ~~until nine o'clock~~.
14. __**F**__ Although I like you. **(dependent clause: doesn't express a complete thought)**
15. __**S**__ (You) Go. **(imperative sentence)**

Name________________________________

Date________________________________

SENTENCES
FRAGMENTS
RUN-ONS

Directions: Cross out any prepositional phrase(s). Underline the subject once and the verb/verb phrase twice. In the space provided, write S for sentence, F for fragment, and R-O for run-on.

Example: __F__ ~~With his brother and friend~~.

1. _____ Down the hall.

2. _____ The sheets and pillowcases.

3. _____ My sister and I.

4. _____ A chimpanzee walked along the wall.

5. _____ A policeman searched a shed and went into the house and he checked the back porch and then left in his car.

6. _____ Standing in line.

7. _____ She peeked into the box, she began to laugh.

8. _____ The visited Mt. Rushmore.

9. _____ Stay with me.

10. _____ The movie director began to speak, everyone looked restless and began to look around and smile at each other and not listen.

11. _____ For the first time in two years.

12. _____ He sits in the park daily.

13. _____ The alarm rang at six, he didn't rise until nine o'clock.

14. _____ Although I like you.

15. _____ Go.

Name________________________________ **SENTENCES**
WORKBOOK PAGE 222 **FRAGMENTS**
Date________________________________ **RUN-ONS**

Note: Be sure to discuss all sentences. Determine what is missing in fragments. Discuss how to correct fragments and run-ons.

Directions: Cross out any prepositional phrase(s). Underline the subject once and the verb/verb phrase twice. In the space provided, write S for sentence, F for fragment, and R-O for run-on.

Example: __S__ Clouds rolled in ~~from the west~~.

1. __**F**__ ~~Before the parade~~.
2. __**F**__ Yes!
3. __**F**__ When you are finished. **(dependent clause: doesn't express a complete thought)**
4. __**S**__ Stores were crowded ~~with holiday shoppers~~.
5. __**F**__ Starred ~~in a musical~~.
6. __**F**__ The boss and his assistant. **(Technically, this may be interpreted differently and not underlined as subject.)**
7. __**R-O**__ We need help this table is too heavy.
8. __**S**__ You are right.
9. __**R-O**__ Our neighbor mows his lawn and pulls weeds, and then he waters it ~~for an hour~~, next, he admires it.
10. __**S**__ (You) Get up, please. **(imperative sentence)**
11. __**F**__ Went ~~to camp~~ last summer.
12. __**S**__ Her flight leaves ~~at midnight~~.
13. __**R-O**__ The American flag is passing, we need (to stand).
14. __**F**__ ~~To Kentucky for a convention~~.
15. __**F**__ Tuning ~~into the radio station during a tornado~~.

Name________________________________

Date________________________________

SENTENCES
FRAGMENTS
RUN-ONS

Directions: Cross out any prepositional phrase(s). Underline the subject once and the verb/verb phrase twice. In the space provided, write S for sentence, F for fragment, and R-O for run-on.

Example: __S__ Clouds rolled in ~~from the west~~.

1. _____ Before the parade.
2. _____ Yes!
3. _____ When you are finished.
4. _____ Stores were crowded with holiday shoppers.
5. _____ Starred in a musical.
6. _____ The boss and his assistant.
7. _____ We need help this table is too heavy.
8. _____ You are right.
9. _____ Our neighbor mows his lawn and pulls weeds, and then he waters it for an hour, next he admires it.
10. _____ Get up, please.
11. _____ Went to camp last summer.
12. _____ Her flight leaves at midnight.
13. _____ The American flag is passing, we need to stand.
14. _____ To Kentucky for a convention.
15. _____ Tuning into the radio station during a tornado.

PAGE 430 = WORKBOOK PAGE 223
PAGE 431 = WORKBOOK PAGE 224

FOR THE TEACHER: Pronouns are difficult. Many students use them incorrectly.

WORKBOOK PAGE 224

PRONOUNS

The "me and Bob" formation is frequently used by students. Often, students have learned this in the family environment. However, continuous correcting in a kind manner will help. When a student uses such a formation, **be sure to have him say the corrected form.** This is important to change.

If a student is making a request and uses the "me and Bob" formation, it is suggested that you look quizzically at him. Frown if necessary, but let the student know in a nonverbal way that you aren't quite understanding his request. You may ask, "Me wants to...?" You may choose to delay granting the request until the student has expressed it correctly.

Another frequent mistake is "John is taller than me." Show students that the sentence could properly be expressed, "John is taller than I am." One would not say, "John is taller than me am." Teaching in this fashion helps the students learn to think and determine proper usage.

∞∞

The Pronoun Finger Trick

Usually, students have learned proper pronouns through speaking the language. (An exception to this is predicate pronouns.) **However, many errors are made with compound (more than 1) pronouns. The following method will greatly help students use correct pronouns in speaking and writing:**

1. In a compound, put your finger or fingers over the first part of the compound.

2. Now, read the sentence and choose the pronoun. In this case, use "sound."

Examples: The baby won't come to Jeremiah and me. Place your finger(s) over *Jeremiah and* . The baby won't come **to me**.

Did Daniel and he finish the project? Place your finger(s) over *Daniel and*. Did **he** finish the project?

∞∞

In this unit, students will be taught that a nominative pronoun will serves as a subject or predicate nominative. They will learn that an objective pronoun will serve as an object of the preposition, direct object, or indirect object. **This is very difficult for some students.** Although a step-by-step approach is provided, don't be discouraged if students do not end the unit with mastery. This will occur as grammar is taught in ensuing years.

PRONOUNS

Pronouns take the place of nouns. They agree in number and gender.

Number: **Austin** and **Hal** visited **their** grandparents. (Two requires their.)

Gender: This means using a female pronoun (she, her) when referring to a girl or woman and using a male pronoun (he, him) when referring to a boy or man.

Examples: **Susan** forgot **her** keys.

He hasn't driven **his** car.

Note: If you aren't sure if the noun is a female or male, you may use *his/her*. However, ***his*** has become acceptable in this situation.

Each **child** must bring his/her birth certificate.
or
Each **child** must bring his birth certificate.

Personal Pronouns:

Nominative Pronouns (Subjective Pronouns)	Objective Pronouns	Possessive Pronouns
I	**me**	**my, mine**
he	**him**	**his**
she	**her**	**her, hers**
you	**you**	**your, yours**
it	**it**	**it, its**
we	**us**	**our, ours**
they	**them**	**their, theirs**
who	**whom**	**whose**
FUNCTION IN A SENTENCE?	**FUNCTION IN A SENTENCE?**	**FUNCTION IN A SENTENCE?**
1. SUBJECT 2. PREDICATE NOMINATIVE	1. OBJECT OF THE PREPOSITION 2. DIRECT OBJECT 3. INDIRECT OBJECT	SHOW OWNERSHIP

PRONOUNS

The nominative or subjective pronouns are **I**, **he**, **she**, **you**, **it**, **we**, **they**, and **who**. Note that ***you*** and ***it*** are in both nominative and objective columns of the pronoun chart. They are considered neutral pronouns and do not change from nominative to objective form.

NOMINATIVE PRONOUNS FUNCTION AS EITHER THE SUBJECT OR PREDICATE NOMINATIVE OF A SENTENCE.

A. **Review of Subjects:**

The subject of a sentence is who or what the sentence is about.

Examples: A large banner is hanging over the podium.

I cannot draw a penguin well.

B. **Review of Predicate Nominatives:**

The predicate nominative is a word that occurs in the predicate (after the verb) which means the same as the subject.

Example: His father is the owner of a small hardware store.

P.N.

His father is the owner ~~of a small hardware store~~.

Proof: The owner is his father.

Predicate pronouns are extremely important. Always invert the sentence to prove a predicate pronoun. This will help you to use correct pronouns.

Examples: The winner was (she, her).

The winner was **she**.

Proof: **She** was the winner. Incorrect: *Her* was the winner.

John's dad is (he, him) in the white hat.

John's dad is **he** ~~in the white hat~~.

Proof: **He** is John's dad.

With predicate nominatives, do not choose by sound. Always invert the sentence for a proof. (If you have heard incorrect usage long enough, it will sound correct.)

When answering the phone, and responding to the question, "Is **Todd** (Sue) there?" your response should be, "This (person) is **he** (she)."

Proof: **He** (She) is this person. Incorrect: Him is this person.

Name________________________________ **PRONOUNS**
WORKBOOK PAGE 225
Date________________________________

Directions: Cross out any prepositional phrase(s). Underline the subject once and the verb/verb phrase twice.

Example: Has one ~~of the ladies~~ wrapped your gift ~~for charity~~?

1. The fire engine raced ~~to the fire~~.

2. We should have gone ~~on the picnic~~.

3. A pail ~~of water~~ is ~~beside the campfire~~.

4. You can*not* take this mug ~~with you~~.

5. Did Sharon send you a "fax" message?

6. I would rather talk ~~to you~~ later.

7. A stewardess must demonstrate airplane safety.

8. Has he given you a bag ~~of chips~~ ~~for lunch~~?

9. Benjamin and she are going downtown ~~to the public library~~.

10. His boots and socks are ~~near the front door~~.

11. You might try the exercise ~~for ten minutes~~.

12. It is a very humid day.

13. May Katie and I help you ~~in the kitchen~~?

14. That woman does *not* leave her children ~~with a babysitter~~.

15. Either Royce or she had *not* removed the clothes ~~from the dryer~~.

Name________________________________ **PRONOUNS**

Date________________________________

Directions: Cross out any prepositional phrase(s). Underline the subject once and the verb/verb phrase twice.

Example: Has one ~~of the ladies~~ wrapped your gift ~~for charity~~?

1. The fire engine raced to the fire.
2. We should have gone on the picnic.
3. A pail of water is beside the campfire.
4. You cannot take this mug with you.
5. Did Sharon send you a "fax" message?
6. I would rather talk to you later.
7. A stewardess must demonstrate airplane safety.
8. Has he given you a bag of chips for lunch?
9. Benjamin and she are going downtown to the public library.
10. His boots and socks are near the front door.
11. You might try the exercise for ten minutes.
12. It is a very humid day.
13. May Katie and I help you in the kitchen?
14. That woman does not leave her children with a babysitter.
15. Either Royce or she had not removed the clothes from the dryer.

Name________________________________

WORKBOOK PAGE 226

Date________________________________

PRONOUNS
Predicate Nominatives

Directions: Cross out any prepositional phrase(s). Underline the subject once and the verb/verb phrase twice. Label any predicate nominative-P.N. Write the proof on the line provided.

P.N.
Example: The judge ~~for the contest~~ was he.

Proof: He was the judge.

P.N.
1. The first person ~~to the finish line~~ was Sarelle.

Proof: Sarelle was the first person.

P.N.
2. The first person ~~to the finish line~~ was she.

Proof: She was the first person.

P.N.
3. The winner was Clara (your name). **(Answers will vary.)**

Proof: (Clara) was the winner.

P.N.
4. The winner was I.

Proof: I was the winner.

P.N.
5. The hostess is the lady ~~in the blue dress~~.

Proof: The lady is the hostess.

P.N.
6. The hostess is she ~~in the blue dress~~.

Proof: She is the hostess.

Name__________________________________

Date___________________________________

PRONOUNS
Predicate Nominatives

Directions: Cross out any prepositional phrase(s). Underline the subject once and the verb/verb phrase twice. Label any predicate nominative-P.N. Write the proof on the line provided.

Example: The judge ~~for the contest~~ was he. (P.N. over "he")

Proof: He was the judge.

1. The first person to the finish line was Sarelle.

   Proof: ____

2. The first person to the finish line was she.

   Proof: ____

3. The winner was ____________________ (your name).

   Proof: ____

4. The winner was I.

   Proof: ____

5. The hostess is the lady in the blue dress.

   Proof: ____

6. The hostess is she in the blue dress.

   Proof: ____

Name____________________________________

WORKBOOK PAGE 227

Date____________________________________

PRONOUNS
Subject or Predicate Nominative?

Directions: Write S on the line if the boldfaced pronoun is the subject of the sentence. Write PN if the boldfaced pronoun is a predicate nominative.

Suggestion: Cross out any prepositional phrase(s). Underline the subject once and the verb/verb phrase twice. Label any predicate nominative-P.N. Using this information, write S or PN in the space provided.

Example: __PN__ The last person ~~on the elevator~~ was **she**. (P.N.)

1. __S__ **They** walked ~~along the beach~~ ~~in the moonlight~~.
2. __PN__ The lady ~~with the most aluminum cans~~ is **Maggie**. (P.N.) **(Proof: Maggie is the lady.)**
3. __PN__ The contestant ~~for the quiz show~~ had been **he**. (P.N.) **(Proof: He had been the contestant.)**
4. __S__ **You** may change your mind.
5. __S__ Later, **I** shall seal the letter ~~to Rae Ellen~~.
6. __S__ ~~At the banquet~~, **we** sat ~~at the head table~~.
7. __PN__ Timothy's teacher is **she** ~~in the red suit~~. (P.N.) **(Proof: She is Timothy's teacher.)**
8. __S__ ~~After his bath~~, **he** wears pajamas.
9. __PN__ Your biggest fans are **we**. (P.N.) **(Proof: We are your biggest fans.)**
10. __S__ Has **he** ever been bitten ~~by a snake~~?
11. __PN__ Her father is that **man** ~~with an umbrella~~. (P.N.) **(Proof: That man is her father.)**
12. __S__ **It** is a pleasure (to know) you.

Name______________________________

Date______________________________

PRONOUNS
Subject or Predicate Nominative?

Directions: Write S on the line if the boldfaced pronoun is the subject of the sentence. Write PN if the boldfaced pronoun is a predicate nominative.

Suggestion: Cross out any prepositional phrase(s). Underline the subject once and the verb/verb phrase twice. Label any predicate nominative-P.N. Using this information, write S or PN in the space provided.

Example: __PN__ The last person ~~on the elevator~~ was **she**. (P.N.)

1. _____ **They** walked along the beach in the moonlight.

2. _____ The lady with the most aluminum cans is **Maggie**.

3. _____ The contestant for the quiz show had been **he**.

4. _____ **You** may change your mind.

5. _____ Later, **I** shall seal the letter to Rae Ellen.

6. _____ At the banquet, **we** sat at the head table.

7. _____ Timothy's teacher is **she** in the red suit.

8. _____ After his bath, **he** wears pajamas.

9. _____ Your biggest fans are **we**.

10. _____ Has **he** ever been bitten by a snake?

11. _____ Her father is that **man** with an umbrella.

12. _____ **It** is a pleasure to know you.

TO THE TEACHER:

PRONOUNS

Pronouns require a thorough understanding of subjects, predicate nominatives, objects of the preposition, direct objects, and indirect objects. All of these will be reviewed.

The terminal objective will be for students to use the proper pronoun according to how the pronoun is functioning in the sentence. (For educational purposes, the terminal objective may have to be stated as: *The student will write (speak) the correct pronoun according to its function in a sentence.*)

You may consider some of this unit too difficult for your students. For example, pages 446-449 require that students determine how the pronoun functions in the sentence. You may choose to omit this part. (It is possible to teach pronoun usage by "sound" as long as students understand the use of predicate nominatives and indirect objects. These two areas are often used incorrectly when students determine a pronoun by "sound.") Don't panic if students do not totally grasp all of the material. As stated previously, these concepts may be mastered in an ensuing year (or years) of grammar study.

PAGE 439 = WORKBOOK PAGE 228
PAGE 456 = WORKBOOK PAGE 237
PAGE 457 = WORKBOOK PAGE 238
PAGE 462 = WORKBOOK PAGE 241
PAGE 463 = WORKBOOK PAGE 242

PRONOUNS

OBJECTIVE CASE:

The objective pronouns include me, him, her, you, it, us, them, and whom.

Look at your pronoun chart. There are only two pronouns that are in both the nominative and objective columns: you and it. These are called neutral pronouns.

Objective pronouns function as one of the following objects:

- **A. Object of the Preposition**
- **B. Direct Object**
- **C. Indirect Object**

1. Review of Object of the Preposition:

The object of the preposition is the noun or pronoun that follows a preposition:

Examples: The bag is *under the **bed***.

This gift is *from **me***.

2. Review of Direct Objects:

A direct object receives the action of the verb.

D.O.
Example: Lucy shoved the ***clothes*** into the drawer.

3. Review of Indirect Objects:

The indirect object "indirectly" receives a direct object. "To" or "for" can be inserted mentally before an indirect object.

Examples: The bride rented each bridesmaid a lovely gown.
for **I.O.**
The bride rented / each **bridesmaid** a lovely gown.

Their grandmother sent them some money.
to **I.O.**
Their grandmother sent / **them** some money.

Name_______________________________ **PRONOUNS**
WORKBOOK PAGE 229 **Object of the Preposition**
Date________________________________

Directions: Cross out any prepositional phrase(s). Label any object of the preposition-O.P.

O.P.
Example: The man ~~without an overcoat~~ is cold.

O.P.
1. The lamp is ~~below the fan~~.

O.P.
2. Loni made a baby blanket ~~with a satin fringe~~.

O.P.
3. A chair was placed ~~beside the fireplace~~.

O.P.
4. Let's wait ~~for Louis~~.

O.P.
5. We looked ~~in the closet~~.

O.P.
6. ~~Throughout the day~~ we played games.

O.P.
7. A post card ~~from him~~ arrived today.

O.P.
8. The children are wading ~~in the stream~~.

O.P. **O.P.**
9. An actor sat ~~beside them~~ ~~during the flight~~.

O.P. **O.P.**
10. This discussion is ~~between Lydia and me~~.

O.P.
11. Set this stand ~~near the door~~.

O.P.
12. The story that the teacher read was ~~about dinosaurs~~.

O.P.
13. ~~After a trip~~, she is always tired.

O.P. **O.P.**
14. Would you like (to go) ~~with Jack and me~~?

O.P. **O.P.**
15. One ~~of the girls~~ left ~~without her purse~~.

Name________________________________

Date________________________________

PRONOUNS
Object of the Preposition

Directions: Cross out any prepositional phrase(s). Label any object of the preposition-O.P.

O.P.
Example: The man ~~without an overcoat~~ is cold.

1. The lamp is below the fan.
2. Loni made a baby blanket with a satin fringe.
3. A chair was placed beside the fireplace.
4. Let's wait for Louis.
5. We looked in the closet.
6. Throughout the day we played games.
7. A post card from him arrived today.
8. The children are wading in the stream.
9. An actor sat beside them during the flight.
10. This discussion is between Lydia and me.
11. Set this stand near the door.
12. The story that the teacher read was about dinosaurs.
13. After a trip, she is always tired.
14. Would you like to go with Jack and me?
15. One of the girls left without her purse.

Name________________________________

WORKBOOK PAGE 230

Date________________________________

PRONOUNS
Direct Objects

Directions: Cross out any prepositional phrase(s). Underline the subject once and the verb/verb phrase twice. Label any direct object-D.O.

D.O.
Example: Stevie hit the ball ~~to the outfield~~.

D.O.
1. The goat chews grass.

D.O.
2. His sister bought a dress.

D.O.
3. Linda has a cute pig.

D.O.
4. The carpenters finished the house.

D.O.
5. A dog followed us home.

D.O.
6. They decorated cookies ~~for the party~~.

D.O.
7. Neil hit me ~~with his ruler~~.

D.O.
8. A musician sang a slow song.

D.O.
9. The milkman put the bottles ~~by the front door~~.

D.O.
10. Several monkeys ate bananas ~~for a snack~~.

D.O.
11. Some boys make a sand castle ~~with a moat.~~

D.O.
12. Harvey sent flowers ~~to his mother~~.

D.O.
13. Do you play a guitar?

D.O.
14. (You) Set this ~~on the table~~, please.

D.O.
15. ~~At the end of the year~~, they chose him (to give) a speech.

Name________________________________

Date________________________________

PRONOUNS
Direct Objects

Directions: Cross out any prepositional phrase(s). Underline the subject once and the verb/verb phrase twice. Label any direct object-D.O.

D.O.
Example: Stevie hit the ball ~~to the outfield~~.

1. The goat chews grass.

2. His sister bought a dress.

3. Linda has a cute pig.

4. The carpenters finished the house.

5. A dog followed us home.

6. They decorated cookies for the party.

7. Neil hit me with his ruler.

8. A musician sang a slow song.

9. The milkman put the bottles by the front door.

10. Several monkeys ate bananas for a snack.

11. Some boys make a sand castle with a moat.

12. Harvey sent flowers to his mother.

13. Do you play a guitar?

14. Set this on the table, please.

15. At the end of the year, they chose him to give a speech.

Name______________________________ **PRONOUNS**
WORKBOOK PAGE 231 **Indirect Objects**
Date______________________________

Directions: Cross out any prepositional phrase(s). Underline the subject once and the verb/verb phrase twice. Label a direct object-D.O. Label an indirect object-I.O.

Remember: Before an indirect object, you can mentally insert *to* or *for*.

Example: Justine handed Tom (I.O.) a slice (D.O.) ~~of watermelon~~.

1. The brother gave the child (I.O.) a kick (D.O.) ~~under the table~~.
2. Ollie loaned me (I.O.) a book (D.O.).
3. A storekeeper sends them (I.O.) a wreath (D.O.) ~~at Christmas~~.
4. A bride handed her bridesmaid (I.O.) some flowers (D.O.).
5. Gregg tells us (I.O.) his problems (D.O.).
6. The doctor wrote her (I.O.) a prescription (D.O.).
7. (You) Give him (I.O.) your ideas (D.O.).
8. The director promised Marietta (I.O.) a chance (D.O.) ~~at the leading role~~.
9. Grandma finds Joey (I.O.) little boats (D.O.) ~~at thrift stores~~.
10. Gina served the guests (I.O.) an iced dessert (D.O.).
11. A dentist sent him (I.O.) a bill (D.O.) ~~for one hundred dollars~~.
12. Their friends gave them (I.O.) a going-away party (D.O.).
13. Lois's grandmother offers her (I.O.) money (D.O.) ~~for good grades~~.
14. I baked my friend (I.O.) a cake (D.O.) ~~for his birthday~~.
15. The agent leased him (I.O.) a store (D.O.) ~~in the new shopping center~~.

Name________________________________

Date________________________________

PRONOUNS
Indirect Objects

Directions: Cross out any prepositional phrase(s). Underline the subject once and the verb/verb phrase twice. Label a direct object-D.O. Label an indirect object-I.O.

Remember: Before an indirect object, you can mentally insert *to* or *for*.

I.O. D.O.
Example: Justine handed Tom a slice ~~of watermelon~~.

1. The brother gave the child a kick under the table.
2. Ollie loaned me a book.
3. A storekeeper sends them a wreath at Christmas.
4. A bride handed her bridesmaid some flowers.
5. Gregg tells us his problems.
6. The doctor wrote her a prescription.
7. Give him your ideas.
8. The director promised Marietta a chance at the leading role.
9. Grandma finds Joey little boats at thrift stores.
10. Gina served the guests an iced dessert.
11. A dentist sent him a bill for one hundred dollars.
12. Their friends gave them a going-away party.
13. Lois's grandmother offers her money for good grades.
14. I baked my friend a cake for his birthday.
15. The agent leased him a store in the new shopping center.

Name________________________________ **PRONOUNS**

WORKBOOK PAGE 232

Date________________________________

Directions: A pronoun appears in boldfaced print. Write the letter that tells how the pronoun functions in the sentence.

1. __A__ **She** has gone.
   A. subject
   B. predicate nominative

2. __B__ He likes **me**!
   A. object of the preposition
   B. direct object
   C. indirect object

3. __A__ Harry received a letter from **him**.
   A. object of the preposition
   B. direct object
   C. indirect object

4. __B__ The last one to leave the room was **I**.
   A. subject
   B. predicate nominative

5. __C__ A businessman sent **them** some free samples.
   A. object of the preposition
   B. direct object
   C. indirect object

6. __B__ Lauren met **me** by the entrance to the mall.
   A. object of the preposition.
   B. direct object
   C. indirect object

7. __B__ The winner was **she**.
   A. subject
   B. predicate nominative

8. __B__ Patricia helped **him** with his homework.
   A. object of the preposition
   B. direct object
   C. indirect object

Name______________________________ **PRONOUNS**

Date______________________________

Directions: A pronoun appears in boldfaced print. Write the letter that tells how the pronoun functions in the sentence.

1. _____ **She** has gone.
   A. subject
   B. predicate nominative

2. _____ He likes **me**!
   A. object of the preposition
   B. direct object
   C. indirect object

3. _____ Harry received a letter from **him**.
   A. object of the preposition
   B. direct object
   C. indirect object

4. _____ The last one to leave the room was **I**.
   A. subject
   B. predicate nominative

5. _____ A businessman sent **them** some free samples.
   A. object of the preposition
   B. direct object
   C. indirect object

6. _____ Lauren met **me** by the entrance to the mall.
   A. object of the preposition.
   B. direct object
   C. indirect object

7. _____ The winner was **she**.
   A. subject
   B. predicate nominative

8. _____ Patricia helped **him** with his homework.
   A. object of the preposition
   B. direct object
   C. indirect object

Name________________________________ **PRONOUNS**

WORKBOOK PAGE 233

Date________________________________

Directions: A pronoun appears in boldfaced print. Write the letter that tells how the pronoun functions in the sentence.

1. __C__ Clyde's brother sold **them** a set of drums.
   A. object of the preposition
   B. direct object
   C. indirect object

2. __A__ Please don't leave without **him**.
   A. object of the preposition
   B. direct object
   C. indirect object

3. __B__ The winner should have been **I**.
   A. subject
   B. predicate nominative

4. __C__ A fiddler played **us** a tune.
   A. object of the preposition
   B. direct object
   C. indirect object

5. __A__ Barb and **she** live in Wisconsin.
   A. subject
   B. predicate nominative

6. __A__ Has **he** entered college?
   A. subject
   B. predicate nominative

7. __A__ **You** are so kind.
   A. subject
   B. predicate nominative
   C. object of the preposition
   D. direct object
   E. indirect object

8. __D__ Take **it** and run.
   A. subject
   B. predicate nominative
   C. object of the preposition
   D. direct object
   E. indirect object

Name________________________________ **PRONOUNS**

Date________________________________

Directions: A pronoun appears in boldfaced print. Write the letter that tells how the pronoun functions in the sentence.

1. _____ Clyde's brother sold **them** a set of drums.
   A. object of the preposition
   B. direct object
   C. indirect object

2. _____ Please don't leave without **him**.
   A. object of the preposition
   B. direct object
   C. indirect object

3. _____ The winner should have been **I**.
   A. subject
   B. predicate nominative

4. _____ A fiddler played **us** a tune.
   A. object of the preposition
   B. direct object
   C. indirect object

5. _____ Barb and **she** live in Wisconsin.
   A. subject
   B. predicate nominative

6. _____ Has **he** entered college?
   A. subject
   B. predicate nominative

7. _____ **You** are so kind.
   A. subject
   B. predicate nominative
   C. object of the preposition
   D. direct object
   E. indirect object

8. _____ Take **it** and run.
   A. subject
   B. predicate nominative
   C. object of the preposition
   D. direct object
   E. indirect object

Name________________________________

WORKBOOK PAGE 234

Date________________________________

PRONOUNS

Directions: Select the correct pronoun.

1. Come sit beside (I, **me**).
2. Donna is going with (she, **her**).
3. (**I**, Me) love a sunny day.
4. A small, laughing child chased after (he, **him**).
5. Have (**we**, us) been given a key?
6. The first one chosen was (**I**, me).
7. (**They**, Them) are having a good time.
8. A guide gave (we, **us**) a tour.
9. (**She**, Her) must have plans soon.
10. Please take (I, **me**) with you.
11. The veteran handed (we, **us**) a small flag.
12. Did he leave (they, **them**) in the sink?
13. The most adventurous child is (**she**, her).
14. Give (I, **me**) your response.
15. The first batter is (**he**, him).

Name________________________________

Date________________________________

PRONOUNS

Directions: Select the correct pronoun.

1. Come sit beside (I, me).
2. Donna is going with (she, her).
3. (I, Me) love a sunny day.
4. A small, laughing child chased after (he, him).
5. Have (we, us) been given a key?
6. The first one chosen was (I, me).
7. (They, Them) are having a good time.
8. A guide gave (we, us) a tour.
9. (She, Her) must have plans soon.
10. Please take (I, me) with you.
11. The veteran handed (we, us) a small flag.
12. Did he leave (they, them) in the sink?
13. The most adventurous child is (she, her).
14. Give (I, me) your response.
15. The first batter is (he, him).

Name________________________________ **PRONOUNS**

WORKBOOK PAGE 235

Date________________________________

Directions: Select the correct pronoun.

1. (**I**, Me) have agreed to help.

2. Georgia tossed (they, **them**) a bag of pretzels.

3. A singer showed (he, **him**) backstage.

4. Bo's teammates are (**they**, them) in the red uniforms.

5. The ladies' club presented (they, **them**) scholarships.

6. The long distance runner zipped past (we, **us**) at great speed.

7. The new model is (**he**, him) in the brown shirt.

8. During the investigation, (**she**, her) talked calmly.

9. Has (**he**, him) been standing on his head again?

10. A travel agent sends (he, **him**) special tickets.

11. A receptionist asked (I, **me**) to be seated.

12. My favorite cousin is (her, **she**).

13. The letter is from (she, **her**).

14. (**We**, Us) answered the door immediately.

15. A fan of that team is (**he**, him) in the team jersey.

Name_______________________________ **PRONOUNS**

Date_______________________________

Directions: Select the correct pronoun.

1. (I, Me) have agreed to help.
2. Georgia tossed (they, them) a bag of pretzels.
3. A singer showed (he, him) backstage.
4. Bo's teammates are (they, them) in the red uniforms.
5. The ladies' club presented (they, them) scholarships.
6. The long distance runner zipped past (we, us) at great speed.
7. The new model is (he, him) in the brown shirt.
8. During the investigation, (she, her) talked calmly.
9. Has (he, him) been standing on his head again?
10. A travel agent sends (he, him) special tickets.
11. A receptionist asked (I, me) to be seated.
12. My favorite cousin is (her, she).
13. The letter is from (she, her).
14. (We, Us) answered the door immediately.
15. A fan of that team is (he, him) in the team jersey.

Name________________________________

WORKBOOK PAGE 236

Date________________________________

PRONOUNS
Compounds

Directions: Select the correct pronoun.

Remember: Place your finger or fingers over the first part of the compound. Then, reread the sentence and choose the proper pronoun.

(In sentences in the present tense, you may have to add <u>s</u> to the verb.)

Example: Nelson and (he, him) want to stay here.
.... (**He**, Him) want**s** to stay here.

1. The sun umbrella beside Randy and (I, **me**) has blown over.

2. Jerry and (**I**, me) want to learn to fly helicopters.

3. Mom and (**she**, her) shop with their children.

4. The two ladies playing bingo were Brandy's aunt and (**she**, her).

5. Mr. Clark sent Ralph and (he, **him**) to Old Tucson.

6. The matter is between Jacob and (they, **them**).

7. Uncle Keith will eat dinner with Vicki and (I, **me**).

8. Levi's dad sent Stephi and (we, **us**) tickets to the game.

9. The mayor handed Mrs. Meadows and (she, **her**) a trophy.

10. The company director wrote the managers and (they, **them**) a letter.

11. Bessie and (**she**, her) like to do crossword puzzles.

12. The dog followed Vic and (he, **him**) to the corner.

13. A handyman and (**she**, her) repaired the leak.

14. The delivery person ran past my friend and (I, **me**).

15. His favorite aunts are Sally and (**she**, her).

Name______________________________

Date______________________________

PRONOUNS
Compounds

Directions: Select the correct pronoun.

Remember: Place your finger or fingers over the first part of the compound. Then, reread the sentence and choose the proper pronoun.

(In sentences in the present tense, you may have to add s to the verb.)

Example: Nelson and (he, him) want to stay here.
.... (**He**, Him) want**s** to stay here.

1. The sun umbrella beside Randy and (I, me) has blown over.
2. Jerry and (I, me) want to learn to fly helicopters.
3. Mom and (she, her) shop with their children.
4. The two ladies playing bingo were Brandy's aunt and (she, her).
5. Mr. Clark sent Ralph and (he, him) to Old Tucson.
6. The matter is between Jacob and (they, them).
7. Uncle Keith will eat dinner with Vicki and (I, me).
8. Levi's dad sent Stephi and (we, us) tickets to the game.
9. The mayor handed Mrs. Meadows and (she, her) a trophy.
10. The company director wrote the managers and (they, them) a letter.
11. Bessie and (she, her) like to do crossword puzzles.
12. The dog followed Vic and (he, him) to the corner.
13. A handyman and (she, her) repaired the leak.
14. The delivery person ran past my friend and (I, me).
15. His favorite aunts are Sally and (she, her).

PRONOUNS

The possessive pronouns are: **my, mine**
his
her, hers
your, yours
its
our, ours
their, theirs
whose

My, his, her, your, its, our, their and whose are placed before nouns and other pronouns and are often called possessive adjectives.

Examples:	Do you have **my** *pencil*?	(noun)
	His *wallet* is on the floor?	(noun)
	Paula gave **her** favorite *one* away.	(pronoun)
	A bird spread **its** *wings*.	(noun)
	Our *car* isn't in the driveway.	(noun)
	Their *leaders* met at the capitol building.	(noun)
	Whose *apron* is this?	(noun)

Mine, **hers**, **yours**, **ours**, and **theirs** do not usually come before the noun or pronoun but refer back in the sentence to it.

Examples: That *pen* is **mine**.

Is the *book* on the shelf **yours**?

The plaid *skirt* is **hers**.

Are those *gerbils* **ours**?

His occurs in the same form at any placement.

Examples: **His** *grandmother* lives in Alabama.

The grilled cheese *sandwich* is **his**.

Possessive Pronouns do NOT have an apostrophe (').

A. It's is not a possessive pronoun. It's is a contraction for it is.

Its is a possessive pronoun. Example: The cat licked its paws.

Suggestion: If you are unsure its or it's should be used in a sentence, read the sentence with the *it is* form. Trust sound to determine your choice.

Examples: It's hot.
Check: It is hot.

The cat licked it's paws.
Check: The cat licked it is paws.
Correct: The cat licked its paws.

B. You're is not a possessive pronoun. You're is a contraction for *you are.*

Your is a possessive pronoun. Example: Where is your coat?

Suggestion: If you are unsure you're or your should be used, read the sentence with the *you are* form. Trust sound to determine your choice.

Examples: You're so funny.
Check: You are so funny.

Is that you're candy?
Check: Is that you are candy?
Correct: Is that your candy?

C. They're is not a possessive pronoun. They're is a contraction for they are.

Their is a possessive pronoun. Example: Their coach talked to them.

Suggestion: If you are unsure they're or their should be used, read the sentence with the *they are* form. Trust sound to determine your choice.

Examples: They're leaving now.
Check: They are leaving now.

They're dad is a plumber.
Check: They are dad is a plumber.
Correct: Their dad is a plumber.

Name________________________________ **PRONOUNS**

WORKBOOK PAGE 239

Date________________________________

Ask students to determine the noun or pronoun a possessive modifies.

Directions: Select the correct word.

Suggestion: Say each sentence separating the contraction.
Use this method to determine your choice.

Example: Do you want to know if (its, it's) ear is infected?

Do you want to know if it is ear is infected? Wrong!

The answer is **its**.

1. (**It's**, Its) a great day.
2. I hope (their, **they're**) coming soon.
3. (You're, **Your**) elbow has black smudges on it.
4. Have you seen (**their**, they're) first home?
5. (**You're**, Your) welcome to stay.
6. A monkey scratched under (**its**, it's) arm.
7. (**Their**, They're) toilet overflowed.
8. Ask if (their, **they're**) ready.
9. I would like (**your**, you're) opinion on this.
10. The dog stopped wagging (**its**, it's) tail.
11. (**You're**, Your) the best skater he has seen.
12. He has (**their**, they're) photographs from camp.

Name________________________________

Date________________________________

PRONOUNS

Directions: Select the correct word.

Suggestion: Say each sentence separating the contraction.
Use this method to determine your choice.

Example: Do you want to know if (its, it's) ear is infected?

Do you want to know if it is ear is infected? Wrong!

The answer is **its**.

1. (It's, Its) a great day.
2. I hope (their, they're) coming soon.
3. (You're, Your) elbow has black smudges on it.
4. Have you seen (their, they're) first home?
5. (You're, Your) welcome to stay.
6. A monkey scratched under (its, it's) arm.
7. (Their, They're) toilet overflowed.
8. Ask if (their, they're) ready.
9. I would like (your, you're) opinion on this.
10. The dog stopped wagging (its, it's) tail.
11. (You're, Your) the best skater he has seen.
12. He has (their, they're) photographs from camp.

Name________________________________ **PRONOUNS**

WORKBOOK PAGE 240

Date________________________________

Ask students to determine the noun or pronoun a possessive modifies.

Directions: Select the correct word.

Suggestion: Say each sentence separating the contraction.
Use this method to determine your choice.

Example: Kenneth and Andrea like (their, they're) new home.

Kenneth and Andrea like they are new home. Wrong!

The answer is **their**.

1. During the high wind, (**their**, they're) chairs blew over.
2. (**It's**, Its) nice to meet you.
3. Do you know that (your, **you're**) the winner?
4. Has anyone taken (**your**, you're) temperature?
5. (Their, **They're**) finished!
6. (It's, **Its**) wings are damaged.
7. A hamster snuggled in the corner of (**its**, it's) cage.
8. (Your, **You're**) kidding me!
9. Sally is (**their**, they're) friend.
10. His mother and (**your**, you're) sister are working at the same place.
11. I believe that (**they're**, their) helping with the move.
12. Do you wonder how (its, **it's**) possible?

Name________________________________ **PRONOUNS**

Date________________________________

Directions: Select the correct word.

Suggestion: Say each sentence separating the contraction.
Use this method to determine your choice.

Example: Kenneth and Andrea like (their, they're) new home.

Kenneth and Andrea like they are new home. Wrong!

The answer is **their**.

1. During the high wind, (their, they're) chairs blew over.
2. (It's, Its) nice to meet you.
3. Do you know that (your, you're) the winner?
4. Has anyone taken (your, you're) temperature?
5. (Their, They're) finished!
6. (It's, Its) wings are damaged.
7. A hamster snuggled in the corner of (its, it's) cage.
8. (Your, You're) kidding me!
9. Sally is (their, they're) friend.
10. His mother and (your, you're) sister are working at the same place.
11. I believe that (they're, their) helping with the move.
12. Do you wonder how (its, it's) possible?

PRONOUNS

Reflexive Pronouns:

Reflexive pronouns end with **self** or **selves**. Reflexive pronouns are **myself**, **himself**, **herself**, **itself**, **yourself**, **ourselves**, and **themselves**.

Hisself and theirselves are incorrect. DO NOT USE THEM!

Reflexive pronouns reflect back to another noun or pronoun in a sentence. (The word to which a reflexive pronoun refers back is called an antecedent.)

Examples: I will do it **myself**.

Ginny finished the job **herself**.

His dad did the roofing **himself**.

Help **yourself** to the food.

The cat licked **itself**.

We want to try it **ourselves**.

They bought all the food for the trip **themselves**.

Antecedents:

An antecedent is the noun or pronoun to which a possessive or a reflexive pronoun refers in a sentence.

Possessives:

A. The man built a large chest for his son.

1. His refers back to **man**. (The man built a large chest for the man's son.)
2. **Man** is the noun to which his refers back in the sentence.
3. **Man** is the antecedent.

B. The boys splashed their friends with a hose.

1. Their refers back to boys. (The boys splashed the boys' friends with a hose.)
2. **Boys** is the noun to which their refers back in the sentence.
3. **Boys** is the antecedent.

Reflexives:

A. The kite wrapped itself around a pole.

1. Itself is the reflexive pronoun.
2. Itself refers back to **kite**.
3. **Kite** is the antecedent.

B. We need to clean ourselves.

1. Ourselves is the reflexive pronoun.
2. Ourselves refers back to **we**.
3. **We** (a pronoun) is the antecedent.

Note: An antecedent will not be a word in a prepositional phrase.
The bird with the broken wing hurt its leg as well.
The bird ~~with the broken wing~~ hurt **its** leg as well.
antecedent for its = bird

Name______________________________________

WORKBOOK PAGE 243

Date______________________________________

PRONOUNS
Reflexive Pronouns

Directions: Select the reflexive pronoun in each sentence.

1. Let Jolynn find it **herself**.
2. I need to go **myself**.
3. Lionel washes his dog **himself**.
4. The guests enjoyed **themselves**.
5. Mickey and I want to listen to the recording **ourselves**.
6. Nita wants to do it **herself**.
7. A little robin perched **itself** on a branch.
8. The lady muttered to **herself** about the weather.
9. The boys hauled the stones **themselves**.
10. We, **ourselves**, must make the decision.
11. May I do it **myself**?
12. One of the boys made **himself** a huge sandwich.
13. A dog chased **itself** in the mirror.
14. Phillip and we managed to do that **ourselves**.
15. Many people volunteer **themselves** for feeding the hungry.

Name______________________________________

Date______________________________________

PRONOUNS
Reflexive Pronouns

Directions: Select the reflexive pronoun in each sentence.

1. Let Jolynn find it herself.
2. I need to go myself.
3. Lionel washes his dog himself.
4. The guests enjoyed themselves.
5. Mickey and I want to listen to the recording ourselves.
6. Nita wants to do it herself.
7. A little robin perched itself on a branch.
8. The lady muttered to herself about the weather.
9. The boys hauled the stones themselves.
10. We, ourselves, must make the decision.
11. May I do it myself?
12. One of the boys made himself a huge sandwich.
13. A dog chased itself in the mirror.
14. Phillip and we managed to do that ourselves.
15. Many people volunteer themselves for feeding the hungry.

Name________________________________ **PRONOUNS**
WORKBOOK PAGE 244 **Antecedents**
Date________________________________

Directions: Write the antecedent for the underlined word on the line.

Example: ______Bridgette______ Bridgette left her books in the truck.

1. ______Dad______ Dad put his tool down.

2. ______I______ I don't know where my sweater is.

3. ______girls______ The girls gave their mom a hug.

4. ______lizard______ A small lizard stuck its tongue out.

5. ______Janie______ Janie does house painting herself.

6. ______Yul/I______ Yul and I don't want our picture taken.

7. ______You______ You must fix this yourself.

8. ______dogs______ Some dogs were lying by their bowls.

9. ______men______ Several men built a church themselves.

10. ______Adam______ Adam must bake a birthday cake himself.

11. ______He______ He found his water gun in the bottom drawer.

12. ______I______ I will find the way myself.

Name____________________________________

Date____________________________________

PRONOUNS
Antecedents

Directions: Write the antecedent for the underlined word on the line.

Example: ______Bridgette__________ Bridgette left her books in the truck.

1. ______________________ Dad put his tool down.

2. ______________________ I don't know where my sweater is.

3. ______________________ The girls gave their mom a hug.

4. ______________________ A small lizard stuck its tongue out.

5. ______________________ Janie does house painting herself.

6. ______________________ Yul and I don't want our picture taken.

7. ______________________ You must fix this yourself.

8. ______________________ Some dogs were lying by their bowls.

9. ______________________ Several men built a church themselves.

10. ______________________ Adam must bake a birthday cake himself.

11. ______________________ He found his water gun in the bottom drawer.

12. ______________________ I will find the way myself.

Name________________________________ **PRONOUNS**
WORKBOOK PAGE 245 **Antecedents**
Date________________________________

Directions: Write the antecedent for the underlined word on the line.

Example: ___He___ He wants to dig the hole himself.

1. ___Hal/she___ Hal and she drove all the way themselves.

2. ___bird___ A bird fluttered its wings and flew off.

3. ___teenager___ The teenager wants to buy a car himself.

4. ___Wendy/I___ Wendy and I left our umbrellas on the bus.

5. ___waiter___ A waiter gave us his pen.

6. ___Gretta___ Gretta needs to give her pet rabbit some food.

7. ___Marion/she___ Marion and she are giving their time to help.

8. ___History___ History often repeats itself.

9. ___I___ I am throwing my old notebook away.

10. ___Amanda___ Amanda gave Jeff her notes.

11. ___model___ The model washes herself with a special soap.

12. ___Logan/he___ Logan and he dished out their lunches.

Name________________________________

Date________________________________

PRONOUNS
Antecedents

Directions: Write the antecedent for the underlined word on the line.

Example: ____He____ He wants to dig the hole himself.

1. ____________________ Hal and she drove all the way themselves.

2. ____________________ A bird fluttered its wings and flew off.

3. ____________________ The teenager wants to buy a car himself.

4. ____________________ Wendy and I left our umbrellas on the bus.

5. ____________________ A waiter gave us his pen.

6. ____________________ Gretta needs to give her pet rabbit some food.

7. ____________________ Marion and she are giving their time to help.

8. ____________________ History often repeats itself.

9. ____________________ I am throwing my old notebook away.

10. ____________________ Amanda gave Jeff her notes.

11. ____________________ The model washes herself with a special soap.

12. ____________________ Logan and he dished out their lunches.

PAGE 471 = WORKBOOK PAGE 246

PRONOUNS

Demonstrative Pronouns:

The demonstrative pronouns are **this**, **that**, **those**, and **these**.

Examples: **This** was a terrific idea!

Will you please give **that** away?

Are you sure **those** are the ones you want?

These are a great buy!

Note: Them is not a demonstrative pronoun.

Incorrect: Them surely are pretty.

Correct: Those surely are pretty.

Incorrect: I like them shoes.

Correct: I like those shoes.

If **this**, **that**, **those**, and **these** modify (go over to) a noun or pronoun, they function as adjectives.

Examples: **This** is terrible. (pronoun)

This spaghetti is terrible. (adjective: this spaghetti)

He bought **that** at a sale. (pronoun)

He bought **that** tire at a sale. (adjective: that tire)

Are **those** yours? (pronouns)

Are **those** socks yours? (adjective: those socks)

I like **these**. (pronoun)

I like **these** chewy bars. (adjective: these bars)

Name______________________________

WORKBOOK PAGE 247

Date______________________________

PRONOUNS

Demonstrative Pronouns

Directions: Write P on the line if the underlined word serves as a pronoun; write A if the underlined word serves as an adjective. Write the adjective and the noun it modifies on the line after the sentence. A sentence marked P will be blank.

Example: __P__ Try these! ______________

1. __A__ This rug is a Native American one. ____This rug____
2. __P__ Please hand me that. ______________
3. __A__ Those machines are complicated. ____Those machines____
4. __P__ We laugh often about that. ______________
5. __P__ Are these what you had in mind? ______________
6. __A__ You may want to read this article. ____this article____
7. __P__ Would you like that heated? ______________
8. __A__ Henry collected these shells on vacation. ____these shells____
9. __A__ You may remove that label from the shirt. ____that label____
10. __A__ This stereo has superb sound. ____This stereo____
11. __P__ I can't seem to do anything with this. ______________
12. __A__ Are these coins rare? ____these coins____
13. __A__ That curling iron is very hot. ____That iron____
14. __P__ We would like two of those. ______________
15. __P__ Zachary removed these with worn pages from the library shelves. ______________

Name______________________________

Date______________________________

PRONOUNS
Demonstrative Pronouns

Directions: Write P on the line if the underlined word serves as a pronoun; write A if the underlined word serves as an adjective. Write the adjective and the noun it modifies on the line after the sentence. A sentence marked P will be blank.

Example: __P__ Try these! ______________________

1. _____ This rug is a Native American one. ______________________
2. _____ Please hand me that. ______________________
3. _____ Those machines are complicated. ______________________
4. _____ We laugh often about that. ______________________
5. _____ Are these what you had in mind? ______________________
6. _____ You may want to read this article. ______________________
7. _____ Would you like that heated? ______________________
8. _____ Henry collected these shells on vacation.______________________
9. _____ You may remove that label from the shirt.______________________
10. _____ This stereo has superb sound. ______________________
11. _____ I can't seem to do anything with this. ______________________
12. _____ Are these coins rare? ______________________
13. _____ That curling iron is very hot. ______________________
14. _____ We would like two of those. ______________________
15. _____ Zachary removed these with worn pages from the library shelves.

____

PAGE 475 = WORKBOOK PAGE 248

<u>PRONOUNS</u>

Interrogative Pronouns:

Interrogative pronouns ask a question.
Interrogative pronouns are **who**, **whom**, **whose**, **which**, and **what**.

Examples: **Who** is that?

To **whom** did you give the money?

Whose is this?

Which do you want?

What is your name?

Who is in the nominative case and will function as the subject or predicate nominative of a sentence.

Who is your best friend? (subject)

The new minister is **who**? (predicate nominative)
Proof: <u>Who is the new minister?</u>

Whom is in the objective case and will function as the direct object, indirect object, and object of the preposition. (**Use <u>whom</u> after *to, for,* and *with.***)

For **whom** did you make this? (object of the preposition)

You called **whom**? (direct object)

Miss Lilt sent **whom** a post card? (indirect object)

<u>Whose</u>, **<u>which</u>**, and **<u>what</u>** are pronouns when they stand alone. However, if they modify (go over to) a noun or another pronoun, they function as adjectives.

Examples: **Whose** is this? (pronoun)
Whose book is this? (adjective)

Which do you want? (pronoun)
Which one do you want? (adjective)

What should I do? (pronoun)
What activity should I do? (adjective)

Name________________________________
WORKBOOK PAGE 249
Date________________________________

PRONOUNS
Interrogative Pronouns

Directions: Write P on the line if the boldfaced word serves as a pronoun; write A on the line if the boldfaced word serves as an adjective.

Example: __A__ **Which** shirt did you buy?

1. __A__ **Which** snake is poisonous?
2. __P__ **Whose** is this?
3. __P__ **What** have I done?
4. __A__ **What** phone number did you dial?
5. __A__ **Whose** cookies are these?
6. __A__ **Which** van do you like?
7. __A__ **What** answer did he give?
8. __P__ **Which** do you want?
9. __P__ **Whose** are these?
10. __A__ **What** animal do you like best?

Directions: Select the correct answer.

Note: Use *whom* after to, for, or with:

1. (**Who**, Whom) was with you?
2. To (who, **whom**) did you speak?
3. (**Who**, Whom) is your favorite?
4. From (who, **whom**) did you receive the gift?
5. The last person in line was (**who**, whom)? (Who was the last person in line?)

Name________________________________

Date________________________________

PRONOUNS
Interrogative Pronouns

Directions: Write P on the line if the boldfaced word serves as a pronoun; write A on the line if the boldfaced word serves as an adjective.

Example: __A__ **Which** shirt did you buy?

1. _____ **Which** snake is poisonous?
2. _____ **Whose** is this?
3. _____ **What** have I done?
4. _____ **What** phone number did you dial?
5. _____ **Whose** cookies are these?
6. _____ **Which** van do you like?
7. _____ **What** answer did he give?
8. _____ **Which** do you want?
9. _____ **Whose** are these?
10. _____ **What** animal do you like best?

Directions: Select the correct answer.

Note: Use *whom* after to, for, or with:

1. (Who, Whom) was with you?
2. To (who, whom) did you speak?
3. (Who, Whom) is your favorite?
4. From (who, whom) did you receive the gift?
5. The last person in line was (who, whom)?

FOR THE TEACHER: AFTER INDEFINITE PRONOUNS, YOU WILL FIND A PRONOUN REVIEW AND A CUMULATIVE REVIEW. THE PRONOUN UNIT TEST FOLLOWS THESE TWO REVIEWS.

PAGE 479 = WORKBOOK PAGE 250

IMPORTANT NOTE

The cumulative review is quite lengthy. You may wish to spend several days completing it.

The cumulative test at the end of this unit may be used as a final exam. However, keep in mind that pronouns, capitalization, and punctuation have not been included.

PRONOUNS

Indefinite Pronouns:

Indefinite pronouns are **some**, **many**, **few**, **several**, **each**, **both**, **either**, **neither**, **someone**, **somebody**, **anyone**, **nobody**, **everyone**, **everybody**, **any**, and **none**.

Examples: **Some** are in the laundry.

Many will be attending the party.

A **few** won't be going.

Each must bring his own lunch.

I want **both**.

You may choose **either**.

Neither is going.

Please share this with **someone.**

Somebody left this.

Has **anyone** seen Kathleen?

They don't want **anybody** to know.

Nobody wants to go.

Everyone is here.

He likes **everybody**.

Do you have **any**?

I want **none**, thanks.

Pronoun or Adjective:

If **some**, **many**, **few**, **several**, **each**, **both**, **either**, **neither**, **someone's**, **somebody's**, **anyone's**, **anybody's**, **nobody's**, **everyone's**, **everybody's**, or **any** modify (go over to) a noun or pronoun, that word functions as an adjective.

Examples: **Several** bunnies hopped into a hole.

She doesn't want to hear **anyone's** story.

I don't like **either** wallpaper.

Name_______________________________
WORKBOOK PAGE 251
Date_______________________________

PRONOUNS
Indefinite Pronouns

Directions: Place P on the line if the underlined word serves as a pronoun; write A on the line if the underlined word serves as an adjective. Write the adjective and noun it modifies on the line after the sentence. A sentence marked P will be blank.

Example: __A__ A few lions prowled around while others slept. __few lions__

1. __A__ Some people enjoy Japanese food. __Some people__
2. __P__ Please give me some. ______
3. __P__ Each must choose a bed. ______
4. __A__ Each partner may take his turn. __Each partner__
5. __A__ Are there many straws in that package? __many straws__
6. __P__ Have many visited Arlington Cemetery? ______
7. __P__ Both want to be teachers. ______
8. __A__ Both men decided to play tennis. __Both men__
9. __A__ I've tried several different mustards. __several mustards__
10. __P__ Are there several in the bin? ______
11. __P__ Has anyone done the dishes? ______
12. __A__ Did anyone's parents come to the meeting? __anyone's parents__
13. __A__ Either boy may come with me. __Either boy__
14. __P__ I don't want either. ______
15. __A__ Do you have any pets? __any pets__

Name________________________________

Date________________________________

PRONOUNS
Indefinite Pronouns

Directions: Place P on the line if the underlined word serves as a pronoun; write A on the line if the underlined word serves as an adjective. Write the adjective and the noun it modifies on the line after the sentence. A sentence marked P will be blank.

Example: __A__ A few lions prowled around while others slept. _few lions_

1. _____ Some people enjoy Japanese food. ____________________

2. _____ Please give me some. ____________________

3. _____ Each must choose a bed. ____________________

4. _____ Each partner may take his turn. ____________________

5. _____ Are there many straws in that package? ____________________

6. _____ Have many visited Arlington Cemetery? ____________________

7. _____ Both want to be teachers. ____________________

8. _____ Both men decided to play tennis. ____________________

9. _____ I've tried several different mustards. ____________________

10. _____ Are there several in the bin? ____________________

11. _____ Has anyone done the dishes? ____________________

12. _____ Did anyone's parents come to the meeting? ____________________

13. _____ Either boy may come with me. ____________________

14. _____ I don't want either. ____________________

15. _____ Do you have any pets? ____________________

PAGE 483 = WORKBOOK PAGE 252

PRONOUNS

A. Often we or us will appear beside a noun. In order to determine which to use, place your finger over the noun following it. Then, decide according to how the word functions in the sentence.

1. (We, Us) girls like to talk together.
   (**We**, Us) like to talk together. (subject)

2. Give (we, us) adults a chance to play, too.
   Give (we, **us**) a chance to play, too. (indirect object)

3. The lucky ones were (we, us) boys.
   The lucky ones were (**we**, us). (predicate nominative)
   Proof: We were the lucky ones.

B. If an indefinite pronoun is plural, the possessive following it needs to be plural.

Many sent **their** best wishes. (Many is called the antecedent.)

Both want **their** baseballs autographed. (Both is called the antecedent.)

If an indefinite pronoun is singular, the possessive following it needs to be singular.

Each wants **his** turn at the bumper cars. (Each is called the antecedent.)

Everyone is taking **her** bathing suit. (Everyone is called the antecedent.)

Note: Everyone may sound plural; however, it is singular. If it were plural, we would say, "Everyone are going." Of course, we say, "Everyone is going."

Everyone is taking **her**, ***not their***, bathing suit.

C. Cross out any prepositional phrase(s). This will help you to determine which possessive is needed.

Each ~~of the children~~ is waiting **his** turn. (Each is called the antecedent.)

This may "sound" wrong; however **his** is singular because the pronoun **each** is singular.

Name________________________________ **PRONOUNS**
WORKBOOK PAGE 253
Date________________________________

A. Directions: Select the correct pronoun.

1. Do you want (we, **us**) teammates to keep score?
2. (**We**, Us) friends will plan to stay together.
3. The elephant came near (we, **us**) children at the zoo.
4. The coach gave (we, **us**) winners trophies.
5. The best people to do that job are (**we**, us) girls.
6. (**We**, Us) workers need a raise.
7. Leave (we, **us**) players alone.
8. Would you like to come with (we, **us**) teenagers?

B. Directions: Select the correct pronoun.

1. Several set (his, **their**) bags on the ground.
2. Everyone must take (**his**, their) books.
3. Many decided to keep (his, **their**) own money.
4. Each ~~of the girls~~ must take (**her**, their) hat.
5. Nobody wants (**his**, their) picture taken.
6. Both have chosen (his, **their**) vehicles carefully.
7. Everyone ~~of the men~~ took (**his**, their) time.
8. Somebody needs to look at (**his**, their) watch.

Name______________________________ **PRONOUNS**

Date______________________________

A. Directions: Select the correct pronoun.

1. Do you want (we, us) teammates to keep score?
2. (We, Us) friends will plan to stay together.
3. The elephant came near (we, us) children at the zoo.
4. The coach gave (we, us) winners trophies.
5. The best people to do that job are (we, us) girls.
6. (We, Us) workers need a raise.
7. Leave (we, us) players alone.
8. Would you like to come with (we, us) teenagers?

B. Directions: Select the correct pronoun.

1. Several set (his, their) bags on the ground.
2. Everyone must take (his, their) books.
3. Many decided to keep (his, their) own money.
4. Each of the girls must take (her, their) hat.
5. Nobody wants (his, their) picture taken.
6. Both have chosen (his, their) vehicles carefully.
7. Everyone of the men took (his, their) time.
8. Somebody needs to look at (his, their) watch.

Name_______________________________

WORKBOOK PAGE 254

Date_______________________________

PRONOUN REVIEW

A. Directions: Write S if the pronoun in boldfaced print functions as the subject; write PN if the pronoun in boldfaced print functions as a predicate nominative.

Suggestion: **Cross out any prepositional phrase(s). Underline the subject once and the verb/verb phrase twice. Then, make your decision.**

Remember: Invert the sentence to prove a predicate nominative.

1. __S__ **We** are sleeping ~~in a tent~~.

2. __S__ ~~In the afternoon,~~ **he** walks two miles.

3. __PN__ The person receiving the award is **she**. (She is the person receiving the award.)

4. __PN__ Our neighbors are **they** ~~by the flag pole~~. (They are our neighbors.)

5. __S__ Soon, **I** shall find it.

B. Directions: Choose the letter that tells how the pronoun functions in the sentence.

1. __a__ The newscaster wants to go with **him**.
   - a. object of the preposition
   - b. direct object
   - c. indirect object

2. __b__ You hit **me**!
   - a. object of the preposition
   - b. direct object
   - c. indirect object

3. __a__ **She** sings constantly.
   - a. subject
   - b. predicate nominative

4. __c__ The banker will give **them** the loan for a car.
   - a. object of the preposition
   - b. direct object
   - c. indirect object

Name________________________________ **PRONOUN REVIEW**

Date________________________________

A. Directions: Write S if the pronoun in boldfaced print functions as the subject; write PN if the pronoun in boldfaced print functions as a predicate nominative.

Suggestion: **Cross out any prepositional phrase(s). Underline the subject once and the verb/verb phrase twice. Then, make your decision.**

Remember: Invert the sentence to prove a predicate nominative.

1. _____ **We** are sleeping in a tent.

2. _____ In the afternoon, **he** walks two miles.

3. _____ The person receiving the award is **she**.

4. _____ Our neighbors are **they** by the flag pole.

5. _____ Soon, **I** shall find it.

B. Directions: Choose the letter that tells how the pronoun functions in the sentence.

1. _____ The newscaster wants to go with **him**.
   a. object of the preposition
   b. direct object
   c. indirect object

2. _____ You hit **me**!
   a. object of the preposition
   b. direct object
   c. indirect object

3. _____ **She** sings constantly.
   a. subject
   b. predicate nominative

4. _____ The banker will give **them** the loan for a car.
   a. object of the preposition
   b. direct object
   c. indirect object

Name________________________________

PRONOUN REVIEW

WORKBOOK PAGE 255

Date________________________________

C. Directions: Select the correct pronoun.

1. (**They**, Them) need a ride.
2. (Him, **He**) likes to sleep late.
3. I can't find (she, **her**).
4. Take (they, **them**) with you.
5. The red team will play against (**us**, we) later.
6. The best choice is (him, **he**).
7. That book belongs to (**me**, I).

D. Directions: Select the correct pronoun.

Suggestion: You may want to place your finger over the first part of the compound.

1. Johnny and (**I**, me) left late.
2. A dog wandered over and sat beside Mack and (he, **him**).
3. A large glass of iced tea had been served to her friend and (she, **her**).
4. The graduating seniors from that area are Cody and (**he**, him).
5. Spectators watched the leader and (**them**, they) water ski.
6. He didn't give that team or (we, **us**) a chance.

E. Directions: Select the correct word.

1. (Their, **They're**) having fun.
2. I wonder why the gerbil runs around in (it's, **its**) cage.
3. Is (**their**, they're) dad a computer expert?
4. We hope that (your, **you're**) chosen.

Name________________________________ **PRONOUN REVIEW**

Date________________________________

C. Directions: Select the correct pronoun.

1. (They, Them) need a ride.
2. (Him, He) likes to sleep late.
3. I can't find (she, her).
4. Take (they, them) with you.
5. The red team will play against (us, we) later.
6. The best choice is (him, he).
7. That book belongs to (me, I).

D. Directions: Select the correct pronoun.

Suggestion: You may want to place your finger over the first part of the compound.

1. Johnny and (I, me) left late.
2. A dog wandered over and sat beside Mack and (he, him).
3. A large glass of iced tea had been served to her friend and (she, her).
4. The graduating seniors from that area are Cody and (he, him).
5. Spectators watched the leader and (them, they) water ski.
6. He didn't give that team or (we, us) a chance.

E. Directions: Select the correct word.

1. (Their, They're) having fun.
2. I wonder why the gerbil runs around in (it's, its) cage.
3. Is (their, they're) dad a computer expert?
4. We hope that (your, you're) chosen.

Name________________________________ **PRONOUN REVIEW**

WORKBOOK PAGE 256

Date________________________________

F. Directions: Fill in the blank.

1. Write an example of a reflexive pronoun. **myself, himself, herself, yourself, itself, ourselves,** or **themselves**

2. An example of a demonstrative pronoun is **this, that, those,** or **these**, and an example of an interrogative pronoun is **who, whom, which, whose, what**.

3. Write two indefinite pronouns. **some, many, several, few, any, most, one everyone, everybody, somebody, anyone, etc.**

G. Directions: Write the antecedent of the underlined pronoun.

1. Mom — Mom irons her tablecloths.
2. I — I can't do this myself.
3. Lani/Al — Lani and Al want their marbles back.
4. girl — One girl carried her own moving boxes.
5. We — We don't have our pets along.

H. Directions: Write A if the underlined word functions as an adjective; write P if the underlined word functions as a pronoun.

1. P Mrs. Hanson wants those.
2. A Are those cups dirty?
3. A Which pear is yours?
4. P Which does he want?
5. P Are there many left?
6. A Many balloons had been blown up for the party.
7. P That is unbelievable!
8. A Are you sure that story is true?
9. A We'd like some water, please.
10. P Would you like some?

Name______________________________

PRONOUN REVIEW

Date______________________________

F. Directions: Fill in the blank.

1. Write an example of a reflexive pronoun. ____________________

2. An example of a demonstrative pronoun is _______________, and an example of an interrogative pronoun is __________________.

4. Write two indefinite pronouns. __________________ and __________________.

G. Directions: Write the antecedent of the underlined pronoun.

1. __________________________ Mom irons her tablecloths.
2. __________________________ I can't do this myself.
3. __________________________ Lani and Al want their marbles back.
4. __________________________ One girl carried her own moving boxes.
5. __________________________ We don't have our pets along.

H. Directions: Write A if the underlined word functions as an adjective; write P if the underlined word functions as a pronoun.

1. _____ Mrs. Hanson wants those.
2. _____ Are those cups dirty?
3. _____ Which pear is yours?
4. _____ Which does he want?
5. _____ Are there many left?
6. _____ Many balloons had been blown up for the party.
7. _____ That is unbelievable!
8. _____ Are you sure that story is true?
9. _____ We'd like some water, please.
10. _____ Would you like some?

Name________________________________ **PRONOUN REVIEW**
WORKBOOK PAGE 257
Date________________________________

I. Directions: Select the correct pronoun.

1. My aunt is (**she**, her) with my dad.
2. A boy sat by (**himself**, hisself).
3. Give (they, **them**) a minute to locate it.
4. Have Harold and (him, **he**) walked home?
5. A ringmaster lifted (**his**, their) megaphone.
6. With (who, **whom**) has Janice gone?
7. Teddy gave Breck and (she, **her**) some rubber bands.
8. Mrs. Thompson and (me, **I**) will sign those papers.
9. (**We**, Us) boys played games all afternoon.
10. Truman and (us, **we**) are writing songs.
11. (**Who**, Whom) is the author of Summer of the Monkeys?
12. One of the blue jays lost a few of (their, **its**) feathers.
13. Please loan (we, **us**) actors your old chest for a prop.
14. To (who, **whom**) should this be sent?
15. Your friend is (**who**, whom)?
16. Split the candy between Gary and (I, **me**).

Name________________________________

Date________________________________

PRONOUN REVIEW

I. Directions: Select the correct pronoun.

1. My aunt is (she, her) with my dad.
2. A boy sat by (himself, hisself).
3. Give (they, them) a minute to locate it.
4. Have Harold and (him, he) walked home?
5. A ringmaster lifted (his, their) megaphone.
6. With (who, whom) has Janice gone?
7. Teddy gave Breck and (she, her) some rubber bands.
8. Mrs. Thompson and (me, I) will sign those papers.
9. (We, Us) boys played games all afternoon.
10. Truman and (us, we) are writing songs.
11. (Who, Whom) is the author of <u>Summer of the Monkeys</u>?
12. One of the blue jays lost a few of (their, its) feathers.
13. Please loan (we, us) actors your old chest for a prop.
14. To (who, whom) should this be sent?
15. Your friend is (who, whom)?
16. Split the candy between Gary and (I, me).

Name________________________________ **CUMULATIVE REVIEW**

WORKBOOK PAGE 258

Date_________________________________

A. Directions: Cross out any prepositional phrase(s). Underline the subject once and the verb/verb phrase twice. Label any direct object-D.O.; label any indirect object-I.O.

1. The father ~~with the twins~~ looks happy.

D.O.

2. ~~At the beginning of the year~~, Earl changed jobs.

D.O.

3. The zoo keeper and his helper feed the animals.

I.O. D.O.

4. An owner ~~of a restaurant~~ offered his customers free sodas.

D.O.

5. One ~~of the women~~ stood and clapped her hands.

D.O.

6. (You) Put this coin ~~into your pocket~~.

B. Directions: Cross out any prepositional phrase(s). Underline the subject once and the verb/verb phrase twice. Label any direct object-D.O.

D.O.

1. Have you (took, taken) your brother ~~to that performance~~?

D.O.

2. He should have (swam, swum) another lap.

3. Her mother-in-law could *not* have (came, come) earlier.

D.O.

4. I must have (drank, drunk) too much water.

5. The mother and son had (gone, went) ~~to a puppet show~~.

D.O.

6. You might have (brung, brought) something (to eat).

7. The cat has (laid, lain) ~~on the bed for an hour~~.

D.O.

8. Some ladies (rose, raised) their hands (to vote).

9. (You) Please (sit, set) here ~~beside me~~.

D.O.

10. (May, Can) we eat popsicles now?

Name________________________________ **CUMULATIVE REVIEW**

Date________________________________

A. Directions: Cross out any prepositional phrase(s). Underline the subject once and the verb/verb phrase twice. Label any direct object-D.O.; label any indirect object-I.O.

1. The father with the twins looks happy.
2. At the beginning of the year, Earl changed jobs.
3. The zoo keeper and his helper feed the animals.
4. An owner of a restaurant offered his customers free sodas.
5. One of the women stood and clapped her hands.
6. Put this coin into your pocket.

B. Directions: Cross out any prepositional phrase(s). Underline the subject once and the verb/verb phrase twice. Label any direct object-D.O.

1. Have you (took, taken) your brother to that performance?
2. He should have (swam, swum) another lap.
3. Her mother-in-law could not have (came, come) earlier.
4. I must have (drank, drunk) too much water.
5. The mother and son had (gone, went) to a puppet show.
6. You might have (brung, brought) something to eat.
7. The cat has (laid, lain) on the bed for an hour.
8. Some ladies (rose, raised) their hands to vote.
9. Please (sit, set) here beside me.
10. (May, Can) we eat popsicles now?

Name________________________________ **CUMULATIVE REVIEW**

WORKBOOK PAGE 259

Date________________________________

C. Directions: Write A if the verb is action; write L if the verb is linking.

Although directions do not include deleting prepositional phrases or underlining subject and verb, they have been included here.

Suggestion: **Write *is*, *am*, *are*, *was*, or *were* above a verb that is on the linking list. If the meaning of the sentence is not changed, the verb is probably linking.**

1. __L__ ~~After the fire~~, the fireman looked (**was**) exhausted.

2. __A__ She looked his way and smiled.

3. __A__ The bell sounded and then stopped suddenly.

4. __L__ This gourd sounds (**is**) hollow.

D. Directions: Write the contraction.

1. how is - __how's__
2. we were - __we're__
3. had not - __hadn't__
4. cannot - __can't__
5. they have - __they've__
6. do not - __don't__
7. I am - __I'm__
8. will not - __won't__

E. Directions: Cross out any prepositional phrase(s). Underline the subject once and the verb/verb phrase twice. Write the tense, *present*, *past*, or *future*, in the space provided.

1. __present__ A crossing guard helps the children.

2. __future__ The children will build houses ~~with sugar cubes~~.

3. __past__ Toby dusted his room.

4. __present__ They make gingerbread houses each Christmas.

F. Directions: Write intj. above each interjection.

1. **Wow!** (**Intj.**) It's all gone!

2. They're here! **Yeah!** (**Intj.**)

Name______________________________ **CUMULATIVE REVIEW**

Date______________________________

C. Directions: Write A if the verb is action; write L if the verb is linking.

Suggestion: **Write *is*, *am*, *are*, *was*, or *were* above a verb that is on the linking list. If the meaning of the sentence is not changed, the verb is probably linking.**

1. _____ After the fire, the fireman looked exhausted.
2. _____ She looked his way and smiled.
3. _____ The bell sounded and then stopped suddenly.
4. _____ This gourd sounds hollow.

D. Directions: Write the contraction.

1. how is - ____________________
2. we were - ____________________
3. had not - ____________________
4. cannot - ____________________
5. they have - ____________________
6. do not - ____________________
7. I am - ____________________
8. will not - ____________________

E. Directions: Cross out any prepositional phrase(s). Underline the subject once and the verb/verb phrase twice. On the line, write the tense, *present*, *past*, or *future*, in the space provided.

1. ____________________ A crossing guard helps the children.
2. ____________________ The children will build houses with sugar cubes.
3. ____________________ Toby dusted his room.
4. ____________________ They make gingerbread houses each Christmas.

F. Directions: Write intj. above each interjection.

1. Wow! It's all gone!
2. They're here! Yeah!

Name________________________________ **CUMULATIVE REVIEW**

WORKBOOK PAGE 260

Date________________________________

G. Directions: Label any conjunction.

conj.
1. Timothy **or** Gary developed the plan.

conj. **conj.**
2. My brother **and** I are coming, **but** we can't stay long.

H. Directions: Write A if the noun is abstract; write C if the noun is concrete.

1. __C__ mole 2. __A__ joy 3. __C__ file 4. __A__ wisdom

I. Directions: Write C if the noun is common; write P if the noun is proper.

1. __C__ STREET 3. __C__ WOMAN 5. __P__ AMY GRANT

2. __P__ ASH STREET 4. __C__ SINGER 6. __P__ MT. SHASTA

J. Directions: Write N if the underlined word functions as a noun; write A if the underlined word functions as an adjective.

1. __N__ A post had been decorated with crepe paper.

2. __A__ Please send me a post card.

3. __A__ That man wears a bow tie.

4. __N__ Her hair bow is purple.

K. Directions: Write N if the underlined word functions as a noun; write V if the underlined word functions as a verb.

1. __V__ Will you nail these boards together?

2. __N__ One nail is needed to finish the jewelry box.

3. __N__ A roll with jelly was served.

4. __V__ They roll dough for sugar cookies.

Name_______________________________ **CUMULATIVE REVIEW**

Date_______________________________

G. Directions: Label any conjunction.

1. Timothy or Gary developed the plan.

2. My brother and I are coming, but we can't stay long.

H. Directions: Write A if the noun is abstract; write C if the noun is concrete.

1. _____ mole 2. _____ joy 3. _____ file 4. _____ wisdom

I. Directions: Write C if the noun is common; write P if the noun is proper.

1. _____ STREET 3. _____ WOMAN 5. _____ AMY GRANT

2. _____ ASH STREET 4. _____ SINGER 6. _____ MT. SHASTA

J. Directions: Write N if the underlined word functions as a noun; write A if the underlined word functions as an adjective.

1. _____ A post had been decorated with crepe paper.

2. _____ Please send me a post card.

3. _____ That man wears a bow tie.

4. _____ Her hair bow is purple.

K. Directions: Write N if the underlined word functions as a noun; write V if the underlined word functions as a verb.

1. _____ Will you nail these boards together?

2. _____ One nail is needed to finish the jewelry box.

3. _____ A roll with jelly was served.

4. _____ They roll dough for sugar cookies.

Name_______________________________ **CUMULATIVE REVIEW**

WORKBOOK PAGE 261

Date_______________________________

L. Directions: Write the possessive form.

1. a shopping cart belonging to a store - store's (shopping) cart
2. dolls belonging to three girls - girls' dolls
3. a luncheon shared by more than one woman - women's luncheon
4. a path used by horses - horses' path

M. Directions: Write the plural of each noun.

1. dish - dishes
2. mouse - mice
3. lime - limes
4. leaf - leaves
5. match - matches
6. goose - geese

N. Directions: Box any nouns.

Nouns are in boldfaced print.

1. A **container** of **yogurt** is in the **refrigerator**.
2. Several **diners** ate two **pieces** of cherry **pie**.
3. I would like glazed **carrots**, several pickled **eggs**, and a **slice** of **Carole's cake**.
4. Their **sister** placed an **arrangement** of **tulips** on that **table**.
5. This **cap** and your old **hat** need to be washed in this **gadget**.

O. Directions: Underline the subject once and the verb/verb phrase. Label any predicate nominative-P.N. Write the proof on the line.

1. Miss Lewis is a teacher (P.N.) ~~at Baltic School~~.

Proof: A teacher is Miss Lewis.

2. *Where the Red Fern Grows* is a famous book (P.N.). (**Book titles are underlined; however, they are placed in italics in printed matter.**)

Proof: A famous book is *Where the Red Fern Grows.*

3. Travis is the boy (P.N.) ~~with the snake~~.

Proof: The boy is Travis.

Name_______________________________ **CUMULATIVE REVIEW**

Date_______________________________

L. Directions: Write the possessive form.

1. a shopping cart belonging to a store - ________________________________

2. dolls belonging to three girls - ________________________________

3. a luncheon shared by more than one woman - ________________________________

4. a path used by horses - ________________________________

M. Directions: Write the plural of each noun.

1. dish - ____________ 3. lime - ____________ 5. match - ____________

2. mouse - ____________ 4. leaf - ____________ 6. goose - ____________

N. Directions: Box any nouns.

1. A container of yogurt is in the refrigerator.

2. Several diners ate two pieces of cherry pie.

3. I would like glazed carrots, several pickled eggs, and a slice of Carole's cake.

4. Their sister placed an arrangement of tulips on that table.

5. This cap and your old hat need to be washed in this gadget.

O. Directions: Underline the subject once and the verb/verb phrase twice. Label any predicate nominative-P.N. Write the proof on the line.

1. Miss Lewis is a teacher at Baltic School.

Proof: ________________________________

2. Where the Red Fern Grows is a famous book.

Proof: ________________________________

3. Travis is the boy with the snake.

Proof: ________________________________

Name_______________________________ **CUMULATIVE REVIEW**

WORKBOOK PAGE 262

Date_______________________________

P. Directions: Circle any adjective(s).

Adjectives are in boldfaced print.

Remember: Read the sentence and circle limiting adjectives first. Then, circle descriptive adjectives.

1. Was **the first California** mission at San Diego?
2. **One** person ordered **two pork** chops and **fried** okra for dinner.
3. **Her older** sister is **an** usher for **a welcome** club.
4. **Their** principal visited **a Japanese** school **last** year.
5. **Marv's new beige** slacks have **black** ink on **the right** cuff.

Q. Directions: Select the correct adjective form.

1. He is (**taller**, tallest) than I.
2. Ray is the (louder, **loudest**) singer in the trio.
3. Brian is (**more talkative**, most talkative) than his partner.
4. Mr. Lyons is the (more successful, **most successful**) lawyer in his office.
5. I was (**more courageous**, most courageous) on my second try.

R. Directions: Read each group of words. Write S for sentence, F for fragment, and R-O for run-on.

Suggestion: Cross out any prepositional phrases, underline the subject once and the verb/verb phrase twice. This helps greatly in making a choice.

1. R-O A ground hog came out ~~of its hole~~ and ran ~~across the meadow~~, then headed ~~toward a woods~~, but turned around and it scampered back ~~into its hole~~.
2. F A waffle iron ~~in the kitchen~~.
3. S Sid sometimes reads ~~during his break~~ ~~at work~~.
4. R-O Nelson continued (to run), we ran ~~after him~~.

Name________________________________ **CUMULATIVE REVIEW**

Date________________________________

P. Directions: Circle any adjective(s).

Remember: Read the sentence and circle limiting adjectives first. Then, circle descriptive adjectives.

1. Was the first California mission at San Diego?
2. One person ordered two pork chops and fried okra for dinner.
3. Her older sister is an usher for a welcome club.
4. Their principal visited a Japanese school last year.
5. Marv's new beige slacks have black ink on the right cuff.

Q. Directions: Select the correct adjective form.

1. He is (taller, tallest) than I.
2. Ray is the (louder, loudest) singer in the trio.
3. Brian is (more talkative, most talkative) than his partner.
4. Mr. Lyons is the (more successful, most successful) lawyer in his office.
5. I was (more courageous, most courageous) on my second try.

R. Directions: Read each group of words. Write S for sentence, F for fragment, and R-O for run-on.

Suggestion: Cross out any prepositional phrases, underline the subject once and the verb/verb phrase twice. This helps greatly in making a choice.

1. _____ A ground hog came out of its hole and ran across the meadow, then headed toward a woods, but turned around and it scampered back into its hole.
2. _____ A waffle iron in the kitchen.
3. _____ Sid sometimes reads during his break at work.
4. _____ Nelson continued to run, we ran after him.

Name________________________________ **CUMULATIVE REVIEW**

WORKBOOK PAGE 263

Date________________________________

S. Directions: Write the sentence type: declarative (statement), interrogative (question), imperative (command), and exclamatory.

1. ____imperative____ Please hurry.
2. ____declarative____ The dog needs to be fed.
3. ____interrogative____ Has the nurse taken his blood pressure?
4. ____exclamatory____ Wow! You received it!

T. Directions: Select the correct adverb.

1. You should chew your food (good, **well**).
2. The limousine driver opened the door (slow, **slowly**).
3. His science project took (**longer**, longest) than yours.
4. This washing machine buzzes (**more shrilly**, most shrilly) than the old one.
5. Don't act so (weird, **weirdly**).

U. Directions: Circle any adverb(s). **Answers are in boldface.**
Suggestion: Cross out any prepositional phrase(s). Underline the subject once and the verb/verb phrase twice. Look for any adverb that tells to what extent. Then, go back and look for any adverb(s) that tell how. Next, look for any adverb(s) that tell when. Then, search for any adverb(s) that tell where.

1. **When** will you arrive **there**?
2. His injured finger hurt **quite badly**.
3. **Tomorrow**, the library will open **early**.
4. Lester cannot find his bag **anywhere** ~~in his room~~.
5. They are **always home** ~~on Saturday~~.
6. He took the dessert **out** ~~of the refrigerator~~ **too soon**.

Name_______________________________ **CUMULATIVE REVIEW**

Date_______________________________

S. Directions: Write the sentence type: declarative (statement), interrogative (question), imperative (command), and exclamatory.

1. ___________________________ Please hurry.
2. ___________________________ The dog needs to be fed.
3. ___________________________ Has the nurse taken his blood pressure?
4. ___________________________ Wow! You received it!

T. Directions: Select the correct adverb.

1. You should chew your food (good, well).
2. The limousine driver opened the door (slow, slowly).
3. His science project took (longer, longest) than yours.
4. This washing machine buzzes (more shrilly, most shrilly) than the old one.
5. Don't act so (weird, weirdly).

U. Directions: Circle any adverb(s).

Suggestion: Cross out any prepositional phrase(s). Underline the subject once and the verb/verb phrase twice. Look for any adverb that tells to what extent. Then, go back and look for any adverb(s) that tell how. Next, look for any adverb(s) that tell when. Then, search for any adverb(s) that tell where.

1. When will you arrive there?
2. His injured finger hurt quite badly.
3. Tomorrow, the library will open early.
4. Lester cannot find his bag anywhere in his room.
5. They are always home on Saturday.
6. He took the dessert out of the refrigerator too soon.

Name________________________________ **PRONOUN TEST**

WORKBOOK PAGE 333

Date________________________________

Part D is difficult. You may wish to count it as part of the test. Weight it according to how important you feel it is for your level. You may wish to count it as extra points.

A. Directions: Select the correct pronoun.

1. The missionary spoke to (**them**, they) about Peru.
2. (**I**, Me) like to read about lizards.
3. The babysitter read (we, **us**) a story about whales.
4. The second speaker is (**she**, her).
5. (**Who**, Whom) has the time?
6. A lifeguard teaches (they, **them**) swimming strokes.
7. With (who, **whom**) has she planned the picnic?
8. The disagreement was between Teresa and (she, **her**).
9. Are (**we**, us) boys invited?
10. Ask (we, **us**) friends to help you.

B. Directions: Write P in the blank if the underlined word serves as a pronoun; write A in the blank if the underlined word serves as an adjective.

1. __P__ Can you imagine <u>that</u>?
2. __A__ <u>This</u> video machine is broken.
3. __A__ <u>Which</u> car is longer?
4. __A__ Have you decided <u>whose</u> shoes are in the laundry room?
5. __P__ <u>What</u> do you want?

C. Directions: Select the correct word.

1. Are you aware that (**it's**, its) raining?

Name______________________________

Date______________________________

PRONOUN TEST

A. Directions: Select the correct pronoun.

1. The missionary spoke to (them, they) about Peru.
2. (I, Me) like to read about lizards.
3. The babysitter read (we, us) a story about whales.
4. The second speaker is (she, her).
5. (Who, Whom) has the time?
6. A lifeguard teaches (they, them) swimming strokes.
7. With (who, whom) has she planned the picnic?
8. The disagreement was between Teresa and (she, her).
9. Are (we, us) boys invited?
10. Ask (we, us) friends to help you.

B. Directions: Write P in the blank if the underlined word serves as a pronoun; write A in the blank if the underlined word serves as an adjective.

1. _____ Can you imagine that?
2. _____ This video machine is broken.
3. _____ Which car is longer?
4. _____ Have you decided whose shoes are in the laundry room?
5. _____ What do you want?

C. Directions: Select the correct word.

1. Are you aware that (it's, its) raining?

WORKBOOK PAGE 334

2. She doesn't know (**their,** they're) address.
3. Joe makes (**his**, their) own bed.
4. The giraffe moved (it's, **its**) neck slowly.
5. Some basketball players help (his, **their**) communities by raising money for charity.
6. Both want (his, **their**) dinner on a paper plate.
7. Everyone ~~of the students~~ took (**his**, their) books. **(Everyone is the antecedent.)**
8. Janice and (**we**, us) talked about our camping trip.
9. The winners of the art contest were Darlene and (him, **he**).
10. The child couldn't reach the cookie jar (hisself, **himself**).

D. Directions: Write the antecedent of the underlined word.

1. ____book____ That book has lost its cover.
2. ____hikers____ Do most hikers take their canteens everywhere?
3. ____Charles/I____ Charles and I eat our dinner early.
4. ____You____ You must take your own money.
5. ____Each____ Each ~~of the spaniels~~ ran to his owner.

E. Directions: Tell how the underlined pronoun functions in the sentence.
A. subject B. direct object C. Indirect object
D. object of the preposition E. predicate nominative

1. __B__ Your aunt helped me.
2. __D__ May I go with them?
3. __C__ A senator gave us a tour of the senate building.
4. __A__ He is playing with his cousin.
5. __E__ The last person in line was she.

2. She doesn't know (their, they're) address.

3. Joe makes (his, their) own bed.

4. The giraffe moved (it's, its) neck slowly.

5. Some basketball players help (his, their) communities by raising money for charity.

6. Both want (his, their) dinner on a paper plate.

7. Everyone of the students took (his, their) books.

8. Janice and (we, us) talked about our camping trip.

9. The winners of the art contest were Darlene and (him, he).

10. The child couldn't reach the cookie jar (hisself, himself).

D. Directions: Write the antecedent of the underlined word.

1. ______________________ That book has lost <u>its</u> cover.

2. ______________________ Do most hikers take <u>their</u> canteens everywhere?

3. ______________________ Charles and I eat <u>our</u> dinner early.

4. ______________________ You must take <u>your</u> own money.

5. ______________________ Each of the spaniels ran to <u>his</u> owner.

E. Directions: Tell how the underlined pronoun functions in the sentence.
A. subject B. direct object C. Indirect object
D. object of the preposition E. predicate nominative

1. _____ Your aunt helped <u>me</u>.

2. _____ May I go with <u>them</u>?

3. _____ A senator gave <u>us</u> a tour of the senate building.

4. _____ <u>He</u> is playing with his cousin.

5. _____ The last person in line was <u>she</u>.

Name______________________________

WORKBOOK PAGE 335

Date______________________________

CUMULATIVE TEST
Pronouns

A. Directions: List 50 prepositions. **Students should list any 50.**

1. about
2. above
3. across
4. after
5. against
6. along
7. amid
8. among
9. around
10. at
11. atop
12. before
13. behind
14. below
15. beneath
16. beside
17. between
18. beyond
19. but (except)
20. by
21. concerning
22. down
23. during
24. except
25. for
26. from
27. in
28. inside
29. into
30. like
31. near
32. of
33. off
34. on
35. onto
36. out
37. outside
38. over
39. past
40. regarding
41. since
42. through
43. throughout
44. to
45. toward
46. under
47. underneath
48. until
49. up
50. upon

with, within, without

B. Directions: Cross out any prepositional phrase(s). Underline the subject once and the verb/verb phrase twice. Label any direct object-D.O.

1. The screen ~~on the back window~~ has several holes. **(D.O.: holes)**

2. The man ~~in the white shirt~~ eats a sandwich ~~at a deli~~ every day. **(D.O.: sandwich)**

3. One lady ~~without an umbrella~~ dashed out ~~into the rain~~.

4. Your fan ~~above the coffee table~~ has five blades. **(D.O.: blades)**

5. Everyone ~~but Claire~~ sat ~~beneath the tree~~ and talked.

Name________________________

Date________________________

CUMULATIVE TEST
Pronouns

A. Directions: List 50 prepositions.

1.	________	14.	________	27.	________	40.	________
2.	________	15.	________	28.	________	41.	________
3.	________	16.	________	29.	________	42.	________
4.	________	17.	________	30.	________	43.	________
5.	________	18.	________	31.	________	44.	________
6.	________	19.	________	32.	________	45.	________
7.	________	20.	________	33.	________	46.	________
8.	________	21.	________	34.	________	47.	________
9.	________	22.	________	35.	________	48.	________
10.	________	23.	________	36.	________	49.	________
11.	________	24.	________	37.	________	50.	________
12.	________	25.	________	38.	________		
13.	________	26.	________	39.	________		

B. Directions: Cross out any prepositional phrase(s). Underline the subject once and the verb/verb phrase twice. Label any direct object-D.O.

1. The screen on the back window has several holes.
2. The man in the white shirt eats a sandwich at a deli every day.
3. One lady without an umbrella dashed out into the rain.
4. Your fan above the coffee table has unusual blades.
5. Everyone but Claire sat beneath the tree and talked.

C. Directions: Cross out any prepositional phrase(s). Underline the subject once and the verb/verb phrase twice.

WORKBOOK PAGE 336

1. That man (go, goes) ~~to his office~~ ~~in the evening~~, too.
2. Has your balloon (busted, burst)?
3. Her arm was (broke, broken) ~~during the fall~~.
4. Several companies (washes, wash) windows ~~in tall buildings~~.
5. Did you (sit, set) the alarm?
6. His little boat had (sank, sunk) ~~in the puddle~~.
7. Several people (walk, walks) ~~through the park~~ each evening.
8. You could not have (chosen, chose) a better one.
9. Have you (drank, drunk) milk ~~for lunch~~?
10. The newspaper is (laying, lying) ~~on the floor~~.
11. Missy has (given, gave) her brother some popcorn.
12. Where have you (laid, lain) the clipper?
13. The sun has already (raised, risen).
14. The mail may have (came, come) early.
15. I should have (went, gone) alone.
16. Joan always (sits, sets) ~~in the back row~~.
17. He could not have (knew, known) that!
18. His answer may have been (wrote, written) ~~on the last page~~.
19. She must have (rode, ridden) her sister's scooter ~~without permission~~.
20. One ~~of the boys~~ (flies, fly) kites frequently.

C. Directions: Cross out any prepositional phrase(s). Underline the subject once and the verb/verb phrase twice.

1. That man (go, goes) to his office in the evening, too.

2. Has your balloon (busted, burst)?

3. Her arm was (broke, broken) during the fall.

4. Several companies (washes, wash) windows in tall buildings.

5. Did you (sit, set) the alarm?

6. His little boat had (sank, sunk) in the puddle.

7. Several people (walk, walks) through the park each evening.

8. You could not have (chosen, chose) a better one.

9. Have you (drank, drunk) milk for lunch?

10. The newspaper is (laying, lying) on the floor.

11. Missy has (given, gave) her brother some popcorn.

12. Where have you (laid, lain) the clipper?

13. The sun has already (raised, risen).

14. The mail may have (came, come) early.

15. I should have (went, gone) alone.

16. Joan always (sits, sets) in the back row.

17. He could not have (knew, known) that!

18. His answer may have been (wrote, written) on the last page.

19. She must have (rode, ridden) her sister's scooter without permission.

20. One of the boys (flies, fly) kites frequently.

WORKBOOK PAGE 337

D. Directions: Write the contraction.

1. I will - I'll 3. has not - hasn't 5. did not - didn't

2. who is - who's 4. we have - we've 6. I am - I'm

E. Directions: Write the sentence type: declarative (statement), imperative (command), interrogative (question), or exclamatory.

1. interrogative When does the bus arrive?

2. exclamatory Drats! I've lost it again!

3. imperative Throw this in the garbage.

4. declarative A bottle was given to the baby.

F. Direction: Write the tense: present, past, or future.

Suggestion: Cross out any prepositional phrase(s). Underline the subject once and the verb/verb phrase twice. This will help you determine tense.

1. future I shall give this ~~to your dad~~.

2. past Several chickens ~~in the yard~~ cackled loudly.

3. present Rena sleeps late ~~on the weekends~~.

4. present The road ~~near the stop sign~~ is curvy.

G. Directions: Write A if the noun is abstract; write C if the noun is concrete.

1. A happiness 3. C cucumber

2. C quilt 4. A peace

H. Directions: Write C if the noun is common; write P if the noun is proper.

1. P MR. BARNES 3. C OAK 5. P CANDLESTICK PARK

2. C TREE 4. C CITY 6. P NEW ORLEANS

D. Directions: Write the contraction.

1. I will - ____________ 3. has not - ____________ 5. did not - ____________

2. who is - ____________ 4. we have - ____________ 6. I am - ____________

E. Directions: Write the sentence type: declarative (statement), imperative (command), interrogative (question), or exclamatory.

1. ______________________ When does the bus arrive?

2. ______________________ Drats! I've lost it again!

3. ______________________ Throw this in the garbage.

4. ______________________ A bottle was given to the baby.

F. Direction: Write the tense: present, past, or future.

Suggestion: Cross out any prepositional phrase(s). Underline the subject once and the verb/verb phrase twice. This will help you determine tense.

1. ______________________ I shall give this to your dad.

2. ______________________ Several chickens in the yard cackled loudly.

3. ______________________ Rena sleeps late on the weekends.

4. ______________________ The road near the stop sign is curvy.

G. Directions: Write A if the noun is abstract; write C if the noun is concrete.

1. _____ happiness 3. _____ cucumber

2. _____ quilt 4. _____ peace

H. Directions: Write C if the noun is common; write P if the noun is proper.

1. _____ MR. BARNES 3. _____ OAK 5. _____ CANDLESTICK PARK

2. _____ TREE 4. _____ CITY 6. _____ NEW ORLEANS

I. Directions: Write the plural.

WORKBOOK PAGE 338

1. solo - solos
2. bush - bushes
3. moose - moose
4. spoof - spoofs
5. baby - babies
6. stitch - stitches
7. wrinkle - wrinkles
8. calf - calves

J. Directions: Write the possessive.

1. a uniform belonging to a nurse - nurse's uniform
2. a bus belonging to tourists - tourists' bus
3. a restroom for more than one man - men's restroom
4. a trail that walkers use - walkers' trail

K. Directions: Box any nouns.

Remember: Finding determining (limiting) adjectives helps you to find some nouns. Nouns are in boldfaced print; determiners have been underlined.

1. Your **pizza** is in a **box** in the **refrigerator**.
2. Several **lamps** had been purchased for **Annie's** new **home**.
3. **Nick** has two **rabbits** and many **cats** in his **yard**.
4. Some **lemons** and an **orange** are needed for that **dessert**.
5. Are those **boys** and **girls** by the **lake** your **relatives**?

L. Directions: Read each group of words. Write F for fragment, S for sentence, and R-O for run-on.

1. F Running down the stairs.
2. S We spent the morning doing laundry.
3. R-O His parents went to England, they saw many castles.

4. F Left without his baseball mitt or bat.

I. Directions: Write the plural.

1. solo - ______________________
2. bush - ______________________
3. moose - ______________________
4. spoof - ______________________
5. baby - ______________________
6. stitch - ______________________
7. wrinkle - ______________________
8. calf - ______________________

J. Directions: Write the possessive.

1. a uniform belonging to a nurse - ______________________
2. a bus belonging to tourists - ______________________
3. a restroom for more than one man - ______________________
4. a trail that walkers use - ______________________

K. Directions: Box any nouns.
Remember: Finding determining (limiting) adjectives helps you to find some nouns.

1. Your pizza is in a box in the refrigerator.
2. Several lamps had been purchased for Annie's new home.
3. Nick has two rabbits and many cats in his yard.
4. Some lemons and an orange are needed for that dessert.
5. Are those boys and girls by the lake your relatives?

L. Directions: Read each group of words. Write F for fragment, S for sentence, and R-O for run-on.

1. ______ Running down the stairs.
2. ______ We spent the morning doing laundry.
3. ______ His parents went to England, they saw many castles.
4. ______ Left without his baseball mitt or bat.

M. Directions: Circle any adjectives.

WORKBOOK PAGE 339

Adjectives will be in boldfaced print.

Suggestion: Read each sentence and first circle limiting adjectives. Then, reread the sentence and circle descriptive adjectives.

1. **A beautiful flower** garden is by **that** stream.

2. **Her older** sister and **one** brother live in **an old country** inn in Vermont.

3. **My German** friend attends **a private** school in **a nearby** town.

4. **Some garlic** potatoes and **glazed** ham were part of **the delicious** buffet.

5. **A talented** student wrote **a true** story about **her strange** vacation.

N. Directions: Select the correct form.

1. Paulette is (younger, **youngest**) in her class.

2. Of all our neighbors, Kim is (kinder, **kindest**).

3. She is the (**rowdier**, rowdiest) twin.

4. Marlo's office is the (larger, **largest**) one in the entire building complex.

5. This scarf is (**more gorgeous**, most gorgeous) than mine.

O. Directions: Circle any adverb.

Adverbs are in boldfaced print.

Suggestion: Cross out any prepositional phrase(s). Underline the subject once and the verb/verb phrase twice. First, look for any adverb telling *to what extent*. (They may be in a prepositional phrase, also.) Then, read each sentence looking for any adverbs that tell *how*. Next, look for adverbs that tell *when*. Last, look for adverbs telling *where*.

1. The boat was rocked **very gently** ~~by the giggling children~~.

2. Mr. and Mrs. Fleming go **there often**.

3. **Patiently**, the clerks searched **in** ~~among the clothes racks~~ ~~for the lost child~~.

4. Those candles did **not** burn **properly**.

5. **Suddenly**, the wind blew **quite hard**.

M. Directions: Circle any adjectives.

Suggestion: Read each sentence and first circle limiting adjectives. Then, reread the sentence and circle descriptive adjectives.

1. A beautiful flower garden is by that stream.
2. Her older sister and one brother live in an old country inn in Vermont.
3. My German friend attends a private school in a nearby town.
4. Some garlic potatoes and glazed ham were part of the delicious buffet.
5. A talented student wrote a true story about her strange vacation.

N. Directions: Select the correct form.

1. Paulette is (younger, youngest) in her class.
2. Of all our neighbors, Kim is (kinder, kindest).
3. She is the (rowdier, rowdiest) twin.
4. Marlo's office is the (larger, largest) one in the entire building complex.
5. This scarf is (more gorgeous, most gorgeous) than mine.

O. Directions: Circle any adverb.

Suggestion: Cross out any prepositional phrase(s). Underline the subject once and the verb/verb phrase twice. First, look for any adverbs telling *to what extent*. (They may be in a prepositional phrase, also.) Then, read each sentence looking for any adverbs that tell *how*. Next, look for adverbs that tell *when*. Last, look for adverbs telling *where*.

1. The boat was rocked very gently by the giggling children.
2. Mr. and Mrs. Fleming go there often.
3. Patiently, the clerks searched in among the clothes racks for the lost child.
4. Those candles did not burn properly.
5. Suddenly, the wind blew very hard.

FOR THE TEACHER:

CAPITALIZATION

1. This unit is designed to study a few capitalization rules at a time. Worksheets following rules will reinforce those just covered. A few rules from preceding lessons may be included. At the end of the unit, students will be given worksheets that cover **all** capitalization rules.

2. Be sure to "teach" each rule and provide your own examples.

3. Go back to former capitalization lessons and review the rules each day. Solicit examples from students.

4. Students may need a review of common and proper nouns.

5. Student writing is necessary to insure application of learned rules.

6. Daily Grams: Guided Review Aiding Mastery Skills offers daily reviews of capitalization. This helps to insure mastery learning. (See last page for list of various levels.)

7. If you are not using a Daily Grams: Guided Review Aiding Mastery Skills, it is suggested that a capitalization unit be taught at least twice during the school year.

NOTE: The following pages correlate with workbook pages:

teacher edition	workbook
521	265
527	268
533	271
539	274
545	277
550	280
551	281

PUNCTUATION

NOTE: The following pages correlate with workbook pages:

teacher edition	workbook
566	287
567	288
571	290
576	293
577	294
580	296
581	297
585	299
588	301
589	302
593	304
606	310
607	311

CAPITALIZATION

RULE 1: Capitalize the first letter of the first word in a sentence.

Example: **C**hicken was baked in an oven.

RULE 2: Capitalize the pronoun I.

Example: Should **I** call you later?

RULE 3: Capitalize the first letter of the first word in most lines of poetry.

Example: **S**he always thought a gallant prince would love her,
Forsaking life itself to please only her.

RULE 4: Capitalize the first word, the last word, and all important words in any title. Do not capitalize a, an, the, and, but, or, nor, or prepositions of four or less letters unless they are the first or last word of a title. (*Memorize this entire rule!*)

Examples: "**S**ilence of the **S**ongbirds"

"**M**issiles to **E**arth from a **C**rater on **M**ars"

Be sure to capitalize all verbs in titles.

Example: "**Y**ou ***A**re* **M**y **S**unshine"

Be sure to capitalize prepositions of five or more letters in titles.

Example: **T**he **M**an ***W**ithout* a **C**ountry

RULE 5: Capitalize people's names and their initial(s).

Examples: **S**haron

Mrs. **M**ary **T**. **B**arkley

Name________________________________ **CAPITALIZATION**

WORKBOOK PAGE 266

Date________________________________

Answers are in boldface.

Directions: Write the capital letter above any word that needs to be capitalized.

H T
Example: has tommy finished?

1. **A**re **S**herry and **I** invited?

2. **T**he musical, **O**klahoma, has been performed many times.

3. **D**o **I** need to sing "**A**mazing **G**race" with you?

4. **S**arah and **I** will read this magazine, **R**anger **R**ick.

5. **H**is mother read him **G**oldilocks and the **T**hree **B**ears.

6. **T**he movie, **L**assie, **C**ome **H**ome, is an old one.

7. (poem) "**E**agle"

Perched upon a ledge,
Gold eyes,
Searching wisely

8. **M**r. **J**ones reads the **B**ible daily.

9. **H**er favorite poem is "**I**f" by **R**udyard **K**ipling.

10. **W**e read the book entitled **New Mexico Is** for **Kids** by **B**obbi **S**alts.

11. **A** grandmother sang "**E**verything **I**s **B**eautiful" to the child.

12. **D**ad enjoyed reading **H**ope for the **T**roubled **H**eart by **B**illy **G**raham.

13. **M**iss **L**iston entitled her speech "**L**iving **W**ithin **Y**our **B**udget."

14. **L**es, **E**lijah, and **C**aleb wrote a song entitled "**W**e **A**re **F**unny."

15. **T**he poem "**W**hy **N**obody **P**ets the **L**ion at the **Z**oo" is by **J**ohn **C**iardi.

Name________________________________ **CAPITALIZATION**

Date________________________________

Directions: Write the capital letter above any word that needs to be capitalized.

H T
Example: has tommy finished?

1. are sherry and i invited?
2. the musical, oklahoma, has been performed many times.
3. do i need to sing "amazing grace" with you?
4. sarah and i will read this magazine, ranger rick.
5. his mother read him goldilocks and the three bears.
6. the movie, lassie, come home, is an old one.
7. (poem) "eagle"

   perched upon a ledge,
   gold eyes,
   searching wisely

8. mr. jones reads the bible daily.
9. her favorite poem is "if" by rudyard kipling.
10. we read the book entitled new mexico is for kids by bobbi salts.
11. a grandmother sang "everything is beautiful" to the child.
12. dad enjoyed reading hope for the troubled heart by billy graham.
13. miss liston entitled her speech "living within your budget."
14. les, elijah, and caleb wrote a song entitled "we are funny."
15. the poem "why nobody pets the lion at the zoo" is by john ciardi.

Name________________________________ **CAPITALIZATION**

WORKBOOK PAGE 267

Date________________________________

Answers are in boldface.

Directions: Write the capital letter above any word that needs to be capitalized.

Suggestion: Review the title rule before assigning this page.

L I T G M W

Example: last summer i read the greatest miracle in the world.

1. **T**he only two people who came were **B**reck and **I**.

2. **R**obert **F**rost wrote "**A**t **W**oodwards's **G**arden."

3. **D**id **C**arl **S**andburg write the poem entitled "**S**ee the **T**rees"?

4. "**T**ravel"

by **R**obert **L**ouis **S**tevenson

I should like to rise and go
Where the golden apples grow.

5. **B**illy **C**oleman is the main character of **W**here the **R**ed **F**ern **G**rows.

6. **R**oger and **I** like children's books with colored pictures.

7. "**A**n **O**ld **W**oman of the **R**oad" is a poem with six stanzas.

8. **H**ave you read "**T**he **L**ady or the **T**iger" by **S**tockton?

9. **D**id **M**iss **L**ogan, **R**egan, or **I** upset you?

10. **T**he class was assigned "**T**he **T**ruth **A**bout **T**hunderstorms."

11. **W**ho wrote "**W**hen **I**cicles **H**ang on the **W**all"?

12. **M**ay **I** read your **P**hoenix **G**azette newspaper?

13. **H**er cousin and she watched the movie, **F**iddler on the **R**oof.

14. **M**y mother read **S**urvival for **B**usy **W**omen by **E**milie **B**arnes.

15. **T**he title of **M**ichelle's essay was "**A** **G**lance **T**hrough **J**efferson's **E**yes."

Name________________________________ **CAPITALIZATION**

Date________________________________

Directions: Write the capital letter above any word that needs to be capitalized.

L I T G M W
Example: last summer i read <u>the greatest miracle in the world</u>.

1. the only two people who came were breck and i.

2. robert frost wrote "at woodwards's garden."

3. did carl sandburg write the poem entitled "see the trees"?

4. "travel"

by robert louis stevenson

i should like to rise and go
where the golden apples grow.

5. billy coleman is the main character of <u>where the red fern grows</u>.

6. roger and i like children's books with colored pictures.

7. "an old woman of the road" is a poem with six stanzas.

8. have you read "the lady or the tiger" by stockton?

9. did miss logan, regan, or i upset you?

10. the class was assigned "the truth about thunderstorms."

11. who wrote, "when icicles hang on the wall"?

12. may i read your <u>phoenix gazette</u> newspaper?

13. her cousin and she watched the movie, <u>fiddler on the roof</u>.

14. my mother read <u>survival for busy women</u> by emilie barnes.

15. the title of michelle's essay was "a glance through jefferson's eyes."

PAGE 527 = WORKBOOK PAGE 268

RULE 6: Capitalize days, months, holidays, and special days.

Examples: **T**uesday — **T**hanksgiving

July — **A**rbor **D**ay

Hanukkah — **S**t. **P**atrick's **D**ay

Christmas **E**ve — **S**unday

RULE 7: Capitalize Mother, Dad, and other titles if you can insert the person's name.

Examples: Has **D**ad gone to the store?

(If Mike is the father's name: Has Mike gone to the store?) You can replace **D**ad with a name; therefore, you capitalize ***D**ad*.

My mom is nice.
(If Amy is the mother's name: My Amy is nice.)
This doesn't make sense; therefore, you do not capitalize *mom*.

Capitalize the title if it appears with a name.

Examples: **U**ncle **D**uane

Aunt **F**ran

Grandma **W**ilson

Lieutenant **J**ackson

RULE 8: Capitalize names of organizations.

Examples: **F**uture **H**omemakers of **A**merica

American **R**ed **C**ross

Organization of **A**merican **S**tates

Name_______________________________ **CAPITALIZATION**

WORKBOOK PAGE 269

Date_______________________________

Answers are in boldface.

Directions: Write the capital letter above any word that needs to be capitalized.

I M

Example: is monday the last day of the trip?

1. **P**lease ask **D**ad to help us.
2. **D**oes **G**randpa **G**rovers belong to the **L**ion's **C**lub?
3. **I**s **U**ncle **A**lvin a leader of the **B**oy **S**couts of **A**merica?
4. **N**ext **F**riday we will celebrate **C**olumbus **D**ay.
5. **M**y mother has joined the **T**ulsa **W**omen's **C**lub.
6. **W**as **A**unt **J**ean born on **S**t. **V**alentine's **D**ay?
7. **Y**esterday, **J**udge **L**ipman announced the verdict.
8. **E**very **W**ednesday, **G**randma and **P**rofessor **S**tone have lunch.
9. **I**s **I**ndependence **D**ay celebrated on **J**uly 4th?
10. **I**n **M**arch, **G**eneral **F**rampton will speak to their class.
11. **H**er mother belongs to **C**oncerned **W**omen of **A**merica*.
12. **H**as **M**ayor **L**exico talked with members of the **C**handler **C**hamber of **C**ommerce*?
13. **W**e learned that **U**ncle **D**on and **A**unt **J**oy will come for a visit at **C**hristmas.
14. **G**arth, **N**ancy, and **C**ousin **L**inda discussed pollution with **S**enator **P**arks.
15. **D**uring the **S**t. **P**atrick's **D**ay celebration, my grandfather wore green.

*name of an organization

Name________________________________ **CAPITALIZATION**

Date________________________________

Directions: Write the capital letter above any word that needs to be capitalized.

I M
Example: is monday the last day of the trip?

1. please ask dad to help us.
2. does grandpa grovers belong to the lion's club?
3. is uncle alvin a leader of the boy scouts of america?
4. next friday we will celebrate columbus day.
5. my mother has joined the tulsa women's club.
6. was aunt jean born on st. valentine's day?
7. yesterday, judge lipman announced the verdict.
8. every wednesday, grandma and professor stone have lunch.
9. is independence day celebrated on july 4th?
10. in march, general frampton will speak to their class.
11. her mother belongs to concerned women of america*.
12. has mayor lexico talked with members of the chandler chamber of commerce*?
13. we learned that uncle don and aunt joy will come for a visit at christmas.
14. garth, nancy, and cousin linda discussed pollution with senator parks.
15. during the st. patrick's day celebration, my grandfather wore green.

*name of an organization

Name________________________________ **CAPITALIZATION**

WORKBOOK PAGE 270

Date________________________________

Answers are in boldface.

Directions: Write the capital letter above any word that needs to be capitalized.

W J

Example: will your grandfather go with us in june?

1. **A**t the **C**hristmas **E**ve service, **P**astor **G**ilman gave a sermon.
2. **N**o one wanted **C**aptain **A**dams or **D**ad to leave.
3. **H**ave you seen my mother or **P**rincipal **G**rady here?
4. **H**is father joined an organization called **P**arents **W**ithout **P**artners.
5. **T**he carnival was held the last **S**aturday of **A**ugust.
6. **A**aron and **I** are planning a party for **A**pril **F**ool's **D**ay.
7. **W**as **P**resident **G**eorge **W**ashington sworn into office in **J**anuary?
8. **A**unt **L**isa and her sister will be here on the weekend after **L**abor **D**ay.
9. **I**s **V**eteran's **D**ay always celebrated on **N**ovember 11th?
10. **R**epresentative **I**rving will be on a television show on **T**hursday.
11. **T**he **N**ational **R**ifle **A**ssociation made a comment about hand guns.
12. **W**e gave **M**om a rose for her **M**other's **D**ay present.
13. **H**as your grandmother ever visited during the **T**hanksgiving holiday?
14. **H**ow long has **D**octor **J**oan **C**arney belonged to the **A**merican **M**edical **A**ssociation?
15. **T**ell your cousin to meet us **S**unday at our church to celebrate **P**alm **S**unday.

Name______________________________

CAPITALIZATION

Date______________________________

Directions: Write the capital letter above any word that needs to be capitalized.

```
           W                                  J
Example:   will your grandfather go with us in june?
```

1. at the christmas eve service, pastor gilman gave a sermon.
2. no one wanted captain adams or dad to leave.
3. have you seen my mother or principal grady here?
4. his father joined an organization called parents without partners.
5. the carnival was held the last saturday of august.
6. aaron and i are planning a party for april fool's day.
7. was president george washington sworn into office in january?
8. aunt lisa and her sister will be here on the weekend after labor day.
9. is veteran's day always celebrated on november 11th?
10. representative irving will be on a television show on thursday.
11. the national rifle association made a comment about hand guns.
12. we gave mom a rose for her mother's day present.
13. has your grandmother ever visited during the thanksgiving holiday?
14. how long has doctor joan carney belonged to the american medical association?
15. tell your cousin to meet us sunday at our church to celebrate palm sunday.

PAGE 533 = WORKBOOK PAGE 271

RULE 9: Capitalize the names of institutions.

Morton School
York College
Samaritan Hospital
Maricopa County Jail

RULE 10: Capitalize business names.

Cross Company
Ameriola Airlines
Beamer Grocery
Sock Store, Inc.
Murray Hotel
Posada Restaurant

RULE 11: Capitalize the names of structures.

Washington Tunnel
London Bridge
Leaning Tower of Pisa
Cumberland Expressway

RULE 12: Capitalize the names of specific geographic places.

Indian Ocean
Baltic Sea
Missouri River
Skunk Creek
Pocono Mountains
Mt. Rushmore
Fox Hill
Roanoke Island
Gulf of Mexico
North America
England
Maryland
Fulton County
Memphis
Mammoth Cave
Dristol Park
Cape Cod
Midwest

Name________________________________ **CAPITALIZATION**

WORKBOOK PAGE 272

Date_________________________________

Answers are in boldface.

Directions: Write the capital letter above any word that needs to be capitalized.

W D P
Example: we like to go to dorado park.

1. **I**s the **G**eorge **W**ashington **B**ridge in **N**ew **Y**ork?
2. **H**e is in **M**emorial **H**ospital on **M**arket **S**treet.
3. **T**he **G**rand **C**anyon is in **A**rizona.
4. **T**he leader of **A**rki **I**ndustries is **M**r. **J**ames **H**orton.
5. **A** group went to **W**ashington and fished in the **C**olumbia **R**iver.
6. **I**s **V**ictoria **F**alls on the continent of **A**frica?
7. **T**hey flew over the **A**rctic **C**ircle on their way to **G**ermany.
8. **H**as **L**ionel ever attended **F**ranklin **S**chool on **M**ilton **A**venue?
9. **T**he class toured **D**esert **H**orizon **P**olice **S**tation in **P**hoenix.
10. **A** post card from **F**lorence **P**rison arrived on **T**uesday.
11. **W**hen **M**iss **H**arlord was in **A**sia, she visited the **G**reat **W**all of **C**hina.
12. **I**s **M**ustang **L**ibrary on **B**ristol **R**oad or **S**hea **B**oulevard?
13. **T**he flight for **A**merica **N**orth **A**irlines was early.
14. **T**he family crossed the **R**io **G**rande **R**iver and drove into **M**exico.
15. **A** girl from the **S**outh plans on going to **H**oover **D**am in **N**evada.

Name________________________________

Date________________________________

CAPITALIZATION

Directions: Write the capital letter above any word that needs to be capitalized.

W D P
Example: we like to go to dorado park.

1. is the george washington bridge in new york?
2. he is in memorial hospital on market street.
3. the grand canyon is in arizona.
4. the leader of arki industries is mr. james horton.
5. a group went to washington and fished in the columbia river.
6. is victoria falls on the continent of africa?
7. they flew over the arctic circle on their way to germany.
8. has lionel ever attended franklin school on milton avenue?
9. the class toured desert horizon police station in phoenix.
10. a post card from florence prison arrived on tuesday.
11. when miss harlord was in asia, she visited the great wall of china.
12. is mustang library on bristol road or shea boulevard?
13. the flight for america north airlines was early.
14. the family crossed the rio grande river and drove into mexico.
15. a girl from the south plans on going to hoover dam in nevada.

Name________________________________ **CAPITALIZATION**

WORKBOOK PAGE 273

Date________________________________

Answers are in boldface.

Directions: Write the capital letter above any word that needs to be capitalized.

T E C F E

Example: the english channel separates france and england.

1. **H**ave you been to **M**oosehead **L**ake in **M**aine?
2. **T**he **B**utte **M**ountains and **B**lack **R**ock **D**esert are in **N**evada.
3. **P**ortia **B**landerson calls her company **C**ottage **C**leaning, **I**nc.
4. **J**oan attended a junior high school before entering **S**unburst **M**iddle **S**chool.
5. **T**he **W**orld **T**rade **C**enter in **N**ew **Y**ork **C**ity is very famous.
6. **T**he town of **B**arnsdall is in **O**sage **C**ounty, **O**klahoma.
7. **T**he new location of **C**oe **R**estaurant is on **W**alker **A**venue.
8. **I**s **G**reat **S**moky **M**ountains **N**ational **P**ark in **N**orth **C**arolina?
9. **A** place called **B**owers **B**each is on the **D**elaware **B**ay in **D**elaware.
10. **L**ast year their family went to **W**rigley **F**ield in **C**hicago for a baseball game.
11. **H**as anyone visited the **K**ennedy **C**enter in **W**ashington, **D**. **C**.?
12. **A**rt traveled to the town of **F**ish **H**aven on **B**ear **L**ake, **I**daho.
13. **D**id you know that **H**omosassa **I**sland is in the **G**ulf of **M**exico?
14. **T**he **T**appan **Z**ee **B**ridge in **N**ew **Y**ork crosses the **H**udson **R**iver.
15. **D**o students from **G**ettysburg **C**ollege sometimes lunch at **W**olfe's **D**iner?

Name________________________________ **CAPITALIZATION**

Date________________________________

Directions: Write the capital letter above any word that needs to be capitalized.

Example:
T E C F E
the english channel separates france and england.

1. have you been to moosehead lake in maine?
2. the butte mountains and black rock desert are in nevada.
3. portia blanderson calls her company cottage cleaning, inc.
4. joan attended a junior high school before entering sunburst middle school.
5. the world trade center in new york city is very famous.
6. the town of barnsdall is in osage county, oklahoma.
7. the new location of coe restaurant is on walker avenue.
8. is great smoky mountains national park in north carolina?
9. a place called bowers beach is on the delaware bay in delaware.
10. last year their family went to wrigley field in chicago for a baseball game.
11. has anyone visited the kennedy center in washington, d. c.?
12. art traveled to the town of fish haven on bear lake, idaho.
13. did you know that homosassa island is in the gulf of mexico?
14. the tappan zee bridge in new york crosses the hudson river.
15. do students from gettysburg college sometimes lunch at wolfe's diner?

PAGE 539 = WORKBOOK PAGE 274

RULE 13: Capitalize the names of historical events and historical documents (papers).

American Revolution | Declaration of Independence
Battle of Shiloh | U.S. Constitution

RULE 14: Capitalize the names of languages.

English | Spanish
Chinese | French

RULE 15: Capitalize the Roman numerals and the letters of the first major topics in an outline.

I.
  A.
  B.

II.
  A.
  B.
  C.

Capitalize only the first word in an outline unless the words are a proper noun.

I. Oceans and seas
  A. Major oceans
  B. Major seas

II. **Land forms**
  A. Western hemisphere continents
    1. North America (proper noun)
    2. South America (proper noun)
  B. Eastern hemisphere continents

RULE 16: Capitalize the first word of a direct quotation.

Examples: Harley asked, "How old is your brother?"

"He is five," said Jodi.

Note: Do not capitalize the word following the quotation unless it is a proper noun.

"He looks older," said Harley.

Name_______________________________ **CAPITALIZATION**

WORKBOOK PAGE 275

Date_______________________________

Answers are in boldface.

Directions: Write the capital letter above any word that needs to be capitalized.

M C E

Example: The magna carta is an important document in england.

1. **S**ome **M**assachusetts colonists signed a document called the **M**ayflower **C**ompact.

2. "**H**ave you seen my magazine?" asked **J**ackie.

3. **I**s **E**nglish spoken in that country?

4. "**D**on't leave me!" shrieked the small child.

5. I. **D**ogs

   A. **T**ypes

   1. **S**hort hair

   2. **L**ong hair

   B. **C**are

   II. **C**ats

6. **T**he **A**merican **R**evolution gave **A**mericans freedom.

7. **I**n **C**anada, both **F**rench and **E**nglish are spoken.

8. **J**udy said, "**Y**our button is open."

9. **G**eneral **A**ndrew **J**ackson led the **B**attle of **N**ew **O**rleans.

10. **B**o asked, "**A**re you ready to leave?"

11. "**W**e will leave in fifteen minutes," **V**incent replied.

12. **B**rook's dad speaks **G**erman and **R**ussian.

Name________________________________ **CAPITALIZATION**

Date________________________________

Directions: Write the capital letter above any word that needs to be capitalized.

M C E
Example: The magna carta is an important document in england.

1. some massachusetts colonists signed a document called the mayflower compact.

2. "have you seen my magazine?" asked jackie.

3. is english spoken in that country?

4. "don't leave me!" shrieked the small child.

5. i. dogs

   a. types

      1. short hair

      2. long hair

   b. care

   ii. cats

6. the american revolution gave americans freedom.

7. in canada, both french and english are spoken.

8. judy said, "your button is open."

9. general andrew jackson led the battle of new orleans.

10. bo asked, "are you ready to leave?"

11. "we will leave in fifteen minutes," vincent replied.

12. brook's dad speaks german and russian.

Name________________________________ **CAPITALIZATION**

WORKBOOK PAGE 276

Date________________________________

Answers are in boldface.

Directions: Write the capital letter above any word that needs to be capitalized.

H

Example: "how did you do that?" asked the smiling lady.

1. I. **A**nimals

    A. **T**hose with one cell

    1. **A**moeba

    2. **P**aramecium

    B. **T**hose with more than one cell

    II. **P**lants

2. **T**he **B**attle of **B**ull **R**un was fought during the **C**ivil **W**ar.

3. "**W**here have you been?" asked **M**iss **P**osey.

4. **T**hey learned **I**talian at their high school.

5. **D**id **T**homas **J**efferson write the **D**eclaration of **I**ndependence?

6. "**Y**ou're right!" yelled **M**rs. **F**rie.

7. **O**ur friend named **M**ario speaks the **S**panish language.

8. **T**he <u>**U**. **S**. **C**onstitution</u> is our nation's written government.

9. **A** weatherman said, "**T**omorrow's weather should be sunny."

10. **D**id **G**eneral **C**ornwallis surrender to **G**eneral **W**ashington at the **B**attle of **Y**orktown?

11. **I**s the **P**ortuguese language spoken in the country of **B**razil?

12. **T**he ballot was written both in **E**nglish and in **S**panish.

Name________________________________ **CAPITALIZATION**

Date________________________________

Directions: Write the capital letter above any word that needs to be capitalized.

H
Example: "how did you do that?" asked the smiling lady.

1. i. animals

   a. those with one cell

      1. amoeba

      2. paramecium

   b. those with more than one cell

   ii. plants

2. the battle of bull run was fought during the civil war.

3. "where have you been?" asked miss posey.

4. they learned italian at their high school.

5. did thomas jefferson write the declaration of independence?

6. "you're right!" yelled mrs. frie.

7. our friend named mario speaks the spanish language.

8. the u. s. constitution is our nation's written government.

9. a weatherman said, "tomorrow's weather should be sunny."

10. did general cornwallis surrender to general washington at the battle of yorktown?

11. is the portuguese language spoken in the country of brazil?

12. the ballot was written both in english and in spanish.

PAGE 545 = WORKBOOK PAGE 277
PAGE 550 = WORKBOOK PAGE 280
PAGE 551 = WORKBOOK PAGE 281

RULE 17: Capitalize brand names but not the products.

Ford van | **S**ony computer disc

Lucerne ice cream | **Bar S** hot dogs

RULE 18: Capitalize religions, religious documents, names of churches, and names for a supreme being.

Christian (religion) | **T**en **C**ommandments (document)

Moslem (religion) | <u>**B**ible</u>

Heavenly **F**ather | **P**almcroft **B**aptist **C**hurch

God | **T**almud (writings of the Jewish religion)

Notes:

A. Capitalize a religious denomination such as **M**ethodist or **B**aptist. If the name of a specific church is not given, capitalize only the denomination.
Example: a **B**aptist church (The name of a church is not given.)

B. Do not capitalize the terms, gods and goddesses.

RULE 19: Capitalize a proper adjective but not the noun it modifies.

a **C**alifornia beach | a **M**emorial **D**ay parade

a **P**ayson music festival | an **A**frican nation

RULE 20: Capitalize the first word of a greeting and closing of a letter.

My dearest friend, | **S**incerely yours,

RULE 21: Capitalize directions when they refer to a region of a country or the world.

Examples: Georgia is in the **S**outh. (region of the U.S.)

He lives in China which is also called the **E**ast. (region of the world)

Name________________________________ **CAPITALIZATION**

WORKBOOK PAGE 278

Date________________________________

Answers are in boldface.

Directions: Write the capital letter above any word that needs to be capitalized.

T N E
Example: they live in the new england states.

1. **H**ave you visited the **W**est?

2. **C**lay's grandmother lives near a **R**hode **I**sland beach.

3. **D**ear **S**usan,

 I just wanted to let you know that my family will be visiting the **E**ast soon.

 Your friend,
 Paula

4. **D**id **G**od tell **M**oses to lead the **J**ewish people out of **E**gypt?

5. **H**as he always liked **W**rigley's spearmint gum and **R**eese's peanut butter cups?

6. **P**astor **J**ones led the service at **S**ilverdale **M**ethodist **C**hurch.

7. **S**ammy lives in **A**rizona, one of the states of the **S**outhwest.

8. **T**he women attended a **C**hristian conference at a **P**resbyterian church.

9. **W**ere the **D**ead **S**ea **S**crolls found in the **M**iddle **E**ast*?

10. **K**enneth likes **O**scar **M**eyer hot dogs with **F**rench's mustard and onion.

11. **T**he **D**obson family goes to the mountains each **L**abor **D**ay weekend.

12. **M**any people in the country of **I**ndia practice the **H**indu religion.

13. **I**s **C**hicago the largest city in the **M**idwest?

14. **H**is parents bought a **M**agnavox television from an appliance store in the **S**outh.

*name of a region of the world

Name________________________________ **CAPITALIZATION**

Date________________________________

Directions: Write the capital letter above any word that needs to be capitalized.

T N E
Example: they live in the new england states.

1. have you visited the west?

2. clay's grandmother lives near a rhode island beach.

3. dear susan,

   i just wanted to let you know that my family will be visiting the east soon.

   your friend,
   paula

4. did god tell moses to lead the jewish people out of egypt?

5. has he always liked wrigley's spearmint gum and reese's peanut butter cups?

6. pastor jones led the service at silverdale methodist church.

7. sammy lives in arizona, one of the states of the southwest.

8. the women attended a christian conference at a presbyterian church.

9. were the dead sea scrolls found in the middle east*?

10. kenneth likes oscar meyer hot dogs with french's mustard and onion.

11. the dobson family goes to the mountains each labor day weekend.

12. many people in the country of india practice the hindu religion.

13. is chicago the largest city in the midwest?

14. his parents bought a magnavox television from an appliance store in the south.

*name of a region of the world

Name________________________________ **CAPITALIZATION**

WORKBOOK PAGE 279

Date________________________________

Answers are in boldface.

Directions: Write the capital letter above any word that needs to be capitalized.

T M D
Example: that school closes before memorial day weekend.

1. **T**o my aunt,

 Thank you for taking me to a **N**ew **J**ersey beach in **J**uly.

 Your nephew,
 Bobby

2. **S**he traveled to **T**hailand, a country in **A**sia.

3. **J**esus delivered a famous sermon called "**S**ermon on the **M**ount."

4. **D**inner consisted of **K**raft macaroni and cheese with **L**ibby's peas.

5. **T**he family read from the book of **G**enesis in the **B**ible.

6. **T**he name of the **W**yoming rodeo was "**O**ld **W**est **C**orral **T**ime."

7. **D**id **T**ommy read about **G**reek goddesses in that book?

8. **H**is mother visited a **S**hinto* temple in **J**apan.

9. **M**itch always buys **L**evi jeans and hiking boots.

10. **D**ear **P**am,

 Will you send me pictures of **B**oise and other places you have visited in the **N**orthwest?

 Your cousin,
 Ross

11. **T**hat **U**tah ski resort is very busy during **C**hristmas vacation.

12. **H**ave you ever eaten **L**ipton's onion soup or **C**ampbell's tomato soup?

*religion

Name________________________________ **CAPITALIZATION**

Date________________________________

Directions: Write the capital letter above any word that needs to be capitalized.

T M D
Example: that school closes before memorial day weekend.

1. to my aunt,

   thank you for taking me to a new jersey beach in july.

   your nephew,
   bobby

2. she traveled to thailand, a country in asia.

3. jesus delivered a famous sermon called "sermon on the mount."

4. dinner consisted of kraft macaroni and cheese with libby's peas.

5. the family read from the book of genesis in the bible.

6. the name of the wyoming rodeo was "old west corral time."

7. did tommy read about greek goddesses in that book?

8. his mother visited a shinto* temple in japan.

9. mitch always buys levi jeans and hiking boots.

10. dear pam,

    will you send me pictures of boise and other places you have visited in the northwest?

    your cousin,
    ross

11. that utah ski resort is very busy during christmas vacation.

12. have you ever eaten lipton's onion soup or campbell's tomato soup?

*religion

DO NOT CAPITALIZE

RULE 1: Do not capitalize the seasons of the year.

spring summer autumn/fall winter

RULE 2: Do not capitalize school subjects unless they have a number or name a language.

We like science, spelling, social studies, geography, and history.

Patrick studies **A**lgebra II, **S**panish, and **B**iology 204 in high school.

If a proper adjective appears with the subject, capitalize only the proper adjective.

American history **G**reek literature

RULE 3: Do not capitalize north, south, east, west, northeast, northwest, southeast, or southwest when they are directions.

Go north on Ludlow Street.

Do not capitalize regions of a state, county, or city.

Are you moving to southern Texas?
Sissy lives in northeastern Anaheim.

RULE 4: Do not capitalize career choices.

Their dad is a teacher.
Hannah wants to be a computer programmer.

RULE 5: Do not capitalize foods.

fudge	beef	apples	lemonade
milk	tacos	lettuce	cookies

If a proper adjective appears with the food, capitalize the proper adjective but not the food.

Swiss cheese **G**erman pancakes

RULE 6: Do not capitalize diseases.

measles	mumps	polio	chicken pox
cancer	flu	hepatitis	arthritis

If a proper adjective occurs with a disease, capitalize the proper adjective but not the name of the disease.

German measles   Parkinson's disease (named after the doctor who first described it.)

RULE 7: Do not capitalize animals.

dog	parrot	sheep	quail
shepherd	leopard	poodle	cat

If a proper adjective appears with an animal, capitalize the proper adjective but not the animal.

Siamese cat   German shepherd

RULE 8: Do not capitalize plants.

grass   tree   flowers   herb

If a proper adjective appears with a plant, capitalize the proper adjective but not the plant.

Bermuda grass   English ivy

RULE 9: Do not capitalize musical instruments.

piano   harp   trumpet   drums

If a proper adjective appears with a musical instrument, capitalize the proper adjective but not the musical instrument.

French horn   Spanish guitar

RULE 10: Do not capitalize games or dances.

cards   chess   two-square   polka

If a proper adjective appears with a game or dance, capitalize the proper adjective but not the game or dance.

Chinese checkers   Mexican hat dance

Capitalize games that are commercial names of products. (Usually these have a trademark.)

Monopoly   Scrabble   Wheel of Fortune

Name________________________________ **CAPITALIZATION**

WORKBOOK PAGE 282

Date________________________________

Answers are in boldface.

Directions: Write the capital letter above any word that needs to be capitalized.

H S

Example: her father plays the saxophone during sunday church service.

1. **T**hose two girls play chess every **S**aturday afternoon during the summer.
2. **D**o you like math better than **E**nglish or science?
3. **M**iss **H**obbs plays a flute for the symphony.
4. **L**ast spring, **T**yler had chicken pox during his **E**aster vacation.
5. **T**hey often eat **C**anadian bacon and eggs for breakfast.
6. **D**uring autumn, leaves fell from the oak trees on **C**entral **A**venue.
7. **S**everal **A**frican daisies were planted in the east flower bed.
8. **T**he group worked on an **A**merican history project several weeks last winter.
9. **S**ome adults play bridge every **T**uesday in the fall.
10. **C**hocolate doughnuts and **D**anish rolls were served at 6 o'clock.
11. **H**as **M**arty planted a **J**apanese privet and tulips?
12. **T**he library is north of the fire department on **T**renton **R**oad.
13. **H**er favorite subjects are reading, art, and **M**ath 101.
14. **T**he couple dancing the tango won a contest in **O**ctober.
15. **L**aurence often gets tonsillitis during the spring.

Name________________________________ **CAPITALIZATION**

Date_________________________________

Directions: Write the capital letter above any word that needs to be capitalized.

Example: her father plays the saxophone during sunday church service. (H above "her", S above "sunday")

1. those two girls play chess every saturday afternoon during the summer.
2. do you like math better than english or science?
3. miss hobbs plays a flute for the symphony.
4. last spring, tyler had chicken pox during his easter vacation.
5. they often eat canadian bacon and eggs for breakfast.
6. during autumn, leaves fell from the oak trees on central avenue.
7. several african daisies were planted in the east flower bed.
8. the group worked on an american history project several weeks last winter.
9. some adults play bridge every tuesday in the fall.
10. chocolate doughnuts and danish rolls were served at 6 o'clock.
11. has marty planted a japanese privet and tulips?
12. the library is north of the fire department on trenton road.
13. her favorite subjects are reading, art, and math 101.
14. the couple dancing the tango won a contest in october.
15. laurence often gets tonsillitis during the spring.

Name________________________________ **CAPITALIZATION**

WORKBOOK 283

Date________________________________

Answers are in boldface.

Directions: Write the capital letter above any word that needs to be capitalized.

```
                S                         I           S P        D
Example:  students danced an irish jig on st. patrick's day.
```

1. **I**n geography we were asked to locate the **C**ape of **G**ood **H**ope.
2. **T**he local golf club held a barbecue on the west lawn for the **J**uly 4th celebration.
3. **H**e learned to play the violin before learning the **S**panish guitar.
4. **H**er uncle had scarlet fever when he was a child.
5. **O**ur family played gin rummy during our summer vacation to **L**aguna **B**each.
6. **H**as **D**r. **B**rock told you about bronchitis?
7. **J**eanette likes **E**nglish, earth science, and **R**oman history.
8. **T**hose children enjoy playing badminton and **C**hinese jump rope.
9. **A** new test can determine if someone has **A**lzheimer's* disease.
10. **S**he pours **I**talian dressing on her **F**rench fries.
11. **D**aily, **F**ran drives east on **L**incoln **D**rive and then takes the freeway south to work.
12. **I**n the morning, the children eat **F**rench toast, **E**nglish muffins, or hot cereal.
13. **H**er cousin who lives in northern **C**alifornia often travels to **L**ake **T**ahoe.
14. **I**n social studies, **I** made a map showing how to get to **P**rentice **P**ark using **M**adison **S**treet.
15. **D**uring spring break, fifty-two students will tour **S**an **F**rancisco, **C**alifornia.

*named for the doctor who first described the disease

Name________________________________ **CAPITALIZATION**

Date________________________________

Directions: Write the capital letter above any word that needs to be capitalized.

S I S P D
Example: students danced an irish jig on st. patrick's day.

1. in geography we were asked to locate the cape of good hope.
2. the local golf club held a barbecue on the west lawn for the july 4th celebration.
3. he learned to play the violin before learning the spanish guitar.
4. her uncle had scarlet fever when he was a child.
5. our family played gin rummy during our summer vacation to laguna beach.
6. has dr. brock told you about bronchitis?
7. jeanette likes english, earth science, and roman history.
8. those children enjoy playing badminton and chinese jump rope.
9. a new test can determine if someone has alzheimer's* disease.
10. she pours italian dressing on her french fries.
11. daily, fran drives east on lincoln drive and then takes the freeway south to work.
12. in the morning, the children eat french toast, english muffins, or hot cereal.
13. her cousin who lives in northern california often travels to lake tahoe.
14. in social studies, i made a map showing how to get to prentice park using madison street.
15. during spring break, fifty-two students will tour san francisco, california.

*named for the doctor who first described the disease.

Name________________________________

CAPITALIZATION REVIEW

WORKBOOK PAGE 284

Date________________________________

Answers are in boldface.

Directions: Write the capital letter above any word that needs to be capitalized.

T D I R F

Example: the racers attended the daytona 500 international race in florida.

1. **J**onas **T**. **P**helps and **G**overnor **A**ndrews met at a local restaurant.

2. **T**he students at a junior high school attended the movie, <u>**T**he **S**ecret **G**arden</u>.

3. **D**id **S**amuel **A**dams lead a group called the **S**ons of **L**iberty?

4. **W**ere the **T**en **C**ommandments given to **M**oses on **M**t. **S**inai?

5. **T**heir **U**ncle **F**ranco who is from **I**taly owns **F**ranco's **S**hoe **R**epair **S**hop.

6. **I**s **D**ulles **I**nternational **A**irport in **W**ashington, **D**. **C**.?

7. **A** **M**others' **D**ay celebration was held at **M**eadowview **E**piscopal **C**hurch.

8. **H**er friend and she ate **G**erman food and danced the polka at a festival in **O**ctober.

9. **T**he **F**irst **C**ontinental **C**ongress met in **P**hiladelphia to ask **K**ing **G**eorge III to get rid of a stamp tax.

10. I. **S**chools below college level

    A. **P**reschools

    B. **E**lementary schools

    C. **S**econdary schools

    II. **C**olleges and universities

    A. **J**unior colleges

    B. **F**our year colleges and universities

Name________________________________ **CAPITALIZATION REVIEW**

Date________________________________

Directions: Write the capital letter above any word that needs to be capitalized.

T D I R F
Example: the racers attended the daytona 500 international race in florida.

1. jonas t. phelps and governor andrews met at a local restaurant.

2. the students at a junior high school attended the movie, <u>the secret garden</u>.

3. did samuel adams lead a group called the sons of liberty?

4. were the ten commandments given to moses on mt. sinai?

5. their uncle franco who is from italy owns franco's shoe repair shop.

6. is dulles international airport in washington, d. c.?

7. a mothers' day celebration was held at meadowview episcopal church.

8. her friend and she ate german food and danced the polka at a festival in october.

9. the first continental congress met in philadelphia to ask king george III to get rid of a stamp tax.

10. i. schools below college level
    - a. preschools
    - b. elementary schools
    - c. secondary schools

    ii. colleges and universities
    - a. junior colleges
    - b. four year colleges and universities

Name________________________________ **CAPITALIZATION REVIEW**
WORKBOOK PAGE 285
Date________________________________
Answers are in boldface.

Directions: Write the capital letter above any word that needs to be capitalized.

T B B H A R
Example: the battle of bunker hill was fought during the american revolution.

1.
23 **H**orton **R**oad
Ruidoso, **N**ew **M**exico 88345
September 30, 20--

Dear **F**lo,

We had a great time on our vacation to **N**ebraska.

Your friend,
Damon

2. **A**unt **J**oy, will you go with me to **D**arby **G**eneral **S**tore?

3. **D**id the **A**xton **B**oys **C**hoir perform at a fair in **J**une?

4. **L**ast spring, **C**aptain **R**eynolds visited the **N**ew **Y**ork **M**useum of **A**rt.

5. **A**t **T**hanksgiving, **G**randma **K**line serves sweet potatoes with a **B**utterball* turkey.

6. **H**ave **M**r. and **M**rs. **S**hatler taken an **A**merican **A**irlines flight to **A**laska?

7. **S**he and **I** attended a <u>**B**ible</u> study at **S**cottsdale **B**ible **C**hurch.

8. **S**hannon attended an elementary school before going to **R**iser **H**igh **S**chool.

9. **T**he **A**rizona **S**tate **F**air occurs each fall in southern **P**hoenix.

10. **W**as the **G**ettysburg **A**ddress written by **P**resident **A**braham **L**incoln?

11. **T**he people of the **M**oslem faith read a book called the <u>**K**oran</u>.

12. **I**n the summer, their uncle works at a **C**olorado cattle ranch near **D**enver.

*brand name

Name________________________________ **CAPITALIZATION REVIEW**

Date________________________________

Directions: Write the capital letter above any word that needs to be capitalized.

T B B H A R
Example: the battle of bunker hill was fought during the american revolution.

1.

23 horton road
ruidoso, new mexico 88345
september 30, 20--

dear flo,

we had a great time on our vacation to nebraska.

your friend,
damon

2. aunt joy, will you go with me to darby general store?

3. did the axton boys choir perform at a fair in june?

4. last spring, captain reynolds visited the new york museum of art.

5. at thanksgiving, grandma kline serves sweet potatoes with a butterball* turkey.

6. have mr. and mrs. shatler taken an american airlines flight to alaska?

7. she and i attended a <u>bible</u> study at scottsdale bible church.

8. shannon attended an elementary school before going to riser high school.

9. the arizona state fair occurs each fall in southern phoenix.

10. was the gettysburg address written by president abraham lincoln?

11. the people of the moslem faith read a book called the <u>koran</u>.

12. in the summer, their uncle works at a colorado cattle ranch near denver.

*brand name

Name________________________________ **CAPITALIZATION REVIEW**

WORKBOOK PAGE 286

Date________________________________

Answers are in boldface.

Directions: Write the capital letter above any word that needs to be capitalized.

A W H
Example: are you allowed to tour the east wing of the white house*?

1. **Th**e gentleman was admitted to **B**ayview **H**ospital for bronchitis.

2. **Th**e state of **O**regon is in the **P**acific **N**orthwest, a region of the **U**nited **S**tates.

3. **H**as **D**ad collected donations for the **A**merican **C**ancer **S**ociety?

4. **Th**e poem entitled "**W**inter **N**ight" begins with the line, "**P**ile high the hickory..."

5. **A**lthough **H**enry lives in **W**est **V**irginia, he was born in the **S**outhwest.

6. **A**t **M**ountain **J**unior **H**igh **S**chool, **C**lark took science, **S**panish, **E**nglish, and **M**ath II.

7. **D**oes **A**ndrea play the trombone for the **M**iller **C**ounty **A**dult **B**and?

8. **Th**e **E**iffel **T**ower in **P**aris, **F**rance, is lighted at night.

9. **Th**e **W**ally **W**orkout **C**lub has a summer special in **A**ugust.

10. **I**s the **C**rown **S**terling **H**otel in **I**rving, **T**exas, near the airport?

11. **I**n **A**merican literature class, **B**ert and **S**andra read <u>**T**he **R**ed **B**adge of **C**ourage</u>.

12. **I**f you go to **P**ike's **P**eak, you will be near **C**olorado **S**prings.

13. **I**s **M**onticello, the name of **Th**omas **J**efferson's home, on the **P**otomac **R**iver?

14.
- I. **B**each activities
  - **A.** **V**olleyball
  - **B.** **S**urfing
- II. **C**amping activities
  - **A.** **H**iking
  - **B.** **M**ountain bike riding

*home of the United States President

Name________________________________ **CAPITALIZATION REVIEW**

Date________________________________

Directions: Write the capital letter above any word that needs to be capitalized.

A W H
Example: are you allowed to tour the east wing of the white house*?

1. the gentleman was admitted to bayview hospital for bronchitis.
2. the state of oregon is in the pacific northwest, a region of the united states.
3. has dad collected donations for the american cancer society?
4. the poem entitled "winter night" begins with the line, "pile high the hickory..."
5. although henry lives in west virginia, he was born in the southwest.
6. at mountain junior high school, clark took science, spanish, english, and math II.
7. does andrea play the trombone for the miller county adult band?
8. the eiffel tower in paris, france, is lighted at night.
9. the wally workout club has a summer special in august.
10. is the crown sterling hotel in irving, texas, near the airport?
11. in american literature class, bert and sandra read the red badge of courage.
12. if you go to pike's peak, you will be near colorado springs.
13. is monticello, the name of thomas jefferson's home, on the potomac river?
14. i. beach activities
        a. volleyball
        b. surfing
    ii. camping activities
        a. hiking
        b. mountain bike riding

*home of the United States President

Name________________________________ **CAPITALIZATION TEST**

WORKBOOK PAGES 340-341

Date________________________________ **Answers are boldfaced.**

You may wish to give one point per correct answer. Total points= 182

You may want to weight certain sections or count each line as a point.

Directions: Write the capital letter above any word that needs to be capitalized.

1.

6228 **E**ast **B**ridge **S**treet
Arlington, **T**exas 76017
December 2, 20--

Dear **D**orothy,

I'm just letting you know that we will definitely be there for **C**hristmas vacation.

Truly yours,
Ann

2. **D**id **K**ing **D**avid write songs to honor **G**od?

3. **O**n the last **S**unday in **J**uly they left for a **P**alm **S**prings hotel.

4. **B**oth **C**oach **B**enson and **G**retta's mom will help with the **B**rightly **B**aseball **C**lub.

5. **J**oanna eats **F**rench toast nearly every morning at **W**ren's **F**amily **R**estaurant.

6. **N**ext spring the **Z**ent family will visit **E**verglades **N**ational **P**ark in **F**lorida.

7. **L**enny and **U**ncle **F**red crossed over the **C**olorado **R**iver at the city of **Y**uma.

8. **I**n reading class, the student read **T**he **C**at **A**te **M**y **G**ym **S**uit for a book report.

9. **D**id **G**eneral **H**arris and **M**iss **B**ronson meet at the **U**niversity of **H**awaii?

10. **H**is home is located north of **M**ustang **L**ibrary on **A**pple **A**venue.

11. **T**he **C**herry **B**lossom **F**estival is held each year in **W**ashington, **D**. **C**.

12. "**P**lease sit beside me," said **R**andy.

13. **A** **C**hristian missionary went to **Z**ambia, a country in **A**frica.

14. **D**id **H**erman fly into **L**os **A**ngeles **I**nternational **A**irport last **F**ather's **D**ay?

Name________________________________ **CAPITALIZATION TEST**

Date________________________________

Directions: Write the capital letter above any word that needs to be capitalized.

1.

6228 east bridge street
arlington, texas 76017
december 2, 20--

dear dorothy,

i'm just letting you know that we will definitely be there for christmas vacation.

truly yours,
ann

2. did king david write songs to honor god?

3. on the last sunday in july they left for a palm springs hotel.

4. both coach benson and gretta's mom will help with the brightly baseball club.

5. joanna eats french toast nearly every morning at wren's family restaurant.

6. next spring the zent family will visit everglades national park in florida.

7. lenny and uncle fred crossed over the colorado river at the city of yuma.

8. in reading class, the student read the cat ate my gym suit for a book report.

9. did general harris and miss bronson meet at the university of hawaii?

10. his home is located north of mustang library on apple avenue.

11. the cherry blossom festival is held each year in washington, d. c.

12. "please sit beside me," said randy.

13. a christian missionary went to zambia, a country in africa.

14. did herman fly into los angeles international airport last father's day?

15. **F**or **S**t. **V**alentine's **D**ay, **M**om received **S**ee's* candy and an **I**talian purse.

16. **D**uring the winter, they volunteered at **R**ose **G**arden **N**ursing **H**ome.

17. **H**is brother sent **D**utch tulips as a gift for **G**randma **P**olley's birthday.

18. **I.** **L**and vehicles
    - **A.** **T**rucks
    - **B.** **V**ans
    - **C.** **C**ars

    II. **A**ir vehicles
    - **A.** **H**ot air balloons
    - **B.** **A**irplanes

19. **I**n **E**nglish class, **P**rofessor **G**ordon taught **T**he **T**ale of **T**wo **C**ities.

20. **A** **B**ible school was held at a **L**utheran church in **B**ergen **C**ounty.

21. **I**s **U**rsala's father the leader of the **P**otts **V**alley **C**hamber of **C**ommerce?

22. **T**hey drive across the **O**akland **B**ay **B**ridge to their office in **S**an **F**rancisco.

23. **H**is neighbor owns **B**arlett **B**owling **A**lley located in the western part of **D**ell **C**ity.

24. **M**r. **A**. **K**ennedy was admitted to **F**airwell **M**emorial **H**ospital for kidney stones.

25. **T**he book, **M**y **M**other **D**oesn't **L**ike to **C**ook, was illustrated by **M**icah **C**laycamp.

26. **H**is grandfather is a sheriff for the **M**aricopa **C**ounty **S**heriffs' **D**epartment.

27. **G**eorgia and **I** are going to **L**ake **O**keechobee and to **D**isneyworld.

28. **D**id the **A**merican **R**ed **C**ross send help to victims of the **M**idwest floods?

29. **W**ilma rode **A**rabian horses on an **A**rizona ranch during her break from **P**enn **S**tate **U**niversity.

30. **M**argot and **R**ay yelled, "**L**ook at our new **C**hrysler* van!"

*brand name

15. for st. valentine's day, mom received see's* candy and an italian purse.

16. during the winter, they volunteered at rose garden nursing home.

17. his brother sent dutch tulips as a gift for grandma polley's birthday.

18. i. land vehicles
    a. trucks
    b. vans
    c. cars

    ii. air vehicles
    a. hot air balloons
    b. airplanes

19. in english class, professor gordon taught the tale of two cities.

20. a bible school was held at a lutheran church in bergen county.

21. is ursala's father the leader of the potts valley chamber of commerce?

22. they drive across the oakland bay bridge to their office in san francisco.

23. his neighbor owns barlett bowling alley located in the western part of dell city.

24. mr. a. kennedy was admitted to fairwell memorial hospital for kidney stones.

25. the book, my mother doesn't like to cook, was illustrated by micah claycamp.

26. his grandfather is a sheriff for the maricopa county sheriffs' department.

27. georgia and i are going to lake okeechobee and to disneyworld.

28. did the american red cross send help to victims of the midwest floods?

29. wilma rode arabian horses on an arizona ranch during her break from penn state university.

30. margot and ray yelled, "look at our new chrysler* van!"

*brand name

PUNCTUATION

PERIOD: (.)

RULE 1: Use a period at the end of a declarative sentence (statement).

We found a bird that had fallen from its nest.

RULE 2: Place a period at the end of an imperative sentence (command).

Please take this with you.

RULE 3: Use a period after initial(s).

Jeremy **J.** Wing is my friend.

RULE 4: Use a period after the letter(s) and number(s) in an outline.

I. Birds
- **A.** Birds that fly
- **B.** Birds that don't fly
  - **1.** Penguins
  - **2.** Ostriches

II. Reptiles
- **A.** Poisonous
- **B.** Non-poisonous

RULE 5: Place a period after an abbreviation.

A. Days of the week:

Sunday- Sun.
Monday - Mon.
Tuesday - Tues., Tue.*
Wednesday- Wed.
Thursday - Thurs., Thur.*
Friday - Fri.
Saturday - Sat.
*The first listing is preferred.

B. Months of the year:

January - Jan.
February - Feb.
March - Mar.
April - Apr.
May
June
July
August - Aug.
September - Sept.
October - Oct.
November - Nov.
December - Dec.

C. Times:

A.M. - Latin ante meridiem (before noon)
P.M. - Latin post meridiem (after noon)

D. Directions:

N. - north   S. - south   E. - east   W. - west

E. Titles:

Mrs. - title used before a married woman's name (plural = Mmes.)
Mr. - Mister
Ms. - title that doesn't show if a woman is married or unmarried
Dr. - Doctor
Gen. - General
Capt. - Captain
Sen. - Senator

F. Places (general):

Ave. - Avenue
Ln. - Lane
St. - Street (or Saint)
Dr. - Drive
Blvd. - Boulevard
Hwy. - Highway
Mt. - Mountain (Mts. - Mountains)
Str. - Strait

Always use a dictionary to check for proper abbreviations.

G: Places (Specific):

Mt. Rushmore - Mount Rushmore
Ft. Lauderdale - Fort Lauderdale
St. Augustine - Saint Augustine
U.S.A. - United States of America
Eur. - Europe
SD - South Dakota*
Penna. - Pennsylvania
(*Using the two letter postal code for each states is suggested; no periods are used.)

H. Associations and Organizations:

Y.W.C.A. - Young Women's Christian Association
Y.M.H.A. - Young Men's Hebrew Association

If the dictionary provides two possibilities, the first given is preferred.

A.M.A. - American Medical Association
E.M.A. - Entrepreneurial Mothers' Association
Madd - Mothers Against Drunk Drivers*
NOW - National Organization of Women*

*If the initials spell out a word, the word is called an acronym. **Do not use periods with acronyms.**

I. Other abbreviations:

MP - Military Police (also M.P.)
Co. - Company
Mgr. - Manager
Assn. - Association

If a sentence ends with an abbreviation, do not place an additional period.

Example: Julius Caesar died in 44 B.C.

Name_______________________________

WORKBOOK PAGE 289

Date_______________________________

PERIODS

Directions: Place a period where needed.

1. Mr. Harmon wants to drive that car.
2. Capt. Stelwell will meet with us this Thurs. at two o'clock.
3. Give your paper about the meeting in Aug. to Miss Fields.
4. King Tutankhamen lived about 1355 B. C. in Egypt.
5. Milly D. Rivers lives at 12 E. Oak Street.
6. I. Presidents

    A. Abraham Lincoln

    B. John Kennedy

    C. George Bush

   II. Famous wives of Presidents

    A. Abigail Adams

    B. Bess Truman

7. They will meet at the Chrysler Bldg. at 9 A. M.
8. Has Dr. Blair J. Adams gone to the A. M. A. meeting?
9. Their new address is 453 N. Ashton, St. Louis, MO 63367.
10. On Sat., Oct. 9th, a fashion show was held by the club.
11. Sen. H. Lipton has lived in the U. S. all of his life.

Name________________________________

Date________________________________

PERIODS

Directions: Place a period where needed.

1. Mr Harmon wants to drive that car
2. Capt Stelwell will meet with us this Thurs at two o'clock
3. Give your paper about the meeting in Aug to Miss Fields
4. King Tutankhamen lived about 1355 B C in Egypt
5. Milly D Rivers lives at 12 E Oak Street
6. I Presidents

   A Abraham Lincoln

   B John Kennedy

   C George Bush

   II Famous wives of Presidents

   A Abigail Adams

   B Bess Truman

7. They will meet at the Chrysler Bldg at 9 A M
8. Has Dr Blair J Adams gone to the A M A meeting?
9. Their new address is 453 N Ashton, St Louis, MO 63367
10. On Sat , Oct 9th, a fashion show was held by the club
11. Sen H Lipton has lived in the U S all of his life

PAGE 571 = WORKBOOK PAGE 290
PAGE 576 = WORKBOOK PAGE 293
PAGE 577 = WORKBOOK PAGE 294
PAGE 580 = WORKBOOK PAGE 296
PAGE 581 = WORKBOOK PAGE 297

Apostrophe: (')

Rule 1: Use an apostrophe in a contraction to show where letter(s) have been omitted.

doesn't = does not
we're = we are
what's = what is

Rule 2: Use an apostrophe when the first two digits are omitted from the year.

'87 = 1987
'98 = 1998
'11 = 2011

Rule 3: Use an apostrophe when referring to letters or words used out of context.

Be sure to dot your i's.
The a in your and's needs to be closed.

Rule 4: Use an apostrophe to show possession (ownership):

A. If the word is singular (one), add apostrophe + s.

a house's roof
one lady's shoes
the teller's smile

B. If the word is plural (more than one) and ends in s, add the apostrophe after the s.

two girls' room
several babies' toy
many students' projects

C. If the word is plural (more than one) and does not end in s, add apostrophe + s.

men's restroom
mice's tails
children's petting zoo

Note: When two people own the same item, add an appostrophe after the **second** name.

Bob and Jan's new home (They own a home together.)

When two people own separate items, add an apostrophe after **both** names.

Tom's and Sue's basketballs (They each have a basketball.)

Name________________________________

WORKBOOK PAGE 291

Date________________________________

APOSTROPHES

Directions: Write the possessive.

Example: skis belonging to her mother: her mother's skis

1. a ferret belonging to Fred: Fred's ferret
2. boots belonging to their dad: (their) dad's boots
3. a horse belonging to Chris: Chris's horse
4. golf clubs belonging to Miss Hand: Miss Hand's (golf) clubs
5. a restaurant owned by two men: men's restaurant
6. a trampoline belonging to three girls: girls' trampoline
7. a work area belonging to several teachers: teachers' (work) area
8. a trail for many walkers: walkers' trail
9. a club formed by several boys: boys' club
10. a park where five geese live: geese's park
11. a balloon belonging to a child: child's balloon
12. the grandfather of Bess: Bess's grandfather

Name________________________________

Date________________________________

APOSTROPHES

Directions: Write the possessive.

Example: skis belonging to her mother: her mother's skis

1. a ferret belonging to Fred: ________________________________
2. boots belonging to their dad: ________________________________
3. a horse belonging to Chris: ________________________________
4. golf clubs belonging to Miss Hand: ________________________________
5. a restaurant owned by two men: ________________________________
6. a trampoline belonging to three girls: ________________________________
7. a work area belonging to several teachers: ________________________________
8. a trail for many walkers: ________________________________
9. a club formed by several boys: ________________________________
10. a park where five geese live: ________________________________
11. a balloon belonging to a child: ________________________________
12. the grandfather of Bess: ________________________________

Name________________________________ **APOSTROPHES**

WORKBOOK PAGE 292

Date________________________________

Directions: Insert any apostrophe where needed.

Example: She was born in '87.

1. Linda's mother walks five miles each day.
2. His answers weren't correct.
3. Who's going to Beverly's house?
4. Cross your <u>t's</u>, please.
5. We aren't finished with Jackie's coat.
6. Your <u>3's</u> look more like <u>8's</u>.
7. That nurses' station is very busy.
8. You're invited to a children's play.
9. One person's luggage hadn't been found.
10. Dot your <u>i's</u> in your name.
11. Was John F. Kennedy's burial in '63?
12. They've learned much about oxen's habits.
13. We've decided to take our two aunts' advice.
14. The artists' convention wasn't held in San Francisco.
15. In '93, Mike's parents went to Denmark.
16. Two puppies' dish had been turned over.
17. The child's grandparents aren't able to attend.
18. Your <u>6's</u> look too much like <u>9's</u>.

Name________________________________

Date________________________________

APOSTROPHES

Directions: Insert any apostrophe where needed.

Example: She was born in '87.

1. Lindas mother walks five miles each day.
2. His answers werent correct.
3. Whos going to Beverlys house?
4. Cross your ts, please.
5. We arent finished with Jackies coat.
6. Your 3s look more like 8s.
7. That nurses station is very busy.
8. Youre invited to a childrens play.
9. One persons luggage hadnt been found.
10. Dot your is in your name.
11. Was John F. Kennedys burial in 63?
12. Theyve learned much about oxens habits.
13. Weve decided to take our two aunts advice.
14. The artists convention wasnt held in San Francisco.
15. In 93, Mikes parents went to Denmark.
16. Two puppies dish had been turned over.
17. The childs grandparents arent able to attend.
18. Your 6s look too much like 9s.

Comma: (,)

Rule 1: Place a comma after the day and year in a date.

April 1, 1987

Place a comma after the day and the date.

Sunday, September 19, 1993

Place a comma after the date if the date doesn't end a sentence.

On Oct. 23, 1946, his father was born.

Rule 2: Place a comma between a town or city and a state.

Reno, Nevada

Place a comma between a city and a country.

Paris, France

In a street address, place a comma after the street and after the city. Do not place a comma between the state and zip code.

They live at 40 Flower Lane, Leeds, AL 35094.

Note that a comma is not placed between the house address and the street address!

Place a comma after the state or country if it appears before the end of the sentence.

Joanna and Paul go to Racine, Wisconsin, for the summer.

Rule 3: Use a comma to set off introductory words.

No, I can't do that.

Yes, this is the best stew ever.

Well, let's decide together.

Rule 4: Use a comma to set off interrupters in a sentence.
(An interrupter usually can be removed from a sentence without changing its meaning.)

His name, by the way, is French.

The cab driver, however, must be paid immediately.

That tie, I believe, is a silk one.

Rule 5: Place a comma after the greeting of a friendly letter.

Dear Uncle Lloyd,

Place a comma after the closing of any letter.

Sincerely yours,
Chelsea

Rule 6: Place a comma after three or more items in a series.

A toothbrush, toothpaste, and mouthwash had been packed.

Do not place a comma after the last item in a series.

Place a comma after phrases in a series.

Miss Harper threw her head back, coughed gently, and began to laugh.

Rule 7: Place a comma after a noun of direct address (a person spoken to).

Cynthia, will you explain this puzzle to me?

I need your help, Dad.

Have you, Betty, seen my notebook?

Name________________________________ **COMMAS**

WORKBOOK PAGE 295

Date________________________________

Directions: Insert commas where needed.

Example: Yes, we will read two stories about snakes.

1. Ronnie and I are coming with you, Teddy.
2. She likes math, spelling, and science.
3. No, don't touch that yet.
4. His cousin lives in Tomball, Texas.
5. Miss Flagg, how are you?
6. Your idea, in fact, is a great one.
7. Their uncle moved to London, England.
8. They were married on August 23, 1990.
9. A cowboy, a cowgirl, and the herd boss talked about the cattle.
10. The tour group will fly to Detroit, Michigan, in the summer.
11. Holly turned twelve on Saturday, February 1, 1992.
12. Dear Earl,

    Marty, Bill, and I are planning a camping trip. Do you want to go?

    Your friend,
    Will
13. On Friday, July 8th, 1990, their family met for a huge reunion.
14. Some children jumped, hopped, and skipped at the park.
15. Her address is 3339 Ridge Drive, Sanford, ME 04073.

Name___________________________________ **COMMAS**

Date___________________________________

Directions: Insert commas where needed.

Example: Yes, we will read two stories about snakes.

1. Ronnie and I are coming with you Teddy.
2. She likes math spelling and science.
3. No don't touch that yet.
4. His cousin lives in Tomball Texas.
5. Miss Flagg how are you?
6. Your idea in fact is a great one.
7. Their uncle moved to London England.
8. They were married on August 23 1990.
9. A cowboy a cowgirl and the herd boss talked about the cattle.
10. The tour group will fly to Detroit Michigan in the summer.
11. Holly turned twelve on Saturday February 1 1992.
12. Dear Earl

    Marty Bill and I are planning a camping trip. Do you want to go?

    Your friend
    Will

13. On Friday July 8th 1994 their family will meet for a huge reunion.
14. Some children jumped hopped and skipped at the park.
15. Her address is 3339 Ridge Drive Sanford ME 04073.

Commas: (,)

Rule 8: Use a comma between two or more descriptive adjectives unless one is a color or a number.

Tall, slender weeds are growing in the garden.
↑
She threw the long, torn coat into a bag.
↑
Some large red roses are growing in the flower bed.

Note: If one of the two adjectives located before a noun is closely related to that noun, a comma is not used. Example: She enjoys spicy Mexican food.

Rule 9: Use a comma to clarify (make clear) a sentence.

During the night owls sat in several trees.

During the night, owls sat in several trees.
↑

Rule 10: Use a comma at the end of most direct quotations.

"Your book is falling," said Millicent.
↑
"I know," replied Harrison.
↑

If the person who is making the statement is given first, place a comma after the person's name + verb that follows:

Mr. Kimble said, "Let's begin."
↑

Mary asked, "Where are we?"
↑

If the quotation is split, place a comma after the first part of the quotation and also after the person + verb (or verb + person).

"My sister," answered Wesley, "did not say that."
↑ ↑

"Listen very carefully," said Miss Zurek, "to these chimes."
↑ ↑

Place any comma within a quotation mark.

After Ann sang "Amazing Grace," the audience applauded.
↑

Rule 11: Use a comma to invert a name. Place the last name, a comma, and a first name.

Washington, George
↑

Madison, Dolly
↑

Kennedy, John F.
↑

Rule 12: If two complete sentences are joined by a conjunction (<u>and</u>, <u>but</u>, or <u>or</u>), place a comma before the conjunction.

The children made snowmen, and the teenagers threw snowballs at each other.
↑

We stopped at Tommy's house, but he wasn't home.
↑

Rule 13: Use a comma to set off an appositive. An appositive is a word or group of words that explains a noun in a sentence. Often, an appositive will give additional information about the noun.

Sal is nice.
Sal, my neighbor, is nice.
↑ ↑

<u>My neighbor</u> is an appositive that explains who Sal is.

Her brother is funny.
Her brother, the boy in the blue sweater, is funny.
↑ ↑

<u>The boy in the blue sweater</u> is an appositive that gives more information about her brother.

Name________________________________ **COMMAS**

WORKBOOK PAGE 298

Date________________________________

Directions: Insert needed commas.

Example: Gloria, my aunt who lives in Denver, is coming to visit.

1. Jane arrived early, but she didn't stay.
2. Your answer, by the way, is right.
3. Mrs. Lionel, a graphic artist, designed an advertisement.
4. Write your name with last name and then first name: **Answers will vary.**

   ___________Last name, first name___________________________

5. "Your hamster needs some water," said Mona.
6. Tiny, soft marshmallows floated in the hot chocolate.
7. With this foil, line the bottom of the pan.
8. "You're just the person," Lollie said, "who can solve this problem."
9. Invert your best friend's name: **Answers will vary.**

   ___________Last name, first name___________________________

10. Have you seen Frisky, my pet canary?
11. Gina took a huge, plaid blanket to the football game.
12. Their trip to the zoo was fun, and they are going again next week.
13. Harry, our Dad's friend, is teaching us how to shoot basketballs.
14. "Turn your project in tomorrow," said Mr. Britton.
15. You may sit here, or you may take your lunch outside.

Name________________________________ **COMMAS**

Date________________________________

Directions: Insert needed commas.

Example: Gloria, my aunt who lives in Denver, is coming to visit.

1. Jane arrived early but she didn't stay.
2. Your answer by the way is right.
3. Mrs. Lionel a graphic artist designed an advertisement.
4. Write your name with last name and then first name:

   ____

5 "Your hamster needs some water " said Mona.

6. Tiny soft marshmallows floated in the hot chocolate.
7. With this foil line the bottom of the pan.
8. "You're just the person " Lollie said "who can solve this problem."
9. Invert your best friend's name:

   ____

10. Have you seen Frisky my pet canary?
11. Gina took a huge plaid blanket to the football game.
12. Their trip to the zoo was fun and they are going again next week.
13. Harry our Dad's friend is teaching us how to shoot basketballs.
14. "Turn your project in tomorrow " said Mr. Britton.
15. You may sit here or you may take your lunch outside.

PAGE 585 = WORKBOOK PAGE 299
PAGE 588 = WORKBOOK PAGE 301
PAGE 589 = WORKBOOK PAGE 302

Semicolon (;)

Rule 1: Use a semicolon to join two complete sentences that are closely related.

Hail began to fall; everyone ran into the building.

↑

complete sentence **complete sentence**

Colon (:)

Rule 1: Use a colon in writing the time.

5:00 P.M. 11:23 A.M.

↑ ↑

Rule 2: Use a colon to set off lists.

Things to take:

↑

shoes
socks
shorts

We need the following: paper plates, plastic forks, and cups.

↑

Rule 3: Use a colon between the chapter and verse(s) in the <u>Bible</u>.

Isaiah 41:10 Mark 3: 5-7

↑ ↑

Rule 4: Use a colon after divisions of topics in a writing.

PLANTS:

↑

Land plants:

↑

Rule 5: Place a colon after the greeting of a business letter.

Dear Sir: Ladies and Gentlemen:

↑ ↑

Name________________________________ **SEMICOLONS AND COLONS**

WORKBOOK PAGE 300

Date________________________________

Directions: Insert needed semicolons and colons.

Example: We read Matthew 9:3 in the Bible.

1. Dear Sir:

2. The football game will begin at 7:30 A.M.

3. Things to do:
   -wash car
   -feed dog
   -take out trash

4. Rule A: Take turns.

   Rule B: Be polite.

5. Homework was given in the following subjects: math, English, and spelling.

6. The cake is cherry; the frosting is cream cheese.

7. Your appointment is at 5:15 or 5:30.

8. Dear Senator Riley:

9. The first verse of the Old Testament is Genesis 1:1.

10. Her hair is very curly; someone must have given her a perm.

11. You may go on these days: Monday, Wednesday, Thursday, and Saturday.

12. Toby's mother answered the phone; she called for Toby to come.

13. People going on the trip:
    -Thomas
    -Lydia
    -Georgette

14. The minister read Luke 10:2 during the 10:30 service.

Name________________________________ **SEMICOLONS AND COLONS**

Date________________________________

Directions: Insert needed semicolons and colons.

Example: We read Matthew 9:3 in the Bible.

1. Dear Sir

2. The football game will begin at 7 30 A.M.

3. Things to do
   -wash car
   -feed dog
   -take out trash

4. Rule A Take turns.

   Rule B Be polite.

5. Homework was given in the following subjects math, English, and spelling.

6. The cake is cherry the frosting is cream cheese.

7. Your appointment is at 5 15 or 5 30.

8. Dear Senator Riley

9. The first verse of the Old Testament is Genesis 1 1.

10. Her hair is very curly someone must have given her a perm.

11. You may go on these days Monday, Wednesday, Thursday, and Saturday.

12. Toby's mother answered the phone she called for Toby to come.

13. People going on the trip
    -Thomas
    -Lydia
    -Georgette

14. The minister read Luke 10 2 during the 10 30 service.

Question Mark (?):

Rule 1: **Use a question mark at the end of an interrogative sentence. (An interrogative sentence asks a question.)**

Is Cape Cod in Massachusetts**?**
May I bring my belongings**?**

Exclamation Point (!):

Rule 1: **Use an exclamation point after an exclamatory sentence. (An exclamatory sentence shows strong feeling.)**

We've been chosen!
Our team is ahead by two points!

Rule 2: **Place an exclamation point after a word or phrase that shows strong feeling (interjection).**

Wow! Yippee! We did it!

Hyphen (-):

Rule 1: **Place a hyphen between fractions and two digit word numbers between 21 and 99.**

four-fifths one-half twenty-two seventy-eight

Rule 2: **Use a hyphen to combine some prefixes with a root word.**

self-concept ex-president

Use a dictionary to determine if words should be hyphenated.

Rule 3: **Use a hyphen to combine some closely related words.**

see-through three-speed

Use a dictionary to determine if words should be hyphenated.

Rule 4: **Use a hyphen when dividing a word of two or more syllables at the end of a line. (Words are divided between syllables.) You must have at least two letters on the first line and three on the following line.**

Check a dictionary if you are not sure where to divide a word.

Correct:

____________________________ re-
fund __________________________
____________________________ jel-
lyfish _________________________
__________________________ divi-
sion __________________________

Incorrect:

____________________________ a- (Two or more letters are required.)
bout __________________________

____
________________________ quick-
ly ____________________________ (Three or more letters are required.)

Underlining ( ):

Rule 1: **Underline the names of ships, planes, and trains.**

Spruce Goose (name of an airplane)
Princess (name of a ship)
Oriental Express (name of a train)

Rule 2: **Underline letter(s), word(s), or number(s) used out of context.**

Please cross your t.
I used too four times in this paragraph.
Your 3's are too small.

Rule 3: **Underline the title of books, magazines, movies, newspapers, plays, television shows, record albums/CD's/tapes, works of art, sculptures, operas, and long poems.**

Note: *An item is usually underlined if you can receive it in the mail.*
Scripts for plays and television shows are long and follow this rule.

Have you read a recent issue of Ranger Rick? (magazine)
He read the book, Old Yeller, and saw the movie, 101 Dalmations.
USA Today is an interesting newspaper.
She wrote a play entitled George Washington and the French.
The child watched a re-run of Mr. Rogers on television.
The tape, In His Time, is very enjoyable.

Note: **In print, a title will be in *italics* rather than underlined.**

Name________________________________

WORKBOOK PAGE 303

Date________________________________

QUESTION MARKS
EXCLAMATION POINTS
HYPHENS
UNDERLINING

Directions: Insert needed punctuation (question marks, exclamation points, hyphens, and underlinings).

Example: Mr. Lampner just bought a ten-speed bike.

1. Hurrah! I found my money!

2. Two-thirds of the flowers have been planted; however, most of the daffodils are still in cartons.

3. Will you please choose a seat?

4. The Queen Mary* is in Long Beach, California.

   *name of a ship

5. The Mertz family bought a tri-level home.

6. Thirty-four people waited in line.

7. Kimberly's mom read the book, Boost Your Brainpower.

8. Mrs. Haas added three-fourths cup of honey to the cookie recipe.

9. Joyce buys a copy of Family Circle* each month.

   *name of a magazine

10. The teacher wrote a gigantic 9 on the board.

11. The woman on the subway was reading The Wall Street Journal*.

    *name of a newspaper

12. The movie, Gone with the Wind, is very long.

13. The man paced to-and-fro in the lobby.

14. Be sure to dot your i and cross your t's in the word mitten.

15. Oh! The fireworks during the half-time celebration were terrific!

Name________________________________

Date________________________________

QUESTION MARKS
EXCLAMATION POINTS
HYPHENS
UNDERLINING

Directions: Insert needed punctuation (question marks, exclamation points, hyphens, and underlinings).

Example: Mr. Lampner just bought a ten-speed bike.

1. Hurrah I found my money

2. Two thirds of the flowers have been planted; however, most of the daf fodils are still in cartons.

3. Will you please choose a seat

4. The Queen Mary* is in Long Beach, California.

   *name of a ship

5. The Mertz family bought a tri level home.

6. Thirty four people waited in line.

7. Kimberly's mom read the book, Boost Your Brainpower.

8. Mrs. Haas added three fourths cup of honey to the cookie recipe.

9. Joyce buys a copy of Family Circle* each month.

   *name of a magazine

10. The teacher wrote a gigantic 9 on the board.

11. The woman on the subway was reading The Wall Street Journal*.

    *name of a newspaper

12. The movie, Gone with the Wind, is very long.

13. The man paced to and fro in the lobby.

14. Be sure to dot your i and cross your t's in the word mitten.

15. Oh The fireworks during the half time celebration were terrific

PAGE 606 = WORKBOOK PAGE 310
PAGE 607 = WORKBOOK PAGE 311

Quotation Marks (" "):

Rule 1: Use quotation marks (" ") to indicate someone's exact words.

"How are you?" asked Miss Dow.
Danny said, "I am fine."

A. In a split quotation, place quotations around each part spoken.

"Your knee," said Mrs. Lincoln, "looks very sore."
"It is sore," said Tom. "I fell and skinned it."

B. In a split quotation, do not place the end quotation mark until the person has finished speaking.

"Let's try," said Jimmie, "Take my hand. Now pull hard on the rope."

C. In dialogue (conversation between two or more people), begin a new paragraph each time a different person speaks.

Roberta asked, "Tom, have you seen the little puppy that I just received for my birthday?"

"What kind is he?" Tom asked.

"He's a cocker spaniel," replied Roberta.

"Would you like to go to my house to show my parents?" asked Tom.

Rule 2: Use quotation marks to enclose the title of short poems, short stories, nursery rhymes, songs, chapters, articles, and essays.

Note: Periods and commas are always placed inside quotation marks. Other punctuation is placed outside unless it is included in the actual quotation.

He read the poem, "Stopping by Woods on a Snowy Evening."
The newspaper article was entitled "Club to Meet."
"Why Mosquitoes Buzz in People's Ears" is the first story they read.
Is their favorite nursery rhyme "Wee Willie Winkle"?
The fifth chapter in the history book is "The Pioneers."
Grandmother's favorite song is "In the Garden."
Nan's essay entitled "Doughboys" is about World War I.

Note: ***Any "item" that is contained within a larger one is usually placed in quotation marks.*** For example: A magazine article is in a magazine.
Chapters are within a book.

Name________________________________ **QUOTATION MARKS**

WORKBOOK PAGE 305

Date________________________________

Directions: Insert needed quotation marks.

Space was left at the end of some sentences so that quotation marks could be placed before the end punctuation.

1. "Let's play together," said Bruce.
2. Molly shouted, "Come here!"
3. The first chapter of that history book is entitled "Native Americans."
4. Mrs. Claire Little said, "Ladies, we are here to discuss the new library."
5. Have you read the poem entitled "The Sands of Dee"?
6. "Give me your hand," said the mother to the child.
7. They listened to the song, "Good Vibrations."
8. "Your facts," said the manager, "are correct."
9. The children read a short story entitled "The Rescue at Sea."
10. Have you memorized the nursery rhyme, "Old Mother Hubbard"?
11. "I know," said the mother, " that you aren't finished. However, it's time for supper."
12. David's essay entitled "Colonial America" won a prize.
13. The magazine article was entitled "Travels in China."
14. "How," asked the lost driver, "do I get to Dover Drive?"
15. Write a dialogue between two people:

Answers will vary. Be sure that a new paragraph is started as each new person speaks. (In oral reading of stories and books, have a student read only one paragraph and then call on another student to read. This process helps to reinforce that a new paragraph begins each time another person speaks.)

Name___________________________________ **QUOTATION MARKS**

Date____________________________________

Directions: Insert needed quotation marks.

1. Let's play together, said Bruce.
2. Molly shouted, Come here!
3. The first chapter of that history book is entitled Native Americans.
4. Mrs. Claire Little said, Ladies, we are here to discuss the new library.
5. Have you read the poem entitled The Sands of Dee ?
6. Give me your hand, said the mother to the child.
7. They listened to the song, Good Vibrations.
8. Your facts, said the manager, are correct.
9. The children read a short story entitled The Rescue at Sea.
10. Have you memorized the nursery rhyme, Old Mother Hubbard ?
11. I know, said the mother, that you aren't finished. However, it's time for supper.
12. David's essay entitled Colonial America won a prize.
13. The magazine article was entitled Travels in China.
14. How, asked the lost driver, do I get to Dover Drive?
15. Write a dialogue between two people:

____

____

____

____

____

Name________________________________
WORKBOOK PAGE 306
Date________________________________

UNDERLINING or QUOTATION MARKS?

Directions: Place quotation marks or underline the following titles:

1. a song, "Red River Valley"
2. a book, Herbs
3. a magazine, National Geographic
4. a magazine article, "Down the Mississippi River"
5. a video tape, Amazon: Land of the Flooded Forest
6. a short story, "Buffalo Bill"
7. a short poem, "I Came to the New World"
8. a ship, Titanic
9. an airplane, Concorde
10. a work of art, Woman with a Child
11. a nursery rhyme, "Hickory Dickory Dock"
12. a newspaper, Chicago Tribune
13. a movie, The Rescuers
14. a magazine article, "The Perfect Diet"
15. an album, Love
16. a play, Columbus
17. an essay, "Why I Believe in America"
18. a television show, Sports
19. a newspaper article, "Suspect Held in Burglary"
20. a chapter, "Adverbs"

Name________________________________

Date________________________________

UNDERLINING or QUOTATION MARKS?

Directions: Place quotation marks or underline the following titles:

1. a song, Red River Valley
2. a book, Herbs
3. a magazine, National Geographic
4. a magazine article, Down the Mississippi River
5. a video tape, Amazon: Land of the Flooded Forest
6. a short story, Buffalo Bill
7. a short poem, I Came to the New World
8. a ship, Titanic
9. an airplane, Concorde
10. a work of art, Woman with a Child
11. a nursery rhyme, Hickory Dickory Dock
12. a newspaper, Chicago Tribune
13. a movie, The Rescuers
14. a magazine article, The Perfect Diet
15. an album, Love
16. a play, Columbus
17. an essay, Why I Believe in America
18. a television show, Sports
19. a newspaper article, Suspect Held in Burglary
20. a chapter, Adverbs

Name________________________________ **PUNCTUATION REVIEW**

WORKBOOK PAGE 307

Date________________________________

Directions: Insert needed punctuation.

1. Yes, my mother is home.

2. His mother and father read the Los Angeles Times*.
   *name of a newspaper

3. Roy, come here.

4. Fifty-nine people boarded a run-down bus.

5. He was born on Jan. 1, 1984.

6. Bonnie said, "Let me help you."

7. Their address is 20874 N. Briar Road.

8. I will call you, and we will plan a party.

9. They saw Bear Country at the 9:30 P. M. movie.

10. Groceries:
    -eggs
    -milk
    -bread

11. Your father, I believe, is looking for you.

12. Thelma Lee's story is called "The Two Huge Pandas."

13. A girls' club was formed by Lollie, her sister, and her cousin.

14. Gentlemen:

    The meeting will be held at 10:30 A. M. in the conference room of the Horton Hotel.

    Sincerely,
    William T. Razz

15. Mona likes to read Weekly Reader magazine.

Name______________________________________

Date______________________________________

PUNCTUATION REVIEW

Directions: Insert needed punctuation.

1. Yes my mother is home

2. His mother and father read the Los Angeles Times*
   *name of a newspaper

3. Roy come here

4. Fifty nine people boarded a run down bus

5. He was born on Jan 1 1984

6. Bonnie said Let me help you

7. Their address is 20874 N Briar Road

8. I will call you and we will plan a party

9. They saw Bear Country at the 9 30 P M movie

10. Groceries
    -eggs
    -milk
    -bread

11. Your father I believe is looking for you

12. Thelma Lees story is called The Two Huge Pandas

13. A girls club was formed by Lollie her sister and her cousin

14. Gentlemen

    The meeting will be held at 10 30 A M in the conference room of the Hor
    ,on Hotel

    Sincerely
    William T Razz

15. Mona likes to read Weekly Reader magazine

Name________________________________ **PUNCTUATION REVIEW**

WORKBOOK PAGE 308

Date________________________________

Directions: Insert needed punctuation.

1. You're my pal, Don.
2. Lowell asked, "May I speak with you**?**"
3. Mrs. E. Babbit is the children's librarian.
4. A fat, chewy brownie is on the plate.
5. At 3:15 P. M. Brenda's game will begin.
6. Mr. Blake drives a two-tone car.
7. Dinah read "Little Miss Muffet"* to her little brother.
   *name of a nursery rhyme
8. "Where's my glove**?**" asked Suzanne.
9. Their new address is 22 Roe Road, Mandeville, LA 70448.
10. Dear Michelle,

    We're going to Norman, Oklahoma.

    Your friend,
    Kelly
11. Ouch**!** I smashed my finger**!**
12. Janell, Cindy, and I did the laundry.
13. Take the umbrella; you'll need it if it rains.
14. The ladies' church group discussed Matthew 5:1-10.
15. Roxanne asked, "Have you pulled the weeds in the garden**?**"

Name________________________________ **PUNCTUATION REVIEW**

Date________________________________

Directions: Insert needed punctuation.

1. Youre my pal Don
2. Lowell asked May I speak with you
3. Mrs E Babbit is the childrens librarian
4. A fat chewy brownie is on the plate
5. At 3 15 P M Brendas game will begin
6. Mr Blake drives a two tone car
7. Dinah read Little Miss Muffet* to her little brother
   *name of a nursery rhyme
8. Wheres my glove asked Suzanne
9. Their new address is 22 Roe Road Mandeville LA 70448
10. Dear Michelle

    Were going to Norman Oklahoma

    Your friend
    Kelly
11. Ouch I smashed my finger
12. Janell Cindy and I did the laundry
13. Take the umbrella youll need it if it rains
14. The ladies church group discussed Matthew 5 1 10
15. Roxanne asked Have you pulled the weeds in the garden

Name________________________________ **PUNCTUATION REVIEW**
WORKBOOK PAGE 309
Date________________________________

Directions: Insert needed punctuation.

1. To do list:
   -feed dog
   -bathe dog
   -wash dog's dish

2. On Nov. 2, 1999, Jim and Lois plan to marry.

3. Chip, our beagle, is short and stout.

4. Have you read the book entitled <u>Angels</u>?

5. You are using too many <u>and's</u> in your writing.

6. Three-fifths of Gregg's baseball cards are valuable.

7. Miss Adams wants the following: a bike, a chain, and a lock.

8. "Whose is this**?**" asked Gen. Morton.

9. Thirty-seven cheerleaders traveled to Richmond, Virginia, for a meeting.

10. You'll enjoy reading the article entitled "Exercise Daily" in that magazine.

11. "I want," said Capt. Bing, "to visit Yellowstone soon."

12. On Thursday, Oct. 21, she will be twenty-one.

13. No, he won't travel to London, England, in the fall.

14. We can sled, ski, or play in the snow, but it will be very cold.

15. Write a friend's name in inverted form: **Answers will vary.** **<u>Last name, first name</u>**

16. "This dish," said the elderly lady, "belonged to my grandmother."

Name________________________________

PUNCTUATION REVIEW

Date________________________________

Directions: Insert needed punctuation.

1. To do list
    -feed dog
    -bathe dog
    -wash dogs dish

2. On Nov 2 1999 Jim and Lois plan to marry

3. Chip our beagle is short and stout

4. Have you read the book entitled Angels

5. You are using too many ands in your writing

6. Three fifths of Greggs baseball cards are valuable

7. Miss Adams wants the following a bike a chain and a lock

8. Whose is this asked Gen Morton

9. Thirty seven cheerleaders traveled to Richmond Virginia for a meeting

10. Youll enjoy reading the article entitled Exercise Daily in that magazine

11. I want said Capt Bing to visit Yellowstone soon

12. On Thursday Oct 21 she will be twenty one

13. No he wont travel to London England in the fall

14. We can sled ski or play in the snow but it will be very cold

15. Write a friend's name in inverted form: ________________________________

16. This dish said the elderly lady belonged to my grandmother

Name________________________________ **PUNCTUATION TEST**

WORKBOOK PAGE 342

Date________________________________

Directions: Insert any needed punctuation.

Example: Dear Sir:

1. Wow! Your ten-speed bicycle is great!

2. Mr. Dave E. Loy, Capt. Fudd, and Dad met in Tucson, Arizona, last fall.

3. A large, unusual monument will be dedicated at 7:30 P. M. today.

4. Dear Lottie,

   I'll go with you to Danny's swim party on Tues., August 4.

   Your friend,
   Bobbie

5. Send the postcard to 24 Briar Lane, Napa, CA 94558.

6. Kirk, we need the following: clay, 3 bottles of paint, and glue.

7. Kay asked, "Where's my lunch sack?"

8. The one boy's grandmother read the nursery rhyme entitled "Jack Sprat" to him.

9. The girls' choir can't meet until next Thursday.

10. Twenty-five people attended the movie entitled Old Yeller.

11. Yes, you must read the magazine article entitled "How to Be a Friend."

12. Write your name in inverted form: Last name, first name

13. Fido, my neighbor's dog, is cute.

14. He has too many but's in his paragraph.

15. One-half of the class attended a pep assembly on Friday, October 8, 1993.

Name________________________________

Date________________________________

PUNCTUATION TEST

Directions: Insert any needed punctuation.

Example: Dear Sir:

1. Wow Your ten speed bicycle is great
2. Mr Dave E Loy Capt Fudd and Dad met in Tucson Arizona last fall
3. A large unusual monument will be dedicated at 7 30 P M today
4. Dear Lottie

   I ll go with you to Dannys swim party on Tues August 4

   Your friend
   Bobbie
5. Send the postcard to 24 Briar Lane Napa CA 94558
6. Kirk we need the following clay 3 bottles of paint and glue
7. Kay asked Wheres my lunch sack
8. The one boys grandmother read the nursery rhyme entitled Jack Sprat to him
9. The girls choir cant meet until next Thursday
10. Twenty five people attended the movie entitled Old Yeller
11. Yes you must read the magazine article entitled How to Be a Friend
12. Write your name in inverted form: ________________________________
13. Fido my neighbors dog is cute
14. He has too many buts in his paragraph
15. One half of the class attended a pep assembly on Friday October 8 1993

IMPORTANT WORDS

THERE, THEIR, THEY'RE:

1. **There is an adverb meaning where.**

   Examples: Have you gone **there**?

   There are five airplanes ready to take off.

2. **Their is a pronoun that shows possession.** When using *their*, you should be able to answer *"their what?"*

   Example: She sang at **their** wedding. (Their what? wedding)

3. **They're is a contraction meaning they are.** If you think *they're* should be used, read the sentence inserting *they are*.

   Examples: **RIGHT:** **They're** leaving in the morning.
   They are leaving in the morning.

   WRONG: Is this **they're** car?
   Is this they are car?

MAY or CAN?:

1. A. **May asks permission.**

   Example: **May** I eat dinner now?
   (asking permission)

   B. **May also suggests a possibility.**

   Example: I **may** return earlier.

2. **Can means that one is able to do something.**

   Example: **Can** you fix this?
   (Are you able to fix this?)

IMPORTANT WORDS

TO, TWO, or TOO?

1. **<u>To</u> is a preposition or part of an infinitive.**

   Examples: Her father went **to** a museum in Chicago.
   (to = preposition; to a museum = prepositional phrase)

   The officer wants **to** receive a medal.
   (to receive = infinitive)

2. **<u>Two</u> is a number.**

   Examples: **Two** countries border Finland.
   We'd like to have **two**, please.

3. **<u>Too</u> is an adverb.**

   A. **<u>Too</u> sometimes means also.**

   Example: Kathy is coming, **too**!

   B. **<u>Too</u> sometimes means to what extent.**

   Examples: He was **too** tired to finish his work.
   (To what extent tired? too tired)

   Your remark is just **too** funny!
   (To what extent funny? too funny)

   C. **<u>Too</u> sometimes is used to emphasize a point.**

   Example: I do **too** want to go!

YOUR or YOU'RE:

1. **Your is a pronoun that shows possession.** When using *your*, you should be able to answer "*your what?*"

   Example: Your wallet is on the couch. (Your what? wallet)

2. **You're is a contraction meaning you are.** If you think *you're* should be used, read the sentence inserting *you are*.

   Examples: **RIGHT:** **You're** funny.
   You are funny.

   WRONG: Are **you're** pencils sharpened?
   Are you are pencils sharpened?

Name_______________________________

WORKBOOK PAGE 312

Date_______________________________

IMPORTANT WORDS

A. Directions: Select the correct word.

1. (Your, **You're**) a great sport!
2. Let's go (their, **there**) later.
3. (**May**, Can) we help you?
4. An ambulance arrived at the accident, (to, two, **too**).
5. (There, Their, **They're**) buying a bed.
6. (**Your**, You're) dream is interesting.
7. A tree has leaned (**to**, two, too) the right.
8. (May, **Can**) you add three-digit numbers in your head?
9. Add (to, **two**, too) chunks of ham to the bean soup.
10. (There, **Their**, They're) team won the championship.

B. Write the correct word in the space provided:

1. **TO, TWO, TOO**:
   - A. Has Brian gone, **too**?
   - B. The businesswoman walked **to** the front of the room.
   - C. There are **two** wheels on the scooter.
2. **THERE, THEIR, THEY'RE**:
   - A. The Douglas family went **there** last summer.
   - B. **Their** car broke down.
   - C. I like it when **they're** playing happily.
3. **MAY, CAN**
   - A. **May** the dog ride in the back seat?
   - B. Jordan **can** repair your bike.

Name________________________________ **IMPORTANT WORDS**

Date________________________________

A. Directions: Select the correct word.

1. (Your, You're) a great sport!
2. Let's go (their, there) later.
3. (May, Can) we help you?
4. An ambulance arrived at the accident, (to, two, too).
5. (There, Their, They're) buying a bed.
6. (Your, You're) dream is interesting.
7. A tree has leaned (to, two, too) the right.
8. (May, Can) you add three-digit numbers in your head?
9. Add (to, two, too) chunks of ham to the bean soup.
10. (There, Their, They're) team won the championship.

B. Write the correct word in the space provided:

1. **TO, TWO, TOO**:
   - A. Has Brian gone,__________?
   - B. The businesswoman walked __________ the front of the room.
   - C. There are _________ wheels on the scooter.
2. **THERE, THEIR, THEY'RE**:
   - A. The Douglas family went _____________ last summer.
   - B. ________________ car broke down.
   - C. I like it when ____________________ playing happily.
3. **MAY, CAN**
   - A. ________________ the dog ride in the back seat?
   - B. Jordan _______________ repair your bike.

Name________________________________ **IMPORTANT WORDS**

WORKBOOK PAGE 313

Date________________________________

A. Directions: Select the correct word.

1. I (may, **can**) change a flat tire.
2. (There, Their, **They're**) with their horses in the corral.
3. The librarian will read (**your**, you're) favorite book.
4. His mother said that he (**may**, can) have to stay inside today.
5. Is it (to, two, **too**) late to call someone?
6. Myla wants (**your**, you're) advice.
7. Bobby is (to, two, **too**) young to go on the roller coaster alone.
8. Does (there, **their**, they're) grandfather live in Idaho?
9. We know that (your, **you're**) in a hurry.
10. Are you going (**there**, their, they're) soon?

B. Write the correct word in the space provided:

1. **TO, TWO, TOO**:
   A. This hot fudge is __**too**__ thick.
   B. It's great to know how __**to**__ read.
   C. Please donate __**two**__ dollars.
2. **THERE, THEIR, THEY'RE**:
   A. The committee members explained __**their**__ plans.
   B. Are you aware that __**they're**__ here?
   C. You may not go __**there**__ without a parent.
3. **MAY, CAN:**
   A. __**Can**__ you be here by nine o'clock?
   B. How __**may**__ we help you?

Name________________________________ **IMPORTANT WORDS**

Date________________________________

A. Directions: Select the correct word.

1. I (may, can) change a flat tire.
2. (There, Their, They're) with their five horses in the corral.
3. The librarian will read (your, you're) favorite book.
4. His mother said that he (may, can) have to stay inside today.
5. Is it (to, two, too) late to call someone?
6. Myla wants (your, you're) advice.
7. Bobby is (to, two, too) young to go on the roller coaster alone.
8. Does (there, their, they're) grandfather live in Idaho?
9. We know that (your, you're) in a hurry.
10. Are you going (there, their, they're) soon?

B. Write the correct word in the space provided:

1. **TO, TWO, TOO**:
   - A. This hot fudge is ___________ thick.
   - B. It's great to know how _____________ read.
   - C. Please donate _____________ dollars.
2. **THERE, THEIR, THEY'RE**:
   - A. The committee members explained ___________________ plans.
   - B. Are you aware that ___________________ here?
   - C. You may not go ___________________ without a parent.
3. **MAY, CAN:**
   - A. ___________________ you be here by nine o'clock?
   - B. How ___________________ we help you?

INDEX

CORRELATION OF

EASY GRAMMAR WORKBOOK 56
with
EASY GRAMMAR: Grades 5 and 6

workbook page 1 - teacher ed. p. 2
workbook page 2 - teacher ed. p. 5
workbook page 3 - teacher ed. p. 3
workbook page 4 - teacher ed. p 7
workbook page 5 - teacher ed. p. 9
workbook page 6 - teacher ed. p. 11
workbook page 7 - teacher ed. p. 13
workbook page 8 - teacher ed. p. 15
workbook page 9 - teacher ed. p. 17
workbook page 10 - teacher ed. p. 19
workbook page 11 - teacher ed. p. 21
workbook page 12 - teacher ed. p. 23
workbook page 13 - teacher ed. p. 25
workbook page 14 - teacher ed. p. 27
workbook page 15 - teacher ed. p. 29
workbook page 16 - teacher ed. p. 31
workbook page 17 - teacher ed. p. 33
workbook page 18 - teacher ed. p. 35
workbook page 19 - teacher ed. p. 37
workbook page 20 - teacher ed. p. 39
workbook page 21 - teacher ed. p. 41
workbook page 22 - teacher ed. p. 43
workbook page 23 - teacher ed. p. 45
workbook page 24 - teacher ed. p. 47
workbook page 25 - teacher ed. p. 49
workbook page 26 - teacher ed. p. 51
workbook page 27 - teacher ed. p. 53
workbook page 28 - teacher ed. p. 55
workbook page 29 - teacher ed. p. 57
workbook page 30 - teacher ed. p. 59
workbook page 31 - teacher ed. p. 63
workbook page 32 - teacher ed. p. 65
workbook page 33 - teacher ed. p. 67
workbook page 34 - teacher ed. p. 69
workbook page 35 - teacher ed. p. 70
workbook page 36 - teacher ed. p. 71
workbook page 37 - teacher ed. p. 73
workbook page 38 - teacher ed. p. 75
workbook page 39 - teacher ed. p. 77
workbook page 40 - teacher ed. p. 78
workbook page 41 - teacher ed. p. 79
workbook page 42 - teacher ed. p. 81
workbook page 43 - teacher ed. p. 83
workbook page 44 - teacher ed. p. 85
workbook page 45 - teacher ed. p. 86
workbook page 46 - teacher ed. p. 87
workbook page 47 - teacher ed. p. 88
workbook page 48 - teacher ed. p. 89
workbook page 49 - teacher ed. p. 91
workbook page 50 - teacher ed. p. 93
workbook page 51 - teacher ed. p. 95
workbook page 52 - teacher ed. p. 97
workbook page 53 - teacher ed. p. 99
workbook page 54 - teacher ed. p. 101
workbook page 55 - teacher ed. p. 102
workbook page 56 - teacher ed. p. 103
workbook page 57 - teacher ed. p. 105
workbook page 58 - teacher ed. p. 107
workbook page 59 - teacher ed. p. 109
workbook page 60 - teacher ed. p. 111
workbook page 61 - teacher ed. p. 113
workbook page 62 - teacher ed. p. 114
workbook page 63 - teacher ed. p. 115
workbook page 64 - teacher ed. p. 117
workbook page 65 - teacher ed. p. 119
workbook page 66 - teacher ed. p. 121
workbook page 67 - teacher ed. p. 122
workbook page 68 - teacher ed. p. 123
workbook page 69 - teacher ed. p. 125
workbook page 70 - teacher ed. p. 127
workbook page 71 - teacher ed. p. 129
workbook page 72 - teacher ed. p. 131
workbook page 73 - teacher ed. p. 133
workbook page 74 - teacher ed. p. 134
workbook page 75 - teacher ed. p. 135
workbook page 76 - teacher ed. p. 137
workbook page 77 - teacher ed. p. 139
workbook page 78 - teacher ed. p. 141

workbook page 79 - teacher ed. p. 143
workbook page 80 - teacher ed. p. 145
workbook page 81 - teacher ed. p. 147
workbook page 82 - teacher ed. p. 148
workbook page 83 - teacher ed. p. 149
workbook page 84 - teacher ed. p. 151
workbook page 85 - teacher ed. p. 153
workbook page 86 - teacher ed. p. 155
workbook page 87 - teacher ed. p. 157
workbook page 88 - teacher ed. p. 159
workbook page 89 - teacher ed. p. 161
workbook page 90 - teacher ed. p. 163
workbook page 91 - teacher ed. p. 165
workbook page 92 - teacher ed. p. 167
workbook page 93 - teacher ed. p. 169
workbook page 94 - teacher ed. p. 171
workbook page 95 - teacher ed. p. 173
workbook page 96 - teacher ed. p. 175
workbook page 97 - teacher ed. p. 183
workbook page 98 - teacher ed. p. 185
workbook page 99 - teacher ed. p. 187
workbook page 100 - teacher ed. p. 189
workbook page 101 - teacher ed. p. 191
workbook page 102 - teacher ed. p. 193
workbook page 103 - teacher ed. p. 195
workbook page 104 - teacher ed. p. 197
workbook page 105 - teacher ed. p. 199
workbook page 106 - teacher ed. p. 201
workbook page 107 - teacher ed. p. 202
workbook page 108 - teacher ed. p. 203
workbook page 109 - teacher ed. p. 205
workbook page 110 - teacher ed. p. 207
workbook page 111 - teacher ed. p. 209
workbook page 112 - teacher ed. p. 211
workbook page 113 - teacher ed. p. 213
workbook page 114 - teacher ed. p. 215
workbook page 115 - teacher ed. p. 216
workbook page 116 - teacher ed. p. 217
workbook page 117 - teacher ed. p. 219
workbook page 118 - teacher ed. p. 221
workbook page 119 - teacher ed. p. 223
workbook page 120 - teacher ed. p. 225
workbook page 121 - teacher ed. p. 227
workbook page 122 - teacher ed. p. 229
workbook page 123 - teacher ed. p. 231
workbook page 124 - teacher ed. p. 233
workbook page 125 - teacher ed. p. 235
workbook page 126 - teacher ed. p. 237
workbook page 127 - teacher ed. p. 239
workbook page 128 - teacher ed. p. 241
workbook page 129 - teacher ed. p. 243
workbook page 130 - teacher ed. p. 245
workbook page 131 - teacher ed. p. 247
workbook page 132 - teacher ed. p. 249
workbook page 133 - teacher ed. p. 251
workbook page 134 - teacher ed. p. 253
workbook page 135 - teacher ed. p. 255
workbook page 136 - teacher ed. p. 257
workbook page 137 - teacher ed. p. 259
workbook page 138 - teacher ed. p. 261
workbook page 139 - teacher ed. p. 263
workbook page 140 - teacher ed. p. 265
workbook page 141 - teacher ed. p. 267
workbook page 142 - teacher ed. p. 277
workbook page 143 - teacher ed. p. 279
workbook page 144 - teacher ed. p. 281
workbook page 145 - teacher ed. p. 283
workbook page 146 - teacher ed. p. 285
workbook page 147 - teacher ed. p. 287
workbook page 148 - teacher ed. p. 289
workbook page 149 - teacher ed. p. 291
workbook page 150 - teacher ed. p. 293
workbook page 151 - teacher ed. p. 295
workbook page 152 - teacher ed. p. 297
workbook page 153 - teacher ed. p. 299
workbook page 154 - teacher ed. p. 300
workbook page 155 - teacher ed. p. 301
workbook page 156 - teacher ed. p. 303
workbook page 157 - teacher ed. p. 305
workbook page 158 - teacher ed. p. 306
workbook page 159 - teacher ed. p. 307
workbook page 160 - teacher ed. p. 309
workbook page 161 - teacher ed. p. 311
workbook page 162 - teacher ed. p. 313
workbook page 163 - teacher ed. p. 315
workbook page 164 - teacher ed. p. 317
workbook page 165 - teacher ed. p. 319
workbook page 166 - teacher ed. p. 321
workbook page 167 - teacher ed. p. 323
workbook page 168 - teacher ed. p. 325
workbook page 169 - teacher ed. p. 327
workbook page 170 - teacher ed. p. 329

workbook page 171 - teacher ed. p. 331
workbook page 172 - lined page
workbook page 173 - lined page
workbook page 174 - lined page
workbook page 175 - lined page
workbook page 176 - lined page
workbook page 177 - teacher ed. p. 343
workbook page 178 - teacher ed. p. 345
workbook page 179 - teacher ed. p. 347
workbook page 180 - teacher ed. p. 349
workbook page 181 - teacher ed. p. 351
workbook page 182 - teacher ed. p. 353
workbook page 183 - teacher ed. p. 355
workbook page 184 - teacher ed. p. 357
workbook page 185 - teacher ed. p. 359
workbook page 186 - teacher ed. p. 361
workbook page 187 - teacher ed. p. 363
workbook page 188 - teacher ed. p. 365
workbook page 189 - teacher ed. p. 367
workbook page 190 - teacher ed. p. 369
workbook page 191 - teacher ed. p. 371
workbook page 192 - teacher ed. p. 373
workbook page 193 - teacher ed. p. 375
workbook page 194 - teacher ed. p. 377
workbook page 195 - teacher ed. p. 379
workbook page 196 - teacher ed. p. 381
workbook page 197 - teacher ed. p. 383
workbook page 198 - teacher ed. p. 385
workbook page 199 - teacher ed. p. 387
workbook page 200 - teacher ed. p. 388
workbook page 201 - teacher ed. p. 389
workbook page 202 - teacher ed. p. 391
workbook page 203 - teacher ed. p. 393
workbook page 204 - teacher ed. p. 395
workbook page 205 - teacher ed. p. 397
workbook page 206 - teacher ed. p. 399
workbook page 207 - teacher ed. p. 401
workbook page 208 - teacher ed. p. 403
workbook page 209 - teacher ed. p. 405
workbook page 210 - teacher ed. p. 407
workbook page 211 - teacher ed. p. 409
workbook page 212 - blank
workbook page 213 - teacher ed. p. 413
workbook page 214 - teacher ed. p. 415
workbook page 215 - teacher ed. p. 417
workbook page 216 - teacher ed. p. 418
workbook page 217 - teacher ed. p. 419
workbook page 218 - teacher ed. p. 420
workbook page 219 - teacher ed. p. 422
workbook page 220 - teacher ed. p. 423
workbook page 221 - teacher ed. p. 425
workbook page 222 - teacher ed. p. 427
workbook page 223 - teacher ed. p. 430
workbook page 224 - teacher ed. p. 431
workbook page 225 - teacher ed. p. 433
workbook page 226 - teacher ed. p. 435
workbook page 227 - teacher ed. p. 437
workbook page 228 - teacher ed. p. 439
workbook page 229 - teacher ed. p. 441
workbook page 230 - teacher ed. p. 443
workbook page 231 - teacher ed. p. 445
workbook page 232 - teacher ed. p. 447
workbook page 233 - teacher ed. p. 449
workbook page 234 - teacher ed. p. 451
workbook page 235 - teacher ed. p. 453
workbook page 236 - teacher ed. p. 455
workbook page 237 - teacher ed. p. 456
workbook page 238 - teacher ed. p. 457
workbook page 239 - teacher ed. p. 459
workbook page 240 - teacher ed. p. 461
workbook page 241 - teacher ed. p. 462
workbook page 242 - teacher ed. p. 463
workbook page 243 - teacher ed. p. 465
workbook page 244 - teacher ed. p. 467
workbook page 245 - teacher ed. p. 469
workbook page 246 - teacher ed. p. 471
workbook page 247 - teacher ed. p. 473
workbook page 248 - teacher ed. p. 475
workbook page 249 - teacher ed. p. 477
workbook page 250 - teacher ed. p. 479
workbook page 251 - teacher ed. p. 481
workbook page 252 - teacher ed. p. 483
workbook page 253 - teacher ed. p. 485
workbook page 254 - teacher ed. p. 487
workbook page 255 - teacher ed. p. 489
workbook page 256 - teacher ed. p. 491
workbook page 257 - teacher ed. p. 493
workbook page 258 - teacher ed. p. 495
workbook page 259 - teacher ed. p. 497
workbook page 260 - teacher ed. p. 499
workbook page 261 - teacher ed. p. 501
workbook page 262 - teacher ed. p. 503

TESTS

PREPOSITION TEST:

VERB TEST:

NOUN TEST:

ADJECTIVE TEST:

ADVERB TEST:

PRONOUN TEST:

CAPITALIZATION TEST:

PUNCTUATION TEST:

Other Books by Wanda C. Phillips:

Easy Grammar: Daily Guided Teaching and Review for Grades 2 and 3 - This text contains 180 **teaching** lessons set up in the same format as the *Daily Grams*. Lessons present learning about capitalization, punctuation, dictionary usage, sentence combining, and grammar concepts and usage. Concepts are introduced, explained, and reintroduced throughout the text.

Easy Grammar: Grades 3 and 4 - This text, introducing just 28 prepositions, uses the prepositional approach to grammar. It includes grammar concepts, capitalization, punctuation, sentence types, and other concepts introduced in an easy format. (See "Scope and Sequence" on the back of this text.) Unit reviews, unit tests, cumulative reviews, and cumulative tests are included. (473 pages) ***Easy Grammar Workbook 34*** - For student use, this book contains worksheets and rules pages found within the text. (230 pages)

Easy Grammar: Grades 4 and 5 - This text, introducing 40 prepositions, uses the prepositional approach to grammar. It includes grammar concepts, capitalization, punctuation, sentence types, and other concepts introduced in a step-by-step manner. (See "Scope and Sequence" on the back of this text.) Unit reviews, unit tests, cumulative reviews, and cumulative tests are included. This text has ample effective teaching strategies to help ensure successful teaching and learning. (521 pages) ***Easy Grammar Workbook 45*** - For student use, this book contains worksheets and rules pages found within the text. (252 pages)

Easy Grammar Plus - This text uses the prepositional approach to grammar. It includes extensive grammar concepts, capitalization, punctuation, sentence types, gerunds, and more. (See "Scope and Sequence" on the back of this text.) Unit reviews, unit tests, cumulative reviews, and cumulative tests in grammar help to insure mastery of concepts. (622 pages) ***Easy Grammar Plus Workbook*** - For student use, this book contains all of the worksheets and rules pages found within the text. (347 pages)

Easy Writing - This text teaches students how to write higher level sentence structures. Students learn, in a step-by-step manner, how to write introductory participial phrases, subordinate clauses, appositives, etc. Two levels make this ideal for intermediate through adult learning.

*All **Daily Grams, 180 daily lessons**, are designed as a **ten minute review** at the beginning of each class and promote mastery learning! Although these may be used with any text, **Easy Grammar** texts are recommended!*

Daily Grams: Guided Review Aiding Mastery Skills for 3rd and 4th Grades - This text is 180 pages of daily reviews. Each lesson contains capitalization review, punctuation review, sentence combining, and review of grammar concepts and usage. Dictionary review is included.

Daily Grams: Guided Review Aiding Mastery Skills for 4th and 5th Grades - Each lesson contains capitalization review, punctuation practice, sentence combining, and general review of grammar concepts and usage.

Daily Grams: Guided Review Aiding Mastery Skills for 5th and 6th Grades - Each lesson contains capitalization review, punctuation practice, sentence combining, and general review of grammar concepts and usage. Phrases, clauses, library skills, and dictionary skills are also important parts of this text.

Daily Grams: Guided Review Aiding Mastery Skills (6th-adult) - Each lesson contains capitalization review, punctuation practice, sentence combining, and general review of grammar concepts and usage.

For ordering information, send a self-addressed, stamped envelope to ISHA Enterprises, Inc., Post Office Box 12520, Scottsdale, Arizona 85267 or call (800) 641-6015. You may wish to contact your local bookstore or teaching center for ordering.